BV4223.M272 1997-98

Property of
INSTITUTE FOR WORSHIP STUDIES
Orange Park, Florida

The Minister's Annual Manual
for Preaching and Worship Planning
1997–1998

Compiled and Edited by
Sharilyn A. Figueroa

**Logos Productions Inc.
6160 Carmen Avenue East
Inver Grove Heights, MN 55076-4422**

Copyright ©1997
LOGOS PRODUCTIONS INC.

First Edition

Eleventh Annual Volume

All rights reserved.

No part of this book may be reproduced or transmitted in any form or by any means, electronic or mechanical, including photocopying and recording, or by any information storage or retrieval system, except as may be expressly permitted by the 1976 Copyright Act or in writing from the publisher or as otherwise permitted herein. Requests for permission should be addressed in writing to Logos Productions Inc., 6160 Carmen Avenue East, Inver Grove Heights, MN 55076-4422.

Permission is hereby granted, however, for the convenience of parish pastors, for reprinting of brief sections of this book in a local congregation's weekly Sunday bulletin or newsletter. Where appropriate, proper acknowledgment should be given as to source.

This book has been typeset by Logos Productions Inc.
Printed by Bolger Publications/Creative Printing,
Minneapolis, Minnesota

Scripture listings in this publication are from *The Revised Common Lectionary—The Consultation on Common Texts* published by Abingdon Press, Nashville, Tennessee, and are used by permission.

The Hymn of the Day for each week has been prepared by the Reverend Kent Gilbert, pastor of Union Church of Christ in Berea, Kentucky. Kent seeks to develop vital worship for people of all ages. He also leads workshops and teacher training events for *The Whole People of God* Sunday school curriculum.

ISBN: 1-885361-04-1
ISSN: 0894-3966

Contents

How to Use This Book 11

Sermons

August 3, 1997
    Working the Work—Andrea La Sonde Anastos 19
August 10, 1997
    Bread of Life—Andrea La Sonde Anastos 26
August 17, 1997
    The Feast of God—Andrea La Sonde Anastos 33
August 24, 1997
    Led in a Harder Way—Andrea La Sonde Anastos 40
August 31, 1997
    Human Precepts, Divine Love
    —Andrea La Sonde Anastos 47
September 7, 1997
    The Woman Who Was Willing to Be a Dog
    —Thomas W. Currie III 54
September 14, 1997
    The Difference between Gossip and the Gospel
    —Thomas W. Currie III 61
September 21, 1997
    Embarrassed into the Kingdom—Thomas W. Currie III 68
September 28, 1997
    The Body of Christ—Thomas W. Currie III 75
October 5, 1997
    Receiving as a Child—Nancy E. Topolewski 82
October 12, 1997
    How High a Price?—Nancy E. Topolewski 89
October 19, 1997
    Pushing in Line—Nancy E. Topolewski 95
October 26, 1997
    Regaining Our Sight—Nancy E. Topolewski 103

October 26, 1997, Reformation
    A Covenant for the Heart—Nancy E. Topolewski 109
November 2, 1997
    Not Far Enough?—William M. Schwein 117
November 2, 1997, All Saints' Day
    What's at the End of the Valley?—William M. Schwein 124
November 9, 1997
    Once and for All—William M. Schwein 131
November 16, 1997
    The Beginning Is Near—William M. Schwein 138
November 23, 1997, Christ the King/Reign of Christ
    Our Mysterious Lord and King—William B. Lawrence 145
November 27, 1997, Thanksgiving Day
    A Grateful Dependent—William B. Lawrence 153
November 30, 1997
    Growing Concerns—William B. Lawrence 161
December 7, 1997
    Preparations for the Underprepared
    —William B. Lawrence 170
December 14, 1997
    Who Do You Expect?—Paul Romstad 178
December 21, 1997
    When Babies Leap in the Womb—Paul Romstad 185
December 24, 1997, Christmas Eve
    God Steps In—Paul Romstad 192
December 25, 1997, Christmas Day
    Announcing Hope—Paul Romstad 200
December 28, 1997
    Words of Faith—John L. Topolewski 207
January 4, 1998
    God's Good Pleasure, and Ours—John L. Topolewski 213
January 6, 1998, Epiphany
    Burden or Gift?—John L. Topolewski 220
January 11, 1998, The Baptism of Our Lord
    Death by Drowning—John L. Topolewski 226
January 18, 1998
    You Can't Shut Up God!—Peter Rosenkvist 232
January 25, 1998
    Needed: A Mission—Paul Lundborg 240

February 1, 1998
    Jesus and His Own People—Paul Lundborg 247
February 8, 1998
    Go Out Where It's Deep—Paul Lundborg 255
February 15, 1998
    Advanced Lessons—Theresa M. Roos 263
February 22, 1998, Transfiguration
    Glory Days—Theresa M. Roos 271
February 25, 1998, Ash Wednesday
    Phoenix from the Ashes—Theresa M. Roos 279
March 1, 1998
    Winning Words—Theresa M. Roos 285
March 8, 1998
    Some Are Enemies of the Cross—Gary L. Walling 293
March 15, 1998
    Examples from the Past—Gary L. Walling 300
March 22, 1998
    No Longer from a Human Point of View
    —Gary L. Walling 307
March 29, 1998
    New Things—Gary L. Walling 314
April 5, 1998, Passion/Palm Sunday
    The Suffering Servant as Teacher—Clyde J. Steckel 321
April 9, 1998, Maundy Thursday
    A Day to Remember—Clyde J. Steckel 329
April 10, 1998, Good Friday
    He Was Wounded for Our Transgressions
    —Clyde J. Steckel 336
April 12, 1998, Easter Day
    The Resurrection Message—Clyde J. Steckel 344
April 19, 1998
    The Benefit of a Doubt—Steven L. Davis 351
April 26, 1998
    A Curious, Uneasy Peace—Steven L. Davis 359
May 3, 1998
    In Good Hands—Steven L. Davis 367
May 10, 1998
    What's Love Got to Do with It?—Steven L. Davis 374

May 17, 1998
   Christ at Home—Steven D. MacArthur 381
May 21, 1998, Ascension Day
   Christ, His Church, and the Angels
   —Steven D. MacArthur 387
May 24, 1998
   That They May Become Completely One
   —Steven D. MacArthur 394
May 31, 1998, Day of Pentecost
   A Festival of Listening—Steven D. MacArthur 402
June 7, 1998, Trinity Sunday
   The Doctrine of the Trinity—Beth Ann Gaede 409
June 14, 1998
   How Can I Make My Life Work?—Beth Ann Gaede 416
June 21, 1998
   Inheriting the Promise—Beth Ann Gaede 423
June 28, 1998
   The Law of Love—Beth Ann Gaede 430
July 5, 1998
   A Guiding Vision—C. Welton Gaddy 437
July 12, 1998
   Love without Limits—C. Welton Gaddy 444
July 19, 1998
   Silent Listening as a Spiritual Discipline
   —C. Welton Gaddy 451
July 26, 1998
   Enough Said—C. Welton Gaddy 457

Children's Object Talks

Date	Title	Page
8/3/97	Finding Fulfillment	18
8/10/97	Always in Sight of God	25
8/17/97	Energy from Jesus, Life's Bread	32
8/24/97	Following Means Doing	39
8/31/97	Inside Clean—Outside Clean	46
9/7/97	Interceding for Others	53
9/14/97	It Isn't Always Easy	60
9/21/97	How Much Are You Loved?	67

Date	Title	Page
9/28/97	Stay Away from Temptation	74
10/5/97	Enter the Kingdom	81
10/12/97	The Role of Possessions	88
10/19/97	The Joy of Serving	94
10/26/97	A Blind Man Sees	102
10/26/97	Knowledge of the Heart	108
11/2/97	Only Two Things Are Important	116
11/2/97	Life from Death	123
11/9/97	Christ Died for Our Sins	130
11/16/97	Follow the Leader	137
11/23/97	Everyone a Priest	144
11/27/97	Consider the Lilies	152
11/30/97	A Caring Letter of Love	160
12/7/97	A Picture Is Worth a Thousand Prayers	169
12/14/97	Waiting without Worrying	177
12/21/97	A Closer Look Inside	184
12/24/97	Only a Baby?	191
12/25/97	An Unbreakable Gift	199
12/28/97	Time to Get Dressed	206
1/4/98	Christmas Every Day	212
1/6/98	Now I Can See	219
1/11/98	A Signpost for Life	225
1/18/98	Better than New	231
1/25/98	Time to Get to Work	239
2/1/98	No Good Reason	247
2/8/98	Fishing for People	254
2/15/98	Fair's Fair	262
2/22/98	The End of the Road	270
2/25/98	Anytime Is Forgiveness Time	278
3/1/98	One for All	284
3/8/98	Dual Citizenship	292
3/15/98	A Fair Test	299
3/22/98	Appealing, Not Repelling	306
3/29/98	Good as New? No, Better than New!	313
4/5/98	Ears to Hear	320
4/9/98	Remember and Celebrate	328
4/10/98	Suffering Servant	335
4/12/98	Jesus Is Lord!	343
4/19/98	Gather Together	350

4/26/98	Work Together	358
5/3/98	Jesus Loves Me	366
5/10/98	Love One Another	373
5/17/98	Keep Learning	380
5/21/98	Watch Jesus	386
5/24/98	Jesus Makes Us One	394
5/31/98	Celebrate and Tell the News	401
6/7/98	Lots Left to Learn	408
6/14/98	Look to Jesus	415
6/21/98	We Are Children of God	422
6/28/98	Love One Another	429
7/5/98	We Boast of the Cross of Christ	436
7/12/98	Mercy	443
7/19/98	Never Too Old to Learn	450
7/26/98	Big Prayers	457

Appendices

Resources for Preparing to Preach
 —Dr. David H. Schmidt 461
1997–1998 Writers 469
Four-Year Church Year Calendar 471
Calendars for 1997 and 1998 472
Index of Sermon Texts 473
Advance Order Form (for 1998–1999) 475

How to Use This Book

This book is intended for use from August 1997 through July 1998. Since many ministers prefer to plan an entire year of preaching and worship during the summer, this manual is designed to assist in summer-to-summer planning.

Every minister develops his or her own style of preaching and worship planning. Methods, planning, study, writing, and delivery are all unique. Preaching practice comes from experiences over the years. Therefore, you will use this book in whatever ways will benefit your worship and sermon preparation most fully. Its usefulness is determined by your own style and manner of preparation. Included in the book are helpful suggestions to guide your worship planning for each Sunday, as well as for several special worship events.

Many ministers prefer to spend time several weeks in advance of a specific Sunday reviewing the texts for that day. The materials in this book will be most helpful for that task. Please read David H. Schmidt's "Resources for Preparing to Preach" on page 440. A variety of resource materials, commentaries, and translations are listed to help you in your exegeses.

For each worship experience, each writer has prepared brief explanatory notes for the lessons, notes that you can use to get a feel for the texts. You can also use these notes in your Sunday bulletins to help your congregation grasp the central idea in the lessons for the day.

As your worship plans develop for a particular Sunday, please note the variety of prayers and calls to worship suggested by our writers to fit in with the theme for the day. You may use these in any way appropriate to your planning.

The children's object talks can be especially useful for those pastors who have difficulty developing ideas and presentations for this important ministry to children. The sermon materials may be used as thought-starters for your own sermon preparation.

Not all preachers use the lectionary lessons on a regular basis. If you don't use these texts for your preaching, the materials in this book can still be extremely useful in providing sermon ideas and illustrations on specific texts appropriate for the time of year. On the other hand, if you are accustomed to using the lectionary lessons, you will find these materials especially suited to your preaching needs.

A large majority of denominations now follow the Revised Common Lectionary. We are, therefore, using the Revised Common Lectionary so that *Minister's Annual Manual* will be helpful to more people. You should have no difficulty adapting these materials to your own church calendar. Consultation on Common Texts asks that we indicate the following:

"For the Sundays following Pentecost (Propers 4 [9] through 29 [34]), the Revised Common Lectionary provides two distinct patterns for readings from the Old Testament. One pattern offers a series of semi-continuous Old Testament readings over the course of these Sundays. The other pattern offers paired readings in which the Old Testament and gospel reading for each Sunday are closely related. In adopting the Revised Common Lectionary, the Presbyterian Church U.S.A., United Church of Christ, and United Methodist Church elected to use the pattern of semi-continuous Old Testament readings. The other pattern of paired readings is found in the Revised Common Lectionary (Nashville: Abingdon Press, 1992)." (The Revised Common Lectionary, 1992, Consultation on Common Texts [CCT].)

The following materials are included for each worship experience:
Lessons are assigned for liturgical preaching.
Introduction to the Lessons, a brief explanation of all texts.
Theme of the day's materials.
Thought for the Day to help set the tone for preaching.
Prayer of Meditation prior to the worship experience.
Call to Worship for the beginning of the service.
Prayer of Adoration for the beginning of worship.
Prayer of Confession asking for forgiveness and pardon.
Prayer of Dedication of Gifts and Self at the offering.
Sermon Summary for the day.
Hymn of the Day suggestions.
Children's Object Talk for conversation with children.
The Sermon including **Hymns**, **Scripture**, and **Sermon Text**.

Hymn of the Day selections were chosen from the following hymnals:
The New Century Hymnal, Cleveland, OH: Pilgrim Press, 1995
Pilgrim Hymnal, Boston: Pilgrim Press, 1958
Presbyterian Hymnal, Louisville, KY: Westminster/John Knox Press, 1990
Chalice Hymnal, St. Louis, MO: Chalice Press, 1995
The United Methodist Hymnal, Nashville, TN: United Methodist Publishing House, 1989
Favorite Hymns of Praise, Chicago, IL: Tabernacle Publishing Co., 1967
Lutheran Book of Worship, Minneapolis, MN: Augsburg Publishing House, 1978
Episcopal Hymnbook 1982, New York, NY: The Church Pension Fund, 1985

With One Voice: A Lutheran Resource for Worship, Minneapolis, MN: Augsburg Fortress, 1995

Hymns for the Living Church, Carol Stream, IL: Hope Publishing Co., 1984

Many of the hymns suggested are available for congregational use through *LicenSing: Copyright Cleared Music for Churches.*™ For more information on *LicenSing,* please call 1-800-328-0200.

Names and addresses for all of the writers who have prepared these materials are listed in the appendix should you wish to write to any of them.

To assist in your planning, a four-year church year calendar is included in the appendix. Calendars for the years 1997 and 1998 are provided as well.

And for even more worship planning helps, you may wish to use the 1997 *May/June Planning Issue* or the regular monthly issues of *The Clergy Journal.* These resources include additional sermons, children's object talks, and hymn selections.

A one-year subscription to *The Clergy Journal* is $29.95, and the *May/June Planning Issue,* when purchased separately, is $16.00. Please call 1-800-328-0200 for ordering information.

Thus, preachers who use this *Minister's Annual Manual 1997–1998* and also subscribe to *The Clergy Journal* will have valuable resources for worship planning that include:

(1) Three complete sets of sermons for every Sunday of the year: this book, the annual planning issue, plus "Preaching on the Lessons" in each issue of *The Clergy Journal.* (The sermon materials in all three publications have been cross-referenced so you will know at a glance which publication to use for a particular passage.)
(2) Two sets of object talks for children.
(3) Almost three dozen additional sermons.
(4) Hymn selections to match the texts.
(5) Prayers and calls to worship.

Both the *Minister's Annual Manual 1997–1998* and the *May/June Planning Issue* of *The Clergy Journal* will make excellent additions to your library.

—Sharilyn A. Figueroa
Spring 1997

August 3, 1997

11th Sunday after Pentecost (Proper 13)
RC/Pres: 18th Sunday in Ordinary Time

Lessons
Pres/Meth/UCC	2 Sam 11:26—12:13a	Eph 4:1–16	Jn 6:24–35
Roman Catholic	Ex 16:2–4, 12–15	Eph 4:17, 20–24	Jn 6:24–35
Episcopal	Ex 16:2–4, 9–15	Eph 4:17–25	Jn 6:24–35
Lutheran	Ex 16:2–4, 9–15	Eph 4:1–16	Jn 6:24–35

Introduction to the Lessons
Lesson 1
(1) *2 Samuel 11:26—12:13a* **(Pres/Meth/UCC)**
When word comes that Uriah is dead, David marries Bathsheba and she bears a son. Nathan comes to David and tells the story of the rich man stealing the poor man's ewe lamb. When David rises in righteous anger against the injustice, Nathan tells him that *he* is the rich man. David confesses his sin against God.

(2) *Exodus 16:2–4, 12–15* **(RC)**; *Exodus 16:2–4, 9–15* **(Epis/Luth)**
The people, traveling through the Sinai, continue to complain about Moses and to resent the fact that they are free in the wilderness rather than enslaved in Egypt. God provides meat (quail) in the evening and bread (manna) in the morning for their feeding. The Roman Catholic reading eliminates the verses when Moses calls the people together before God.

Lesson 2
(1) *Ephesians 4:1–16* **(Pres/Meth/UCC/Luth)**
This passage is an appeal to the church to maintain unity because there is "one Lord, one faith, one baptism." Gifts are given to each for the good of all until the whole congregation attains maturity of faith and grows into the one body which has Christ as its head.

(2) *Ephesians 4:17, 20–24* **(RC)**; *Ephesians 4:17–25* **(Epis)**
Since the people of the church no longer live lives in which they do not know God (like the Gentiles), they are called to "put off" the old

nature and "put on" the new, which is created in God's own likeness. The Roman Catholic reading eliminates the verses that describe the former life as callous and unclean.

Gospel
John 6:24-35 **(Pres/Meth/UCC/RC/Epis/Luth)**
Following the miracle of the bread and fish, the people again seek Jesus, wanting more miracles. Jesus suggests that they stop worrying about their stomachs and seek to do the work of God. Now they ask for manna as a sign that they should follow Jesus. Jesus proclaims that he is the bread of life offered by God to feed their spirits and souls.

Theme
Christians are called to "walk God's walk" and to "work God's work."

Thought for the Day
"The test of love is not feeling, but obedience." —William Ullathorne

"Work is love made visible." —Kahlil Gibran

Prayer of Meditation
Loving God, you have invited me to seek the Christ who goes with me in each moment of my life. Let me never tire of finding him in the children and women and men you have invited into the community I serve. Give me grace this day to walk as a faithful disciple so that others who are seeking Christ may find him in me. Amen.

Call to Worship
> Leader: God's gift to our ancestors was manna in the wilderness.
> People: Praise God for bread from heaven!
> Leader: God's gift to us is the bread broken at the table of the Lord.
> People: Praise God for the bread of heaven!
> All: Praise God for living bread which feeds both bodies and spirits.

Prayer of Adoration
Holy, Holy, Holy One, your open hand was over our ancestors in the wilderness. Your overflowing generosity fed those who came to Jesus

August 3, 1997
11th Sunday after Pentecost (Proper 13)
RC/Pres: 18th Sunday in Ordinary Time

for bread for their bodies and souls. Your grace-filled abundance drenches us with good things. Holy, Holy, Holy One, we kneel before you in gratitude, we dance before you in joy, we lift our voices before you in praise. Holy, Holy, Holy One, we bless you for the blessings you pour out upon your whole creation. Amen.

Prayer of Confession

We confess, God of abundance, that we have taken the gifts you gave us so freely and hoarded them for our own use. We confess that we have not trusted that there will always be enough, and so we have clung to what needed to be passed on to others. We confess that gathering has been more important to us than scattering. We confess our unhealthy desire, even now, for *more*. Forgive us our childish fears. Forgive us our lack of faith in your promise. Grant us the courage to open our hearts and hands, God of abundance, so that we may be true stewards of your bounty. Amen.

Prayer of Dedication of Gifts and Self

Jesus spoke to those who were his friends and students and called them to work on your behalf. Through the prophets and the saints across the ages, he has called us to do your work. Accept these gifts we bring that are made possible by our work, our ministries outside the church. Accept our lives offered to minister in your name wherever we see opportunity. Bless our labor and our lives, Most Holy One, that they may be worthy of your commonwealth. Amen.

Sermon Summary

Being a disciple does not involve following a rule book. Rather, it means committing oneself to being intentionally engaged in relationship and at one with God and the universe.

Hymn of the Day

"Guide Me, O Thou Great Jehovah (Guide Me, O My Great Redeemer)." This hymn is filled with the powerful imagery of deliverance for the people. Often called forth to reference the Exodus from Egypt, it is also a strong song of our own deliverance through communion with Jesus. Verse one praises God for the strength of holy manna in the desert, but verse two is a beautiful evocation of the text from Revelation about the new Jerusalem (Rev 22:1-2) yet to come. The text written in 1745 by William Williams appears in many early hymnody collections, including *Southern Harmony*, and many shape-note hymnals. "Cwm Rhondda," the tune most often associated with these words, is a Welsh tune written in 1907 and composed by John Hughes, a railway worker, for the anniversary of his church. For variety, the older tune "Zion" written in 1830 offers a pleasing alternative.

Children's Object Talk

Finding Fulfillment

Object
None.

Lesson
Jesus is the bread of life that satisfies forever. (Pause for children's responses. Accept all responses.)

How many of you had breakfast this morning? Were you hungry? Were you still hungry when you finished eating? Will you be hungry again at lunchtime? So, you'll eat some lunch, and then you won't be hungry anymore, right? Then why will you have dinner later on? Oh—you'll get hungry all over again! And again tomorrow morning, and tomorrow noon, and tomorrow night, and the next day, and the next. We just get hungry over and over again, don't we?

Did you ever want a certain present for your birthday or for Christmas? What happened when you got it? You never wanted another present again, right? You did? Well, why weren't you happy with that first present? We just always want more stuff, don't we?

In the story I just read from the Bible, Jesus tells us that when we really accept him, we won't want things ever again. Jesus' love is so wonderful that once you have it, you just never need to want anything again. It's like eating a piece of toast for breakfast, and never having to eat again. Or like getting a wonderful gift and never wanting another one ever again. How wonderful it is that you have found Jesus while you're just a little child. Now you don't have to spend your whole life hunting and wanting. You know Jesus' love already. You can grow up sharing that love with everybody you know instead of hunting. Jesus loves you now and always. You remember that, okay?

—*Lois Brokering*

August 3, 1997
11th Sunday after Pentecost (Proper 13)
RC/Pres: 18th Sunday in Ordinary Time

The Sermon

Working the Work

Hymns
Beginning of Worship: "Hope of the World"
Sermon Hymn: "Break Now the Bread of Life"
End of Worship: "O God of Earth and Altar"

Scripture
John 6:24–35 (For additional sermon materials on this passage, see the April 1997 and the *1997 May/June Planning Issue* of *The Clergy Journal*.)

Sermon Text
"Then they said to him, 'What must we do, to perform the works of God?'" (vs. 29).

The text for this morning is part of the peculiarly disjointed conversation between Jesus and the crowd of people who follow him across the Sea of Galilee. This crowd has heard the teachings of Jesus and has seen the miracle of the loaves and fishes. Now they ask what appears to be a completely reasonable question, *"What must we do, to perform the works of God?"*

A cursory reader might assume that the persons standing before Jesus have, indeed, been transformed by what they have seen and heard and are now requesting guidance for the next stage of their discipleship.

Looking further into the passage where the same people go on to demand further signs and miracles of Jesus suggests that the question may be something other than what it seems on the surface.

"What must we do, to perform the works of God?"

In fact, when we hear the question in the larger context of the whole story, it suddenly sounds decidedly odd. There is an implication in the words that somehow Jesus can give the crowd (or us) a handy list of behaviors that constitute "the works of God." Then, if we just check off the items on the list, we will be "good," we will be "doing the right things."

How nice it would be if it were all as simple as taking a vitamin pill or remembering to brush our teeth. How nice it would be if we never had to *think* about God, or God's hope for creation. How convenient it would be if we we never had to *listen* to the needs of our neighbors and consider our response deeply, prayerfully, faithfully. How pleasant it would be to know that, simply by following the instructions, we could count on getting lots of little gold stars on our "righteousness chart."

"What must we do, to perform the works of God?"

Jesus doesn't offer the crowd a simple answer in Scripture. His way is not simple if, by that, we mean we can walk it on automatic pilot. Jesus, instead, invites us to ask a different question, a question which will lead us to consider living by a different paradigm. Jesus invites the crowd (and us) to believe in, to partake of, to participate with the Anointed One whom God has sent us as a model.

The whole meaning of the incarnation is that God is not distant from us, but present with us. Jesus invites us to be at one with him, to be part of his incarnate presence which is God in the world. Doing the works of God involves being at one with God, with the Anointed of God, with the people of God, and with the universe of God. It means feeling as God feels, giving as God gives, hoping as God hopes, loving as God loves.

The African-American churches define the parameters of discipleship very clearly when they say, "It's no good to talk the talk, if you don't walk the walk."

The people in the crowd ask Jesus a question about discipleship and Jesus invites them (invites us) not only to "walk the walk," but to "work the work."

"What must we do, to perform the works of God?"

What would the world look like if we were to take Jesus seriously, if we were to accept that he has poured himself out for us to show us what it means to live into God's hope for a commonwealth of equity and justice? What if we were to take up our mandate to work in his name toward that reign, that commonwealth? What would our social programs to alleviate hunger look like if we approached them with faith-filled focus and an awareness that our solutions need to offer not only temporal bread, but eternal bread? What would welfare look like if we looked at it with God's eyes and shaped it so that through it, we would be accomplishing God's work? How would we handle health care, housing, the environment, or stewardship of resources if we saw ourselves as God's agents, seeking to preserve and nurture God's universe with the love God brought to its creation?

"What must we do, to perform the works of God?"

Jesus doesn't give us a simple answer because there is no simple answer. He gives us a way toward a divine vision. *"Do not work for the food that perishes* [Do not work on

August 3, 1997
11th Sunday after Pentecost (Proper 13)
RC/Pres: 18th Sunday in Ordinary Time

behalf of your—*our*—passing desires and fancies and fads], *but for the food that endures for eternal life* [but for that which sustains and enables God's promise of wholeness for the universe]."

Jesus doesn't give us a simple answer because there is no simple answer. He gives us a way toward a divine vision.

—*Andrea La Sonde Anastos*
The First Church of Deerfield
Deerfield, Massachusetts

August 10, 1997

12th Sunday after Pentecost (Proper 14)
RC/Pres: 19th Sunday in Ordinary Time

Lessons

Pres/Meth/UCC	2 Sam 18:5–9, 15, 31–33	Eph 4:25—5:2	Jn 6:35, 41–51
Roman Catholic	1 Kings 19:4–8	Eph 4:30—5:2	Jn 6:41–51
Episcopal	Deut 8:1–10	Eph 4:(25–29), 30—5:2	Jn 6:37–51
Lutheran	1 Kings 19:4–8	Eph 4:25—5:2	Jn 6:35, 41–51

Introduction to the Lessons
Lesson 1
(1) *2 Samuel 18:5-9, 15, 31-33* **(Pres/Meth/UCC)**
This passage tells of the battle between David's army and the forces of Absalom. It concludes with David's grief at the death of his son.

(2) *1 Kings 19:4–8* **(RC/Luth)**
This brief passage contains the story of Elijah, fleeing Jezebel, being fed twice by God to prepare him for his journey to Mount Horeb.

(3) *Deuteronomy 8:1–10* **(Epis)**
In one of Moses' last addresses to the people, he reminds them of God's providence while they were in the wilderness. He speaks of the tempering of that experience and of the abundance of God's grace.

Lesson 2
Ephesians 4:25—5:2 **(Pres/Meth/UCC/RC/Luth)**;
Ephesians 4:(25–29), 30—5:2 **(Epis)**
As Jesus loved us, we are to love one another. The writer gives instructions about the church: we are encouraged to speak in wisdom and truth, to labor honestly so that we can give generously, and to put away bitterness or wrath lest we grieve the Holy Spirit.

The shorter lesson gives as optional verses the more specific instructions in the passage about how we are to live in relationships.

August 10, 1997
12th Sunday after Pentecost (Proper 14)
RC/Pres: 19th Sunday in Ordinary Time

Gospel
John 6:35, 41–51 **(Pres/Meth/UCC/Luth)**;
John 6:41–51 **(RC)**; *John 6:37–51* **(Epis)**

Following the feeding of the 5,000, the authorities "murmur" against Jesus. He speaks to them of temporal and eternal bread and further develops his statement that he is the living bread of life. The Common Lectionary and the Lutheran readings add the original verse in which Jesus calls himself the bread of life. The Episcopal reading adds the verses in which Jesus speaks about those who see and believe in him having eternal life.

Theme
No matter how abundant the food we provide for our bodies, we will continue to need until we realize our soul-hunger and seek God's abundance to feed us spiritually.

Thought for the Day
"Before we can begin to understand the symbolism of the Eucharist or try to fathom the message it conveys, we need to remember hunger . . . To understand very well what it means to be very hungry over a long period of time. To understand in starkly revelatory depth what hunger means is to be starving . . ."

—Monica Hellwig

Prayer of Meditation
Bountiful God, I have come here this day, believing in your promise, to be fed with holy food, so that I will never again hunger or thirst. May it strengthen me to such faithful response that the good bread that is your living word can, in turn, feed others through the ministry to which you have called me. Amen.

Call to Worship
Leader:	Jesus blessed bread and said, "This is my body, broken for you."
People:	Jesus blessed bread and gave it to us saying, "Take, eat."
Leader:	Those who feed on this bread are promised eternal life.
People:	O let us taste and see that the Lord is good
All:	and God's promise endures forever!

Prayer of Adoration
Wondrous God, you have taken this ordinary day and consecrated it to renewal and refreshment. You have taken our ordinary lives and consecrated them to your work. You have taken our ordinary hopes and consecrated them to your eternal vision. You have taken ordinary bread and made it heavenly food. You have blessed the mundane and the ordinary, making it wonderful and holy. Wondrous God, we rejoice in the grace you offer us and stand in awe of your power to fill all things with glory. Amen.

Prayer of Confession
We confess, merciful God, that we do not always believe you when you promise that we will have our daily bread. We confess that we often trust more in the bread we buy than we do in the freely given bread of heaven. We confess that we prefer to eat bread that will not change us rather than the bread you offer, which will transform hearts and minds. Give us the faith to eat at your table, merciful God, where our hunger for self-fulfillment will be met by your desire to fill us with yourself. Amen.

Prayer of Dedication of Gifts and Self
Incarnate God, who chose to be enfleshed even as we are flesh and blood, we thank you for your gracious choice to share the joys and sorrows of being a physical being. Incarnate God, we rejoice that you showed us how, through loving relationship with our sisters and brothers, we can nourish others as you nourish us with your body and your blood. Accept the work of our hands, the love of our hearts, the faith of our souls to be food and drink for others as you are food and drink for us. Amen.

Sermon Summary
We are what we eat. When we "inwardly digest" the word of God, the bread of heaven, we become new people.

Hymn of the Day
"Bread of Life." This is a hymn from Timothy Tingfang Lew, a noted Chinese Protestant lay musician and poet. "Bread of Life" is standard in many hymnals because of its haunting oriental melody that is nonetheless easy to learn and sing. Writing this hymn in 1934, Lew

August 10, 1997
12th Sunday after Pentecost (Proper 14)
RC/Pres: 19th Sunday in Ordinary Time

specifically included imagery and terms familiar to Buddhists to make the hymn accessible to the Chinese culture. In so doing, however, he has sharpened the passion and the mystery of the traditional Christian understanding. For congregational use, "Bread of Life" is best sung at a moderate, stately tempo. Sung too slowly, the line of the melody can be lost, distracting from this fascinating hymn.

Children's Object Talk

Always in Sight of God

Object
Picture of a mother cat and kittens.
Lesson
God never gives up wanting us as God's own children.

Have you ever seen a mother cat with very young kittens like those in this picture? Let me tell you a true story about a mother cat and her kittens. The mommy's name was Tee Wee. When Tee Wee had her very first litter of kittens, she was given a large grocery box to keep them in. After a couple of weeks, the little kittens grew bigger. Their legs grew stronger, and they got rather curious.

Pretty soon the strongest one climbed up the side of the box and peeped over the edge. Then it slid down inside again. But before long, it tried again—and again—and pretty soon it went right over the top.

Now it was outside the box. But Tee Wee was nearby, watching carefully. She hurried right over and put her kitten back inside the box where she knew it would be safe. And then do you know what happened? That kitten did it again.

And pretty soon another kitten climbed over. In a few days, all the kittens were able to climb out of the box. At first, Tee Wee patiently put each one back. But they kept right on climbing out, setting out to see what was in that big, big world outside the box. After a while, Tee Wee just gave up. It was too hard to keep four kittens inside that box anymore. She no longer paid any attention to their climbing out. They could go wherever they wanted to go.

But God is not like that. In the story I just read in the Bible, Jesus tells us that he will never turn away from us. God wants all of us to be with God in heaven someday. God will never give up, like the mother cat did. God will never stop paying attention to you—and you—and you—(touch each child, and if possible, say their names). Isn't that wonderful?

—*Lois Brokering*

The Sermon

Bread of Life

Hymns
Beginning of Worship: "Day by Day the Manna Fell"
Sermon Hymn: "Bread of the World"
End of Worship: "All Who Hunger"

Scripture
John 6:35, 41–51 (For additional sermon materials on this passage, see the *1997 May/June Planning Issue* of *The Clergy Journal* and on Ephesians 4:25—5:2, see the April 1997 issue of *The Clergy Journal*.)

Sermon Text
"I am the bread of life. Whoever comes to me will never be hungry, and whoever believes in me will never be thirsty" (vs. 35).

In these latter days of the twentieth century, we are perhaps more aware than in any previous generation of the value of what we eat. Many of us are almost obsessively concerned with nutritional soundness. A proliferation of health magazines and books stirs up our concern about food additives and contaminants. This obsession is somewhat ludicrous in a country where our accepted social use of such addictive drugs as nicotine, caffeine, and alcohol has contributed to skyrocketing chronic illness. It is equally ludicrous where our short-sighted pollution of the air, the earth, and the water supply far outweigh any benefits we gain from consuming organically grown fruits and vegetables.

Yet, while millions in the world have inadequate food every day, lawyers in Boston, models in New York, doctors in Los Angeles, and bankers in Chicago worry about which vitamins in what quantity will guarantee unending youth and vigor. Many of us have taken to heart the adage, You are what you eat.

Therefore, we should be able to recognize ourselves easily in the crowds who followed Jesus to Capernaum. They, too, were looking for the magic potion that would make everything all better. They, too, were looking for temporal human answers to eternal questions. Like us, they were not really looking for food to eliminate physical hunger, but food to end spiritual hunger.

August 10, 1997
12th Sunday after Pentecost (Proper 14)
RC/Pres: 19th Sunday in Ordinary Time

It is not our physical needs that compel us to read the ingredients list on the container of Ben and Jerry's ice cream or the wrapper of our Carr's Water Table Biscuits; it is a spiritual "dis-ease," a sense that we are out of control in a hostile environment and in need of protection. We try to guarantee perfect health and wholeness by depending on ingredients or farming methods—still our hunger grows and gnaws within us.

"I am the bread of life. Whoever comes to me will never be hungry, and whoever believes in me will never be thirsty."

We are what we eat. If we eat of the bread of life, the true bread of which Jesus speaks; if we eat of Jesus himself, how can he fail to become part of who we are? But, as with nutritionally balanced meals in an environment polluted by airborne carcinogens, Jesus has only limited effect if we expect him to be a magic panacea leading to spiritual peace and wholeness in spite of the roadblocks of conscious materialism, sin, and idolatry we throw in his way.

Christianity makes the audacious claim that the individual matters, and that what the individual chooses matters. To be Christian is to accept responsibility. We cannot expect health if we consume the nutritious food that is Jesus while simultaneously polluting our bodies with the drugs of pride, or lust, or greed, or fear. We must choose. *We choose* whether to surround ourselves with a clean, balanced physical environment and *we choose* whether to surround ourselves with an environment that will nurture our souls and spirits.

Just as we cannot expect others to protect us from the consequences of our greed and carelessness in relation to our physical environment, so we cannot continue to indulge our prejudices; our lust for power, for money, for physical luxury; our fears that allow us to oppress one another, and think that one hour in church on Sunday will sanctify our behavior and set us right with the created order. Partial Christianity is no Christianity at all. What happens in your spiritual environment must be empowered to influence every other choice you make in your life . . . or it is useless. We are what we eat. Cheating rarely fools anyone but ourselves. It never fools God.

The crowds go to Jesus, demanding that he provide them with manna, the bread of heaven, as proof that he is the Christ. He explains to them that manna is not a gift from one human being to another. "Moses," he reminds them, "did not give your ancestors manna—God did. And I cannot give you the bread of heaven; the true bread comes only from my Father." It is God who creates and shares the bread of life and God has given all creation new bread more healthful than manna. Any other food (once digested) will continue to leave us hungry.

Jesus taught his followers a prayer. We use that prayer in our own worship: "Give us this day our daily bread." My godmother has often told me, "Beware what you pray for; you may get it!" Jesus himself is the bread of life. He was incarnate and still lives among us, offering himself as the answer to the prayer he taught us. We have been given the very bread of life; if we eat we shall never again hunger. But we must choose, and we must provide, at very least, a neutral environment in which the bread can begin to work its health.

You are what you eat. If you feed on anger or pride, you will not only *be* aggressive, but you will see the world as part of a hostile and antagonistic creation. If you feed on lust or greed, you will not only turn to domination as a way of being with others, but you will find creation violent and predatory. If you feed on Jesus, the word of God, the bread of life, you will not only be satisfied, but you will know creation as abundant and life-giving.

But there is a cost.

In seeing creation's abundance, you will be unable to watch others starve. In knowing the fulfillment of empowering life, the death that is silence and apathy and disregard in the face of inequity and injustice will be impossible for you to maintain. You will be unable to compromise with worldly values. You will be compelled to act on behalf on that abundant, life-giving commonwealth. You will be changed; essentially, ultimately changed.

Knowing that, I pray for you and for myself, that terrifying prayer: O God, our God, beloved God, abundant God: Thy will be done on earth. Give us (O, yes, and again, yes) give us this day our daily bread.

—*Andrea La Sonde Anastos*
The First Church of Deerfield
Deerfield, Massachusetts

August 17, 1997

13th Sunday after Pentecost (Proper 15)
RC/Pres: 20th Sunday in Ordinary Time

Lessons

Pres/Meth/UCC	1 Kings 2:10–12; 3:3–14	Eph 5:15–20	Jn 6:51–58
Roman Catholic	Prov 9:1–6	Eph 5:15–20	Jn 6:51–58
Episcopal	Prov 9:1–6	Eph 5:15–20	Jn 6:53–59
Lutheran	Prov 9:1–6	Eph 5:15–20	Jn 6:51–58

Introduction to the Lessons
Lesson 1
(1) *1 Kings 2:10–12; 3:3–14* **(Pres/Meth/UCC)**
Solomon assumes the throne after the death of David. He goes to Gibeon to offer a sacrifice to God and, while there, he has a dream in which he asks God for the gift of wisdom. God, in delight, gives not only discernment, but riches, power, and a long life.

(2) *Proverbs 9:1–6* **(RC/Epis/Luth)**
Wisdom invites the unwise to her banqueting table where they will learn insight and leave simple-mindedness behind.

Lesson 2
Ephesians 5:15–20 **(Pres/Meth/UCC/RC/Epis/Luth)**
The writer invites the church to walk in wisdom, seeking to understand the will of God. This involves being filled with the Spirit and with gratitude.

Gospel
John 6:51–58 **(Pres/Meth/UCC/RC/Luth)**;
John 6:53–59 **(Epis)**
The longer reading overlaps the lesson from last Sunday, picking up the final verse in which Jesus proclaims that he is living bread. The verses continue with an explanation of the necessity of the Eucharist (the act of eating and drinking) which enables the participant to "take in" the word of God and the teachings of Jesus and, so, to live

eternally in God. The shorter lesson eliminates the repetitive first verse and adds the statement that Jesus taught this in the synagogue.

Theme
Whether we understand the meal we share at God's table as a memorial or as a literal sacrifice, it is *the* act by which we are transformed into true disciples.

Thought for the Day
>And I will clothe myself in your eternal will,
>and by this light I shall come to know that you, eternal Trinity, are table
>and food
>and waiter for us. —Catherine of Siena

Prayer of Meditation
O Holy Wisdom, you have called me to walk in the ways of the wise and in all things to be taught by you. Grant this day that I may be so filled with your Spirit and with your desire for me that, in everything I do, I may will what you will, and, thus, be your presence manifest in this place. Amen.

Call to Worship
Leader:	The young lions suffer want and hunger;
People:	but those who open their hearts to God's hope lack no good thing.
Leader:	O stand in awe before the Lord, all you who are saints of God;
People:	and receive abundant bounty from God's own hand.
All:	We receive so that we may share! Let all creation feast and be filled!

—Adapted from Psalm 34:9–10

Prayer of Adoration
God of both the wise and the unwise, the mature and the immature, the faithful and the unfaithful, you are our God when we are reaching for the divine within us and when we have been tempted to brokenness. You are our God when we can rejoice before you and when we have fallen into despair. You are our God when we are seeking you

August 17, 1997
13th Sunday after Pentecost (Proper 15)
RC/Pres: 20th Sunday in Ordinary Time

and when we are running from your presence. In gratitude we lay our frightened selves and our courageous selves, our confident selves and our trembling selves, our loving selves and our angry selves before you, knowing that you will look with compassion on whatever we bring. In gratitude, we come, just as we are knowing that your great heart will accept us and welcome us. Amen.

Prayer of Confession

We confess, Holy One, that we have not always eaten the healthy food you put before us that has the power to make us whole and holy. We confess that we have often eaten the bitter fruit of anger or envy, the poisoned fruit of pride or covetousness, the sickly fruit of lust, or sloth, or gluttony. We ask your forgiveness for the hungers we do not even try to control. Grant us the will to accept the good food your Son died to provide for us, and to put away from us the temptation to be fed on evil. Amen.

Prayer of Dedication of Gifts and Self

Generous God, you have given us such overflowing plenty. You have filled our lives without measure. Grant that we may learn to give even as you give, without counting the cost. Accept and bless what we bring this day and help us to grow in maturity until the day comes when we lay *everything* before you: all that we have, all that we are, all that we will become. Amen.

Sermon Summary

The sacrament of the Lord's Supper (Eucharist, communion) means nothing if it does not transform us continually into beings who reveal more fully the divine image in which we are created.

Hymn of the Day

"Rejoice Ye (You) Pure in Heart." A well-loved favorite, this hymn carries the festive atmosphere of the Choral Festival at Peterborough Cathedral for which it was written in 1865. The text is based on Philippians 4:4, and conveys the strong sense of Paul's admonition to rejoice always. No matter what the circumstances of the present may be, God's victory and our part in it is won already by our faith. The latter verses spoken either by pastor or antiphonally with the congregation work very well as a fitting benediction at the close of worship.

Children's Object Talk

Energy from Jesus, Life's Bread

Object
Small pieces of bread in a napkin-lined basket, possibly one used for communion.

Lesson
Jesus is the bread of life. Feeding on him changes us.

(Pass the bread as the children assemble, and invite each to choose a piece and eat it slowly.)

What is happening to that piece of bread you just put into your mouth? Where is it going? Will it change inside of you? What will it become? It will become your blood, your muscles, your eyes, your teeth, your fingernails, and so on. The food you eat turns into you, doesn't it? What marvelous bodies we have that turn food into eyes and ears, mouths and hands, and energy to use them!

In the story I just read in the Bible, Jesus tells us that he becomes part of us, too. You can keep all the stories you hear about Jesus in your mind. You can think of them. You can remember how they sound. You can remember how they feel. You can remember them whenever you want to. When someone is unkind to you, you can remember that Jesus loves you. You can remember that Jesus said to love each other. You can remember how Jesus shared food. You can remember how he loved the poor, and how he healed the sick. You can remember what Jesus tells you do to.

That's how Jesus is inside you—in your head—in your mind. When you remember all the things you've been told that Jesus said—all these things in your head—then your eyes will want to look at good things, not nasty things. Your hands will want to do happy things, not hurtful things. Your mouth will want to say kind things, not harmful, or sneaky things. Keep on remembering. Keep thoughts of Jesus inside your head.

—*Lois Brokering*

August 17, 1997
13th Sunday after Pentecost (Proper 15)
RC/Pres: 20th Sunday in Ordinary Time

The Sermon

The Feast of God

Hymns
Beginning of Worship: "Now Thank We All Our God"
Sermon Hymn: "O Jesus, Joy of Loving Hearts"
End of Worship: "Jesus Took the Bread"

Scripture
John 6:51–58 (For additional sermon materials on this passage, see the *1997 May/June Planning Issue* of *The Clergy Journal* and on Ephesians 5:15–20, see the April 1997 issue of *The Clergy Journal*.)

Sermon Text
"*So Jesus said to them, 'Very truly, I tell you, unless you eat the flesh of the Son of Man and drink his blood, you have no life in you'*" (vs. 53).

Although almost every Christian participates regularly in the sacrament of the Eucharist, there is no commonly held belief that explains what is *actually* happening during the event. At one end of the spectrum, some understand this act as a literal sacrifice directly comparable to the ancient temple sacrifice of a bull or a sheep; they understand the eating and drinking to be a literal consuming of the literal body and literal blood of Jesus, as participation in a sacrifice that was made once and for all centuries ago and is, mysteriously, made over and over again in the sharing of the elements each time we gather at the altar.

At the other end of the spectrum are those who hold that communion is a memorial of the life and death of Jesus, a time of remembrance of the self-sacrifice he made on our behalf and that we are called to imitate as his disciples. The bread and wine are symbols of a life poured out in love for others. There are those who call this ritual Eucharist, others who refer to it as communion, some for whom it is the Lord's Supper. Each name nuances the event differently, emphasizing one aspect over another, putting the participants into a different context.

For many persons, it can be profoundly unsettling to realize that something this central to our Christian faith can be as open to interpretation as is this meal.

Yet, when we return to Scripture for illumination, we are not comforted by finding a single, simple truth. Indeed, what is interesting about this text in the Gospel of John is that, although it seems quite specific on first reading (even, to our twentieth-century ears, a little overly graphic), it doesn't *explain* anything at all, nor does it tell us definitely what we are about.

It is even more confusing to note that John is the one gospel that does not contain the story of the Last Supper with the familiar act of breaking and blessing bread, pouring and blessing wine. This strange, ambiguous passage is the closest John comes to including that piece of our faith history. It is clear that the evangelist, writing many years after the death of Jesus, is trying to help the disciples of his own era understand something profound, something not easily captured in words, about this meal that they share with one another at God's table. It seems he was trying to communicate something that would renew and enrich them (and us) by inviting us all to let go of the "facts" and catch a glimpse of the truth.

It can be helpful to remember that to the people—primarily Jews—among whom Jesus moved and taught when he was alive in Palestine two millennia ago, God was present in the reality of life itself. It was God's Spirit, God's Breath, the *ruach*, breathed into *adham* at the time of creation that made a living being.

In this sense, God was and is present in *every* being at *all* times. In addition, the ancient Hebrews, in common with most of the people of the Mideast, understood that the Holy One became present in the act of sacrifice at the temple. They believed that when God accepted the blood as a renewal of the covenant, God entered into the body of the sacrificial animal and, by eating the flesh at the feast following the ritual, each participant partook of the power and being, the essence, of God.

It is these two ideas, still very much part of our own belief system, that begin to cast light on the passage both for Christians who hold the Lord's Supper to be a memorial as well as for those who hold it to be literal sacrifice.

First, we acknowledge that it is God's Spirit, incarnate in Jesus, that filled him with God's own power, enabling him to be God's anointed Christ. It is this divinity that we recognize when we call him Lord and Savior.

Second, we know that we partake of the power and essence of what we eat. If we don't believe that, why do we worry about balanced diets? or with getting the proper amount of protein and other nutrients?

August 17, 1997
13th Sunday after Pentecost (Proper 15)
RC/Pres: 20th Sunday in Ordinary Time

Why are we concerned that our children eat healthy foods? and enough food? We are concerned because we know that our body takes and transforms those elements into bone and muscle, into the chemicals that allow our brains to function, our hearts to beat, our lungs to fill.

The words John reports in his gospel, *"Very truly, I tell you, unless you eat the flesh of the Son of Man and drink his blood, you have no life in you,"* are inviting us to welcome God's presence with us as Jesus himself welcomed it.

First, we are invited to see and know God permeating every fiber of our being, every breath we take. Unless we know God with that intimacy and that wholeness of knowing, we do not begin to comprehend the miraculous gift we have been given and the meaning of that gift.

Second, just as we know that healthy physical food transforms and strengthens our physical bodies, so we are invited to know God as the holy spiritual food, as the flesh and blood that *is* our eternal body and that *sustains* our eternal body. Unless we know God with that level of dependence, we cannot begin to resonate to God's essential being, which can be incarnate in the temporal, but is known without veils only when we are willing to risk touching the eternal.

The sacrament itself means nothing if it is an event locked in time that leaves us exactly as it found us. Its power (whether as sacrifice or as memorial) is in its power to change our very beings. When we know God truly as creator, redeemer, sustainer, one whose breath breathes in us, whose flesh is our flesh, whose power is that by which we act, then—and only then—do we *live* as Christ called us to live, at one with the God who called us by name.

John reports that Jesus used this image, these words, *"Very truly, I tell you, unless you eat the flesh of the Son of Man and drink his blood, you have no life in you."* In our ultra-scientific age, we would perhaps use others, less ambiguous or mysterious. Whatever the image, it is asking the same thing of us: to be willing to allow Christ to enter into us, enter into the deepest depths of our beings, into our hearts and minds, into our bodies, into our very cells, where he can be the elements that transform us from those who hear and see, but do not understand, into fully aware humans manifesting the divine image in which we are created.

—Andrea La Sonde Anastos
The First Church of Deerfield
Deerfield, Massachusetts

August 24, 1997

14th Sunday after Pentecost (Proper 16)
RC/Pres: 21st Sunday in Ordinary Time

Lessons

Pres/Meth/UCC	1 Kings 8:(1, 6, 10–11) 22–30, 41–43	Eph 6:10–20	Jn 6:56–69
Roman Catholic	Josh 24:1–2a, 15–17, 18b	Eph 5:21–32	Jn 6:60–69
Episcopal	Josh 24:1–2a, 14–15	Eph 5:21–33	Jn 6:60–69
Lutheran	Josh 24:1–2a, 14–15	Eph 6:10–20	Jn 6:56–69

Introduction to the Lessons
Lesson 1
(1) *1 Kings 8:(1, 6, 10–11) 22–30, 41–43* **(Pres/Meth/UCC)**
The optional verses tell of bringing the ark of the covenant to Solomon's Temple. Verses 22–30, 41–43 are Solomon's prayer that God will dwell on earth and hear the prayers of both the Israelites and foreigners so that the whole earth may, in time, worship the Lord.

(2) *Joshua 24:1–2a, 15–17, 18b* **(RC)**;
 Joshua 24:1–2a, 14–15 **(Epis/Luth)**
The shorter reading is simply the choice Joshua sets before the people of Israel between the Lord and the other gods previously served by them. The longer reading includes the affirmation of the people to serve God.

Lesson 2
(1) *Ephesians 6:10–20* **(Pres/Meth/UCC/Luth)**
This passage speaks of putting on the spiritual armor of God to be prepared to stand against the enemies of the Spirit. With the exception of the word of God (referred to as a sword), none of the armor is offensive. It prepares the wearer not to attack, but to stand (the word is used four times in these verses) firmly, with confidence and perseverance.

August 24, 1997
14th Sunday after Pentecost (Proper 16)
RC/Pres: 21st Sunday in Ordinary Time

(2) *Ephesians 5:21–32* **(RC);** *Ephesians 5:21–33* **(Epis)**
The analogy of wives and husbands can make this a highly problematic reading for contemporary churches. Verse 32 is essential in that it explains back onto the passage that the writer is referring not to marital relationship, but to the relationship between Christ and the church.

Gospel
John 6:56–69 **(Pres/Meth/UCC/Luth);** *John 6:60–69* **(RC/Epis)**
The shorter reading tells of the disciples beginning to fall away from Jesus as they are forced to confront the harder sayings. It concludes with the confession of Peter that at least some of the disciples recognize Jesus as the Messiah. The longer reading includes four verses that many scholars consider a redaction concerning the body and blood of Jesus being essential to eternal life.

Theme
Our power to be transforming agents in the world comes from a deep knowledge that we reflect the loving presence of God in us and manifest it by our wise choices and compassionate acts.

Thought for the Day
"If we were willing to learn the meaning of real discipleship and actually to become disciples, the Church in the West would be transformed, and the resultant impact on society would be staggering."
—David Watson

Prayer of Meditation
Sustaining God, I come before you today in my belief and in my unbelief. I come before you wanting the easy way and knowing that the strength you offer me will only come through my struggles to be faithful to the hard way. Grant me courage, O you who are my redeemer and sustainer, to follow where you lead, even when I am tempted to turn away. Amen.

Call to Worship
We who would valiant be: let us not waver,
but in true constancy, follow the Savior.
There's no discouragement shall make us once relent
our first avowed intent to live as pilgrims.   —John Bunyan

Prayer of Adoration
We kneel before the magnitude of your service to us, Almighty One. We kneel in awe that you choose humility before power, and the form of a servant when you are our sovereign. We lift our hearts in joy that you have shown us that we can be your people, incarnations of your presence, called by your name, no matter how humble our work in the eyes of the world. We lift our hearts in joy that we can serve you. Amen.

Prayer of Confession
In sorrow, we acknowledge that we have sometimes been among those who questioned the authority of your Christ to ask us for faithful service. In sorrow, we acknowledge that we have sometimes been among those who turned away from him when such commitment seemed too hard. In sorrow, we acknowledge that we have sometimes worked to appear valuable in the world's eyes rather than in your eyes. Pour out your compassion upon us, God of mercy, and guide us to deeper and more trusting life. Amen.

Prayer of Dedication of Gifts and Self
As Christ offered himself without measure on behalf of your desire for humanity, so we seek to learn how to offer ourselves without measure. Accept these offerings as part of our learning, encouraging us and supporting us in our desire to be ever more generous with the gifts that come from you and which we are called to return to your work. Amen.

Sermon Summary
What stands in the way of committed discipleship is often not self-satisfaction, but a sense of worthlessness.

Hymn of the Day
"Stand Up, Stand Up for Jesus," written by George J. Webb in 1837, was originally composed for a secular piece, "'Tis Dawn, the Lark Is Singing." It was combined with George Duffield Jr.'s text taken from Philippians 6:10–17 in the mid-1800s and was a revival favorite. Controversial because of its militaristic imagery, it is worth noting that Paul's original text speaks to those who indeed need the defense of God, the armor of the gospel. The war imagery is contrasted to militaristic battle gear: the belt of truth (not of knives) and the sword of the Spirit (the word of God) as our weapons.

August 24, 1997
14th Sunday after Pentecost (Proper 16)
RC/Pres: 21st Sunday in Ordinary Time

Children's Object Talk

Following Means Doing

Object
None.

Lesson
God enables us to be followers of Jesus.

Let's play follow the leader. You do what I do, okay? I'm going to fold my hands. (Fold your hands where all children can see them.) Can you do it too? That's the way. Now watch—do exactly what I do. (Place your hands on your head. Hold them up in front of you close to your body, and wiggle your fingers. Scratch your ear. Pat your cheeks. Make a tube with both hands and blow through it. Watch to see that the children follow your actions and encourage them.) Good! You are good followers. That game is called "Follow the Leader." I was the leader. You followed me. That means you did what I did.

Jesus wants to be your leader and mine too. What does that mean? We can't see Jesus and watch what he does? How can we find out what it means to follow Jesus? How do we know what Jesus does? (Elicit answers: read the Bible, pray, etc.) There are many stories in the Bible where Jesus tells us what to do Even though we can't see him, we can remember these stories, and try to do all those good things Jesus does.

Can you think of some things Jesus tells us to do in the Bible? (Elicit answers, and repeat them if possible so adults can hear.) He tells us to share. He tells us to be peacemakers. He tells us to say kind things. He tells us to do kind things. When we do these things because Jesus tells us to, we are followers of Jesus.

—*Lois Brokering*

The Sermon

Led in a Harder Way

Hymns
Beginning of Worship: "When We Are Tempted to Deny Your Son"
Sermon Hymn: "You Are the Way"
End of Worship: "The Church's One Foundation"

Scripture
John 6:56–69 (For additional sermon materials on this passage, see the April 1997 and the *1997 May/June Planning Issue* of *The Clergy Journal*.)

Sermon Text
"When many of his disciples heard it, they said, 'This teaching is difficult; who can accept it?'" (vs. 60).

The context of this verse is the audacious claim, read over the past three Sundays, that Jesus is the living bread come down from heaven to nourish the world. It is no wonder that we, today, grapple with our faith when even those who listened to Jesus in the flesh, who were willing to call themselves his first disciples, found his teachings difficult and wondered who would accept them.

Indeed, it could be argued that we, in our era, have legitimate reason to struggle with Jesus' claim. After all, he came among us almost two thousand years ago and, yet, he does not seem to have fed the world as he promised. Millions of us go to bed physically hungry every night. Millions die having never known anything *but* physical hunger. The vast majority of the rest of us are starved spiritually in spite of Jesus' incarnate presence long ago in Palestine.

What are we to make of this —we who call ourselves Christians? William Barclay, the brilliant Scottish theologian, suggests that what makes Jesus' claim hard to hear and difficult to do is not that we *cannot* grasp the image of a human being as living bread, but that we do not *want* to grasp the implications of that possibility. We do not want to accept that Jesus, in offering himself to us over and over as living bread, is offering to transform us.

He is offering to be the conduit by which we are connected body, mind, and spirit to God and God's overflowing

August 24, 1997
14th Sunday after Pentecost (Proper 16)
RC/Pres: 21st Sunday in Ordinary Time

graciousness. He is offering us an alternate paradigm. He is asking us to see that the resources of the world are experienced as limited because those in power distribute them inequitably rather than because they are not sufficient, even abundant. By participating in his act of self-sacrifice and allowing it to change us radically (change us into living bread ourselves), he is offering *us* the opportunity to feed the world.

This is, indeed, a hard teaching and in this passage, Jesus tells us why it is so easy to fall away. He says, *"I have told you that no one can come to me unless it is granted by the Father."* Lest there be any confusion, Jesus is not suggesting that God chooses to keep some people eternally separate from Christ or from "at-one-ment" with Christ. What he is saying is that unless we are willing to be defined by that which is God in us, we will always be unable to comprehend the fullness to which Christ invites us.

What makes this hard for us to understand is that many of us have been taught that pride is the deadliest of the sins. We think of pride as seeing ourselves as more important than God, beyond the need of God, able to do it on our own.

However, what often causes us to fall away from Christ, is not our sense of self-importance, but quite the opposite: our sense of worthlessness. What causes us to find the way of Christ too difficult is not being too full of ourselves (our true selves which is God's living presence), but feeling totally empty and helpless and disempowered. Pride, you see, can also be the perverse belief that we are so far beneath God's care, so far outside God's love, that we are not capable of being true children of God. It can be the belief that since we can never measure up, why should we try?

Our brokenness can overwhelm us when we believe that we are outside the power of love. Gradually we begin to feel resentful of those who appear to us to be particularly blessed (those who, unlike us, *are* loved by God). Our resentment and insecurity spawns a need to justify our very existence. This quickly leads to contempt for those who seem even more miserable than we are; after all, if we have someone in relation to whom we can feel superior, we must have *some* worth!

Jesus asks his disciples to step outside that tragic pattern of relationship, to be healed, and to be fed by that which will truly satisfy. He asks us to eat of his body and his blood, to be nourished with all that is divine, so that we will know our God-named selves as persons of God, as persons of authority and compassion, able to manifest God's presence in our families and cities and nations.

When we stop ourselves as helpless unconnected creatures, and truly know ourselves as members of the body of Christ on earth, we know ourselves as transformed individuals, instruments through whom God can work to build the commonwealth which is only hidden from us by that which is still unhealed in the here and now. When we truly know ourselves as members of the body of Christ on earth, we know that God's authority can act through us on behalf of all God's people. We know that God's power can act through us to change that which is dysfunctional. We know that God's power can act through us to redistribute resources so that everyone will be adequately fed and housed and clothed. We know that God's power of discernment can lead us to re-vision worn-out political and economic structures. In solidarity with our brother and rabbi, we willingly allow ourselves to be used as living bread to feed the hungry.

When we can allow God to define us as whole and beloved heirs, when we can truly know ourselves as members of the body of Christ on earth because we have been radically altered, we are neither puffed up by a sense of our own importance nor paralyzed by a sense of our own worthlessness. We are able to reflect God's light and truth with joy and confidence. The way of the cross is no longer the harder way. It is the *only* way because it is the way that allows us to die to that which would come between us and our sisters and brothers. The way of the cross is the *only* way because it is the way that allows us to share with a pure and open heart our wealth of body, mind, and spirit with those in need.

When we truly know ourselves as members of the body of Christ on earth, we will be able to say with Peter, *"Lord, to whom can we go? You have the words of eternal life."* So be it.

—*Andrea La Sonde Anastos*
The First Church of Deerfield
Deerfield, Massachusetts

August 31, 1997

15th Sunday after Pentecost (Proper 17)
RC/Pres: 22nd Sunday in Ordinary Time

Lessons

Pres/Meth/UCC	Song 2:8–13	Jas 1:17–27	Mk 7:1–8, 14–15, 21–23
Roman Catholic	Deut 4:1–2, 6–8	Jas 1:17–18, 21b–22, 27	Mk 7:1–8, 14–15, 21–23
Episcopal	Deut 4:1–9	Eph 6:10–20	Mk 7:1–8, 14–15, 21–23
Lutheran	Deut 4:1–2, 6–9	Jas 1:17–27	Mk 7:1–8, 14–15, 21–23

Introduction to the Lessons

Lesson 1
(1) *Song of Solomon 2:8–13* (**Pres/Meth/UCC**)
This passage tells of the exquisite call of the bridegroom to the beloved to arise and come away. Whether read as a metaphor for Christ and the church or as love poetry, it is an invitation to leave the winter behind and respond to the greening of creation.

(2) *Deuteronomy 4:1–2, 6–8* (**RC**); *Deuteronomy 4:1–9* (**Epis**); *Deuteronomy 4:1–2, 6–9* (**Luth**)
The shorter readings are the prologue to the Law, explaining that nothing should be added to it or taken from it because the Law is given by God and, therefore, perfect. The Episcopal reading includes the verses about what happened to some of the people who followed Baal.

Lesson 2
(1) *James 1:17–27* (**Pres/Meth/UCC/Luth**);
James 1:17–18, 21b–22, 27 (**RC**)
The lesson begins with the reminder that the Christian lives by grace. The writer goes on to say that it is not possible to truly *hear* the word without being affected in behavior. One acts because of the grace one has received.

(2) *Ephesians 6:10–20* **(Epis)**
This passage speaks of putting on the spiritual armor of God to be prepared to stand against the enemies of the Spirit. With the exception of the word of God (referred to as a sword), none of the armor is offensive. It prepares the wearer not to attack, but to stand (the word is used four times in these verses) firmly, with confidence and perseverance.

Gospel
Mark 7:1–8, 14–15, 21–23 **(Pres/Meth/UCC/RC/Epis/Luth)**
Jesus addresses the issue of traditions that are worshiped as more sacred than God's word. He points out that spiritual defilement comes from within and we must look to changing those behaviors that spring from an unclean heart or impure spirit rather than expecting rituals to "purify" us.

Theme
We want our Christianity to keep us safe and comfortable, but Christ asked us to live in open and risky relationship with God and with each other.

Thought for the Day
"The Christian ideal has not been tried and found too difficult; it has been found difficult and left untried." —G. K. Chesterton

Prayer of Meditation
By grace, O gracious God, I have been brought to your house. By grace, I have been empowered to service on your behalf. May my every word and deed be a word or a deed of grace this day. Amen.

Call to Worship
Leader:	Who shall dwell in the house of the Lord?
People:	Those who speak truth, who walk blamelessly, who do right.
Leader:	Who shall dwell in the house of the Lord?
People:	Those who offer mercy, who do justice, who forgive hurts.
Leader:	Shape us all, O Lord, that we may be a people of your house of peace.
People:	Shape us to your will so that we may dwell in your house forever. —Adapted from Psalm 15 and Micah 6

August 31, 1997
15th Sunday after Pentecost (Proper 17)
RC/Pres: 22nd Sunday in Ordinary Time

Prayer of Adoration

Beloved God, you have blessed us with the amazing promise that nothing outside us can separate us from you. You have promised that no sin, no brokenness, no uncleanness can cause you to stop loving us. We sing aloud with gratitude that such hope can be ours! Grant that your love so transforms us that *our* love and purity reach ever further and more confidently to meet your love. Then, we will know the blessing of your promise that nothing can separate us from your presence in our neighbors, and every pain will drop away until we dance together in your glory. Amen.

Prayer of Confession

We confess that we have often judged others harshly, when we were in need of mercy ourselves. We confess that we have often judged others by outward things and missed the inward grace of your being manifest in them. We confess that it has been easier to condemn others for not following our human rules than it has been to follow your commandment to love our neighbor as ourself. Wash us again in the cleansing waters of baptism. Make us new again, renewing God, and help us leave behind our judgmentalism to make room for your compassion. Amen.

Prayer of Dedication of Gifts and Self

We ask your blessing, O God, on our hearts and minds, on our visions and missions, on our labor and stewardship. We dedicate all we are and all we have to your work with whole and thankful hearts, knowing that it has been entrusted to us by you, to be wisely used in your name. Amen.

Sermon Summary

Jesus invites us (as he invited the religious people of his own time) to let go of our human rules and regulations and risk the radical freedom of living faithfully into a relationship of divine love.

Hymn of the Day

"Just as I Am, without One Plea." Important as a statement of Jesus' saving care for us wherever we are in our spiritual journey, this hymn had particular significance for English author, Charlotte Elliot (1789–1871). Disabled by disease at the age of thirty-two, she nevertheless wrote over 150 hymns in collections like *The Invalids' Hymn Book*, and *Hours of Sorrow Cheered and Comforted*. The words for the first line came to her from a visiting Swedish minister who assured her in a letter that no matter how useless she felt, surely Jesus would come to her "just as you are." Disabled in the use of her body, her spirit continues to grace us with the gospel of her words.

Children's Object Talk

Inside Clean—Outside Clean

Object
Moist towelettes for all the children.
Lesson
Clean thoughts and clean actions are not the same.

(Hold up a moist towel packet.) Does anybody know what this is? (Pause for answers. To incorrect guesses, reply, "It looks a little like that, doesn't it?" or "It could be. What else could it be?") Well, it's actually one of those little wet paper things that you can use to get your dirty hands clean again. (Open one and demonstrate.) There. Are my hands cleaner than they were? I think so. Everyone take one of these, but DO NOT OPEN IT. Just hold it with both your hands. (Pass the towelettes quickly. Use two baskets if there are many children.)

Now, can you close your eyes really tight, so you can't see anything at all? Try to imagine your hands are *really* dirty. What have you got on your hands? Have you been outside playing, and gotten mud on them? Did you go fishing and get smelly fish stuff on them? Did you eat a *Big Mac* and get the gooey dressing on your fingers? Did you just finish painting a picture, and get paint on your hands? What's on your hands? (Wait for responses.) Now open your eyes. Are your hands really dirty? No. You just imagined it.

In the story we heard from the Bible a minute ago, Jesus tells us that God doesn't like us to do unkind things. God wants us to do loving things. But . . . not only that. God doesn't even want us to *think* about doing things that are not loving and kind. God doesn't like us to imagine we are doing nasty things. God doesn't want us to imagine we're calling someone an unkind name. He doesn't want us to think about stealing something that isn't ours. God doesn't want us to do unloving things. He doesn't even want us to think about doing them. That's really hard, isn't it? Think about loving things. Do loving things.

And save your towelette for the next time your hands are actually dirty.

—*Lois Brokering*

August 31, 1997
15th Sunday after Pentecost (Proper 17)
RC/Pres: 22nd Sunday in Ordinary Time

The Sermon

Human Precepts, Divine Love

Hymns
Beginning of Worship: "Great Is Your Faithfulness"
Sermon Hymn: "Just as I Am, without One Plea"
End of Worship: "As a Chalice Cast of Gold"

Scripture
Mark 7:1–8, 14–15, 21–23 (For additional sermon materials on this passage, see the April 1997 and the *1997 May/June Planning Issue* of *The Clergy Journal*.)

Sermon Text
"[Jesus] said to them, 'Isaiah prophesied rightly about you hypocrites, as it is written, "This people honors me with their lips, but their hearts are far from me; in vain do they worship me, teaching human precepts as doctrines"'" (vss. 6–7).

As a student of Scripture, I find it baffling whenever parishioners or other clergy suggest that church is (or should be) a place of comfort. I am puzzled when I hear some Christian groups speak of Jesus as if his teachings uphold a Christian status quo based on such apparently unassailably good things as "family values." I wonder how passages such as this one from the Gospel of Mark fit such a paradigm.

My own experience of faith has been disconcerting and *uncomfortable*. As soon as I think I have my Christianity whipped into shape and I finally understand how I'm supposed to behave, I come across a text like this . . . and I need to reassess everything. My own experience has been that the phrase "status quo" doesn't apply to the faithful life, although I would love to believe that there *is* a Christian status quo and that, someday, I could settle into it and feel "finished" as a Christian.

Indeed, the Pharisees must be my fathers and mothers into the faith because, like them, in my quest to be a *good* Christian and to do my Christianity "right," I find it so easy to fall into behaviors that make rules and regulations into idols. Frankly, it is less challenging to follow a rigid rule than it is to listen attentively for the good news of God to come to me each day.

Jesus, sharing our daily round with us, reminds us that our relationship with God is not a convenient set of rules and regulations that we can memorize and then perform by rote for the rest of our lives. Jesus reminds us forcefully in passages such as this one from Mark that our grace-filled relationship with YHWH—the one who called Godself "I Will Be Who I Will Be"—is a living entity, rich and ever-changing, stretching and bending and adjusting and deepening as we mature. An important spiritual discipline at one time in our lives may be a roadblock at another. What is an appropriate act of faith in one setting may be unkind or thoughtless or, even, abhorrent in another. A careful attentiveness to God's voice (and to God's presence manifest in God's people) will always lead us more deeply into lively choices based on *love* rather than legalism.

"This people honors me with their lips, but their hearts are far from me; in vain do they worship me, teaching human precepts as doctrines."

We need to remember that the questions of the Pharisees in this particular passage are questions of orthopraxis (correct religious behavior). They are not speaking here about physical cleanliness or dirt, but about the sacred categories of clean and unclean which they understood to affect their righteousness or their defilement as people in relationship with God. Although most Christians today would find this a peculiar thing to be worried about, it was not a stupid or ridiculous concern.

In fact, Jesus doesn't criticize the Pharisees for seeking righteousness per se; he calls them to account for the extremes to which they carry it because those extremes do exactly the opposite of what the Pharisees intended. Rather than liberating them to worship the God whose service is perfect freedom and to rejoice in the radical newness to which God calls them, they have locked themselves into a lifestye that is almost obsessive. In trying to understand and follow faithfully the broad and overarching commandments that God gave to them through Moses, they have imprisoned themselves in layer after layer of "human precepts."

Two thousand years later, Christians seeking the living God are still making the same very human mistakes, still imprisoning ourselves and others in layer after layer of "human precepts" so that we can consider ourselves righteous people (and, by the way, judge whether our neighbor is righteous, too). Although Jesus himself turned the status quo on its head and questioned every religious rule and regulation he had been taught, it seems that we choose to honor him as our rabbi

August 31, 1997
15th Sunday after Pentecost (Proper 17)
RC/Pres: 22nd Sunday in Ordinary Time

and mentor by clinging to rigid understandings of his literal words and creating a new status quo with new rules and regulations. Although he went to his death so that we would know that *nothing* (*no* thing, *no* sin, *no* behavior) stands between the human soul and its creator-redeemer-sustainer, we spend most of our religious life designing methods by which we can separate those with access to God from those who are outside the pale.

Our new categories of clean and unclean are based on such things as gender and whether we need to protect God from the ministry of women, and whether we need to protect God from the ministry of those whose sexual love and fidelity is expressed toward one who is like them rather than different from them. When we use such concerns to allow or disallow certain relationships with God, we are judging righteousness by an outward indicator, something we can *see*—just as we used to judge people with different skin colors as more or less worthy.

In this passage (and many others like it throughout the Gospels), Jesus calls our judgments to account. Over and over, he breaks from the old understandings, the old rules, the old legalism which are all fear-based choices, into freedom and love. He invites us to leave behind rigid regulations that trap us into believing that God relates to us through reward and punishment, through clean and unclean. He invites us to relate to God and to God's presence in each other through liberating love that freely grows and changes and is expressed in different ways in each succeeding generation. He invites us to take the risk of setting aside our human precepts of good and bad, right and wrong, and being attentively aware of the divine uniqueness in each person.

Jesus himself was accused of blasphemy and sacrilege by the religious establishment and, by the human precepts of his time, he was guilty of both. Given his own choices, we should not be surprised that over and over in the Gospels he has invited those who follow him to risk such judgment in their own times in order that they, that *we*, may witness to God's love which always moves beyond such categories.

—*Andrea La Sonde Anastos*
The First Church of Deerfield
Deerfield, Massachusetts

September 7, 1997

16th Sunday after Pentecost (Proper 18)
RC/Pres: 23rd Sunday in Ordinary Time

Lessons

Pres/Meth/UCC	Prov 22:1–2, 8–9, 22–23	Jas 2:1–10 (11–13), 14–17	Mk 7:24–37
Roman Catholic	Isa 35:4–7a	Jas 2:1–5	Mk 7:31–37
Episcopal	Isa 35:4–7	Jas 1:17–27	Mk 7:31–37
Lutheran	Isa 35:4–7a	Jas 2:1–10 (11–13), 14–17	Mk 7:24–37

Introduction to the Lessons

Lesson 1

(1) *Proverbs 22:1–2, 8–9, 22–23* **(Pres/Meth/UCC)**
This passage emphasizes themes common in the wisdom tradition—its superiority to wealth, the claims that the poor have on the rich, reaping what is sown whether for good or ill, and the importance of having a generous heart.

(2) *Isaiah 35:4–7a* **(RC/Luth)**; *Isaiah 35:4–7* **(Epis)**
A vision of a future is told in which nature itself will be healed, participating in and witnessing to the redemption of Israel and the messianic fullness that "the day of the Lord" will bring.

Lesson 2

(1) *James 2:1–10 (11–13), 14–17* **(Pres/Meth/UCC/Luth)**;
  James 2:1–5 **(RC)**
Resist the temptation to split God's gifts from God and make them our own, thus splitting faith from works, worship from work, and word from deed. God is the one who, in Jesus, holds everything together.

(2) *James 1:17–27* **(Epis)**
Deep connections are rooted in God: between faith and works, between worship and life, and between word and deed.

September 7, 1997
16th Sunday after Pentecost (Proper 18)
RC/Pres: 23rd Sunday in Ordinary Time

Gospel
Mark 7:24–37 (**Pres/Meth/UCC/Luth**); *Mark 7:31–37* (**RC/Epis**)
Both passages deal with Jesus' ministry among the Gentiles, specifically, "in the region of Tyre and Sidon" where he encounters "a Greek, a Syrophoenician" woman and a man from the Decapolis who is deaf and dumb. In both instances he responds to expression of faith, healing the woman's daughter who was demon-possessed, and unstopping the ears of the deaf man and healing him of his impediment. In part, these stories constitute messianic signs that Jesus' ministry provokes, and in part they witness to the universal scope of his mission and life.

Theme
The grace of our Lord Jesus Christ turns the world upside down. The last become first, Gentiles faithfully interpret Torah, and the dumb plainly speak good news.

Thought for the Day
The gospel is upsetting. It is most upsetting to the world our virtues work so hard to uphold: the world of right and wrong, of merit and class, of doing good. Part of the gospel's scandal is that all the "wrong" people respond to Jesus in faith—e.g., gentile women, deaf and dumb men—while all those who concern themselves with keeping the law are offended by him. Yet being offended by him seems to be the only way to receive his grace, which is why, in the end, it is a marvelous gift that the gospel is so upsetting.

Prayer of Meditation
Grant us, O Lord, the gift of being small, as small as leaven, or a mustard seed, or even the eye of a needle. We work so hard to make ourselves big, to add a cubit to our span of life, an inch to our height. We would even work hard to make ourselves small, growing big with our own humility. Grant us, O God, what we cannot give ourselves, the gift of being a child of God. We ask this in Christ's name. Amen.

Call to Worship
"*. . . he has filled the hungry with good things, and sent the rich away empty*" (Lk 1:53). Come, all you who are hungry and thirsty, who spend money for that which is not bread and who labor for things that do not satisfy. Come! Come to him who feeds the hungry and gives drink

to those who thirst. Come to the fountain of living waters, to the bread of life. Come let us worship God!

Prayer of Adoration
O God who scatters the proud in the imagination of their hearts, who fills the hungry with good things and sends the rich empty away, receive our adoration and praise. Lift us up to celebrate the gift of your presence and humble us to discover that singular angle of vision that is able to discern your kingdom. We ask this confident of the grace which is ours in Jesus Christ, the love of God, and the fellowship of the Holy Spirit. Amen.

Prayer of Confession
We work so hard, O Lord, to keep this world in decent order, to keep our virtues away from our vices, our good moments from our weaker ones. But we confess that all our labors have only bound us more deeply to ourselves and we are quite unable to set ourselves free. Show us again and anew what is good, we pray, and what the Lord requires of us that by his grace we may risk doing good, love mercy, and walk humbly with our God. We pray in Jesus Christ's name. Amen.

Prayer of Dedication of Gifts and Self
What are we ever called upon to do in response to your grace, O Lord, but to offer ourselves? Indeed, we confess that we belong to you already and what we give in the form of gift or self is always yours. Save us from the poverty of selfishness, the hell of being unable to give, and teach us, we pray, that generosity which did not spare even his own Son but gave him up for us all. We ask this in his name. Amen.

Sermon Summary
It is one thing for the blind to see, the deaf to hear, the poor to hear good news, but it is quite another for Gentiles to praise the God of Israel. And a woman to boot? What kind of sign is this? Can the dogs who eat the crumbs of the table know better than the children who are to be fed first? So may we become such a *Domini Canis*, such a hound of the Lord.

September 7, 1997
16th Sunday after Pentecost (Proper 18)
RC/Pres: 23rd Sunday in Ordinary Time

Hymn of the Day

"If You But Trust in God to Guide Thee." This traditional German hymn was written in the seventeenth century by Georg Neumark, taking its theme from Psalm 55:22. Like many of the psalms, the poetry expresses assurance even in the darkest of times. In Neumark's case, the Thirty Years' War caused much suffering and death. The tune at first seems to carry the lament, but with an inexorable sweep takes the voice to a note of hope at the end of each stanza. Played not too slowly, this is a meditative hymn of the highest caliber.

Children's Object Talk

Interceding for Others

Object
A list of parishioners who need prayers.

Lesson
God hears when we pray for others' needs.

The gospel lesson we just heard was about two sick people. Do you remember what was wrong with each of them? (Wait for responses.)

There was a little girl whose mother came to Jesus. The little girl was sick, and her mother knew Jesus could make her well. She was brave enough to go up to him and ask him. The second person was a man who could not hear. This time it was friends who came to Jesus to ask for help. Please fix this man's ears so he can hear. Because he can't hear, he has never learned to speak correctly. He can't hear how he sounds. Please help him. The mother and the friends begged for someone else—not for themselves. They did it out of kindness for someone they loved. And Jesus heard them. Jesus answered their requests—their prayers.

Sometimes we pray for ourselves. And sometimes we ask Jesus to help our friends and loved ones. We know people who are sick and need God's help to get well. (Name someone who is close to one of the children. Hold up the prayer list.) This is a list of people we know who are sick or grieving. These people belong to our congregation. Or they are friends or relatives of one of us. Let's ask God to help these people feel better. (Say a short prayer of intercession, saying each person's name aloud, slowly and thoughtfully.) Take this list home with you. This week when you have your times to talk to God, ask God to help these people to feel good again. Know that God will hear you like Jesus heard the mother and the friends in the story.

—*Lois Brokering*

The Sermon

The Woman Who Was Willing to Be a Dog

Hymns
Beginning of Worship: "Now Thank We All Our God"
Sermon Hymn: "Ah, Holy Jesus, How Hast Thou Offended"
End of Worship: "Christ Is Made the Sure Foundation"

Scripture
Mark 7:24–37 (For additional sermon materials on this passage, see the April 1997 and the *1997 May/June Planning Issue* of *The Clergy Journal*.)

Sermon Text
"But she answered him, 'Yes, Lord; yet even the dogs under the table eat the children's crumbs'" (vs. 28).

Why is it that all the people who should have been drawn to Jesus had such trouble with him, while those who were "beyond the pale" so to speak, came to him like filings to a magnet? In this passage in Mark, Jesus has just finished a series of hostile encounters with the Pharisees. They had criticized Jesus' disciples for departing from tradition and eating without first partaking of the ritual washing of the hands. In response, Jesus fairly explodes, accusing them of following the traditions of men but betraying the commandments of God. Turning to the people, he concludes that it is not what is outside of a man that makes him unclean but what is inside his heart. And then, perhaps as much in sorrow as in anger, he leaves the land of the Pharisees, the familiar land of Israel, and ventures into gentile country into the region of Tyre and Sidon.

In Mark's Gospel, geography becomes theology; that is, the place where Jesus is reveals his true mission and purpose—far from serving as a mere backdrop to his ministry. Here his rejection by his own people opens the door to the Gentiles, indeed, makes it possible for the Gentiles to do what his own people were called upon to do but could not: confess him the embodiment of Israel's life and

September 7, 1997
16th Sunday after Pentecost (Proper 18)
RC/Pres: 23rd Sunday in Ordinary Time

calling. Strangely, what happens in this story is not that the Gentiles become "Christians" or that they supersede the Jews, but rather they are given a place in the economy of God which makes them what Krister Stendahl has called, "honorary Jews."

Look. Jesus' glory could not be hid, we are told, even from the Gentiles (vs. 24). In a house, seeking quiet, Jesus is approached by a person with two strikes against her: she is a Gentile and she is a woman. She is, in other words, the least of the last. And worse than that, she is dying. "Oh not so," you say, "it's her daughter who is dying. Her daughter is possessed of a demon." Perhaps so, but for any mother to be in such a situation is to die a hundred times a day. Moreover, a sick child, a dying child is, we think, "unnatural," and the grief a parent bears in such a circumstance is almost unbearable. Such a parent might well conclude that he or she has nothing to lose, that saving one's life seems utterly pointless in view of the possibility of losing the one life that matters.

So, with the enormous courage and almost reckless freedom, this gentile woman asks Jesus for help. No talk of ritual cleansing, no question of credentials, no bitter disputes, only begging him to cast the demon out of her daughter.

Jesus' reply has troubled some folks. It sounds almost cold or indifferent. "Let the children first be fed," he tells her, "for it is not right to take the children's bread and throw it to the dogs." A harsh reply to a beggar woman? Perhaps. But this reply could also be a confession of faith in the God of Israel, the God who chose Israel to be a light to the nations, who covenanted first with Abraham that all the nations of the earth would be blessed through him. In this economy of grace Israel does have a certain priority, as God's chosen people, as the ones through whom salvation is to come. As children of a liberal democracy we may find such a "priority" offensive; we may even be scandalized by its particularity. But there it is, and Jesus has no hesitation in laying it before this gentile woman.

Then a miracle occurs. This woman has no problem with being last or least, no problem even with being called a dog. To a hungry dog, scraps from the table look pretty good. So she is willing to be a dog, to die even, to confess that she has no right to this grace and cannot, in any case, preserve her life or justify her claims before God. Nevertheless, like a dog who refused to quit digging up the backyard for a bone, this woman digs deeper and deeper into God's grace. "Yes, Lord: yet even the dogs under the table eat the children's crumbs." Yes, Lord. This gentile woman has confessed the faith of Israel and seen in Jesus Christ God's covenant with Abraham fulfilled. "Go your way," Jesus tells her; "the demon has left your daughter."

In a sermon on this text Martin Luther called this woman the woman who could hear the Yes in the No; that is, the woman who could hear in God's covenant with Israel good news for herself. Perhaps only dogs can hear such a high-pitched frequency, or perhaps only dogs are foolish enough to believe that there is a treasure hidden in the field. May God make us dogs like that, happy to dig even amid the negatives we hear every day, certain that at the bottom there is a word of grace for us.

—Thomas W. Currie III
First Presbyterian Church
Kerrville, Texas

September 14, 1997

17th Sunday after Pentecost (Proper 19)
Pres: 24th Sunday in Ordinary Time
RC: The Holy Cross—Not listed

Lessons

Pres/Meth/UCC	Prov 1:20–33	Jas 3:1–12	Mk 8:27–38
Episcopal	Isa 50:4–9	Jas 2:1–5, 8–10, 14–18	Mk 8:27–38
Lutheran	Isa 50:4–9a	Jas 3:1–12	Mk 8:27–38

Introduction to the Lessons
Lesson 1
(1) *Proverbs 1:20–33* **(Pres/Meth/UCC)**
Israel's rejection of Yahweh brings judgment according to the wisdom of Proverbs, and falls in the most terrible manner, i.e., Yahweh lets those who reject this gift "be sated with their own devices," truly one definition of hell.

(2) *Isaiah 50:4–9* **(Epis)**; *Isaiah 50:4–9a* **(Luth)**
Israel's rejection of the suffering servant is disclosed in the vindication of that servant by Yahweh.

Lesson 2
(1) *James 3:1–12* **(Pres/Meth/UCC/Luth)**
Chapter three begins by noting the peril of teaching the Christian faith, for who is in a position to give lessons? Especially of concern here is what James considers the almost uncontrollable threat to faithful discipleship—the tongue.

(2) *James 2:1–5, 8–10, 14–18* **(Epis)**
Temptation exists to show partiality, especially to the rich, to love those whom it is in our interest to love.

Gospel
Mark 8:27–38 **(Pres/Meth/UCC/Epis/Luth)**
These verses record Mark's telling of Peter's confession of faith at

Caesarea Philippi, along with Jesus' description of his own mission and identity, and his subsequent rebuke by Peter and his rebuking of Peter. As if to spell things out even more clearly, Jesus adds the familiar if difficult words about self-denial and taking up one's cross and following him, along with the less familiar but even more difficult admonition that whoever is ashamed of him in this life, of him will the Son of Man be ashamed in glory.

Theme
Faith is not information. It is more costly.

Thought for the Day
The difference between expressing an insight, perhaps even a profound and true insight, and confessing the faith is the difference between, as Kierkegaard might say, a genius and an apostle. The genius makes a great discovery and just so enlightens all humankind. But there is no genius in following a genius. The second person to "discover" gun powder does not so much discover it as merely repeat a formula already discovered. But faith, on the other hand, is just as difficult for the second person as it is for the genius. The answer to the question "Who do people say that I am?" requires only an accurate summarizing of received opinion. In some ways it is like the quest for the historical Jesus: opinions, even scholarly opinions, differ. But the question "But who do you say that I am?" requires more of us. Such a question is a question of faith and requires our lives.

Prayer of Meditation
Grant us, O Lord, what flesh and blood cannot give us, what only comes to us by your Holy Spirit; grant us faith in Jesus Christ, the Son of Mary, the Son of God. Him we would confess; him we would follow; him we would adore. Grant us this gift of faith, for we ask this in his name. Amen.

Call to Worship
"Who has believed what we have heard? And to whom has the arm of the Lord been revealed?" (Isa 53:1). Who, indeed, has believed, yet this gift has come to us nevertheless, and even now invites faith. Pray for the strength to follow; pray for the courage to believe; pray for the joy to celebrate this gift. And come, come let us worship God!

September 14, 1997
17th Sunday after Pentecost (Proper 19)
Pres: 24th Sunday in Ordinary Time

Prayer of Adoration

O God, who remains hidden to the wise and yet wonderfully open to babes, whose mystery is never more mysterious than in its clarity and light, we give you thanks and praise for the gift of Jesus Christ. In him all hearts meet and all voices find their true song of praise. Receive our thanks and our hearts and make of us happy followers of your own. We ask in Jesus Christ's name. Amen.

Prayer of Confession

How much would we prefer flesh and blood to the freedom of your grace; how much would we prefer to believe in the sincerity of our own expressions than in the work of the Holy Spirit; how much of our own creatures do we seek to become, rather than to receive our faith and life from your own hand, O Lord. Forgive us, we pray. We say and do lethal things to ourselves and others in the vain attempt to save ourselves. Forgive us, and grant that the death of Jesus Christ might be the end of all our lethal ways, and his resurrection might be the beginning of our own happy and obedient life in your presence. We ask this in his name. Amen.

Prayer of Dedication of Gifts and Self

What else do we have to give but our hearts, O Lord? Receive then these gifts, not because we find them useful or lavish or even particularly generous, but because they tell part of the story of our belonging to you, and because they remind us how much we are your own. So make of us, we pray, gifts to be spent in your service, for we ask in Jesus Christ's name. Amen.

Sermon Summary

As long as Peter is repeating received opinion, he does not risk being wrong; indeed, he does not risk much of anything at all. His position only becomes vulnerable when he confesses his faith. When he does that he is placed directly before the danger of believing. Faith always asks the hardest questions, which is why Job is a person of such great faith. But faith is always asked the hardest questions too, questions which Job could also tell us about. Until Peter believed enough in Jesus to confess him as Lord, he did not believe enough in him to deny him, to fail him, to place himself under the judgment of his grace. But once he made his confession, his whole life became vulnerable, and just so, useful to the Lord he confessed.

Hymn of the Day

"Nearer My God to Thee." The text of his hymn especially evokes the story of Jacob and his vision of angels ascending and descending, reminding us as we sing of the grace of God that allows us to step outside of our present grief. The gospel lesson for today is about Jesus asking us to take up their cross and follow, if we would truly be nearer to God. The story that claimed this was the hymn played by the orchestra as the *Titanic* sank is probably apocryphal.

Children's Object Talk

It Isn't Always Easy

Object
A large bag of a familiar brand of small, wrapped candies.
Lesson
It isn't always easy to resist temptation.

In the gospel lesson today, we heard Jesus tell that it isn't always easy to follow him. We would like to be Jesus' followers. But sometimes other people want us to do something Jesus wouldn't like. Sometimes we want other people to like us so much we want to do what *they* ask us to do. Then we may forget what Jesus asks us to do.

(Hold up the candy.) What do I have here? (Wait for response.) Ummm! I have candy. You like candy? Me, too. This is my candy. (Wait a few seconds, looking smug, then change your expression to serious.) What if I said I will *not* share this candy with you? And what if a couple of kids said to you, "She's (he's) nasty. She won't share. When she isn't looking, let's take some. She'll never know."

What could you do? What could you say? (Elicit answers. Be sure at least two alternatives are posed: first, go along with the tempters; or second, refuse, even if they don't like you anymore.) Sometimes it seems easier to do what others suggest. But even if it is lonely, or gets us in trouble, or causes us to lose our friends, we should do what Jesus would like. We have a choice. Jesus will always be our friend. Jesus will still be our friend when we get to heaven. Jesus will love us forever and ever. But Jesus tells us it won't always be easy to follow him.

Now about this candy . . . (Choose to give each child a piece to take away now, or say that the ushers will give it out as the children leave the service later.)

—*Lois Brokering*

September 14, 1997
17th Sunday after Pentecost (Proper 19)
Pres: 24th Sunday in Ordinary Time

The Sermon

The Difference between Gossip and the Gospel

Hymns
Beginning of Worship: "Holy, Holy, Holy! Lord God Almighty!"
Sermon Hymn: "O Master, Let Me Walk with Thee"
End of Worship: "I'm Not Ashamed to Own My Lord"

Scripture
Mark 8:27–38 (For additional sermon materials on this passage, see the July 1997 and the *1997 May/June Planning Issue* of *The Clergy Journal*.)

Sermon Text
"He asked them, 'But who do you say that I am?' Peter answered him, 'You are the Messiah'... Then he began to teach them that the Son of Man must undergo great suffering..." (vss. 29–31).

"Why," I was asked recently, "are the only people who know how to run this world cutting hair and driving taxis?" The pleasure of good conversation is not to be dismissed, but in truth one of the nice things about "just talking" is that it is just that, talk. Solving the problems of the world is fun and sometimes even illuminating so long as we do not have to do anything about it. But when the talk ceases, when at some point we have to declare our responsibilities and pursue them, then the situation changes and our talk can seem trivial and cheap.

"Who do people say that I am?" Jesus asks his disciples. The question is harmless enough. What do others say? What is the received opinion, the conventional wisdom? Repeating what others are saying is not difficult: John the Baptist, Elijah, one of the prophets. Almost like gossip, the names are thrown about.

But then Jesus turns the tables and asks, "But who do you say that I am?" Why is that such a difficult question? And why is it so different from citing the opinions of others? Perhaps it has something to do with the difference between the gospel and gossip. What Jesus is asking has very little to do with information about him. The disciples have enough information; indeed, they have just summarized the prevailing wisdom *about* Jesus. But what Jesus is asking for is a decision, a judgment, even a taking of responsibility for what they know. "But who do you say that I am?"

Once we answer that question, we put ourselves under a kind of judgment, a judgment which strips away any illusion of neutrality, any sense that Jesus' identity is a matter of mere historical or social interest that we might determine, and instead is a judgment in which we are judged, a confession in which Jesus' identity is a matter of worship and adoration, a telling of the truth in which to tell it we must lay ourselves open to this particular way and life and truth. Such a judgment scares us because it knocks us out of our accustomed position of judging who and what Jesus can be or do. It reverses things and places us in the role of following after.

Peter, bless him, is unafraid of that reversal. He knows that there is much more at stake here than received opinion, and so he happily and gladly confesses. The gospel is not gossip, he says: it is the truth. "You are the Christ." You are the Christ.

And so Jesus begins to unfold what it means to tell the truth. The truth, he says, *"must undergo great suffering, and be rejected by the elders, the chief priests, and the scribes, and be killed, and after three days rise again"* (Mk 8:31). And he said this not in parables but, as Mark points out, "plainly."

Such plain-spokenness is too much for Peter, who takes Jesus aside to rebuke him. A marvelous scene! Peter rebuking Jesus for not knowing what the truth is, for not knowing how messiahs are to behave. But also a marvelous scene because Peter is unafraid of rebuking Jesus, so wonderfully falling under the judgment of his own confession, a confession which compels Peter to hear Jesus' even stronger rebuke: *"Get behind me, Satan! For you are setting your mind not on divine things but on human things"* (Mk 8:33).

Believing is dangerous. I am not sure the church has ever fully appreciated how dangerous it is, or how secure neutrality can seem to some people. Faith, confessing Jesus as Lord, opens one up to that terrible possibility of betraying the truth, of failure, of risking being called "Satan." Jesus does not even call the Pharisees that. Bystanders, spectators, interested parties do not risk his wrath; he never calls them "Satan." After all, they do not place themselves under the obligation to the truth. Only people of faith are so foolish as to open themselves to that kind of risk.

Indeed, people of faith are often just as wrong as Peter is. The Inquisition was put on by Christians, not neutral bystanders;

September 14, 1997
17th Sunday after Pentecost (Proper 19)
Pres: 24th Sunday in Ordinary Time

witches were burned by people of faith, not disinterested observers; segregation was enforced by devout believers, not sophisticated skeptics. We are at our most dangerous when we believe, which is why skepticism, unbelief seems to be attractive to many. It offers the illusion of not taking anything seriously enough to get into trouble or do any damage. The modern world is full of such aspirations to neutrality and is, consequently, very loath to busy itself with anything so binding as the truth.

Yet, this story in Mark suggests that the truth is much more costly than mere information; that the truth, while it does embarrass us, also sets us free. Unless and until we are wounded by it, even as a seed might fall onto the ground and die, we will never be able to bear any real fruit, but instead will lead only a kind of sterile, comfortless existence, an existence that is condemned to live without either joy or passion.

"If any want to become my followers," Jesus concludes, *"let them take up their cross and follow me . . . For what will it profit them to gain the whole world and forfeit their life?"* (Mk 8:34b–36). Confessing Christ opens us up to the reality, and were he someone other than the crucified, it would be a reality which we could scarcely call gospel. Even so, the temptation is always to remain in the realm of gossip, in a studied neutrality that will not obligate us by calling us to account. That way, we think, we can save our lives and never do anything dreadfully wrong; that way, we can preserve our innocence and never be called "Satan." That way, we can be safe.

But what if only sinners are saved? What if only those who dreadfully misunderstand the gospel are the only ones redeemed by it? What if the true judgment on the Inquisition, on the burning of witches, on segregation is not a studied neutrality but the gospel itself? There are worse things than being called "Satan" evidently, and one of them is the illusion that the gospel is not worth confessing. Peter, in both his triumph and in his painful failure to understand and follow, suggests that there is a dignity in being a sinner, even a joy, which neutrality knows not. And in that, he is a gift to us who also misunderstand and often fail to follow a gift that gives us hope in the one who bids us to love him and feed his sheep.

—*Thomas W. Currie III*
First Presbyterian Church
Kerrville, Texas

September 21, 1997

18th Sunday after Pentecost (Proper 20)
RC/Pres: 25th Sunday in Ordinary Time

Lessons

Pres/Meth/UCC	Prov 31:10–31	Jas 3:13—4:3, 7–8a	Mk 9:30–37
Roman Catholic	Wis 2:12, 17–20	Jas 3:16—4:3	Mk 9:30–37
Episcopal	Wis 1:16—2:1	Jas 3:16—4:3	Mk 9:30–37
Lutheran	Jer 11:18–20	Jas 3:13—4:3, 7–8a	Mk 9:30–37

Introduction to the Lessons
Lesson 1
(1) *Proverbs 31:10–31* **(Pres/Meth/UCC)**
This passage celebrates the "good wife," that wise woman who manages well the work of her household, who assists her husband, who provides for her children, who is generous of heart and industrious of spirit.

(2) *Wisdom 2:12, 17–20* **(RC)**; *Wisdom 1:16—2:1* **(Epis)**
This book of Wisdom sketches how the world tends to scorn wisdom and kindness, thinking that death answers all things and that those who trust in God are just whistling past the graveyard.

(3) *Jeremiah 11:18–20* **(Luth)**
This passage decribes what happens when Israel forgets that the fear of the Lord is the beginning of wisdom and trusts, rather, in herself. When that happens, the prophet who speaks the dangerous word of truth, is put in danger himself.

Lesson 2
James 3:13—4:3, 7–8a **(Pres/Meth/UCC/Luth)**;
James 3:16—4:3 **(RC/Epis)**
The wisdom motif is carried further in these passages in James, all of which emphasize that the "wisdom from above" is full of "good fruits," whose harvest is not strife but peace. The wise person is one who recognizes the war going on within and who submits to God's purifying grace.

September 21, 1997
18th Sunday after Pentecost (Proper 20)
RC/Pres: 25th Sunday in Ordinary Time

Gospel

Mark 9:30–37 (**Pres/Meth/UCC/RC/Epis/Luth**)
This passage contrasts Jesus' prophecy concerning his own death with the disciples' preoccupation with their future success. It ends with Jesus speaking to his disciples about the downward trajectory of true discipleship, and indeed, the superior wisdom of babes and infants.

Theme

The downward trajectory of Christian discipleship leads to true joy.

Thought for the Day

Jesus' disciples are instructive not just in their occasional moments of faithfulness, but even more in their frequent and embarrassing failures. In this they resemble Israel. Their bafflement at Jesus' words concerning his own death is exceeded only by their interest in discussing their own careers. Those who are so preoccupied with themselves can only enter the kingdom through embarrassment, a form of dying which Jesus introduces to his disciples by means of a little child, whose presence important people like the career-minded disciples might have missed, and whose joy they would have, otherwise, not have known.

Prayer of Meditation

By your Spirit, O Lord, we are made small enough to glimpse your kingdom, and without it we will always be too big and too important and too full of ourselves. Send us your Spirit, we pray, that we might become like a child and so know the joy of trusting in thee for all things. We ask this in Christ's name. Amen.

Call to Worship

"... *where shall wisdom be found? And where is the place of understanding?* ...
'Truly, the fear of the Lord, that is wisdom; and to depart from evil is understanding'"
(Job 28:12–28). Come, let us worship God!

Prayer of Adoration

For your wisdom, O Lord, we give you thanks and praise. For your wisdom, which did not save this world but hid itself in the foolishness of the cross, we give you thanks and praise. Grant us such wisdom, we pray, that we might know the joy of infants, the happy service of the children of God. We ask this in Christ's name. Amen.

Prayer of Confession
Forgive us, O Lord, for trusting in ourselves. Our careers, our futures, our responsibilities seem so much more important than your grace. Forgive us our wisdom; it has become yet another way we have sought to hide ourselves from you. Grant us, we pray, that embarrassment, that shame, that dying from which alone we might be raised, from which alone we might discover true joy. For we ask this gift in the name of him who died, for our sakes, in whose resurrected life our very selves are hid, even Jesus Christ, the Lord. Amen.

Prayer of Dedication of Gifts and Self
Unless we receive your gift of grace, we cannot even give aright, O Lord. Grant us, we pray, your Spirit that we might offer what we long to give back to you: ourselves, our hearts, our lives. From you we have received these gifts and to you they belong, and to give them back has become our great joy. Receive these gifts, our offerings, and help them to find their place in serving you. In Jesus Christ's name we pray. Amen.

Sermon Summary
It was characteristic of Jesus that he was not afraid to embarrass his disciples, whether by asking them hard questions or by engaging in some kind of embodied parable. Embarrassment is a form of dying, which in Jesus' hands becomes a "learning experience," i.e., the means by which he teaches us of death and resurrection as the way to true wisdom, indeed, true joy. On the surface it seems a hard sell, as hard as the "foolishness of the cross," but only through such foolishness are we ever delivered from the seriousness of our own careers, agendas, and projects, and enabled to be small enough to discover the joy Jesus wants us to have.

Hymn of the Day
"Be Now My Vision." The epistle lesson for today inspires the choice of this eighth-century text. Set to a traditional Irish melody, this familiar hymn adapts itself wonderfully to additional instrumentation. Fiddle/violin, recorder or flute recall the folk origin of the Irish melody. Ancient as the text is, it still speaks to a remarkable array of modern spiritual problems. Like all who seek God, we often try to see with our own eyes, exercising our own plans, instead of remaining centered on God's sight, God's wisdom, God's providence.

September 21, 1997
18th Sunday after Pentecost (Proper 20)
RC/Pres: 25th Sunday in Ordinary Time

Children's Object Talk

How Much Are You Loved?

Object
Pictures of yourself as an infant and/or small child, photos of confirmation or graduation, and a recent portrait. They should be large enough for all the children to see. Mount them so they can all be seen at once.

Lesson
God thinks children are important.

Who do you think this is? (Point to recent picture.) And how about this one? Do you know this person? (Point to the pictures one at a time, establishing that all are of you, although your appearance has changed considerably. Point to the most recent picture again.) Do you think this is an *important* person? I hope I'm important to this congregation. I hope I can be important in your life. Do you think I was more important when I was a baby? Or am I more important now? Or do you think I was more important when I was this age? Which time of my life do you think I was the most important?

In the gospel lesson we read a minute ago, we heard Jesus say a surprising thing. Do you remember what the story said? Jesus' disciples had argued about which one of them was the most important. And you know what Jesus did? Jesus asked a little child to come over and stand in the middle of all those big men he was talking with. He took that child in his arms. Then he told those big men that this little child was so important that if someone was kind to this child, it was just like being kind to Jesus himself. If someone welcomed this little child, it was just like welcoming Jesus himself. That's how important Jesus said little children are.

Do you see how important you are to Jesus? Right now, you are as important as you will ever be in your life. If ever you feel like nobody loves you, just remember, God thinks you're very important.

—*Lois Brokering*

The Sermon

Embarrassed into the Kingdom

Hymns
Beginning of Worship: "Blessing and Honor and Glory and Power"
Sermon Hymn: "Fairest Lord Jesus"
End of Worship: "Who Trust in God a Strong Abode"

Scripture
Mark 9:30–37 (For additional sermon materials on this passage, see the July 1997 issue of *The Clergy Journal* and on James 3:13—4:3, 7–8a, see the *1997 May/June Planning Issue* of *The Clergy Journal*.)

Sermon Text
"He sat down, called the twelve, and said to them, 'Whoever wants to be first must be last of all and servant of all'" (vs. 35).

When a stand-up comedian tells a joke and no one laughs, there is often a painful silence, an embarrassing self-consciousness in which the comedian feels as if he or she is dying. In fact, that is what they call it: "dying out there." The phrase is aptly descriptive of what happens when the laughing stops. All of a sudden, instead of being able to direct their attention to what is funny, the comedian is the exposed, "dying" to the pretense of magic and revealed as a quite flawed though otherwise normal human being. As most comedians could tell us, "dying" like that is no fun. They will go to great lengths to keep the pretense of their comedy alive.

The truth is, we are all comedians who fear "dying" and who will go to almost any lengths to get a laugh. In that sense we are like the disciples, the disciples who were absolutely convinced that they would have the last laugh. So often they just didn't get it, not even when Jesus spelled it out for them and told them that the whole trajectory of his life would lead to the cross. Like any successful, career-minded group, the disciples "did not understand" what Jesus was saying, though they must have suspicioned it was not what they had in mind, for, we read "they were afraid to ask him."

With good cause, we might think. But not even their bafflement at Jesus' words could slow them down for long; soon they were debating who was going to

September 21, 1997
18th Sunday after Pentecost (Proper 20)
RC/Pres: 25th Sunday in Ordinary Time

be senior vice-president in the kingdom. We might laugh at such silliness, but in many ways ambition for "great things" is the stock in trade of pastors and leaders today.

The church is, among other things, a place to have a career, and Jesus' disciples are not above comparing notes as to who is ahead. Again, however, Jesus' disciples suspicion that this is not what he is about since they were ashamed to tell him when he asked what they were discussing along the way. *"He sat down, called the twelve and said to them, 'Whoever wants to be first must be last of all and servant of all.' Then he took a little child and put it among them; and taking it in his arms, he said to them, 'Whoever welcomes one such child in my name welcomes me, and whoever welcomes me welcomes not me but the one who sent me'"* (Mk 9:35-37).

How embarrassing! Could you imagine such a thing happening at a presbytery meeting, or a synod, or church council? Perhaps we could, thinking that what Jesus is offering the disciples and us is a lesson in humility. We would like to think that. That would moralize things and reduce the gospel's threat to a matter of good behavior. That, however, is not what Jesus is doing. He is not offering here a slice of humility so much as he is talking about the futility of saving your own life. He is talking about dying to our project of self-creation, most especially our religious project of self-realization. Instead he is offering what Nicodemus found so difficult to believe: becoming small enough to enter your mother's womb and be born anew. He is talking about receiving that smallness, even that death from his own hands, and finding in it what we can scarcely credit: joy, happiness, freedom.

We often read this passage as if Jesus were sadly calling the reluctant disciples to share his tragic view of life, to embrace martyrdom as a kind of courageous act of despair. Their refusal to join him in this embrace we often put down to cowardice or some other base form of denial. But in truth, what Jesus is offering is not tragedy but joy; he actually believes that receiving a child in his name is a happier activity than puffing ourselves up into an important career. He even thinks, and perhaps this is why he keeps on reminding the disciples of the cross, that his dying will be the liberation of the world, the embodiment of a joyful life.

Consumers that we are, we find it difficult to believe that happiness comes from giving your life away. It sounds like death to us. Which is why Jesus has to embarrass us again and again with his cross, with his placing of a child in our midst, with his giving a child to us to love, with his embodied life in the church (there is nothing more embarrassing!) to make us small, to make us laugh, even to show us our death so that we can find our life in his happy service.

The disciples were right about one thing: they would have the last laugh, only not quite the way they thought. Theirs would be the laughter of grace, the laughter of those who have died and whose lives are hidden in the clown of God, that fool on the hill, that crucified Lord.

—Thomas W. Currie III
First Presbyterian Church
Kerrville, Texas

September 28, 1997

Nineteenth Sunday after Pentecost (Proper 21)
RC/Pres: 26th Sunday in Ordinary Time

Lessons

Pres/Meth/UCC	Esth 7:1-6, 9-10; 9:20-22	Jas 5:13-20	Mk 9:38-50
Roman Catholic	Num 11:25-29	Jas 5:1-6	Mk 9:38-43, 45, 47-48
Episcopal	Num 11:4-6, 10-16, 24-29	Jas 4:7-12 (13—5:6)	Mk 9:38-43, 45, 47-48
Lutheran	Num 11:4-6, 10-16, 24-29	Jas 5:13-20	Mk 9:38-50

Introduction to the Lessons

Lesson 1
(1) *Esther 7:1-6, 9-10; 9:20-22* **(Pres/Meth/UCC)**
These verses tell the story of Esther's disclosure of Haman's plot against her own people and her request to her husband, King Ahasueras, for redress.

(2) *Numbers 11:25-29* **(RC)**;
Numbers 11:4-6, 10-16, 24-29 **(Epis/Luth)**
Israel's day in the wilderness found the people growing tired of eating manna and longing for the days spent in Egypt. Both Moses and the Lord are fatigued with this "murmuring," with Moses lashing out at the Lord for giving him such impossible burdens.

Lessons 2
(1) *James 5:13-20* **(Pres/Meth/UCC/Luth)**
Because we are one in Christ we do not have the option of ignoring one another or being indifferent to each other's needs. Those who are well are to pray for and take care of the suffering and the sick, just as those who are rich have deep obligations to the poor and those who are reconciled to Jesus Christ must not let barriers of anger or sin get in the way of practicing the forgiveness that binds us all together.

(2) *James 5:1–6* **(RC)**
This passage deals with prayer in the midst of suffering and tribulation, and the judgment that is coming on the rich who have exploited the poor.

(3) *James 4:7–12 (13—5:6)* **(Epis)**
These verses are an entreaty of submission and ressistance to evil. We are to be judged, not to judge.

Gospel
Mark 9:38—50 **(Pres/Meth/UCC/Luth)**;
Mark 9:38–43, 45, 47–48 **(RC/Epis)**
This passage begins with a complaint by Jesus' disciple, John, that there were those who were casting out demons in Jesus' name but who were not disciples. It ends with Jesus' invitation to "be at peace with one another." In between are words praising those who do mighty works in the name of Jesus, whoever they might be, as well as harsh words of judgment on those who would lead little ones astray.

Theme
Our unity in Christ is a gift from which we cannot escape and against which not even our much-prized cultural and religious divisions can prevail.

Thought for the Day
It is a recurring embarrassment to Jesus' disciples to discover his presence in places outside of their control or direction. It is an even greater embarrassment to discover that our need for each other is greater than our achievements in going it alone, and that our skillful use of "hand" or "eye" or "foot" can be an actual impediment to perceiving Christ's presence in our midst. The salt that gives season is salt that has been salted by the fire of chastening judgment and therefore, the salt that is embarrassed into the humility of being content to love and to be at peace with one another.

Prayer of Meditation
Grant us, O Lord, the gift of being at peace with one another. We ask this, not because it is easy or because we even know what we are asking, but because such peace is rightfully ours in Jesus Christ and

September 28, 1997
19th Sunday after Pentecost (Proper 21)
26th Sunday in Ordinary Time

is the only way we can discern his presence in our midst. Grant us the gift, we pray, for we ask it in the name of him who has promised to be with us always, even Jesus Christ our Lord. Amen.

Call to Worship
"O Lord, open my lips, and my mouth will declare your praise" (Ps 51:15). Come, let us worship God!

Prayer of Adoration
For the gift that is ours in Jesus Christ, the gift of life together, we give thee thanks and praise. Receive the offering of our worship, we pray, for we render it as a sign that we are not our own but belong body and soul, in life and in death, to Jesus Christ our Lord, in whose name we ask this. Amen.

Prayer of Confession
Most merciful and gracious creator, we confess that we have sinned against thee and against one another. With sharp words and thoughtless acts, in selfish despair and cheerless joy, we have built our little kingdoms unto ourselves. Subvert us with thy grace, we pray, that we might be conquered by thy Son and his cross and be overcome in genuine repentance and true hope. We ask this in the name of the crucified and risen Lord, even Jesus Christ. Amen.

Prayer of Dedication of Gifts and Self
As the windmill depends upon the wind, so our lives are fruitless unless they are breathed upon by thy Spirit, O Lord. We offer unto thee the fruit of thy Spirit, the grist which our lives have milled in thy name. Receive these gifts, we pray, and bless and forgive and heal all that is amiss in them, and use and prosper and fulfill all that they contain of thy purpose and promise. We ask this in Christ's name. Amen.

Sermon Summary
What explains the presence of good in the world? Philosophers sometimes try to explain what they call "the problem of evil," but why is there good? How is it that Jesus Christ is proclaimed often in spite of us and in any case, quite without us? How is it that we take so little notice of cups of cold water given in his name, yet find interesting only what our hand

or foot or eye is doing? Might it be that Jesus is alive and loose in the world, and that discerning his presence there is an embarrassment to us, yet our one hope of joy? Maybe, just maybe the body of Christ contains more than my hand or foot or eye, and maybe, just maybe it is a happier, more joyful presence in the world than I could ever admit.

Hymn of the Day
"God of Grace and God of Glory." This is perhaps the best known hymn of Harry Emerson Fosdick, preacher and writer, who taught at Union Theological Seminary and was pastor of Riverside Church in New York City. The words are in the form of a prayer for the tools to evade the evils of our day, and seek the life God would have us lead. The Welsh tune *"Cwm Rhondda"* (pronounced approximately "coom run-tha") is both lyrical and moving.

Children's Object Talk

Stay Away from Temptation

Object
Optional—a good-sized, attractive toy truck.
Lesson
It's better to leave people who cause you to be unkind.

Today I want to tell you a true story about two brothers. Martin and Noel liked to play in the sand with their sand pails and shovels and toy trucks. (Something like this one.)

One day, two boys the same ages moved in down the street. The new boys came out to play, too. They took the trucks away from Martin and Noel. One boy threw a truck against a tree and broke it. He hit Martin. His little brother threw sand into Noel's hair. Noel was surprised. He had never seen anyone play like this before. When the older boy threw a rock at Martin, Martin picked up a rock and threw it back. It was not fun. The next day, the new boys came out again. Again they took Martin and Noel's toys. They threw rocks at Martin and Noel. They threw sand into their hair. Some got into Martin's eye. Crying, he went into the house to find his mother. As she gently washed the sand from Martin's eye, Mother talked about what had happened.

"You know, Martin, I don't like it that you and Noel are throwing rocks and sand at the new children."

"But they did it first!" Martin pouted.

September 28, 1997
19th Sunday after Pentecost (Proper 21)
26th Sunday in Ordinary Time

"Next time," Mother suggested, "try this. Tell the boys *you* do not play like that. Breaking toys, throwing rocks and sand are not happy ways to play. Tell the new boys that you are coming into the house. When they are ready to play in a happy way, they may ring our doorbell and you will come out again. Then leave them. Jesus tells us to love our neighbors."

Of course, the next day, the new brothers again threw rocks and sand, and grabbed toys. This time they even called names. But this time Martin and Noel left them and went into their house. Soon the new boys were ringing the doorbell. "We will only play if you stop being unkind," Martin said. What do you think happened? Now everyone played happily in the sand lot.

—*Lois Brokering*

The Sermon

The Body of Christ

Hymns
Beginning of Worship: "All People That on Earth Do Dwell"
Sermon Hymn: "Make Me a Captive, Lord"
End of Worship: "Ask Ye What Great Thing I Know"

Scripture
Mark 9:38–50 (For additional sermon materials on this passage, see the July 1997 and the *1997 May/June Planning Issue* of *The Clergy Journal*.)

Sermon Text
"'For everyone will be salted with fire. Salt is good; but if the salt has lost its saltiness, how will you season it? Have salt in yourselves, and be at peace with one another'" (vss. 49–50).

The end of the ninth chapter of Mark seems to be a kind of grab bag of sayings of Jesus, almost as if Mark had some material, but didn't know where to fit in—so he just threw it in here.

It starts out with one of the disciples, John, complaining that there are folk using Jesus' name to exorcise demons, folk who were not "following us." From that the passage segues into a discussion of "little ones" and the judgment that will fall on those who cause them to sin. Then it moves rapidly to some rather harsh words about what will happen when one's hand or foot or eye causes one to sin, ending with a discussion on being salted by fire and finally, curiously enough, being "at peace with one another." "Huh?" we are tempted to comment. What on earth is going on here?

The key, I think, is in the first and last verses. John is upset because he has discovered that it is possible for folk to know of Jesus Christ without "following us." The implication is that Jesus Christ is alive and loose in the world, gathering all manner of folk into his service and into his life. His body is present in the world, and our task is not so much to *bring* him to others as to discover his presence amidst them. He precedes us. That has always been scandalous news to missionaries in foreign countries, to pastors who are surprised to learn that Jesus has been in the hospital room before we ever arrive there, to churches who make the alarming discovery that Jesus is already at work in the community in which they find themselves. Notice that the cup of water that Jesus says is there waiting for us is one which is given to us as the bearers of the name of Christ. Christ feeds his body and nourishes us all, wherever and whomever we are.

Are these words of judgment? If John's temptation was to identify the cause of Jesus Christ with himself and the ministry to the disciples, might our temptation be to do the same? Unless our hand does it, does it really ever get done? Unless we bird-dog it, will this ministry ever get off the ground? Unless we see the big picture, will this body have any life? As a minister I can say that nothing is easier than wanting to work by myself, wanting to disconnect from the body of Christ and simply be a very efficient hand or foot or eye. That is the way careers are built, both in the church and without. But that is precisely the way we lead little ones to stray and cause them to think that life without the body is possible.

In a parable told by the prostitute, Grushenka, to Alyosha, the saintly one of the brothers Karamazov, she tells of an old woman condemned to hell who pleads for deliverance night and day. Her guardian angel is told that she can be delivered if it can be shown that the old woman has ever done a good deed. The guardian angel knows that once, the old woman gave an onion to a beggar. Find that onion, the angel is told, and it will be strong enough to pull the woman out of hell. The angel finds the onion and reaches down to the old woman who grabs and is slowly pulled up. As the others in hell see her rising, they grab hold of

September 28, 1997
19th Sunday after Pentecost (Proper 21)
26th Sunday in Ordinary Time

her. Fearful that the onion will break, she kicks them away telling them that it is her onion, not theirs. At that very moment the onion does break and she falls back into hell.

It is a kind of hell to want salvation apart from other sinners, or even to lust for it above all. "Those who wish for their salvation," Simone Weil has written, "do not truly believe in the reality of the joy within God." Which is why we must die to our desire to be everything, to be "salted with fire" as it were, so that we can truly receive the gifts God chooses to give us and so "be at peace with one another."

There is no more tasteless porridge than the constant effort to turn God's grace into our own achievements. To be salty in this world is to know "the joy within God," the pleasures of life within the body of Christ, the practices of grace and gratitude. So are little ones put on the right path and so do our eyes and hands and feet take up the happy task of serving their master, even Jesus Christ the Lord.

—Thomas W. Currie III
First Presbyterian Church
Kerrville, Texas

October 5, 1997

20th Sunday after Pentecost (Proper 22)
RC/Pres: 27th Sunday in Ordinary Time

Lessons

Pres/Meth/UCC	Job 1:1; 2:1–10	Heb 1:1–4; 2:5–12	Mk 10:2–16
Roman Catholic	Gen 2:18–24	Heb 2:9–11	Mk 10:2–16
Episcopal	Gen 2:18–24	Heb 2:(1–8) 9–18	Mk 10:2–9
Lutheran	Gen 2:18–24	Heb 1:1–4; 2:5–12	Mk 10:2–16

Introduction to the Lessons
Lesson 1
(1) *Job 1:1; 2:1–10* **(Pres/Meth/UCC)**
Job, an upright, God-fearing man, is singled out by Satan for special afflictions in the hope that suffering so intensely will make Job curse God.

(2) *Genesis 2:18–24* **(RC/Epis/Luth)**
The Lord God allows the man he has created to name the living creatures of the earth, then creates for the man a helper and companion in the form of a woman.

Lesson 2
(1) *Hebrews 1:1–4; 2:5–12* **(Pres/Meth/UCC/Luth)**
God's son is identified in his majesty and as a reflection of God's glory as well as by his humiliation through suffering and his exaltation.

(2) *Hebrews 2:9–11* **(RC)**; *Hebrews 2:(1–8) 9–18* **(Epis)**
By speaking of the son's superiority to the angels, the author of Hebrews warns readers against neglecting their salvation, a salvation that was bought at a very high price by the one who came to be one of us.

October 5, 1997
20th Sunday after Pentecost (Proper 22)
RC/Pres: 27th Sunday in Ordinary Time

Gospel
Mark 10:2–16 (**Pres/Meth/UCC/RC/Luth**);
Mark 10:2–9 (**Epis**)
Jesus is in Judea and the region beyond the Jordan when he is questioned by some Pharisees about the legality of divorce. Afterward, the disciples query him about the teaching and are interrupted by people who bring their children to Jesus to be blessed.

Theme
Receive the kingdom of God as a little child.

Thought for the Day
"If there is anything that we wish to change in the child, we should first examine it and see whether it is not something that could better be changed in ourselves."
—Carl Gustav Jung,
The Integration of the Personality, 1939, p. 285,
quoted in John Bartlett, *Familiar Quotations*, 15th ed.,
Boston: Little, Brown and Company, 1980, p. 754

Prayer of Meditation
"Abba, call us from death to life, call us from inertia to energy, call us from all that lulls us and soothes us into mediocrity and sameness into the brash, bold, splendid eccentricities that make us each unique. Call us from the falsely adult to the truly mature, from our self-important agendas to your eternally important work. Call us your children, Abba-God, and gift us with the wonder of childhood. Amen."
—Andrea La Sonde Anastos, *Lectionary Prayers*,
Inver Grove Heights, MN:
Logos Productions Inc., 1993, p. 199

Call to Worship
Our feet stand on level ground; in the great congregation we will bless the Lord.
—Adapted from Psalm 26:12

Prayer of Adoration
Loving Jesus, gentle Lamb,
In thy gracious hands I am;
Make me, Saviour, what thou art;
Live thyself within my heart.

—Charles Wesley (1707–1788),
Hymns and Psalms: A Methodist and Ecumenical Hymn Book,
London: Methodist Publishing House, 1983, #738, verse 1

Prayer of Confession
Gracious God, together we confess the superiority and meanspiritedness that make us believe we need not change to receive your kingdom. You have told us, through your Son Jesus Christ, that we must become as little children to receive the kingdom, but we are wary of letting ourselves become that vulnerable. Forgive us, we pray. Help us to become as children, for the sake of your promised kingdom; through Jesus Christ our Lord. Amen.

Prayer of Dedication of Gifts and Self
Bless, O Lord, these offerings which we, your children, bring to you. Help us, through the offering of ourselves and our substance, to draw closer to your kingdom. We ask these things in Jesus' name. Amen.

Sermon Summary
Receiving the kingdom of God as a little child means being outcast and lowly, able to see through the eyes with simple clarity, and coming with hearts of imagination.

Hymn of the Day
"When Love Is Found." This is a contemporary hymn by the well-known author Brian Wren who wrote this for his own wedding and set it to the very familiar English folk tune "O Waly Waly (The Water Is Wide . . .)." Noted particularly for his striking and insightful language, Wren remarked that this hymn should be the hope of all Christian relationships "that love may reach out beyond the nuclear family, rather than the more cozy and familiar theme of inviting others into 'home's warmth and light.'" This hymn makes a fine choir anthem or solo piece as well as being very accessible for congregational worship. The poetry makes excellent reading, even without the musical accompaniment.

October 5, 1997
20th Sunday after Pentecost (Proper 22)
RC/Pres: 27th Sunday in Ordinary Time

Children's Object Talk

Enter the Kingdom

Object
A large picture of Jesus and the children.
Lesson
God treasures children.

Can you close your eyes for a minute and imagine with me? Pretend you are sitting on someone's lap. It is someone you love very much and who loves you very much. Who is it? Whose lap do you love to sit on? Is it grandfather's? a babysitter's? your mom's? your dad's? Santa Claus' at Christmas? (Wait for responses and accept all.) How does it feel?

How would you like it if you could sit on Jesus' lap? Or maybe just have Jesus put his arm around you and pull you close? Wouldn't that be a wonderful, warm thing to happen to you? Wouldn't you feel really special?

In the story we just read from the Bible, that's exactly what did happen to some children. They were probably with their parents who wanted Jesus to bless their children.

But when they brought the children close to Jesus, the disciples tried to send them away. In those days people didn't think women and children were important, so the men told them not to bother Jesus. Do you remember what Jesus said when he saw what was happening? He told the disciples to *let the children come to him*. Once again he told them that it is children who come to God's kingdom. If grown-ups don't come to God like children do, they probably won't be part of God's kingdom.

So, if anyone treats you like you're not very important, just remember that you *are* important to God. Close your eyes. Imagine you are sitting on Jesus' lap, and he is holding you in his loving arms.

—*Lois Brokering*

The Sermon

Receiving as a Child

Hymns
Beginning of Worship: "I Sing the Almighty Power of God"
Sermon Hymn: "Children of the Heavenly Father"
End of Worship: "All My Hope Is Firmly Grounded"

Scripture
Mark 10:2–16 (For additional sermon materials on this passage, see the July 1997 and the *1997 May/June Planning Issue* of *The Clergy Journal*.)

Sermon Text
"'Let the little children come to me; do not stop them; for it is to such as these that the kingdom of God belong'" (vs. 14).

Today we find Jesus in a familiar situation. He has gone to Judea and the region beyond the Jordan where he is surrounded by crowds. While he is teaching the multitudes, some Pharisees come to test him by asking him a potentially explosive question about divorce. After Jesus deals with the challenge, in private the disciples ask him what the teaching means.

In the midst of this very intense atmosphere of controversy and verbal sparring, people bring little children to Jesus for his touch and blessing. The disciples treat the children's appearance as an intrusion, but an indignant Jesus says to them, *"Let the little children come to me; do not stop them; for it is to such as these that the kingdom of God belongs. Truly I tell you, whoever does not receive the kingdom of God as a little child will never enter it"* (Mk 10:14b–15). The world of Jesus is full of surprises; no one knows what he is going to say or do next, except that it will reverse the usual order under which we live.

What does receiving the kingdom of God as a little child mean? First, it means *receiving the kingdom as one who is outcast and lowly.*

Throughout the ancient world, and in first-century Palestine in particular, children were entirely dependent upon their fathers. Like women, children were property that belonged to the male head of the household until they were released into the world (if male), or became their husband's property (if female). Children

October 5, 1997
20th Sunday after Pentecost (Proper 22)
RC/Pres: 27th Sunday in Ordinary Time

had no legal rights. They occupied the very bottom rungs of the social ladder. The people of the first century cherished none of our romantic notions about children and the blessedness of childhood. Children had duties to perform, a place to keep.

That is why the disciples tried to shoo away the people bringing their little children to Jesus. Why interrupt the master's important work for this low-life, these first-century equivalents of contemporary street people?

Jesus cut through the class and legal structure by bidding the children to come to him. He identified with the outcast and the oppressed, reminding the disciples that the kingdom does not belong to them, is not only their gift, but comes by God's grace to all those who are willing to receive it. To receive the kingdom of God as a child is to be outcast and lowly.

What does receiving the kingdom of God as a little child mean? It means *seeing the kingdom through the eyes of simple clarity.*

My first parish was in a former coal-mining village set back in the hills. I encountered people there whose world did not include female clergy, and who let me know in both subtle and overt ways that I would never be their pastor.

After seven years, the time came to move. The women of the church put on a coffee-and-cookies reception for me after worship to which the whole congregation was invited. I was asked to say a few words. I could see the children growing restless and decided to talk to them as representing the whole church family.

"Soon you'll have a new minister," I told them, "one who will love you and take care of you. The new minister might even be a man."

A hush followed my remarks. Finally, seven-year-old Victor spoke up. "You mean," he said, his voice filled with questioning awe, "that men can be ministers, too?"

To receive the kingdom as a child is to see through the eyes of simple clarity.

What does receiving the kingdom of God as a little child mean? It means *coming to the kingdom with a heart of imagination.*

Up until the time of her fourth birthday, our granddaughter Erin and her parents lived with us. Erin loved to spend time with us. One of her favorite activities was to ride along with Jack and me as we made the rounds of the three hospitals in our area.

Erin was a remarkably patient child, but the time would come when she would grow bored with sitting in the car; she would need some entertainment. Our routine was to play the "alphabet game," trying to find words or objects whose names began with successive letters of the alphabet. (Usually we were lucky, and Erin's interest would flag before we got to "q.")

On this particular day, we breezed through the beginning of the alphabet; we even found a "q" word on a billboard, and then an "r" word, "road." "S" was the next letter.

We were stopped at a traffic light when Erin pointed out the window exclaiming, "Look, Grampie, schwings! There must be children!" Sure enough, there in the front yard stood a shiny, new metal swingset, complete with slide. In this, her first experience of inductive reasoning, Erin moved from what she could see (the swings) to what she knew must be there (the children). And she was totally confident of her "leap of faith."

To receive the kingdom of God as a child is to come to the kingdom with the heart of imagination.

What does receiving the kingdom of God as a little child mean? The good news is that everyone past the age of ten has not missed the kingdom just by getting older. What it does mean is that Jesus announces the kingdom to come will be for those who are willing to come as the outcast and lowly, to come as those who see through the eyes of simple clarity, to come with the heart of imagination.

In our more pessimistic moments, we may wince at approaching God's kingdom with the smudged faces and boisterous self-centeredness of children. We need to remember that is not the way Jesus encountered children.

Martin Luther, whose views on a number of subjects represented a departure from earlier church attitudes and teaching, believed in the importance of children to the community of faith: "Children are better informed in the faith than adults, for they believe very simply and without any question in a gracious God and eternal life . . . Children live altogether in faith, without reason." (Theodore G. Tappert, ed., *Luther's Works,* Volume 54, "Table Talk" [Philadelphia: Fortress Press, 1967], No. 4367, February 26, 1539, p. 335.)

Can we cast aside the pretenses of status, knowledge, and fact and receive the kingdom of God as a little child?

—*Nancy E. Topolewski*
Vestal United Methodist Church
Vestal, New York

October 12, 1997

21st Sunday after Pentecost (Proper 23)
RC/Pres: 28th Sunday in Ordinary Time

Lessons

Pres/Meth/UCC	Job 23:1–9, 16–17	Heb 4:12–16	Mk 10:17–31
Roman Catholic	Wis 7:7–11	Heb 4:12–13	Mk 10:17–30
Episcopal	Amos 5:6–7, 10–15	Heb 3:1–6	Mk 10:17–27 (28–31)
Lutheran	Wis 7:7–11	Heb 4:12–13	Mk 10:17–30

Introduction to the Lessons
Lesson 1

(1) *Job 23:1–9, 16–17* **(Pres/Meth/UCC)**
Believing God to be hiding from him, Job is afraid that God has abandoned him and expressed longing for relief from his afflictions.

(2) *Wisdom 7:7–11* **(RC/Luth)**
Solomon, describing wisdom and his search for it, calls wisdom a gift to be valued above all else.

(3) *Amos 5:6–7, 10–15* **(Epis)**
Amos warns the nation to return to the Lord while there is still time, describing dire consequences to come.

Lesson 2
(1) *Hebrews 4:12–16* **(Pres/Meth/UCC)**;
   Hebrews 4:12–13 **(RC/Luth)**
The author of the letter to the Hebrews describes the power of the word of God who is also our high priest in the heavens.

(2) *Hebrews 3:1–6* **(Epis)**
Jesus and Moses are compared for their faithfulness to God: Moses as servant, and Jesus as the Son.

Gospel
Mark 10:17–31 **(Pres/Meth/UCC)**;
Mark 10:17–30 **(RC/Luth)**; *Mark 10:17–27 (28–31)* **(Epis)**
Jesus is setting out on a journey when he is met by a man who asks what he must do to inherit the kingdom of God. Jesus speaks of the difficulties those with wealth will have in entering the kingdom of God, and points out that his followers will receive the true rewards.

Theme
The gift of eternal life is a costly gift.

Thought for the Day
"A rejection, or in Scripture's strong language, a crucifixion of the natural self is the passport to everlasting life. Nothing that has not died will be resurrected."
—C. S. Lewis, "Membership," *The Weight of Glory and Other Addresses*, New York: The Macmillan Company, 1949, p. 39

Prayer of Meditation
"O Most Generous Giver, help us to see that we can only answer your call with a whole heart when we are willing to spend all that we are and all that we have in your service, using *all* our strengths and gifts without regard for cost. Beloved Giver, whose gift is life itself, teach us to be worthy of your abundance by accepting it wholly and sharing it freely. Lay your hand upon our hearts so that we may find peace and courage to give all that we have and follow you. Amen."
—Andrea La Sonde Anastos, *Lectionary Prayers*, Inver Grove Heights, MN: Logos Productions Inc., 1993, p. 201

Call to Worship
In God our ancestors trusted;
> they trusted, and God delivered them.
To God they cried and were saved;
> in God they trusted, and were not put to shame.
—Adapted from Psalm 22:4–5

October 12, 1997
21st Sunday after Pentecost (Proper 23)
RC/Pres: 28th Sunday in Ordinary Time

Prayer of Adoration

    O more and more thy love extend,
        My life befriend
        With heavenly pleasure;
    That I may win thy paradise,
        Thy pearl of price,
    Thy countless treasure;
        Since but in thee
        I can go free
    From earthly care and vain oppression,
        This prayer I make
        For Jesus' sake
        That thou me take
    In thy possession.

—Robert Bridges (1844–1930),
Hymns and Psalms: A Methodist and Ecumenical Hymn Book,
London: Methodist Publishing House, 1983, #40, verse 3

Prayer of Confession

We confess to you, O God, this day, that we are preoccupied with material things. Our lives are filled with whatever money can buy, leaving little room for you and your gifts. Help us to know that your kingdom and eternal life in your presence cannot be bought, but come to us at the cost of the death and resurrection of your Son, in whose name we pray for forgiveness. Amen.

Prayer of Dedication of Gifts and Self

Your kingdom comes to us as a gift, gracious God—a costly gift without price. In your giving, you have taught us to give. We ask you to accept these our offerings as signs that we seek to follow your example, made real to us in Jesus Christ our Lord. Amen.

Sermon Summary

Contrary to what is believed by the rich man who comes to Jesus, eternal life is not something to be earned, but is an inheritance, a gift that comes to us by the grace of God.

Hymn of the Day

"Are Ye Able?" Familiar to many, Earl Marlatt's hymn is a reflection on the questions asked of Jesus throughout the Gospels: what must we do to inherit eternal life? The answer is often harder or less glamorous than we would choose as the text reminds us, but it also reminds us of the everlasting life and light that comes from the loyalty of risk and endeavor. This irregular tune from the first part of this century may not be familiar. Consider having a soloist sing the first verse, and then have everyone join on the refrain.

Children's Object Talk

The Role of Possessions

Object
Items your congregation is collecting to give away: food from a food-shelf collection, clothing from a clothing drive, quilts made by members to be sent overseas, etc. (This would be a good time to start or complete a drive children can participate in.)

Lesson
We share what God has given us so generously.

Look at all this stuff! What is all this? (Help children really look at the items.) What do you think is going to happen to these things? (Elicit a few answers for each question to lead the discussion to the point that as Jesus' followers, we share what God has given us.) These (quilts, boxes of food, etc.) are going to people who don't have enough food or clothing, or money to buy them. Who brought these things to our church?

Have you ever been hungry? Have you ever been really hungry when there wasn't anything at all to eat in the house? Do you know that happens to some people? God put enough food on this earth for everybody to eat. God expects people to share so everyone has food. We do God's work when we share what we have with people who don't have much. (Tell them where the items will be sent, and who will receive them. Mention other programs your congregation participates in and how they can help.)

This is one way we show we are Jesus' followers. We share what we have. We could keep it all for ourselves, but our gospel story today shows us that doesn't make us happy. People in God's kingdom know that sharing is God's happy way.

—*Lois Brokering*

October 12, 1997
21st Sunday after Pentecost (Proper 23)
RC/Pres: 28th Sunday in Ordinary Time

The Sermon

How High a Price?

Hymns
Beginning of Worship: "Rejoice, the Lord Is King"
Sermon Hymn: "On Jordan's Stormy Banks I Stand"
End of Worship: "I Love Thy Kingdom, Lord"

Scripture
Mark 10:17–31 (For additional sermon materials on this passage, see the July 1997 and the *1997 May/June Planning Issue* of *The Clergy Journal*.)

Sermon Text
"Jesus, looking at him, loved him and said, 'You lack one thing; go, sell what you own, and give the money to the poor, and you will have treasure in heaven; then come, follow me'" (vs. 21).

As Jesus sets out on a journey, he is accosted by a man who has a burning question: "Good teacher, what must I do to inherit eternal life?" Jesus may be a bit annoyed, or merely seeking to set the records straight. "No one," Jesus retorts, "is good but God alone."

The man's question yawns before them like an abyss. Jesus tells the man to keep the commandments, which the man can say he has done since his youth. This is not an ordinary pupil; this is a gifted student with the potential for greatness. Jesus looks at him and loves him, then tells him what the extra credit problem will be, *"'Go, sell what you own, and give the money to the poor, and you will have treasure in heaven; then come, follow me'"* (Mk 10:21). Mark reports that the man is "shocked" when he hears the requirement, for he *"has many possessions"* (Mk 10:22).

But what if . . .

What if the man had been able to reply, "I just did all that. My stocks and bonds are being cashed in by my broker even as we speak. My house is sold; my car has been turned back to the dealer. Every penny I had has gone to support the local soup kitchen. Is there anything else I must do?"

How might Jesus have responded? One possibility is that Jesus could say to the assembled disciples, "Children, how hard it is to enter the kingdom of God. But right here is a man who has passed the entrance exam with flying colors. Move over. This man has earned a place in our midst." If this story were merely a morality play, warning us that wealth is a roadblock in our relationship with God, then this hypothetical response might have been appropriate.

But there is another possibility. Jesus might respond, "Have you really sold everything and endowed the soup kitchen? Bravo! But the test isn't over yet. You have one more task to perform. Take your pick from the following list: stop the sun from setting tonight, change yourself from a man into a woman, create some new stars for the heavens. When you've fulfilled the assignment, come back. Then we'll talk about what you can do to inherit eternal life."

I think Mark has more on his mind than the hazards of wealth. He is really talking about human arrogance that believes eternal life is something to be earned.

What is an inheritance? The word conjures up the picture of God as a rich, old uncle whom everybody is trying to impress so they will be in his will. But is not an inheritance a gift, entirely out of the hands of those on whom it is bestowed?

Jesus is not saying that one can earn eternal life if one does the right things. His reason for bringing up the Ten Commandments is entirely different. Think back on the Ten Commandments:

You shall have no other gods before me.

You shall not make for yourselves graven images.

You shall not take the name of the Lord your God in vain.

Remember the sabbath day to keep it holy.

Honor your father and your mother.

You shall not kill (or, commit murder).

You shall not commit adultery.

You shall not steal.

You shall not bear false witness against your neighbor.

You shall not covet anything that belongs to your neighbor. (Look at Ex 20:1–17 or Deut 5:6–21.)

These are rigorous, all-inclusive laws that we continually fail to keep. And if the law is so difficult, how can we expect to use it to gain eternal life? The man wants something only God can bestow. Eternal life is a gift. It must be inherited, waited for until the appropriate time.

The man must be something of a hero if he has, indeed, kept all the commandments since his youth. He has won the spiritual decathlon. He has probably come to Jesus with great confidence. With riches in his possession, this man is at risk of missing the entire point of Jesus' preaching about wealth. Would the man

October 12, 1997
21st Sunday after Pentecost (Proper 23)
RC/Pres: 28th Sunday in Ordinary Time

come to Jesus in such confidence if his wealth was taken away?

Self-confidence, self-reliance, self-sufficiency are attributes admired in American culture. We learn early in life to rely upon our own accomplishments. Dependence is not often seen as a laudable trait.

There was a time in my life when I could have been the man who comes to Jesus. In high school, I excelled at mathematics and science. I convinced myself that I was going to make great discoveries, to win the Nobel Prize. I learned easily and had no patience with others who didn't work at the same level as I did.

Then I went to college. I discovered that others were much better at math than I. I didn't have a clue how to deal with the physics problems on the force of gravity, but I refused to ask anyone for help. In my self-sufficiency, I got a D in physics my first semester. Suddenly, my confidence was gone.

After prolonged inner struggle, I ended up going in another direction entirely from science and math. I had to unlearn my arrogance and give up the wealth of long-cherished dreams. I ended up, not in a laboratory, but in the church, and I have not looked back.

For someone else, the requirement will be different from mine. There are as many ways of relying on our own worthiness as there are individuals. No wonder the man leaves Jesus grieving. For him, the cost of eternal life (as for many of us) seems exorbitant indeed.

He cannot pay for it.

He cannot earn it.

By God's amazing grace, it is free.

—*Nancy E. Topolewski*
Vestal United Methodist Church
Vestal, New York

October 19, 1997

22nd Sunday after Pentecost (Proper 24)
RC/Pres: 29th Sunday in Ordinary Time

Lessons

Pres/Meth/UCC	Job 38:1–7 (34–41)	Heb 5:1–10	Mk 10:35–45
Roman Catholic	Isa 53:10–11	Heb 4:14–16	Mk 10:35–45
Episcopal	Isa 53:4–12	Heb 4:12–16	Mk 10:35–45
Lutheran	Isa 53:4–12	Heb 5:1–10	Mk 10:35–45

Introduction to the Lessons

(1) *Job 38:1–7 (34–41)* **(Pres/Meth/UCC)**
Job encounters God in the whirlwind. God remarks on the wonders of creation and Job's insignificance in comparison to God's activities.

(2) *Isaiah 53:10–11* **(RC)**: *Isaiah 53:4–12* **(Epis/Luth)**
Isaiah describes the work of the suffering servant in atonement for human sin, bearing in his own body the sin of many.

Lesson 2
(1) *Hebrews 5:1–10* **(Pres/Meth/UCC/Luth)**
The author of Hebrews compares the work of a human high priest with that of the Great High Priest who suffered obediently and thereby made salvation possible.

(2) *Hebrews 4:14–16* **(RC)**; *Hebrews 4:12–16* **(Epis)**
Jesus is described as the Great High Priest who knows human shortcomings and suffers on human behalf.

Gospel
Mark 10:35–45 **(Pres/Meth/UCC/RC/Epis/Luth)**
Following the third prediction of the passion, James and John approach Jesus and ask him for special honor. When the other ten disciples learn of their request, they are furious, but Jesus uses the occasion to teach the twelve about servanthood.

October 19, 1997
22nd Sunday after Pentecost (Proper 24)
RC/Pres: 29th Sunday in Ordinary Time

Theme
Move to the back of the line for salvation.

Thought for the Day
". . . They also serve who only stand and wait."
—John Milton (1608–1674),
"On His Blindness," in *The English Spirit: The Little Gidding Anthology of English Spirituality*, Paul Handley, Fiona MacMath, Pat Saunders, and Robert Van de Weyer, eds., Nashville: Abingdon Press, 1987, p. 98

Prayer of Meditation
"O God, you have given me a will so that I may freely will to obey the inspiration of your Holy Spirit moving in heart and mind and soul.
   Grant me the courage to be.
   Grant me the strength to bend.
   Grant me the grace to follow.
   Grant me the love to obey. Amen."
—Andrea La Sonde Anastos, *Lectionary Prayers*, Inver Grove Heights, MN: Logos Productions Inc., 1993, p. 203

Call to Worship
   I will sing to the Lord as long as I live;
      and I will sing praise to my God while I have being.
—Psalm 104:33

Prayer of Adoration
   But who can speak thy wondrous deeds?
   Thy greatness all our thoughts exceeds;
      Vast and unsearchable thy ways,
      Vast and immortal be thy praise.
—Isaac Watts (1674–1748),
in *Hymns and Psalms: A Methodist and Ecumenical Hymn Book*, London: Methodist Publishing House, 1983, #12, verse 5

Prayer of Confession
Gracious God we confess that we, like James and John, want places of honor in your kingdom. We count up our little merits, hoping someday that they will be enough to put us at the head of the line. Forgive the competitiveness that drives our ambition. Help us to see ourselves, not as competitors with our brothers and sisters, but as servants each to one another. We ask these things in the name of your son who came not to stand at the head of the line, but to show us where the line ends—in service to others. Amen.

Prayer of Dedication of Gifts and Self
Gracious God, we come before you as those who would lead through service. Do with us and with these our offerings what you will, enlivening us and our gifts for the work of your kingdom. Amen.

Sermon Summary
James and John, like most of us, are fiercely competitive people, wanting Jesus to extend them special privileges of leadership. Jesus points out that leadership is not a matter of where one stands in line, but of service.

Hymn of the Day
"Jesus Comes Down to the Lakeshore." This hymn is a gift from Spanish songwriter Cesáreo Gabarain, a parish priest known for working with youth. Translated into eight languages, this elegant tune with its refrain is an excellent way to bring the gifts of cultural exchange to a congregation, especially if the Spanish can be sung first by a soloist or small group with the congregation singing the remaining verses in English. The text and gentle folk tune remind us that Jesus came not to the rich or powerful, but to the poor and humbled among God's people, and that our love is for each person in every nation, rich or poor.

Children's Object Talk

The Joy of Serving

Object
Some items children might use to help around the house such as a dust cloth, a small vacuum, a pet food dish, a coat hanger, etc., all in a clothes basket.

October 19, 1997
22nd Sunday after Pentecost (Proper 24)
RC/Pres: 29th Sunday in Ordinary Time

Lesson
Helping each other is a way of showing love.

I have a basket of things here I know you've seen before. At our house we use these things often. What do you think this is? (Hold up items one at a time.) What do we use all these things for? When do you think we use them? We use them for our daily chores. Do you know what chores are? Chores are those things we have to do over and over like cleaning our rooms, picking up our toys, washing the dishes, feeding the pets. Who is supposed to do these things in any home? Only moms? Only the big kids?

Sometimes people think they are too important or too helpless to do things for other people. They expect other people to do things for them. I can't put my socks in the laundry basket; I'm just a little kid. I can't clean up the kitchen; I'm the one who earns the money. I don't want to feed the dog; he's not my dog. It was my sister who wanted him; she can feed him. I can't help make supper; I have swimming practice. Have you ever heard anyone talk like that, or act like that?

In our gospel story today, two brothers wanted to be sure everyone knew they were important. They were two of the disciples, James and John. They asked Jesus if they could sit on each side of him when they got to heaven—in the most important places. Jesus told them something really surprising.

"If you want to be great in God's kingdom," Jesus said, "you will serve."

Then he told them that even he came to this world to be a helper, someone who serves. There has never been anyone more important than Jesus. But he came to serve, to be a helper. So he tells us to help each other, to serve each other. When we do that, we show we love each other, and we show we love God.

—Lois Brokering

The Sermon

Pushing in Line

Hymns
Beginning of Worship: "O Worship the King"
Sermon Hymn: "Are Ye Able?"
End of Worship: "Father, We Thank You"

Scripture

Mark 10:35-45 (For additional sermon materials on this passage see the July 1997 and the *1997 May/June Planning Issue* of *The Clergy Journal*.)

Sermon Text

"'. . . But whoever wishes to become great among you must be your servant, and whoever wishes to be first among you must be slave of all'" (vss. 43b-44).

For some time now, I have been closely examining myself and my attitudes to find out what shaped and molded the adult I have become. One of my most disturbing discoveries (or, more accurately, rediscoveries) is that I am a fiercely competitive person.

Most of the neighbors, in the rural area where I grew up, were retired. I had two sisters, and the only other playmates were three boys in one family whose ages roughly mirrored ours, and two boys two years older than I who lived farther up the road. Once I started school, I learned very quickly that if I wanted to play with anyone, I would have to play with the boys.

Being a girl was a distinct disadvantage, especially since I was small for my age and wore thick glasses. But it was keep up or shut up. So I did everything the boys did. When we played baseball, I was typically the last one chosen, but I still played. When we were into what we called "survival" games, I had to be careful to hide myself better than anyone else, to make up for my lack of running speed when found. When we played football (always tackle, never touch, and no one had any protective gear), I made it a matter of pride never to let them see when they hurt me.

I practiced jumping, climbing trees, and running through the brook down the hill from our house until I almost convinced myself it was no use trying to play with anyone; I was never going to be good enough. The more inept I showed myself to be, the more desperately I wanted to win at something—at anything.

Quite by accident, I learned that I did better in school than everyone else in the neighborhood—even the oldest boys. When they would taunt me for my lack of physical prowess, I would come right back and ridicule their poor performance in class. (Children can be incredibly cruel to one another.) This went on the whole time I was in elementary school. Competitiveness, wanting to be the best, became my singular motivation.

October 19, 1997
22nd Sunday after Pentecost (Proper 24)
RC/Pres: 29th Sunday in Ordinary Time

Maybe it was because I got hurt or put down too often, or because I was tired of the way people rolled their eyes when they saw my grades. Whatever the reason, I pulled inside myself and stopped competing with everyone but myself. To look at me now, you'd never know I have this dark secret in my past.

Our grandchildren become exasperated with me because I won't play games of any kind with them. I don't want to put them, or myself, through the humiliation of my having to beat them. I avoid being measured against others. I seldom watch sports, either on television or in person, because even as a spectator, I can be terribly partisan. I now shrink from situations in which people push in line, where once that pushing defined my whole life.

Like me, James and John in today's gospel lesson show a fiercely competitive side. Jesus has given his third and most detailed prediction of his passion, of the suffering and death which he surely faces, right before today's lesson. It seems as if for people with any sensitivity at all, this news should be terrifying. Instead, we find James and John coming to Jesus on the sly and asking him to do them a favor. When Jesus asks them what they want, they say, *"Grant us to sit, one at your right hand and one at your left, in your glory"* (Mk 10:37). Were these men listening, paying any attention at all, when Jesus spoke of being condemned to death, mocked, spat upon, flogged, and killed?

In the minds of these two disciples, a strange transformation has taken place, turning the firing squad Jesus knew awaited him into a party in their honor. James and John show by their question that they have no understanding that the ones who ultimately will be on Jesus' left and right will be criminals. James and John are merely interested in getting ahead of the others, in pushing their way to the front of the line.

The invitation Jesus gives about his coming triumph is an easy one to accept, until we find out that the route from here to there is a winding, meandering, twisting road. Jesus does not take the interstate highway directly to exaltation with his Father. He takes the single-lane dirt road, pitted with chuck holes, to the Upper Room, the Garden of Gethsemane, the prison in the Antonia Fortress, and Golgotha. What kind of fool would want to compete to follow Jesus on this journey, much less to sit at his right hand and his left? Jesus reminds James and John that even if they think they can follow him down the narrow dirt road, they haven't a clue where that road is going.

The inevitable happens. The other disciples find out about

James and John and their request for a favor, and they are furious. Jesus realizes that in spite of his best efforts, they are all confused about the nature of God's reign. Martyrdom is but one of the ways in which God's realm will call them to live and to give. Once again, expectations are reversed. The way to become great, Jesus says, is to be a servant, even as he himself came *"not to be served but to serve"* (Mk 10:45). To all who are pushing in line, Jesus turns the competition upside down.

In Margaret Craven's novel *I Heard the Owl Call My Name* (New York: Dell Publishing Co., Inc., 1973), we follow the story of Mark Brian, a newly ordained Anglican priest, who has (unbeknownst to him) been diagnosed as terminally ill. His bishop could tell him of the diagnosis and send him home to his family to die. Instead, the bishop sends him to the most difficult parish in his diocese, so that Mark will be able to experience the totality of ministry in a relatively short time.

Mark is assigned a circuit of remote Canadian Indian villages. He must learn to pilot a boat, to fix things for himself when they break, to live among his parishioners as one of them. When the people of Kingcome Village are cold because of severe winter weather, Mark is cold. When there is food in abundance because the salmon are running, Mark learns that he knows nothing of fishing and so must depend on others in the village, but he does eat. When an ancient cemetery must be relocated, Mark helps to move the bodies of the tribe's ancestors. When members of the village are lost or in trouble, he joins in seeking them.

Shortly after Mark discovers the diagnosis for himself, he is mercifully killed in an avalanche while looking for a missing logger. After his body is recovered, the villagers lovingly anoint him for burial, in his parish, as one of them.

Margaret Craven's young priest knows what James and John and the rest of us must be taught: that pushing our way through lines is not the way we are called to live in God's realm. From time to time, we need to hear, with James and John and all the others:

"... whoever wishes to be great among you must be your servant, and whoever wishes to be first among you must be slave of all" (Mk 10:43b–44).

The back of the line is this way.

—*Nancy E. Topolewski*
Vestal United Methodist Church
Vestal, New York

October 26, 1997

23rd Sunday after Pentecost (Proper 25)
RC/Pres: 30th Sunday in Ordinary Time

Lessons

Pres/Meth/UCC	Job 42:1–6, 10–17	Heb 7:23–28	Mk 10:46–52
Roman Catholic	Jer 31:7–9	Heb 5:1–6	Mk 10:46–52
Episcopal	Isa 59:(1–4) 9–19	Heb 5:12— 6:1, 9–12	Mk 10:46–52
Lutheran	Jer 31:7–9	Heb 7:23–28	Mk 10:46–52

Introduction to the Lessons
Lesson 1
(1) *Job 42:1–6, 10–17* (Pres/Meth/UCC)
After hearing God's rebuttals to his lamentations, Job acknowledges his own ignorance, but even then does not curse God, thereby prevailing against Satan's temptations. Having won the contest, God restores Job's fortunes twice over.

(2) *Jeremiah 31:7–9* (RC/Luth)
Jeremiah, speaking on God's behalf, proclaims the eventual restoration of the people of Israel to their homeland after their time of exile in Babylon.

(3) *Isaiah 59:(1–4) 9–19* (Epis)
Isaiah points out the iniquities of the nation and shows that those sins are barriers to the people's relationship with God. Later, the community admits their shortcomings and hears how their transgressions have affected God.

Lesson 2
(1) *Hebrews 7:23–28* (Meth/Pres/UCC/Luth)
The author of the letter to the Hebrews describes the Levitical priesthood in comparison with the high priesthood of Jesus Christ.

(2) *Hebrews 5:1–6* (RC)
The human high priest deals gently with people and offers sacrifices for their sins and his own. Like the human high priest, Jesus the Great High Priest was called and set apart by God; his priesthood is everlasting.

(3) *Hebrews 5:12—6:1, 9–12* (Epis)
The readers of Hebrews are still spiritually immature; the author asserts that they need to go on to perfection. God will not overlook their good work in relation to their salvation.

Gospel
Mark 10:46–52 **(Pres/Meth/UCC/RC/Epis/Luth)**
Jesus heals blind Bartimaeus, after Bartimaeus reminds Jesus of his place in the Davidic line and asks Jesus to let him see again.

Theme
Restoring our ability to see past, present, and future.

Thought for the Day
"We are as much as we see. Faith is sight and knowledge. The hands only serve the eyes."
—Henry David Thoreau (1817–1862),
Journal, April 9, 1841, quoted in John Bartlett, *Familiar Quotations,*
15th ed., Boston: Little, Brown and Company, 1980, p. 557

Prayer of Meditation
"O Perfect Light, inspire us to rest confidently in your healing promise given us through the life of Jesus and through the lives of his disciples. Thus, dispose us to cherish your word and accept your invitation to follow your Son so that our every thought and deed may be blessed to bring closer the time of your reign. Amen."
—Andrea La Sonde Anastos, *Lectionary Prayers,*
Inver Grove Heights, MN:
Logos Productions Inc., 1993, p. 205

Call to Worship
O magnify the Lord with me,
and let us exalt his name together.
—Psalm 34:3

October 26, 1997
23rd Sunday after Pentecost (Proper 25)
RC/Pres: 30th Sunday in Ordinary Time

Prayer of Adoration

> Father, in whom we live,
> In whom we are and move,
> Glory and power and praise receive
> Of thy creating love.
> Let all the angel throng
> Give thanks to God on high;
> While earth repeats the joyful song,
> And echoes to the sky.
>
> —Charles Wesley (1707–1788),
> in *Hymns and Psalms: A Methodist and Ecumenical Hymn Book*,
> London: Methodist Publishing House, 1983, #4, verse 1

Prayer of Confession

We confess to you, O God, the blindness that has kept us in a wilderness of darkness, unable to see you or your works. We confess that our feet are not firmly planted in your time, but that we seek to create time and meaning for ourselves. Open our eyes, and in so doing, open our hearts, so that we may see and respond to the pain of your children that is all around us. We ask these things through Jesus Christ, who made the lame to walk and the blind to see. Amen.

Prayer of Dedication of Gifts and Self

We bring to you, O God, the best we have to give: ourselves and our substance. Put our offerings to work in the world, so that others through us might see your salvation; through Jesus Christ our Lord. Amen.

Sermon Summary

Like Bartimaeus, we, too, live in blindness and captivity. If Bartimaeus could be given his sight again, and with it his perception of time, then so can we.

Hymn of the Day

"A Mighty Fortress Is Our God." *"Ein' feste Burg"* was written by Martin Luther himself. Luther, both spiritually and practically, felt the need for a hymn that could be sung by the people in the native language that would express the principles of faith so long carried by purely Latin texts. Inspired by Psalm 46, there is debate about whether this hymn was written in 1527 when a friend of Luther's was burned at the stake for heresy, or in 1529 when the German Lutheran princes objected to the limitations placed on their liberties. In either case, the image of God as a place of refuge in time of war and struggle is an important image to a world yet wracked by war, hatred, and personal tragedy.

Children's Object Talk

A Blind Man Sees

Object
An old pair of eyeglasses with masking tape covering the lenses.
Lesson
We can see and hear to follow Jesus.

Look at these funny glasses I have. Glasses are supposed to help you see better. (Put on the glasses.) But when I put these on, I don't see better! Actually, I can't see at all. Why can't I see? I have to take off this covering from the glass, don't I? (Peel off the tape.) Yes! Now I can see.

In the story we just heard from the Bible, there was a beggar who could not see. He was sitting by the side of the road when he heard that Jesus was coming. He yelled and yelled to get Jesus' attention. Blind Bartimaeus knew that Jesus could fix his eyes. He might never be near Jesus again. Jesus was just traveling through Bartimaeus' town. This was the chance of a lifetime, so he was not going to let it pass.

"Jesus, son of David, have mercy on me," he called.

People told him to be quiet. But he wanted so badly to have Jesus help him that he went right on yelling. And Jesus heard him. Jesus stopped. He asked that the blind man be called. Bartimaeus was so eager to get to Jesus, he threw down the robe he was wearing and went as fast as he could to him.

"What do you want me to do for you?" Jesus asked.

Bartimaeus answered, "I want to see." Jesus said, "Your faith has healed you."

Bartimaeus wasn't blind anymore! He could see. It was as though someone had taken the tape off his glasses. (Hold up the glasses.) Then you know what he did? He followed Jesus. The Bible says he followed after Jesus. He didn't just run home to show his family that he could see. He stayed with Jesus.

We want to follow Jesus, too. We can know what it means to follow Jesus when we read the Bible. Can you think of some

October 26, 1997
23rd Sunday after Pentecost (Proper 25)
RC/Pres: 30th Sunday in Ordinary Time

things we do when we follow Jesus? (Elicit answers and repeat them. Include such ideas as being kind, praying, taking care of the poor, forgiving, etc.).

—*Lois Brokering*

The Sermon

Regaining Our Sight

Hymns
Beginning of Worship: "O for a Thousand Tongues to Sing"
Sermon Hymn: "Pass Me Not, O Gentle Savior"
End of Worship: "We Would See Jesus"

Scripture
Mark 10:46-52 (For additional sermon materials on this passage, see the July 1997 and *1997 May/June Planning Issue* of *The Clergy Journal*.)

Sermon Text
"Jesus said to him, 'Go; your faith has made you well.' Immediately he regained his sight and followed him on the way" (vs. 52).

On a trip to England in 1992, Jack and I had occasion to visit the Greenwich Observatory on the Thames estuary outside London. In addition to its fine collection of astronomical instruments, the Observatory boasts a unique marker of time and space: the Prime Meridian, or Greenwich Meridian, zero degrees longitude, from which distances and time over the rest of the earth are measured. Visitors can straddle the brass strip in the floor, demarcating the eastern and western hemispheres, to be in both hemispheres simultaneously—in past and in future, with the brass marker, signifying the present moment, in between.

As people of God, we find ourselves often straddling the line, as well: the line between past and future. The past has a powerful claim upon us. In the past, our "firsts" seem to be the easiest events to recall: a first boy/girlfriend, a first paying job, the birth of a first child, the arrival of a first grandchild. There is a great deal to be said for returning to the old. The old holds a history. For better or worse, we are linked to that history. Sooner or later, the foot on the historical side of the meridian must be attended to.

It is crucial to faith to know that God is on both sides of the meridian, as well as on the line. God *was* before us, God *is* before us, and God is in this exact moment. So what is Bartimaeus regaining in this lesson? He could very well be regaining experiences, memories, even fears about being blind. In regaining his sight, Bartimaeus once again has a foot in the past, and is able to put a foot in the future. In regaining his sight, he is regaining the rich-ness of the life he once knew. In regaining his sight, Bartimaeus has a reborn opportunity to see across the wide world of time and space.

A college classmate of mine was blind. He had a guide dog, read his textbooks in Braille, and studied by listening to tapes of lectures he made in class. Because he could not see, his other senses became highly developed to compensate. What I remember best about him was that he had perfect pitch, which helped since he was a music major.

Several years after we graduated, I heard that Jim had undergone delicate eye surgery. Miraculously, he could see again —an experience he had not had since early childhood. A mutual friend told me that not only had Jim retained all the sensitivity he had acquired while blind, he had also become a much more motivated person, because he remembered what being blind meant. The operation had allowed him to jump off the brass strip in the floor. Jim once again was able to straddle the meridian, with a foot in the richness of his life in the past, a foot in the wide-open possibilities of the future, and the marker of the present in between.

We, too, have wandered in the wilderness of darkness, unable to see the line of demarcation. Perhaps we have been in physical captivity, as were the Israelites in Egypt, before the Exodus, or have been under the rule of alien principalities and powers, like the Jews of first-century Palestine. Perhaps we have been physically blind, as was Bartimaeus, or have simply been confused, depressed, or aimless in our lives. Nevertheless, we are called, not only to fix our gaze on the future, but to return to the place we once had through God's creating, redeeming grace, and to look toward the kingdom promised to us in the future by the presence of Jesus Christ here on earth.

I have spent most of my life being unable to see. My blindness has not been of a physical sort, although I have worn glasses since the age of three. My blindness has resulted from years of physical, verbal, psychological, and sexual abuse. I have grown to adulthood believing that nothing about my life has any value. Most of the time, I am afraid of

October 26, 1997
23rd Sunday after Pentecost (Proper 25)
RC/Pres: 30th Sunday in Ordinary Time

people, because everyone I meet has the potential to revisit the abuse, to cause me bodily harm. I know that fear is irrational, but it persists nonetheless. The abuse has hurt me very deeply. For years, I didn't care if there was a past or a future; all I wanted was to have an end to the pain of the present.

About ten years ago, my past began to intrude into my life in the form of flashbacks and nightmares. I had no control over it. I was going to wander in a wilderness of inner terror. Confusion and depression have been my constant companions. Through the help of a gentle spiritual director and a caring therapist, I am beginning to have the courage to step off the metal strip of the present, putting one foot back into the past, and one foot forward into the future. The process is both painful and time-consuming, and no one has guaranteed its outcome. I can only hope that, as it did for Bartimaeus, the blindness will someday pass.

Bartimaeus had been able to see once, but now he only remembered seeing. He had learned of God's promises in the past to David; that is why he placed Jesus in the historical context of the faith by calling him "Son of David." To some, Bartimaeus was simply a nuisance. People told him to be quiet and not to bother Jesus. But his need was so great that he called out all the louder, "Son of David, have mercy on me."

Something about the situation interested Jesus. He asked the disciples to bring Bartimaeus to him. Then, he inquired what the man wanted. Bartimaeus had lost something precious. He had once known both sides of the meridian, and he was part of the heritage of Abraham, Isaac, Jacob, and Joseph, of David and Solomon and Jeremiah, waiting for renewal and redemption, laying a moral claim upon Jesus. "I want to see again," he said.

We, too, live in blindness and captivity, immobile on the brass meridian of the present: captive to jobs in which we feel more trapped than fulfilled, or in which our employers seem to lack any compassion; captive to family responsibilities that might have begun as a joy but which have become burdensome; captive within ourselves and blind to the pain of so many around us, persons who, like ourselves, have been created in the image of God.

We, too, cry out, "Son of David, I want to see again."
Bartimaeus did.
So can we.

—Nancy E. Topolewski
Vestal United Methodist Church
Vestal, New York

October 26, 1997

Reformation

Lessons
Jer 31:31–34   Rom 3:19–28   Jn 8:31–36

Introduction to the Lessons
Lesson 1
Jeremiah 31:31–34
The prophet promises that God will make a new covenant with God's people, one not dependent upon stone tablets, but one which will be written on the human heart.

Lesson 2
Romans 3:19–28
Paul points out that in the old order, under the law, no one can be justified; but now, apart from the law, God's righteousness has been declared through the atoning death of Jesus Christ.

Gospel
John 8:31–36
Jesus, speaking to Jews who had believed in him, promises that the Son will set them free from bondage to the law.

Theme
God's new covenant will be written on the hearts of believers.

Thought for the Day
"Do you ask, 'What is faith in Him?' I answer, the leaving of your way, your objects, your self, and the taking of His and Him; the leaving of your trust in men [sic], in money, in opinion, in character, in atonement itself, *and doing as He tells you.* I can find no words strong enough to serve for the weight of this obedience."
—George Macdonald (1824–1905), in *Unspoken Sermons*, 2nd series, "The Truth in Jesus," quoted in C. S. Lewis, *George Macdonald: An Anthology,* New York: The Macmillan Co., 1947, p. 75, #165, "Faith"

October 26, 1997
Reformation

Prayer of Meditation

"In Jesus Christ we have been given a true mentor; one who, in his humanity, understands our most human fears and torments. Give us grace to take courage from his life and from those who have followed in his footsteps through service to honor.

"We offer thanksgiving for all who have offered their pain, their physical limitations, their emotional wounds for your healing touch, and have become grains of wheat, dying to fear and rising to holy confidence. We offer thanksgiving for all who have offered the changes and chances of their lives, their disappointments, their public humiliations for redemption and have become grains of wheat, dying to personal aspirations and rising to faith in your providence. We offer thanksgiving for all who have offered their mistakes, their misunderstandings, their ignorance for your correction and become grains of wheat, dying to sin, and rising to obedience to your will.

"We are one body in our humanity and in our suffering. In clinging to one another in love, and to Jesus who is our head, let us become a whole and holy body. Amen."
—Andrea La Sonde Anastos, *Lectionary Prayers,*
Inver Grove Heights, MN:
Logos Productions Inc., 1993, p. 142

Call to Worship

Create in us clean hearts, O God,
    and put a new and right spirit within us.
Do not cast us away from your presence
    and do not take your holy spirit from us.
Restore to us the joy of your salvation,
    and sustain in us a willing spirit.
—Adapted from Psalm 51:10–12

Prayer of Adoration

Give to our God immortal praise,
Mercy and truth are all his ways:
    Wonders of grace to God belong,
    Repeat his mercies in your song.
—Isaac Watts (1674–1748), based on Psalm 136,
Hymns and Psalms: A Methodist and Ecumenical Hymn Book,
London: Methodist Publishing House, 1983, #22, verse 1

Prayer of Confession
We confess to you, O Lord, this day, the divisions that have rent your church since its earliest years. In our zeal to reform, we have often lost the truth and beauty of the old. We follow your law when it is convenient and go our own way when we wish. Inscribe your new covenant upon our hearts, we pray. Help us to know you, not only in words, but in Jesus Christ your living word. Amen.

Prayer of Dedication of Gifts and Self
We come to you as ever-changing people, O God. Renew us according to the example of Jesus Christ, the pioneer and perfecter of our faith, as we come before you with our gifts. We here dedicate our gifts and ourselves to your ever-reforming church; through Jesus Christ our Lord. Amen.

Sermon Summary
Jeremiah foretells a time when our covenant with God will not be an external one, based on a binding, indisputable pact calling for trust in and obedience to God, but when God will write a new covenant on our hearts.

Hymn of the Day
"I Greet Thee, Who My Sure Redeemer Art (I Greet You, Sure Redeemer)." This hymn is from the 1454 *Strasbourg Psalter* attributed to Calvin for whom the grace of God was the supreme gift. His words are a prayer for the sustaining gift of faith and a hymn of praise for God who has the "true and perfect gentleness."

Children's Object Talk

Knowledge of the Heart

Object
>An enlarged copy of the Ten Commandments on firm paper, and a small copy for each child.

Lesson
>The law of God shall be written on our hearts. (Note: Because children think concretely, the use of the word "heart" in this context is often confused with the organ that pumps blood. Use the word "mind" instead when talking to children.)

October 26, 1997
Reformation

(Hold up an enlarged copy of the Ten Commandments.) On this piece of paper is a list of rules. Do you know what rules are? Rules are things we all should do to be safe, to be fair, and to be happy with each other. These ten rules were given to us by God. These are ten things God tells us to do or not to do. God knows we will not be happy together unless we do what he tells us here.

I can hang this piece of paper on my wall, or I can fold it up and keep it in my pocket. I could put it into a wooden box with a lock and a key. I could put these rules on a gigantic banner and hang it on a flag pole in front of my house. But is that going to help me do these things God wants me to do? No.

If I am going to do this list of rules, I have to put them inside my head, don't I? I have to hear this list with my ears or read it with my eyes. I have to get it into my mind, and then I have to remember it. I have to think about it. One of these rules is to take a rest every seven days. Keep it holy. All of us in this room had that rule in our minds today. That's why we decided to come here to our church to worship God together.

There are other rules in this list. Respect God's name. Respect your parents. Don't take other people's things. Don't kill another person. Don't say something that isn't true. There are lots of things to remember—not easy, is it? But God will help us. God will put these things in our minds. Learn these rules. Put them inside your head so you can be the kind of person God wants you to be. (Give each child a copy.)

—Lois Brokering

The Sermon

A Covenant for the Heart

Hymns
Beginning of Worship: "A Mighty Fortress Is Our God"
Sermon Hymn: "Out of the Depths I Cry to You"
End of Worship: "The Church's One Foundation"

Scripture
Jeremiah 31:31–34 (For sermon materials on John 8:31–36, see the July 1997 issue of *The Clergy Journal* and on Romans 3:19–28, see the *1997 May/June Planning Issue* of *The Clergy Journal*.)

Sermon Text

"But this is the covenant that I will make with the house of Israel after those days, says the Lord: I will put my law within them, and I will write it on their hearts; and I will be their God, and they shall be my people" (vs. 33).

Jeremiah is in a rather unusual position. He has spent many chapters, as the prophet of God, lamenting the unfaithfulness of Israel with the God who brought them out of captivity in Egypt. The fall of Jerusalem is now imminent, but instead of continuing his condemnation of his fellow Israelites, Jeremiah offers them a word of hope.

They will, he tells them, be taken off to exile in Babylon. But they should *"consider well the highway, the road by which [they] went"* (Jer 31:21). Jeremiah affirms that God will protect God's people and then sets forth his astounding claim. In spite of a history of faithlessness among God's chosen ones, God is faithful. God will make a new covenant with Israel, one which will not be written on stone tablets, as was the Sinai covenant, but which will be written on each individual heart.

Covenants with God, and the Israelites' inability to keep them, have been the source of much trouble. Let us look for a few moments at the characteristics of covenants, to see what makes the new covenant proclaimed by Jeremiah such a departure from the past.

First, a covenant is not a contract; it is not an agreement mutually worked out between two parties of equal stature. A covenant is not the deal we make at the used car lot, or an exchange of money for services rendered. *A covenant is a binding pact between God and God's people.*

Think back on all the instances of covenants up to this point in the Old Testament. After the great flood that obliterated the world, God made a covenant with Noah never again to destroy the world by water. The sign of this covenant is the rainbow.

After asking Abram to leave his home and his native land, God made a covenant that if Abram (later Abraham) would obey God, God would give him land, descendants, and blessings. God repeated this covenant with Isaac, Jacob, and Joseph, in spite of all the treachery and double-dealing that marked each of their generations.

After leading the Hebrew people out of slavery in Egypt, God made a covenant with Moses on Mount Sinai that showed God was claiming this people for God's own. There is never a time in this long sweep of history when God does not uphold his end of the covenant. God is both covenant-maker and covenant-keeper. Human beings both make and break covenants. A covenant is a binding pact between God and God's people.

Second, *a covenant is not open to debate.* The only choice human beings have is either to accept the covenant or to reject it. This represents a departure from what we know to have been (and continues to be) the economic system of the Middle East. Each time we have visited Israel, we have gone into the *suk,* or marketplace, in the Muslim Quarter of Old Jerusalem. Shopkeepers and street vendors are highly aggressive in calling attention to their wares. It is tacitly expected that the visitor will argue the price of goods with the seller. Not to barter is a sign of bad manners.

We once watched a shopkeeper try to sell a leather purse to a woman in our Holy Land tour group. He started out at fifty dollars; she was not interested. As the price was successively lowered in ten-dollar increments, the woman continued to walk away. Finally, the exasperated shopkeeper told the woman to take the purse for nothing, for she had beaten him at his own game—and still she refused him! A covenant, by contrast, is not open to debate.

Third, *a covenant brings blessings to those who trust in God's promises and obey God's conditions.* Covenants were not made one-sidedly; that is, so that God could make infinite demands upon people without providing anything in return. Covenants offered benefits to those who kept them.

Up until Jeremiah's time, the blessing had been the land and the protection of God for the nation. The Israelites, however, had been neither trusting nor obedient. They had come to interpret the Sinai covenant very narrowly, as a way of getting around it. Now, with the Babylonian invasion, God is chastening the people for their infidelity. The blessings of covenant life with God will be removed, until Israel learns trust and obedience. A covenant brings blessings to those who trust in God's promises and obey God's conditions.

"But this is the covenant that I will make with the house of Israel after those days, says the Lord: I will put my law within them, and I will write it on their hearts; and I will be their God, and they shall be my people" (Jer 31:33).

In spite of all that has gone on before, God still believes in God's people. The new covenant will not be some external instrument, like the tablets of the Sinai covenant; it will be written on the hearts of believers. Not only will they not have to be taught the covenant; the covenant will be part of their very nature.

This text has been seen as a foreshadowing of the coming of

Jesus Christ, God's new covenant. But it can also be applied to the beliefs of our ancestors in the Protestant Reformation.

To greatly simplify the historical situation, persons like Martin Luther and John Calvin saw the church of their day as becoming more and more narrowly focused. Church tradition about the word, and not the word of God itself, was viewed as primary to Christian belief.

Martin Luther, for one, did not throw out the idea of covenant; in fact, he saw God's covenant as most readily present for Christians in the sacrament of baptism.

"In the act of baptism, [God] makes a new covenant with us and gives us the assurance that he will forgive us our sins throughout our entire life and at the same time that he will put our sins to death . . . He trains us for that death in which sin finally dies." (Paul Althaus, *The Theology of Martin Luther* [Philadelphia: Fortress Press, 1966], p. 355.)

For Luther, the sacrament of baptism becomes the covenant written on the heart.

On this day when we remember the work of those who have gone before us in faith, let us, like Jeremiah, try to see our covenant as God's people in new ways, moving from seeing the covenant as a binding pact not open to debate, bringing blessings for those who trust God's promises and obey God's conditions. Let us focus instead upon the graciousness of a God who puts the covenant within our hearts, allowing that covenant to be constantly known and refined, and providing us, with that covenant, the assurance of forgiveness of sins and a new, renewed, constantly changing life in Jesus Christ, who is, himself, God's new covenant.

—*Nancy E. Topolewski*
Vestal United Methodist Church
Vestal, New York

November 2, 1997

24th Sunday after Pentecost (Proper 26)
Pres: 31st Sunday in Ordinary Time
RC: Commemoration of All the Faithful Departed
(All Souls)—Not listed

Lessons

Pres/Meth/UCC	Ruth 1:1–18	Heb 9:11–14	Mk 12:28–34
Episcopal	Deut 6:1–9	Heb 7:23–28	Mk 12:28–34
Lutheran	Deut 6:1–9	Heb 9:11–14	Mk 12:28–34

Introduction to the Lessons
Lesson 1
(1) *Ruth 1:1–18* **(Pres/Meth/UCC)**
The two main characters of this story, traditionally read during the Feast of First Fruits (celebrating the spring barley harvest), are introduced against the backdrop of death and famine. Ruth, the Moabite, and her Israelite mother-in-law, Naomi, are remembered for their loyalty to one another.

(2) *Deuteronomy 6:1–9* **(Epis/Luth)**
Moses restates the first commandment in positive form. If it and all of God's commands are heard and obeyed, God's promises will be fulfilled and the faithfulness of the people rewarded. First and foremost in the response to God is an undivided allegiance to the one God.

Lesson 2
(1) *Hebrews 9:11–14* **(Pres/Meth/UCC/Luth)**
Through the sacrifice of his life, Jesus Christ made possible the new covenant which replaced the old covenant. There are several contrasts between the "old" and "new," including the blood of the sacrificial animals and Christ's own blood. In every way, Christ's sacrifice is superior to the offering of the high priests up to that time.

(2) *Hebrews 7:23–28* **(Epis)**
Continuing the "new covenant" theme, the writer of Hebrews draws a

contrast between the inadequacy of the Levitical priesthood and the role of Jesus Christ as the permanent and perfect priest.

Gospel
Mark 12:28–34 **(Pres/Meth/UCC/Luth/Epis)**
In the only positive reference to a scribe in Mark, an encounter with Jesus provides a link between Judaism and Christianity. Both hold as central tenets, love of God and love of neighbor. Faith and ethical behavior are more important than ritual.

Theme
How close are we to the kingdom of God?

Thought for the Day
We may wonder about the future coming of the kingdom of God and how far away it is, but we should also be personally concerned with how close to it we are right now.

Prayer of Meditation
How do we love you, Lord? Let us consider and count the ways: Do we love you with all our heart or are we halfhearted in our devotion? Do we love you with all our soul or are we rich in things and poor in soul? Do we love you with all our mind or do we have our doubts? Do we love you with all our strength or is our commitment weak? Are all our powers engaged in loving you? Do we love you enough? Can we ever love you as much as you love us? Amen.

Call to Worship
Leader:	Happy are those whose way is blameless.
People:	Who walk in the law of the Lord.
Leader:	Happy are those who keep his decrees,
People:	Who seek him with their whole heart.
Leader:	You have commanded your precepts to be kept diligently.
People:	O that my ways may be steadfast in keeping your statutes! —Psalm 119:1–2, 4–5

Prayer of Adoration
You are our God, and you are the one and only God we need. You are

November 2, 1997
24th Sunday after Pentecost (Proper 26)
Pres: 31st Sunday in Ordinary Time

enough to satisfy our longings and fulfill our desires. Your goodness is sufficient for our every trouble and your guidance for our every trial. Your love covers the multitude of our sins. There is no time when we do not need you. There is no time or place when you are far from us. You are everywhere, involved in everything, and we pray that you will become everyone's God. Amen.

Prayer of Confession

God, forgive us if we have never really let you be God for us or let you do everything you want to do for us. Keep us from listening to other voices, seeking to learn other truths, leaning on others for the strength only you can give, looking in other places for the love which only you can give, loving anything and anyone more than we love you, and allowing ourselves to be led in so many wrong directions in life. Give us renewed loyalty as followers of him whom you sent to be *the* way, *the* truth, and *the* life for us all, Jesus Christ. Amen.

Prayer of Dedication of Gifts and Self

Loving Lord, if we have tried to love you without loving others, forgive us. Remind us that it is in giving to others that we fulfill our responsibilities for using what you have given us, and are more responsive to your will for us. Help our offerings to show we mean it when we pray and sing, "take my life and let it be consecrated to you." May this sharing of the resources you have entrusted to us be the means by which we are brought closer to you. May these gifts become a ministry of bringing your children closer to one another. Amen.

Sermon Summary

It is perhaps because we have stopped short of a total devotion to God that we are no closer than "not far from the Kingdom of God."

Hymn of the Day

"Sing a New Church into Being." Sung to the tune "Nettleton," this hymn has the familiar and uplifting character of the 1813 original piece more commonly known as "Here I Raise My Ebeneezer." Exemplifying unity and inclusivity, images of God and God's people abound in this piece. In particular, the words remind us that we serve a greater church than just the one we attend, and that God's grace strengthens us all through the diversity of individual gifts. As we sing of the "saints" of the church, this hymn so aptly expresses the hope of all their work. This hymn is easy to sing and is especially easy to learn by virtue of a repeating refrain.

Children's Object Talk

Only Two Things Are Important

Object
The enlarged copy of the Ten Commandments from October 16 and a pair of scissors.

Lesson
The Ten Commandments can be summed up in two basic rules.

A couple of Sundays ago, we talked about the ten important rules that God wants us to do. These rules are called commandments—the Ten Commandments from God. In the gospel lesson we just read from the Bible, a very smart man asked Jesus about those rules. This man asked Jesus which rule was the most important. What do you suppose Jesus answered? (Accept all answers.)

Jesus said the most important rule or commandment was this: *Love God as much as you possibly can.* That's the most important thing we are to do all the time, every day, all night, at school, at day care, at home, especially outside playing with friends—love God.

Then Jesus went on. The second most important rule or commandment is this: *Love other people just the way you love yourself.* God wants us to love each other. We forgive each other. We are kind to each other. We do all the things to the people around us that we wish they would do to us. Do you like it when someone hits you? No? Then you shouldn't hit anyone either. Love each other the way you love yourself, Jesus told us.

Now, if we look at God's list of Ten Commandments (hold up the large list) we can see that the first rules are about loving God. Then these rules (point) are about loving other people. So we can put them together into two important rules: (Cut the sheet in two between the two sections.)

We should love God (hold up the first section) and we should love each other (hold up the second section). That makes it easier to remember the Ten Commandments. They tell us how to love God and how to love each other. I hope you are working hard on learning them with your parents. Put them inside your mind and remember them. Then you can be the kind of person God planned for you to be.

—*Lois Brokering*

November 2, 1997
24th Sunday after Pentecost (Proper 26)
Pres: 31st Sunday in Ordinary Time

The Sermon

Not Far Enough?

Hymns
Beginning of Worship: "I Love Thy Kingdom, Lord"
Sermon Hymn: "I Am Thine, O Lord"
End of Worship: "More Love to Thee, O Christ"

Scripture
Mark 12:28–34 (For additional sermon materials on this passage, see the August 1997 and *1997 May/June Planning Issue* of *The Clergy Journal*.)

Sermon Text
"... 'You are not far from the kingdom of God'" (vs. 34).

We were on a bus taking us from the hotel to Disney World. A family with two young boys sat across from us. It was obviously their first visit, though they had already purchased and put on all the shirts, caps, and shoes that indicated they were ready for a great adventure in the Magic Kingdom. As the bus turned the corner, one of the little boys exclaimed, "It's the Kingdom! There it is! I see the Kingdom!" We had arrived. The boys got off the bus and ran as fast as they could to enter.

Wouldn't it be wonderful if it were as obvious to know when we were getting close to the kingdom of God! Or that easy to see it and know that we had arrived. Like children seated in the back seat of a car, asking "Are we there yet?" a thousand times, we want to know how far we have to go before we get to where we are going. Or to know when our daily prayer, "Thy kingdom come ... ," might be answered.

Only God, of course, knows how far away the kingdom is or how far from it any of us might be. When the scribe in our Scripture reading entered into a conversation with Jesus, and was able to affirm his understanding of the great commandments of God, Jesus pronounced him "not far from the kingdom of God." We can only guess what kept him for "having arrived" and from fully entering it. Certainly he knew the importance of loving God wholly and of loving one's neighbor. He had already figured out that relationships were far more fundamental to the faith than religious rituals (as exemplified by his statement, "this is much more important than all whole burnt offerings and sacrifices"). He had shown a genuine and quite sincere desire to listen and to learn. What kept him from being told, "You're there!"

What keeps us? Might it be that we have not gone "far enough" in our faith? Might it be that we have some "unconverted areas"? or that we do not love God with our minds, our hearts, our souls, and our strength? The whole law was summed up as total devotion to God and love for one's neighbor. Some of us do better at loving God than we do loving our neighbor. Others of us do better at loving our neighbor than we do loving God. We end up as halfway Christians.

Or we might be "almost Christians." That is a phrase from the writing of John Wesley. He drew a contrast between an "almost Christian" and being "altogether, a Christian." He spoke from his own experience, noting that for much of his life, his conscience led him to believe he was "but almost a Christian." Wesley offered, by way of a checklist for those who would become "altogether, a Christian," the importance of loving God and loving neighbor. In addition, he listed knowing we are forgiven and reconciled to God, obedience to God's commandments, and a sincere desire to please God in all things. He called for us never to stop short of achieving the goal—of being 100 percent Christian.

Another checklist is provided in 2 Peter:

". . . make every effort to support your faith with goodness, and goodness with knowledge, and knowledge with self-control, and self-control with endurance, and endurance with godliness, and godliness with mutual affection, and mutual affection with love" (2 Pet 1:5–7).

Or maybe we need to move beyond equating religion with ritual and routine—even rules—to seeing it as involving relationships. That surely is the lesson of the encounter between Jesus and the good scribe. The Hebrews had been told that the proper response to God was to be involved in a personal, intimate, and trusting relationship. It called for a total commitment and a wholehearted loyalty. No other religion had anything to compare to that way of relating to God. That kind of devotion was to dominate every aspect of our lives.

Maybe we have not gone far enough into what an intimate relationship with God requires. Long enough in our study. Often enough in prayer. Far enough in our trust. Deep enough in our knowledge. Maybe we are being called to move ahead in our prayer, our service, our stewardship—or

November 2, 1997
24th Sunday after Pentecost (Proper 26)
Pres: 31st Sunday in Ordinary Time

our faith, hope, or love. Thomas Carlyle is quoted as saying that what every church needs is a preacher "who knows God at more than second-hand." I would add that every church also needs members who know God on a firsthand basis.

Clarence Jordan once responded to his brother's admission that he followed Jesus up to a point with "I don't think you are a disciple. I think you are an admirer of Jesus, not a disciple." Do we, too only follow Jesus up to a point? Have we given up, turned back, stopped short of being permanent residents of the kingdom of God by our desire to only visit occasionally?

What if we began to act as if we were already residents of the kingdom, as if it had fully come—at least in our lives? That means seeking first the will of God to be done in our lives. That means becoming more interested in fulfilling God's needs than in having God fulfill our needs.

A Russian youth once felt he could not serve in the army. He was hauled before a Russian judge. The young man stood up to give his defense, basing it on his belief that military service was not permissible within the rule of God. The judge looked at him and said, "All this is true—but the kingdom of heaven has not come!" To that the youth replied, "Your honor, it may not have come for you, but it has come for me."

Are we ready to enter the realm of God's ultimate and absolute rule in our lives? To pray "thy will be done," and mean it? Too often, we turn back before we are there. A story is told about a young man who saw a beautiful girl on the road and followed her. Annoyed, she finally turned to ask him, "Why do you dog my footsteps?" He answered, "Because you are the loveliest thing I have ever seen and I have fallen madly in love with you at first sight. Please be mine!" The young lady answered, "But you have merely to look behind you to see my young sister who is ten times more beautiful than I am." Of course, the man whirled about and his gaze fell on as homely a girl as anyone had ever seen. "What mockery is this?" he demanded. "You lied to me!" "So did you," she replied. "If you were so madly in love with me, why did you turn around?"

God says to us, "If you are so madly in love with me, if you have promised to follow me always, why do you turn back? Why did you stop short of entrance into the kingdom of God? Why haven't you gone far enough?

—*William M. Schwein*
Carmel Un. Methodist Church
Indianapolis, Indiana

November 2, 1997

All Saints' Day

Lessons

Pres/Meth/UCC	Wis 3:1–9 or Isa 25:6–9	Rev 21:1–6a	Jn 11:32–44
Roman Catholic	Rev 7:2–4, 9–14	1 Jn 3:1–3	Mt 5:1–12a
Episcopal	Eccl 44:1–10, 13–14	Rev 7:2–4, 9–17	Mt 5:1–12
Lutheran	Wis 3:1–9 or Isa 25:6–9	Rev 21:1–6a	Jn 11:32–44

Introduction to the Lessons
Lesson 1
(1) *Isaiah 25:6–9* **(Pres/Meth/UCC/Luth)**
In this part of Isaiah (chapters 24–27), the prophet often speaks in less optimistic tones than in the other sections. He gives an "end time" vision of salvation that depends less on our efforts than on God's intervention. Isaiah offers the vision of a new world order in which God will break into history by hosting a banquet for all persons and by defeating death.

(2) *Revelation 7:2–4, 9–14* **(RC)**
John's vision includes an assurance that God's people would be protected from the effects of the tribulation. The symbolic number of the faithful indicates completeness. Those who receive the sign of God's protection ascribe praise to God.

(3) *Eccl 44:1–10, 13–14* **(Epis)**
The heroes of the faith are praised. Those receiving special recognition and remembrance were the ones who had been examples of personal piety and righteousness. God's gift of wisdom had guided them.

Lesson 2
(1) *Revelation 21:1–6a* **(Pres/Meth/UCC/Luth)**
John sees the ultimate triumph of God at the end of time in a vision of a new Jerusalem, a new heaven, and a new earth. God's redemptive

November 2, 1997
All Saints' Day

activity will be completed when the old has passed away and the new has come, evidenced by the disappearance of suffering, pain, and death.

(2) *1 John 3:1–3* **(RC)**
The promise is made that the children of God will be transformed into God's likeness, including their moral purity.

(3) *Revelation 7:2–4, 9–17* **(Epis)** (see Lesson 1)

Gospel
(1) *John 11:32–44* **(Pres/Meth/UCC/Luth)**
The presence and power of God are evidenced in the sensitivity of Jesus Christ at the grave of Lazarus and in his miraculous raising of Lazarus from the dead.

(2) *Matthew 5:1–12a* **(RC)**; *Matthew 5:1–12* **(Epis)**
In what is perhaps the most familiar of all of Jesus' teachings, which we know as the Sermon on the Mount, he begins with the Beatitudes. Happiness comes to those who live in ways that mark their inclusion in the kingdom of God.

Theme
Our faith allows us to face death confidently.

Thought for the Day
Though we try to bypass the valley of shadows by denying death, it cannot be avoided. Christianity assures us that we do not have to make that journey alone, and even offers us the belief that we can defy it.

Prayer of Meditation
On this day of remembrance, our thoughts are naturally drawn to those who are no longer with us except in spirit and in memory. This is the time when we have to think long and hard about what it means to affirm that you are the Lord of life and of death. Give us a different way to look at both life and death. As aware as we are of the absence of loved ones, let us also be attentive to your comforting presence. Let us hear more clearly than ever before our Savior say to us, "I am the resurrection and the life." Amen.

Call to Worship

> Leader: Those who have clean hands and pure hearts,
> People: Who do not lift up their souls to what is false,
> Leader: They will receive blessing from the Lord,
> People: And vindication from the God of their salvation.
> Leader: Such is the company of those who seek him,
> People: Who seek the face of the God of Jacob.
> —Psalm 24:4–6

Prayer of Adoration

From generation to generation, you are to be praised. All the saints adore you! It is the faith and faithfulness of those who have gone before us that often moves us to join in unending praise. It is the assurance that we are surrounded by a cloud of witnesses that often makes our praise of you more meaningful and memorable. It is the awareness of the communion of saints that can make our praise more contagious to those who are hesitant to join in our singing, our praying, and our rejoicing. Let those who have gone before us set the example for how we should come before you in honor and glory. Amen.

Prayer of Confession

We confess to you, God, how reluctantly we have given up loved ones into your hands. We have denied so much of what we have said we believed when actually faced with death's reality. We have even said we did not want to go on living ourselves. We have wanted more than just the promises of Jesus; we have wanted precise answers to all our questions: Why did they have to leave so soon? Why have they been taken from us? Where are they now? When will we see them again? Beyond our vain questioning, help us to know what it means to let our faith, our hope, and your love be the sources of comfort and peace for our troubled spirits and saddened hearts. Amen.

Prayer of Dedication of Gifts and Self

How will we be remembered, God? For our selfishness or for our selfless giving? For our affluence or for our compassion? For our generosity or for our accumulation of wealth? May the offering of these gifts be an expression of our sincere desire to be known as people of generosity and goodwill. Amen.

November 2, 1997
All Saints' Day

Sermon Summary
Jesus not only spoke words of comfort and assurance, but embodied the "thou art with me" promise of the Twenty-third Psalm that reassures us when we have to walk through the valley of the shadow of death.

Hymn of the Day
"O What Their Joy and Their Glory Must Be." "He will wipe away every tear" in the New Jerusalem promises the Revelation of John when the saints gather in that place. Peter Abelard, one of the medieval church's most innovative and controversial thinkers, wrote this hymn contemplating our reunion with God. Nearly a thousand years later, his words still bring comfort as we remember those who have gone before us into the wider life with Christ.

Children's Object Talk

Life from Death

Object
A pot of soil or a bulb vase of water, a dormant bulb with *no green* protruding and a sprouted bulb, especially a blooming one such as an amaryllis, oxalis, daffodil, hyacinth, or even an onion.

Lesson
God brings life from death.

(Show the dead bulb. Keep the growing bulb covered.) What do you suppose this funny looking thing can be? This is a _____ bulb. Does it look dead or alive to you? It looks pretty dead, doesn't it? Have you any idea what I could do to make this bulb look alive again? (Wait for children to answer.) Suppose I put it in some earth and watered it, or even into a vase of water. (do so as you speak)

What do you think? Does it look alive now? No, it doesn't look alive now either, does it? What else do you think I have to do? Yes, I have to wait, don't I? (Uncover the sprouted bulb.) Here is a bulb that was planted some weeks ago. It looked dead and brown, just like this one. But now see what happened! God put a bit of life inside that bulb. Along with the bit of life, there was food to help it grow. But it needed water. When it got water, the bit of life grew and grew into this beautiful plant, and that took time.

In our gospel story today, we heard about a man who died.

His name was Lazarus. His sisters, Mary and Martha, cried and cried because they missed him so much.

When Jesus came they said, "If only you had been here, Lazarus would not have died."

But Jesus called to Lazarus, and he got up again. He was alive again. Jesus promises us that when we die, we will still be alive in a different way. We will live in heaven with him. Today we are celebrating people who have died—people who followed Jesus. Now these people are living in heaven with Jesus.

—*Lois Brokering*

The Sermon

What's at the End of the Valley?

Hymns
Beginning of Worship: "Rejoice in God's Saints"
Sermon Hymn: "Shall We Gather at the River?"
End of Worship: "O Love That Wilt Not Let Me Go"

Scripture
John 11:32–44 (For additional sermon materials on this passage, see the August 1997 and the *1997 May/June Planning Issue* of *The Clergy Journal.*)

Sermon Text
"Then Jesus, again greatly disturbed, came to the tomb" (vs. 38).

As I was leaving the church one afternoon, a man stopped me and asked, "Are you the preacher?" "Yes," I replied, with a hesitancy that comes from years of having been confronted in that way because someone wanted a handout. "Well, this is what I want to know. Where is my wife?"

"I don't understand. What happened to your wife?"

"She died last year. I want to know where she is now."

He told me that visiting his wife's grave had meant nothing to him. He added that he had never thought a thing about heaven until "all this happened." We talked awhile about heaven, and I stumbled through my explanation of its location. I apologized that I could not be more specific in my description of its geography. I suggested that Jesus had spoken of being "in paradise" with him. He asked where paradise is. I mumbled

November 2, 1997
All Saints' Day

something about "having to trust in God," and slipped away.

Where do we go from here? What *is* at the end of the valley anyway? Some would suggest it is nothing more than a dead end. There is nothing beyond. Others compare it to a tunnel. Still others think of it as a connecting route from the here to the hereafter.

We all try to bypass it—or at least postpone ending up there. We would rather not think about it. A young mother once sent me a note that said, "I still feel very uncomfortable with the thought of my own death. Eternity—that concept alone can start an unpleasant round of middle-of-the-night panic attacks. Not many people want to think or talk about it. I don't know how they can avoid doing so." She was obviously having what have been called "night questions"—those that go through our minds when we are lying awake at night. Many people today fear extinction, the thought of "when I am not."

Death is often considered to be the obscenity of our day. Some people are like William Randolph Hearst who would not permit the word to be spoken in his presence.

One survey indicated 35 percent of us refuse to think about our own death. We resort to any number of euphemisms: passed away, gone, at home with the Lord. It's almost a part of our American tradition to never say "die."

And yet, no matter where we were born, where we have been, where our travels have taken us, we all end up converging at the same place. Sooner or later we must all walk through the "valley of the shadow of death." Before we walk down it ourselves, we walk it with any number of our friends and loved ones. Coming off the mountaintops, fresh from green pastures and still waters, or maybe after weeks and months trying to avoid it, we must hold the hand of someone very dear to us and face that inevitable journey through the valley of the shadows.

Too many of us act as if God goes with us to that valley and then abandons us. In fact, God has probably given us as much assurance for that time of our lives as for any other. Paul wrote to the Thessalonians, *"But we do not want you to be uniformed, brothers and sisters, about those who have died, so that you may not grieve as others do who have no hope"* (1 Thess 4:13). Surely the Christian has a different perspective from which to grieve. We might even call it "good grief." And if we have been given a new way of looking at death, we have also been given a way of getting through it when a loved one dies.

The question on our minds should not be "what is at the end of the valley?" but "who is at the end of the valley?"

And so the psalmist assures us, *"Even though I walk through the darkest valley, I fear no evil; for you are with me"* (Ps 23:4).

Surely one of the messages of Jesus' visit to the grave of Lazarus is a reminder that we do not go there alone. I do not remember who gave me the idea, but I often use this story as the outline for committal services. I have always been struck with the fact that no more than a few moments are spent there, sometimes after long services and longer drives to the cemetery. It always feels so routine and too brief to me. Even including a time for silent prayers of gratitude offered to God for the person being buried does not keep it from being much too short.

In a sense this was the first graveside service. It begins where most of us end up when faced with the death of a loved one, with Mary saying to Jesus, "Lord, if you had been here, my brother would not have died." "If only" is as much a part of grief as are our tears. How many regrets and how much guilt are associated with it! We are encouraged to acknowledge that.

That is why I begin the committal service with Martha's words to Mary, *"The Teacher is here..."* (Jn 11:28). It is so important that a gathering of mourners be reminded of the presence of Jesus Christ, and that God's "goodness and mercy" have followed them all the way to the grave.

Then John tells us Jesus "was greatly disturbed in spirit and deeply moved." Later, he began to weep. The Jews standing by said, "See how he loved him!" It is important for us to remember—especially when standing by the grave—that not only is Jesus present, he stands by us and shares in our suffering.

There is not only God's presence that gives us comfort, but also God's power—the same power with which he raised Lazarus from the grave. We are to recall three things Jesus said: "Your brother [sister] will rise again," "Lazarus, come out!" and "Unbind him, and let him go." The grave is not a dead end, nor a permanent "resting place." We are called to be with God in heaven. Death is the way God provides for us to be set free from the struggles and illnesses of this earthly life. I once heard someone say God whispers to us at our death, "You do not need to carry your burdens any longer. You can leave them with me." We are, in fact, "unbound," set free!

Do not overlook the word "through" the valley in the psalmist's great hymn of trust. We go through it and come out the other side. We can also get through our experience of grief when we have to go there with a loved one. That is because God is there "to see us through." God did it, through Jesus, for Mary, Martha, and Lazarus.

God will do it for you and me.
—*William M. Schwein*
Carmel Un. Methodist Church
Indianapolis, Indiana

November 9, 1997

25th Sunday after Pentecost (Proper 27)
Pres: 32nd Sunday in Ordinary Time
RC: Dedication of the Latern Basilica in Rome—
Not listed

Lessons
Pres/Meth/UCC	Ruth 3:1–5 —4:13–17	Heb 9:24–28	Mk 12:38–44
Episcopal	1 Kings 17:8–16	Heb 9:24–28	Mk 12:38–44
Lutheran	1 Kings 17:8–16	Heb 9:24–28	Mk 12:38–44

Introduction to the Lessons
Lesson 1
(1) *Ruth 3:1–5—4:13–17* **(Pres/Meth/UCC)**
In a desire to help Ruth find a spouse, Naomi instructs her daughter-in-law to win the favor of Boaz, who was related to Naomi's deceased husband. This appears to be an extension of the Levirate laws in which next-of-kin were to marry widows. As a result, a son is born to Ruth and Boaz who will be the grandfather of David.

(2) *1 Kings 17:8–16* **(Epis/Luth)**
As the story of Elijah begins during the reign of Ahab, the prophet meets a widow who participates in the miraculous provision of food and drink as evidences of the power of God. Through the prophet's words, and the widow's trust and generosity, God's word is fulfilled.

Lesson 2
Hebrews 9:24–28 **(Pres/Meth/UCC/Epis/Luth)**
The Christian covenant was superior to the old covenant of the Hebrews and, as such, required a greater sacrifice. It was through the sacrifice of Christ himself that the requirements of the new covenant are fulfilled. Because the sacrifice was "once for all," there is no longer a need for the repeated sacrifices of the cultic community.

Gospel
Mark 12:38–44 **(Pres/Meth/UCC/Epis/Luth)**
As the public ministry of Jesus concludes, he issues warnings about public shows of piety and a lack of humility. In contrast to a need to be the center of attention, a humble, generous widow is presented as the model of genuine faith.

Theme
The "once for all" sacrifice of Jesus Christ is sufficient for our salvation.

Thought for the Day
There are some religious acts that we do not have to do over and over again for God because of what Jesus has already done for us.

Prayer of Meditation
We are often more aware, God, of what we do in this place of worshp than we are of what you can do here. We become so caught up in all the things going on around us that we forget what you want to do within us. We become so concerned with who is seated next to us, how the choir sounds, whether we know and like the hymns, how inspiring the sermon is, whether or not we put enough in the offering plate, that we foget you are in our midst to save us. Do not let us be as worried about whether others speak to us, as we are that we speak to you and listen openly as you speak to us. May your word to us this day be one of challenge, forgiveness, and new life. Amen.

Call to Worship
> Leader: Praise the Lord!
> Praise the Lord, O my soul!
> People: I will praise the Lord as long as I live;
> I will sing praises to my God all my life long.
> Leader: Do not put your trust in princes, in mortals, in whom there is no help.
> When their breath departs, they return to the earth; on that very day their plans perish.
> People: Happy are those whose help is the God of Jacob, whose hope is in the Lord their God.
> —Psalm 146:1–5

November 9, 1997
25th Sunday after Pentecost (Proper 27)
Pres: 32nd Sunday in Ordinary Time

Prayer of Adoration

We thank you, Lord, that what we cannot do for ourselves, you do for us. We cannot save ourselves, but you save us. We cannot heal ourselves, but you heal us. We cannot change ourselves, but you change us. We cannot become the best that we can be, but you are constantly at work in us to accomplish that. Accept us as we are, but do not let us stay the same as when we came. Help us accept all that you would do for us so that we may, in turn, be willing to do more for you as your people. Amen.

Prayer of Confession

We are creatures of habit. We keep doing the same thing over and over, committing the same sins, nursing the same grudges, carrying the same guilt. We wonder why we do not seem to feel our sins are forgiven, no matter how many times assurances of pardon are spoken in these hours of worship. Is it because we forget that entering a place of worship really means coming into your presence? Is is because we seek fellowship with others more than a relationship with you? Is it because our busyness in the church does not always bring us closer to you? May we be reminded again that our salvation comes through our faith, not our good works, and that the sacrificial death of your Son Jesus Christ has taken away our need to earn your forgiveness and love. May the words we have heard so many times finally have the power to work in us your miracles of healing and grace. Amen.

Prayer of Dedication of Gifts and Self

God, may the sacrifice of your son, Jesus Christ, be the standard by which our gifts are measured. If we have withheld anything from you, may we be reshaped by the spirit of him who gave his all to you and for us. May we never be content until we have offered you all that we have and all that we are. Amen.

Sermon Summary

There is no need for us to keep repeating so many of the things that make up our religion, for Jesus Christ has taken away not only our sins, but also much of what we believe God requires.

Hymn of the Day

"We Give Thee but Thine Own." The gospel lesson today speaks of the widow's mite—her willingness to contribute all that she had. Written by

William How around 1858, this hymn is an appropriate accompaniment to the question of stewardship raised by the gospel text. As the fourth stanza expresses so clearly, we do the work of God because we have been given God's gifts. To free the captive, find the lost, teach of life and peace: these things are most worthy of our best efforts and finest treasures.

Children's Object Talk

Christ Died for Our Sins

Object
A basket full of apples, a backpack or gym bag.
Lesson
We are forgiven because Christ took our punishment as he died on the cross.

(Place the basket of apples on your left side, the empty bag on your right.)

Today I want to tell you a story about a little boy who liked apples so much that he forgot about the commandment God gave us: do not steal. That means do not take things that belong to someone else.

Every day Zach walked to school by a big lot where apple trees grew. One day Zach noticed that an apple had rolled onto the road. He picked it up and rubbed it on his sleeve. Umm! It looked good. He decided to taste it. Before he knew it, the apple was just an apple core.

The next day Zach looked for another apple on the road, but he didn't find one. So on the way home he just climbed over the fence and pulled one off the tree. Then he remembered that his mother said he should wash apples before he ate them, so he put it in his bag. (Move apples, one at a time, to the bag.) The next day Zach climbed the fence again. He put another apple in his bag, and the following day he did it again. For two weeks Zach put an apple in his bag every day. Then one night while his family was eating dinner, the doorbell rang. It was the man who owned the apple trees.

"This boy has been taking my apples," he said, pointing to Zach. "I mean to punish him for it. He must come and help me pack the apples to sell, but with *no pay*."

Zach's big brother stepped forward. "I will do it for Zach," his brother said. Today we read in the Bible that Jesus did that for us. Jesus said *he* would be

November 9, 1997
25th Sunday after Pentecost (Proper 27)
Pres: 32nd Sunday in Ordinary Time

punished for all the times *we* do not do what God asks us to do. Zach's brother was not the one who stole the apples, but he took Zach's punishment. We tell Jesus we are sorry, and we try to love God and each other. Then God forgives us because of Jesus.

—*Lois Brokering*

The Sermon

Once and for All

Hymns
Beginning of Worship: "Blessed Assurance"
Sermon Hymn: "Alas! and Did My Savior Bleed"
End of Worship: "Come, Thou Fount of Every Blessing"

Scripture
Hebrews 9:24–28 (For additional sermon materials on this passage, see the *1997 May/June Planning Issue* of *The Clergy Journal* and on Mark 12:38–44, see the August 1997 issue of *The Clergy Journal*.)

Sermon Text
"*. . . But as it is, he has appeared once for all at the end of the age to remove sin by the sacrifice of himself*" (vs. 26).

During their retirement, my father and stepmother lived next door to a young boy who would frequently bring them food and desserts that his mother had made. One day, Todd brought some cheesecake, and after the usual "Tell your mother how good this is and how much we appreciate her thoughtfulness," he replied, "You know, my mom can give you her recipe for it, and then I won't have to keep bringing it over all the time!"

When my father shared that little incident with me, it started me thinking. On the one hand, it is easier for us to have someone bring us the finished product; but on the other hand, it is probably easier for them if we had the recipe and made it ourselves. All too often, we depend upon God and God's church for easy answers, instant solutions, and finished products. We would rather have someone else do the work for us so we do not have to do the difficult work ourselves. It is much harder to have someone say, "here's my recipe; you go put it together yourself."

There are times when God tells us to answer our own prayers, to seek solutions to our problems, or to use the brains God has given us. But there are some instances when God says to us, "I have taken care of it. You can quit working so hard." It sounds as if the writer of Hebrews tells us that our salvation from sin is one of those gifts. As he said, *". . . Christ, having been offered once to bear the sins of many, will appear a second time, not to deal with sin, but to save those who are eagerly waiting for him"* (vs. 28). Though this is generally thought to be a reference to the "second coming" of Christ at some future time, there is a sense in which it can refer to that time in our lives when we simply accept through faith what Christ has done for us.

That may mean we can give up trying to earn God's forgiveness and salvation by our good works and accept it as a "given" through faith. Following the theme of Hebrews that Christ is "better" in every respect than the old ways of achieving reconciliation with God and salvation from our sins, it becomes obvious to us that there may be a better way than any we have known and practiced before.

Isn't it a recurring dream of ours to find "a better way" of doing things? Especially those activities that are repeated? Think of all those repetitious activities that consume our lives: cleaning, doing the dishes, shaving, driving to work, preparing meals. Even preparing sermons and confessing our sins! Would it not be better if we could find a better way of doing them, maybe even getting to the point when we did not have to keep doing them over and over again?

That is exactly what is promised for our sinfulness, because Christ's sacrifice was better than those practiced by the priests in the old cultic ritual whose repetition was evidence of the inherent failure of our attempts to "do it ourselves." Earlier, the writer of Hebrews had affirmed that *". . . without the shedding of blood there is no forgiveness of sins"* (vs. 22b). That tradition held that God required blood to satisfy the need for justice and gave rise to all sorts of theories of "atonement." Human redemption had a costly price tag attached to it. Human sinfulness and alienation are never overcome with anything less than sacrificial love. Love that pays the ultimate price of the shedding of one's own blood.

Why was the sacrifice of Jesus Christ better than those of the earthly priests? This letter (really more like a sermon) was written at a time when the priesthood was held in highest regard. Thousands and thousands of Jewish priests were designated to preside over cultic functions. Their role was basically to provide access to God. The priest was like an advocate who stood before God. The priest was a go-between, an intermediary who mediated between people and God through liturgy and sacrifice.

November 9, 1997
25th Sunday after Pentecost (Proper 27)
Pres: 32nd Sunday in Ordinary Time

In a sense, the writer of Hebrews said they were dispensable, passé. Christ had become the High Priest *par excellence*, the final dispensation of salvation. Jesus did not just enter a human-made sanctuary; he entered into the actual presence of God. Jesus did not come into the presence of God for his own glory; he did it in order to intercede for us. Jesus did not stand before God holding an animal to be sacrificed; he sacrificed himself.

We are not, for the most part, comfortable talking about the sacrifice of Christ in terms of "blood." We are not so clear about how the suffering of Christ could be divine punishment for the sin of the world either through the "ransom" or "satisfaction" theories of atonement. Most of us think of Christ's redemptive work in terms of his love and example.

When my father, a minister, used to try to explain the suffering love of Christ, he would tell the story of an incorrigible boy. In spite of all sorts of punishment—the denial of things he liked, confinement, and every other means of discipline nothing was effective. But then, on a hot summer afternoon, the boy was trying to teach his little dog a trick. When the dog did not respond as the boy wanted, the boy kicked the dog in the mouth until it bled. The dog tried again and again to do the trick. Finally, he tried to lick the little boy's hand with his blood-stained tongue. The boy broke down and cried. He ran to his mother, and she asked, "What's the matter?" He sobbed, "I have done an awful thing." Nothing else had ever made him cry, but suffering love did, and that was because of the love of a little dog!

Think how much greater was the suffering love of God that demands nothing from us except for us to surrender to it.

A friend of mine told me about attending a funeral mass for a man who was Roman Catholic. The man's wife was Protestant. When it came time for the sacrament, the priest told the assembled mourners, "Now, I know that many of you here are not Catholic. We would not ordinarily invite you to participate in this sacrament, but because this is a gathering to celebrate the life of our good friend whose wife is not Catholic, I want you all to come forward and receive the bread and wine. I want all of you to feel a part of the celebration. I will take upon myself whatever sin that might result."

Jesus Christ took all our sins upon himself. That was the only sacrifice that was needed to be made. When our High Priest identified with us and suffered for us, our salvation was assured. For he did not come just to deal with our sins but to do something better—to give us salvation.

—*William M. Schwein*
Carmel Un. Methodist Church
Indianapolis, Indiana

November 16, 1997

26th Sunday after Pentecost (Proper 28)
RC/Pres: 33rd Sunday in Ordinary Time

Lessons

Pres/Meth/UCC	1 Sam 1:4–20	Heb 10:11–14 (15–18), 19–25	Mk 13:1–8
Roman Catholic	Dan 12:1–3	Heb 10:11–14, 18	Mk 13:24–32
Episcopal	Dan 12:1–4a (5–13)	Heb 10:31–39	Mk 13:14–23
Lutheran	Dan 12:1–3	Heb 10:11–14 (15–18), 19–25	Mk 13:1–8

Introduction to the Lessons
Lesson 1
(1) *1 Samuel 1:4–20* (**Pres/Meth/UCC**)
Barren women who bear offspring in their old age are mentioned several times throughout the Bible. Hannah promised God that if she were to bear a son, she would dedicate him to the Lord. The priest, Eli, reassured her and her prayers were answered with the birth of Samuel.

(2) *Daniel 12:1–3* (**RC/Luth**); *Daniel 12:1–4a (5–13)* (**Epis**)
Daniel speaks of the great tribulations that would be a prelude to the end of the age at which time Michael, the Jews' patron angel, would protect and deliver them. This passage contains the first obvious reference to resurrection in Scripture.

Lesson 2
(1) *Hebrews 10:11–14 (15–18), 19–25* (**Pres/Meth/UCC/Luth**);
Hebrews 10:11–14, 18 (**RC**)
The writer continues to draw the contrast between the priestly work of the Christ and other human priests. It is through faith in the sacrifice of Christ that sins are taken away and believers are sanctified—making unnecessary the ritual sacrifices of the old covenant. In response, those living under this new covenant are encouraged to live the Christian life.

November 16, 1997
26th Sunday after Pentecost (Proper 28)
RC/Pres: 33rd Sunday in Ordinary Time

(2) *Hebrews 10:31–39* **(Epis)**
This is a call to confidence, endurance, and patience, for those who seek to live in faith until the day of Christ's second coming.

Gospel
(1) *Mark 13:1–8* **(Pres/Meth/UCC/Luth)**
Jesus predicts the destruction of Jerusalem as an event that will take place before the end time. In speaking of God's future, Jesus also warns the disciples not to be concerned with misleading pronouncements of the end or with an exact timetable.

(2) *Mark 13:24–32* **(RC)**
Jesus teaches about the end of the age. He speaks of his second coming and the eternal nature of his words.

(3) *Mark 13:14–23* **(Epis)**
In the second of three of Jesus' discourses on the end of time, he warns against false prophets and advises the disciples to remember his words.

Theme
When something ends, something else begins.

Thought for the Day
Is this Lord's Day the end of your week or the beginning of your week? Where we feel we are in our lives depends upon our perspective. Are you "winding down" or "gearing up"?

Prayer of Meditation
Lord, our lives feel like an endless round of reruns. We know too much of routine and rut. We have seen it all before. We have heard it all before. In so many experiences, we shrug our shoulders and say, "This is where I came in." It's always the same thing all over again. Is there a way out of all this, Lord? Can we have a fresh start? Speak to us of clean slates and second chances. Help us to let the past be past so that the future may come alive, and we may truly begin to live. Amen.

Call to Worship

> Leader: All your works shall give thanks to you, O Lord,
> People: And all your faithful shall bless you.
> Leader: They shall speak of the glory of your kingdom,
> People: And tell of your power,
> Leader: To make known to all people your mighty deeds,
> People: And the glorious splendor of your kingdom.
> Leader: Your kingdom is an everlasting kingdom,
> People: And your dominion endures throughout all generations.
> Leader: The Lord is faithful in all his words,
> People: And gracious in all his deeds.
> —Psalm 145:8–13

Prayer of Adoration

God who makes all things new, make us new persons. May your power evidenced in creation be as powerful in recreating us. May your power we see in the changing of the seasons change us. May your power we witness in the gift of each new day make this a new day for us. May your power we celebrate in the raising of Jesus Christ from the grave raise us to new life. May the power we see in everything you do be seen in the way we believe we are just beginning the best of our lives this day. Amen.

Prayer of Confession

We give up too easily, don't we, God? We put down periods where you put down a comma. We close the book before the last chapter has even been written. We think the curtain has come down to end the play, but it is only intermission. We worry about doors that are closing, rather than walk through those that are opening. We see "exit" signs over passageways where you have put "entrance." Forgive us for doubting that you can bring something new out of the old. Let there be no person, no experience, no situation, no problem on which we give up until you have finished working your renewing power. Amen.

Prayer of Dedication of Gifts and Self

When we look around us and see so many desperate situations, it is easy for us, God, to throw up our hands in hopeless resignation. Move us this day to join our hands, to offer the works of our hands, and to provide opportunities for your purposes to be fulfilled and your children to be given more hopeful lives. Amen.

November 16, 1997
26th Sunday after Pentecost (Proper 28)
RC/Pres: 33rd Sunday in Ordinary Time

Sermon Summary
God is in the business of recycling, making something new from something old. God can turn anything we are tempted to call "trash" into a "treasure."

Hymn of the Day
"Joys Are Flowing Like a River (Blessed Quietness)." This hymn was written by Manie Payne Ferguson in the mid-nineteenth century. Married to a Weslyan evangelist, she moved from her native Ireland to help found Methodist missions on the west coast of England. The wonderful words of this hymn evoke the same sense of gratitude that Hannah expresses in her song from 1 Samuel 2 recalling the saving and comforting power of God. Available in several versions and a favorite of quartets and choirs, the refrain is particularly nice for four-part harmony.

Children's Object Talk

Follow the Leader

Object
A picture of a duck, preferably with ducklings in a row.
Lesson
It's important to choose the right leader. Christ asks us to have him as our leader and follow him.

(Show the picture of the duck so all the children can see it.) Did you know that when a baby duck comes out of its eggshell it thinks the first animal it sees is its mother?

Once there was a boy named Jason who hatched a duck egg for a school project. He and his dad built an incubator to keep the egg warm. Since the mother duck who laid the egg didn't live with Jason, he had to try to care for the egg like a mother duck. That meant that Jason had to keep the egg warm until the little duck inside grew big enough to live outside the shell. One day while Jason was watching his egg, the shell began to crack. Little by little the crack got bigger, and finally the baby duck stepped outside, all fuzzy and damp. It looked at Jason. "Quack," it said— that meant, "Hi, Mom!"

The duck thought Jason was its mother. All spring and summer Ducky followed Jason around the yard. But Jason couldn't teach Ducky how to catch bugs or how to swim. When fall came, and it was time for school again, Jason left the gate open one day. His duck was quite grown up now. She followed him happily out the gate, up the hill, and down again.

Suddenly Ducky saw something she had never seen before—a lake! Ducky began to run. She ran down the hill and right into the water. There were other ducks swimming there. Ducky was so happy. She quacked good-bye to Jason, and Jason waved good-bye to her. Ducky would make friends with the other ducks. She would fly south with them when they left for the winter; now she would have a new leader to follow.

Jesus told his disciples that many people would ask them to follow. But the disciples knew they should just follow Jesus. Following Jesus means *doing what he teaches*. Other leaders may ask us to do what is not right. Let's follow Jesus. Jesus is *our* leader.

—*Lois Brokering*

The Sermon

The Beginning Is Near

Hymns
Beginning of Worship: "This Is a Day of New Beginnings"
Sermon Hymn: "God Moves in a Mysterious Way"
End of Worship: "Hymn of Promise"

Scripture
Mark 13:1–8 (For additional sermon materials on this passage, see the August 1997 and the *1997 May/June Planning Issue* of *The Clergy Journal.*)

Sermon Text
"... 'This is but the beginning of the birthpangs'" (vs. 8).

An inn sits on the border between England and Scotland. As you approach it from the south the sign reads, "This is the last hotel in England." In a few yards, there is a sign that says, "This is the first hotel in Scotland." It makes a difference how you look at things.

A member of the World Future Society is quoted as saying that as we approach January 1, 2000, we will see a "heightened interest in the future ... the end of every decade gives a mini-

November 16, 1997
26th Sunday after Pentecost (Proper 28)
RC/Pres: 33rd Sunday in Ordinary Time

version of it. People see something ending and something about to begin, the same as we do on birthdays, anniversaries, etc." Futurists predict a renewal of excitement, optimism, energy, creativity, and the confidence that we can find solutions to our common problems as this century comes to a close.

Do you have the same optimistic attitude about your own future? Is this the first day of the rest of your life, or the last day of the first of your life? Are you playing "taps" or "reveille"? Is this time of your life marked by "recessionals" or "processionals"?

We often tell graduates that their "commencement" is not the end of school, but actually the beginning of a new chapter. *Commencing* means "to have a beginning, to initiate, to enter upon, to start."

We have all seen cartoons picturing those "prophets of doom" carrying posters that warn, "The end is near!" In your life, is this the beginning of the end, or the end of the beginning?

It would be easy to assume that Jesus was only speaking of the end being near. The temple in Jerusalem would be destroyed. There would be wars and rumors of wars. Nation would rise against nation, kingdom against kingdom. There would be earthquakes and famines. Would those signal the beginning of the end or a new beginning? What did Jesus mean by speaking of "the beginning of the birthpangs"? Birthpangs are the recurring pains accompanying childbirth. They also refer to experiences of disorder and distress, social upheaval. Paul chose the same image in Romans: *"We know that the whole creation has been groaning in labor pains until now"* (Rom 8:22). Jesus' words called for hopefulness. Why else would he choose the image of childbirth and not death? Perhaps he saw something beyond the appearance of the end since he had warned against misreading the signs. He saw the promise of a new heaven, a new earth, his own second coming, and the time when God would vindicate the faithful and achieve final victory.

Change, especially when it results in something being born, is painful. Change is often disruptive. Something is often uprooted before something new can be planted. Something must be plucked up before something new is planted according to Ecclesiastes. Some things are broken down before others can be built up. Have you watched the destruction of some buildings that are blown up to make room for new construction? Change, when it results in something being born, is worth it. Rather than focus on the pain, what if we focused on what follows? Not the end, but the beginning?

What if in closing one chapter of our lives, we knew we were beginning a new one? What a difference it would make in our lives if we could see in every "end" of things the possibility for a new "beginning." Not just to focus on an experience as a time when something is dying, but when something is being born. God helps us to begin again.

Illustrations abound. There was an item in our daily paper about a young student who received a $20,000 scholarship. Nothing unusual about that, except that this boy had been misdiagnosed and sent to special education classes his first four years of school. A fall when he was six months old had impaired his ability to speak. From then on, he was labeled as one "who would never make it." But he became editor-in-chief of his student newspaper, president of the science club, vice-president of the computer club, and a tutor for other students. The superintendent of schools said of him: "Someone told him he couldn't succeed. But he kept saying, 'I'm bright. I'm talented.' In May he will graduate second in his class."

We mistakenly label people and write them off. We give up on them too early. A young boy was estimated at having an IQ of eighty-one. He was considered too backward for formal schooling. He was losing his hearing. His emotional health was poor. He burned down his father's barn. He used very poor grammar. Was it all over for him? No! That was Thomas A. Edison.

A young girl showed little promise. She was sickly, bedridden, considered erratic and withdrawn. She wore a backbrace from a spinal defect. She was a daydreamer with no goals in life. Was it all over for her? No! That was Eleanor Roosevelt.

Charlie Chaplain couldn't get a job in Hollywood because his odd style of pantomime was considered "nonsense." Albert Einstein flunked out of a Swiss school and was considered "non-intelligent." Charles Schulz had every cartoon rejected by his high school yearbook staff.

Perhaps nothing illustrates this better than how many people approach old age with a renewed sense of value. Immanual Kant wrote his best philosophical works at age seventy-four. Michelangelo completed his finest work at eighty-seven. Moses began the exodus at age eighty.

An old Italian proverb says it best, "When God shuts a door, he opens a window." Even the worst things that happen to people have in them the possibility for good. Every problem bears the seeds of some benefit, some possibility, something that can be born in or through us.

—*William M. Schwein*
Carmel Un. Methodist Church
Indianapolis, Indiana

November 23, 1997

Christ the King/Reign of Christ

Lessons

Pres/Meth/UCC	2 Sam 23:1–7	Rev 1:4b–8	Jn 18:33–37
Roman Catholic	Dan 7:13–14	Rev 1:5–8	Jn 18:33b–37
Episcopal	Dan 7:9–14	Rev 1:1–8	Jn 18:33–37
Lutheran	Dan 7:9–10, 13–14	Rev 1:4b–8	Jn 18:33–37

Introduction to the Lessons

Lesson 1
(1) *2 Samuel 23:1–7* **(Pres/Meth/UCC)**
Set within the midst of the narrative recounting David's reign, these verses follow the royal psalm in chapter twenty-two (which repeats Psalm 18) with a prophetic statement about the character of David's reign. Called into a covenant by God, David affirms his office and warns his adversaries. Identified as his dying words, these verses offer not a blessing but a theological ideology which his successors and foes must face.

(2) *Daniel 7:13–14* **(RC)**; *Daniel 7:9–14* **(Epis)**;
Daniel 7:9–10, 13–14 **(Luth)**
The apocalyptic vision of judgment in verses 9–10 sees God as the ancient one whose age and authority surpass any of the nations to be judged. This "Ancient of Days" who sits enthroned in glory with countless thousands of attendants does not have human characteristics except those associated with age. Older, and thus more to be respected than others, the ancient one is nevertheless unstained and pure. To this ancient one is presented in a second vision (vss. 13–14), one like a human being who will reign forever after the judgment. These verses date from the second century B.C. and offer a messianic hope which Christians see realized in Jesus.

Lesson 2
Revelation 1:4b–8 **(Pres/Meth/UCC/Luth)**;
Revelation 1:5–8 **(RC)**; *Revelation 1:1–8* **(Epis)**
This overture to the book extends greetings to the specific churches addressed, gives thanks for the person and work of Jesus Christ,

affirms the mission of the church as Christ has provided it, and anticipates his universally recognizable return. God is the timeless one in whom the past, the present, and the future are a unity and by whom the beginning and the end are defined.

Gospel
John 18:33–37 **(Pres/Meth/UCC/Epis/Luth)**;
John 18:33b–37 **(RC)**

The dialogue between Pilate and Jesus becomes a faithful witness to the nature of authority. With each interchange in the conversation, Pilate's governance diminishes. Instead of being the one who judges Jesus, Pilate is judged and his authority is reduced to a fragment of what Jesus holds. By the end of the conversation, Pilate seems no longer to be sure that he can even discern what is the truth.

Theme
Any authority we have, even the authority of faith, is the gift of the Lord of all ages.

Thought for the Day
"The New Testament proclaims that at some unforeseeable time in the future God will ring down the final curtain on history, and there will come a Day on which all our days and all the judgments upon us and all our judgments upon each other will themselves be judged. The judge will be Christ. In other words, the one who judges us most finally will be the one who loves us most fully."

—Frederick Buechner

Prayer of Meditation
O God, from whom every moment of our lives comes as a gift and whose power precedes the first of our moments and surpasses the last of them: grant that we might honor each opportunity to praise you, claim every occasion to proclaim your word, and seize every setting to serve you; in the name of the one who came as servant of all and Savior of all, Jesus Christ our Lord. Amen.

Call to Worship
> Leader: Grace to you, and peace, from the one who is and who was and who is to come.

November 23, 1997
Christ the King/Reign of Christ

People: Thanks be to God!
Leader: And from Jesus Christ the firstborn of the dead, the Lord of all creation.
People: Praise the Lord!
Leader: He is coming as our redeemer and our judge.
People: Amen. Come, Lord Jesus.

Prayer of Adoration

O God, whose glory gives birth to the light that fills all creation and whose power is the author of the promises that fill us with hope, we praise you with our word, our music, our silence, and our service. Draw near to us in this hour and let us all be drawn to you. Let the children sense that they can trust you. Let the youth trust that they can talk with you. Let the mature among us take their secrets to you and let all receive the blessings of your grace, through Jesus Christ our Lord. Amen.

Prayer of Confession

O Lord, we do not find it easy to come in confession. We do not respond well to the guilt that others place upon us. And we do not feel as if our ways of living have been so terribly wrong. We know we are not perfect. But if we judge ourselves by the standards of others' behavior, we are not your most wicked creatures. So let us confess first that we are reluctant confessors. We have done some things that we would undo if we could. We would like to forget them. We would prefer not to be judged for them. So let us confess also that we are prisoners of our pride. We see ourselves as doing the best we can. Forgive us for trying to design the faith according to our own desires. Forgive the pride that holds us hostage. By your grace, come and judge our faults, and then we shall truly be free. Amen.

Prayer of Dedication of Gifts and Self

To you, Lord, we offer our gifts. Remind us that these are not the contributions that sustain your church, for it endures only because you sustain it. Remind us that these are not the means to bless your church, for it is blessed only by the spiritual gifts you provide. Remind us, Lord, that these are the signs by which we offer ourselves to you in thanksgiving for all of the ways that we have been graced by your blessings. Now, O Lord, guide the church in the use of these gifts. Grant that they might be used to honor your will, to serve your people, and to bear witness in all creation that Jesus Christ is Lord. Amen.

Sermon Summary
One of the problems facing us when we read the book of Revelation is that it seems to be overwhelmingly mysterious. It is indeed a mystery, but that mystery is the person of Jesus Christ who is our Lord and king. The mystery is strange because it is so unlike what we find in the world. That is why it is so filled with hope.

Hymn of the Day
"Now Thank We All Our God." A favorite hymn of thanksgiving, *"Nun danket alle Gott"* was written by German Lutheran pastor Martin Rinkart in 1647. A musician by training, he served the church in Eisleben during the devastating years of the Thirty Years' War. Appropriate for those celebrating Reign of Christ Sunday, the words and tune evoke the very best tradition of Christ bearing the gifts of God to the people. If you have access to a hymnal with the German words, a solo or spoken reading of them is a powerful reminder of God's care for all the world, no matter where we come from.

Children's Object Talk

Everyone a Priest

Object
Your minister's pulpit manual, the organist's enlarged hymnal, and a pew version of the hymnal.

Lesson
We can all come to God through Jesus—we are all priests.

(Show your manual.) This is a book that belongs to me. It belongs to me because I am the minister (pastor, priest) of this congregation. I need it to know what I am supposed to say when I stand over there by the altar and up there at the lectern to lead our worship. (Show the organist's hymnal.) And this book belongs to _____, our organist (pianist). _____ has this book because he/she is the leader of the singing. (Show the congregational hymnal.) Now, can you tell me what we call this book? (Wait for answers. Repeat, "hymnal" or "hymnbook.") It is a book of songs we sing to praise God. Where do we find this book? Can you have one at home? Yes, you can sing the hymns and pray the prayers in this book at home too. Anyone can buy a hymnal to use at home.

In our gospel lesson today we read that Jesus made all of us priests. *Priest* is another word for *minister*. When Jesus lived on earth, priests gave animals to God *for* the people. It was their offering. Today, we don't give animals. We give money to do God's work. And *you* put it in the offering basket. I don't have to do it for you, do I? Priests talked to God *for* the people. Jesus said you can pray to God anytime you want to. You don't have to wait for _____ to play the organ for you to sing praises to God.

Jesus tells us that all of us are priests. Each of us can come to God all by ourselves. When we come to church, we do come to God together. Then _____ and I help by being the worship *leaders*. But always remember, *you* can talk to God anytime *you* want to, all by *yourself.*

—Lois Brokering

The Sermon

Our Mysterious Lord and King

Hymns
Beginning of Worship: "All Praise to Thee, for Thou O King Divine"
Sermon Hymn: "At the Name of Jesus"
End of Worship: "Lift High the Cross"

Scripture
Revelation 1:4b–8 (For additional sermon materials on this passage, see the *1997 May/June Planning Issue* and on John 18:33–37, see the August 1997 issue of *The Clergy Journal*.)

Sermon Text
"Blessed is the one who reads aloud the words of the prophecy, and blessed are those who hear and who keep what is written in it . . . Grace to you and peace . . ." (vss. 3–4).

The Christian life would be a whole lot simpler if the New Testament did not include the book of Revelation.

For one thing, it is hard to get the title right. Good, church-going folks still can be heard referring to it as the "book of revelations," as if it were a list of things that have been revealed to us secretly. But since the Bible is still the most widely sold publication in the world, the contents of its last book are hardly a big secret. Now if someone were to publish the actual recipe for *Coca-Cola*, that would be a revelation. Or if someone were to teach the average grandparents how to play the video game that their grandchildren will be able to master by the day after Christmas, that would be a revelation. Those truly are secrets. But the last book of the New Testament is not a private recipe, and it is not a collection of information whose revelations are accessible to a certain generation.

It is not a secret. But it is a mystery. Unraveling the mystery has befuddled biblical scholars for two thousand years, some of whom have traveled down strange paths in an effort to resolve the mystery. The book of Revelation has been interpreted as a code for use by a first-century force of religious revolutionaries. It has been explained as a schematic diagram for all of human history, with a precise timetable to tell when events in the structure of our salvation will occur. It has been used as a census of the population of heaven to demonstrate that only 144,000 will get inside the pearly gates. In fact, it has even been the source of countless jokes that typically begin with a line about some soul arriving at those pearly gates. The book of Revelation has been used as the consummate Christian text, a culmination of the New Testament witness. And it has been interpreted as a pirated and modified version of a manuscript that was crafted by a group who continued to believe that John the Baptist, not Jesus, was the Messiah.

The book of Revelation is not a secret, but it is a mystery.

Part of the mystery lies in the fact that the book of Revelation is not user-friendly. Anyone who decides to read the whole Bible and starts reading the last book of the New Testament without having a thorough appreciation of the Old Testament will find it a rough ride. Even a slow reader would probably complete the entire twenty-two chapters in less time than it takes to watch a typical Hollywood feature film, and in far less time than it takes to watch a pro football game on a Sunday afternoon. However, absorbing those chapters would require a certain amount of digging elsewhere in the Bible, as well as more patience than most of us can muster. So the mystery seems inaccessible.

Besides, the book of Revelation is not laid out in a nice, neat narrative. It is filled with pictures—not pictures like those in the oversize books that decorate our coffee tables, but pictures described by words and then painted in our imaginations. One cannot read the book of Revelation at a fast pace, because one has to spend time examining the panorama developing in our

November 23, 1997
Christ the King/Reign of Christ

minds. Here are four living creatures, each with six wings. There is a pregnant woman in labor and a red dragon with seven heads poised to devour the child at its moment of birth. It takes energy to read this stuff. After a chapter or two, one has to take a break or fall exhausted.

Today we have to contend with only a few verses, and those are at the very beginning of the book. In these few verses we find a greeting followed by some words about God and Jesus. How mysterious can it be? Plenty!

Here we encounter something that is at the core of the Christian faith. It is certainly possible for churchgoers and Bible study attendees to come away from their experiences with the impression that the Scriptures simply share with us some stories: about the comings and goings of Jesus in his earthly ministry; about the acts of the apostles in the book of that name; about the letters of Paul and others concerning activities in the early church.

But the core of the Christian faith is a conviction that these stories, these letters, these comings and goings only matter because they bear witness to one person who stands at the center of human history. The problem with the book of Revelation is that it bears witness to Jesus Christ as the one whose word arches over everything. So to unfold the mystery of the book of Revelation, all we have to do is confront the mystery of Jesus Christ. All we have to do is recognize his resurrection. All we have to do is accept the premise that there is no authority on earth that lies beyond the scope of his authority. All we have to do is stake our claim to the role he has given us and find our destiny in serving God.

That's all. In just these few verses, we can find our place in this world and in eternity. In just these few verses, we can face death because we come face to face with the one who conquered death. In just these few verses, we can feel the pointlessness of our own pride, since the sovereign of the universe has show us that we are not in charge—he is.

Before that thought terrifies us or exhausts us, let's look again at the way these verses begin. The fourth verse of the first chapter of the book of Revelation greets us this way: *"Grace to you and peace."* The one who reigns over us and over all things, Christ the King, greets us with greater love than we deserve and with greater peace than our prideful efforts could ever make possible.

And he greets all of us that way. The writers of the New Testament fashioned that form of greeting in the name and spirit of Christ. *Grace* is based on a Greek word that means "loving gift."

Peace is based on a Hebrew word *shalom*, which means "a wholeness of community and contentment." In the era of the New Testament writers, there were only two cultures that mattered, the Greek and the Hebrew. So the expression *"grace to you and peace"* intentionally incorporated everybody in the mystery of Christ Jesus who comes to us with a loving gift by which we are united with one another and with him.

His is not a troubling or terrifying mystery. In fact, it is an offer which, if accepted, would bring an end to hatred and bitterness, war and racism, and all those other evils that bewilder the human heart and bedevil the human community. That is why Christ's gift is such a mystery. It is so unlike what we face every day in this world. And it is ours from the sovereign Lord of all creation if we will dare to accept its mysterious joy.

—*William B. Lawrence*
Duke Divinity School
Durham, North Carolina

November 27, 1997

Thanksgiving Day

Lessons

Pres/Meth/UCC	Joel 2:21–27	1 Tim 2:1–7	Mt 6:25–33
Roman Catholic	Joel 2:21–27	1 Tim 2:1–7	Mt 6:25–33
Episcopal	Deut 8:1–3, 6–10 (17–20)	Jas 1:17–18, 21–27	Mt 6:25–33
Lutheran	Joel 2:21–27	1 Tim 2:1–7	Mt 6:25–33

Introduction to the Lessons
Lesson 1
(1) *Joel 2:21–27* **(Pres/Meth/UCC/RC/Luth)**
The entire chapter sets the judgment and the promises of God in the framework of the whole creation. Using the vivid imagery of a colossal army of locusts, verses two through eleven discuss the punitive onslaught, verses twelve through seventeen define the faithful liturgical response, and verses eighteen through twenty offer the restoration of a promise. Then the rest of the passage proclaims the ways that the whole creation (soil, animals, pastures, trees, vines, and the children of God) will thrive again.

(2) *Deuteronomy 8:1–3, 6–10 (17–20)* **(Epis)**
This text is characterized by the main theological emphasis of Deuteronomy. Its theme is that diligent adherence to the commandments of God will yield blessings from the Lord. In particular, these blessings will be manifest in abundant agricultural harvests and mineral riches. However, they will only come through humility and obedience to God.

Lesson 2
(1) *1 Timothy 2:1–7* **(Pres/Meth/UCC/RC/Luth)**
These verses contain the first set of instructions given to Timothy to guide him toward a faithful and fruitful ministry and to help him avoid the corruptions that have caused others in ministry to go astray. He is to offer four types of prayer on behalf of governing authorities. The theological basis for this resides in the fact that there is one mediator between God and humanity. Therefore, prayers even for Gentiles in public office will be effective.

(2) *James 1:17–18, 21–27* **(Epis)**
Every act of giving is itself the result of a gift. However, it is the responsibility of believers to be accountable to the gift of faith they have received by being doers of the word and not just hearers. Doing the word involves both restraining actions such as keeping oneself pure and bridling the tongue, and outreaching actions such as care for widows and orphans.

Gospel
Matthew 6:25–33 **(Pres/Meth/UCC/RC/Epis/Luth)**
This portion of the Sermon on the Mount offers the assurance that everything necessary for life comes as a gift from God, and that the same Lord who cares for all other creatures cares for us. Therefore, no effort of our own can add anything to the beauty or the durability of creation; not even our anxieties or our worries can do so.

Theme
Our lives are defined by the gifts and promises of God.

Thought for the Day
"You are a word about the Word before you ever say a word."
—Barbara Brown Taylor

Prayer of Meditation
O God, whose blessings are beyond our capacity to count but not beyond our capacity to enjoy, we give you thanks for the treasures of this day and the fruits of this season. Grant that we will prepare hearts to worship you with thanksgiving for all that we have received and in humility for the manner in which we have become receivers, not by our own merits but by your grace. In Jesus' name we pray. Amen.

Call to Worship
> Leader: Let us give thanks to the Lord.
> People: It is right to give God our thanks and praise.
> Leader: Let us give thanks to the Lord for the gift of life.
> People: And for all the gifts that nourish and sustain us.
> Leader: Let us give thanks to the Lord for the certainty of hope.
> People: And for the promises of redemption in which our hope is sure.

November 27, 1997
Thanksgiving Day

Prayer of Adoration

O Lord, who has brought the saints through the journey of another season and has kept the promise that we would not travel alone, we persist in our path of faith because of the grace by which you continue to travel with us. Our struggles would leave us too weary were it not for your strengthening presence. Our hopes would be too easily dashed, were it not for your enduring promise. Our hearts would break were it not for the love in which you embrace us. Accept our praises, in Jesus' name. Amen.

Prayer of Confession

O God, whose word is truth and whose will is that we should declare the truth before you, we confess that we are not eager to give you thanks for all the ways that we have been blessed. If our tables will be laden with food this holiday, we know we have labored long and struggled hard to reap the harvest of the year. If our blessings seem few and our riches small, we know that there are those who say we will have to work longer and struggle harder. We confess this day that our pride is strong. Pardon and deliver us from this bondage to ourselves. Open our hearts to receive your mercy and be reconciled to your ways. Transform us from proud laborers to humble servants and grant that we will keep faith with your promises for ourselves and for the sake of your world, through Christ our Lord we pray. Amen.

Prayer of Dedication of Gifts and Self

O God, whose love for us is never less than total, accept these offerings as a portion of the blessings that we have received on earth and as a sign of our complete commitment of ourselves to you. With a part of our wealth, we offer all of our lives. Take our gifts and bless them. Take our lives and direct them. Take our promises and enable us to keep them, by the guidance and correction and discipline of your Holy Spirit. In Jesus' name we pray. Amen.

Sermon Summary

Our occasions for giving thanks and the traditions through which we exercise our thanksgiving are planned, shaped, and structured by our families as well as by the culture of which we are a part. But thanksgiving to God is most profound when it is spontaneously responsive to the unexpected ways we experience God's work.

Hymn of the Day

"Many and Great, O God, Are Your Works." This powerful hymn in praise of God's creation comes from the Dakota tribes, now in a variety of English translations. With its strong and deliberate beat, it was mistaken as a pagan war chant of defiance when sung by thirty-eight Dakota prisoners of war when they were taken to their execution in Mankato, Minnesota, in 1862. Instead, it was and is a moving affirmation of God's bounty and blessing.

Children's Object Talk

Consider the Lilies

Object
A live lily from the florist.

Lesson
Be thankful for what you have, rather than fret over what you want.

(Elicit answers and accept all.) What are you going to wear tomorrow? Do you think you may have to go barefoot to school on Monday? Why not? How many pairs of shoes do you have? Do you have enough? How many can you wear at the same time? It's funny, isn't it—we only have two feet but how many shoes do you have in your closet? Me, too! And how many do I need?

In our gospel story today, Jesus tells us we shouldn't worry about what to wear or what to eat. We should just ask God to give us what we *need.* We do that when we pray, "Give us this day our daily bread." So then, what should we be spending our time thinking about? First, look for the kingdom of God, Jesus says. That means we should think about all those things that show we are Jesus' followers, and God will give you what you need. (Hold up the lily.) Isn't this a beautiful flower? Jesus said this flower doesn't worry one bit about what to wear, and yet look how beautiful it is! God has given it these beautiful colors to wear.

Today we have come together especially to thank God for all the good things he gives us: our families, our food, clothes to keep us warm and dry, our homes—all the things we need. Shall we do that now? Let's close our eyes and fold our hands. Think of something you like to do (pause), or someone you love (pause), or something you especially like to eat (pause). If you want to, each of you can say out loud what you want to thank God for. I'll touch you when it's your turn.

November 27, 1997
Thanksgiving Day

Dear Lord, today we all want to thank you for taking care of us, for giving us everything we have. We especially want to thank you for:_____. Amen.

—*Lois Brokering*

The Sermon

A Grateful Dependent

Hymns
Beginning of Worship: "All Creatures of Our God and King"
Sermon Hymn: "Now Thank We All Our God"
End of Worship: "What Gift Can We Bring?"

Scripture
Matthew 6:25–33 (For additional sermon materials on this passage, see the August 1997 issue and the *1997 May/June Planning Issue* of *The Clergy Journal*.)

Sermon Text
"'... do not worry... why do you worry?... do not worry...'" (vss. 25–31).

Among the memorable people whom I have been privileged to serve as a pastor was a couple who were in their mid-seventies when I first met them. They had already passed their golden wedding anniversary by that time. One day they shared with me their story about the day they were married in 1917.

They had been raised in neighboring communities, belonged to the same church, and had courted for a while before he asked for her hand in marriage. But global events intruded into their wedding plans. The young bridegroom was in the Navy and was scheduled for sea duty in the First World War, so they went to see the preacher and decided to be married in a small ceremony on Thanksgiving Day.

A service was scheduled to be conducted in the church that morning, so the wedding could conveniently be held shortly after worship. The couple would arrive at the parsonage where his wife would greet them and their attendants. They could wait in the parlor until the service ended. Then the preacher would come to the parsonage, escort them into the sanctuary where their invited guests would gather, and the ceremony would proceed. He would ask the organist to stay after the Thanksgiving Day service and play for the wedding.

153

When Thanksgiving Day arrived, everything proceeded according to plan—with one exception. Just before pronouncing the benediction at the close of the congregation's service, the preacher announced that a beloved and well-known couple from the community were to be married later that morning in the sanctuary, and he invited everyone to stay for the service.

Then he went next door to the parsonage. He escorted the couple to the church, as planned. But when he led them into the sanctuary, they found it filled with family and friends, sisters and brothers in the faith. All of these folks had decided to remain and give thanks to God for the love that these two young people had found and for the promises that human beings can make in God's name to one another.

Such a thing could happen in 1917. It could never happen today. Not because it would be difficult to fill a sanctuary for a service on Thanksgiving morning, though it might be. Not because a congregation would be unwilling to linger for an extra half-hour on a holiday, though they might be. But because it would be impossible to hide the presence of an entire congregation from an unsuspecting couple. In 1917, almost everyone who came to worship on Thanksgiving or any other day would have walked to the service. Few, if any automobiles would have been parked near the church. The notion of a parking lot on the church grounds would never have occurred to a pastor or board of trustees at that time. So there would have been no physical evidence that a crowd would greet the couple or share their wedding day.

We structure Thanksgiving in our cultural, commercial, and community calendars now in such a way that everything about it is quite predictable. We know that the president of the United States will be given a turkey that he will ceremoniously pardon and protect from execution. We know that the day before Thanksgiving will be the busiest travel day in the country. We know that church and community groups who scarcely lift a finger to feed the hungry or tend to the homeless during the rest of the year will try to find a way to do something. We know that families will overeat and then divide into two groups: one will wrap the leftovers and clean up the mess; the other will find a television set and watch football. We know that the morning newspaper will be thick with retail store advertisements luring a barrage of shoppers to early-bird sales on the day after Thanksgiving.

There is a power in such rituals.

But the act of giving thanks may not always be successfully

November 27, 1997
Thanksgiving Day

programmed or packaged into such predictable patterns. The act of giving thanks needs an element of spontaneity, of surprise, of sensitivity to the immediate circumstances that cause us to feel the need to give thanks.

In the early days of America's Thanksgiving celebrations, there were no pre-calendared annual events. People were called to give thanks to God when the occasion demanded it. When the pilgrims survived a first year and faced the prospect of a hard winter not knowing if they would survive the second, they gave thanks. When a storm passed, doing little or no damage to a community, people gave thanks. When a terrible scourge (like slavery) ended, people gave thanks. And so it was that Abraham Lincoln called the American people to hold a day of thanksgiving in November 1863 —after Gettysburg, after emancipation, after the prospects for an end to the war began to brighten.

When we limit our lives to what we can schedule, plan, or calendar, we may succeed in organizing our time clearly. But we lose the freedom to recognize how dependent we are on the things we cannot control, or structure, or package.

Our traditional Thanksgiving Day hymns and symbols tend to draw heavily upon agricultural imagery. We sing of "harvest home" and echo that "all is safely gathered in." But most of us have long grown accustomed to the plan that our well-being depends upon a predictable monthly or biweekly paycheck. Except for a few farmers or builders among us, we are not dependent upon the idiosyncrasies of the weather for our welfare. We depend on what is automatic.

But when the harvest may or may not come, when the river may or may not flood, when the check may or may not be in the mail, that's when our dependency upon the unexpected becomes so clear. That's when the act of giving thanks is so spontaneous, so certain, so pure.

In the fall of 1996, the residents of my community spent a long night listening to the winds, and the falling trees, and the pounding rain of a hurricane. For days afterward, besides facing the physical cleanup and repairs to damaged property, people once again had to learn what it meant to live without electricity.

One of the first discoveries was just how dependent we were on one another. The need for food turned into unplanned neighborhood picnics as households discovered that food would not keep in the freezer or refrigerator very long. So those with charcoal and gas grills cooked food provided by others. Someone who knew how to make coffee over an open fire served the neighbors. In spontaneous acts of thanksgiving, people shared meals, prayed in gratitude for safety through the storm, and rediscovered the joy of being grateful dependents.

That's what all of us are: dependent on the gifts of a benevolent Lord who provides everything we need and to whom we offer in response a gift of thanks. Not because we planned it, but because we recognized the beautiful truth of it. We live and hope not because of all that we can do, but because of what has been done for us by a creative God and a saving Lord named Jesus.

—William B. Lawrence
Duke Divinity School
Durham, North Carolina

November 30, 1997

1st Sunday of Advent

Lessons
Pres/Meth/UCC/Luth	Jer 33:14–16	1 Thess 3:9–13	Lk 21:25–36
Roman Catholic	Jer 33:14–16	1 Thess 3:12—4:2	Lk 21:25–28, 34–36
Episcopal	Zech 14:4–9	1 Thess 3:9–13	Lk 21:25–31

Introduction to the Lessons
Lesson 1
(1) *Jeremiah 33:14–16* **(Pres/Meth/UCC/Luth/RC)**
The ancient promises are renewed (see 29:10) for the exiles in the form of a prophecy that focuses upon a shoot, branch, or "scion" of David. As it stands, the prophecy poses some interesting questions: whether the scion is one person or the revived dynasty in David's line; whether the name, a homonym for the king Zedekiah, a puppet ruler whom the Babylonians had controlled, is intended to suggest that Zedekiah will be the promised scion or that a real (rather than a shadow) sovereign will occupy the throne of Israel.

(2) *Zechariah 14:4–9* **(Epis)**
Here the promises of God are framed in terms of geocosmic battle where the whole earth and the whole universe will undergo climactic (as well as climatic) change. In effect, creation will be undone, with light filling the scene continuously rather than light and darkness, distinguishing day and night. At the end, the Lord will reign over a new earth dominated by a secure and victorious Jerusalem.

Lesson 2
1 Thessalonians 3:9–13 **(Pres/Meth/UCC/Luth/Epis)**;
1 Thessalonians 3:12—4:2 **(RC)**
The bond among Christians is strong and viable because of the encouragement that they offer one another. For this, the apostle offers thanks to God, asks that God will make possible a personal visit with them, and expresses the hope that their love for one another will increase. Further, the apostle indicates that one aspect of this loving unity is holiness of heart in a blameless life.

Gospel
Luke 21:25–36 (**Pres/Meth/UCC/Luth**);
Luke 21:25–28, 34–36 (**RC**); *Luke 21:25–31* (**Epis**)

With a set of apocalyptic images concerning the coming of the "Son of Man," we are told to be prayerfully alert. The whole cosmos will be involved with geophysical signs like the roaring of the sea as well as signs in the skies. However, while dread and foreboding will overtake the people of the nations, believers are to rise, raise their heads, and anticipate their redemption.

Theme
The coming of the Lord is not only a heartfelt, personal experience, but it also involves every aspect of our lives.

Thought for the Day
"Christ, come quickly. There's a danger at the door. There's poverty aplenty. Hearts gone wild with war. There's hunger in the city and famine on the plain. Come, Lord Jesus, the light is dying, the night keeps crying."

—Sr. Miriam Therese Winter

Prayer of Meditation
God of power and glory, let us not look upon this time of worship as an hour filled with songs, prayers, and gifts that we offer to you unless we also look upon it as an hour in which you begin to prepare us for your coming again. Work on our hearts, so that we will get ready for more than the festivities of Christmas. Instead, let us get ready for the continuing journey of being Christians who engage in faithful service while awaiting a faithful Savior. Amen.

Call to Worship
> Leader: Lift up your head, people of God!
> People: We have heard that the promised one of God is coming.
> Leader: Arise and be alert, for the redeemer is coming soon!
> People: Amen. Come, Lord Jesus.

November 30, 1997
1st Sunday of Advent

Prayer of Adoration
O Lord whose infinite presence is grander than the vastness of the universe, yet smaller than the tiniest unseen cell, we know there is no limit on the ways you can reveal yourself to us or come to us. We praise you for the promise of your coming, and we pray that we will keep alert for the infinite array of possibilities for us to notice your glorious arrival. In Jesus' name we pray. Amen.

Prayer of Confession
O God, we confess that we are more ready to have you come as our redeemer than we are to have you come as our judge. Our sins are many, and we confess them. Our wills are stubborn, and we admit it. Our faithfulness is flawed, and we acknowledge that we have not always been your obedient servants. We prefer to believe that you are coming to redeem us, not that you are coming like a fire to consume our ways. Hear us, O Lord, as we confess that we would rather make you in our image than have you make us in yours. Then we shall be even more ready to receive you when you come again. Amen.

Prayer of Dedication of Gifts and Self
O Lord, from whom every gift comes and to whom any gift of ours can add nothing, we place these offerings in the care of your church as a sign of our gratitude for your gifts to us, and in the confidence that your Spirit will guide the church in their use. As we have been blessed, so we bless and praise you with our lives. As we have been served, so we offer to serve you with our selves. As we have been saved, so we ask that your church will be enabled to share the good news of salvation, through Jesus Christ our Lord. Grant that in our giving and in our serving we will remain grateful and faithful to you, through Jesus Christ our Lord. Amen.

Sermon Summary
One of the dominant concerns facing many churches is the matter of growth. Many denominations are facing declining membership. Many congregations accustomed to being influential in their communities are finding that other forces dominate the cultural and social patterns of the day. The apostle Paul offers some principles for church growth in today's epistle lesson, but he has more than numerical growth in mind.

Hymn of the Day

"Come, Thou Long-Expected Jesus." Charles Wesley was the brother of the famous evangelist John Wesley. Prolific beyond words, he wrote hymns for many of the Methodist movement student gatherings at Oxford in the early eighteenth century. This hymn has many suitable tunes including the familiar *"Stuttgar"* and *"In Babilone."* If you have access to an older hymnal, a particularly interesting setting of this hymn comes from the Southern Harmony version. Its minor tune captures the sense of anticipation appropriate for the "longing" of Advent.

Children's Object Talk

A Caring Letter of Love

Object
A letter in a used envelope.
Lesson
Christians of long standing mentor newer Christians.

Who brought you here today? (Accept all answers.) Why do you suppose those people brought you today? Why didn't they take you shopping or to the zoo instead? I think someone brought you to church today because they want to be sure you learn as much as possible about Jesus. They want to be sure that as you grow, your faith in God grows too. They want you to be strong followers of Jesus. They want you to do what Jesus teaches us. Do you think they will still care when you grow up and have your own home? I think they will always care.

I have here a letter from my (choose: mother, father, grandma, etc.). When I was a small girl (boy) my _____ told me Bible stories. My _____ taught me to pray and prayed with me. I knew that _____ really cared about me and wanted me to love Jesus. But now I'm all grown up. Do you think _____ still wants me to follow Jesus? Listen to the letter, and then see what you think.

"Dear_____, Today I am thinking of you and wondering how you are. Each day I pray that you continue to grow in the love of our Lord Jesus. I know your work takes much time. But I hope you always remember to read your Bible and to pray each day. May you show the love of Jesus Christ to every one you meet. I love you. _____

Do you think my _____ still cares about my love for Jesus? Someone cares about your

November 30, 1997
1st Sunday of Advent

faith too—someone who brought you here this morning.

In the Bible story we just read, a man named Paul is writing a letter to some friends in another city called Thessalonica. He is very concerned and interested in how they love Jesus. So he writes to tell them how he is praying for them. When you go home, ask your family if they ever pray for you, and you can pray for them too.

—Lois Brokering

The Sermon

Growing Concerns

Hymns
Beginning of Worship: "O Come, O Come, Emmanuel"
Sermon Hymn: "Hail to the Lord's Anointed"
End of Worship: "Come, Thou Long-Expected Jesus"

Scripture
1 Thessalonians 3:9–13 (For sermon materials on Luke 21:25–36, see the September 1997 and the *1997 May/June Planning Issue* of *The Clergy Journal*.)

Sermon Text
"... may the Lord make you increase and abound in love... And may he so strengthen your hearts in holiness that you may be blameless..." (vss. 12–13).

Among the things that cause piles of material to accumulate on every pastor's desk is a torrent of mail from companies who are in the religious publishing business. These are catalogs and brochures arriving all the time from firms with sermon ideas for preachers, classroom suggestions for Sunday school teachers, and practical plans for a local church financial campaign.

But, of all the topics that seem to be featured in these items, none is more common than the business of church growth. Books appear with titles like *Marketing the Congregation* and *Forty-four Ways to Increase Church Attendance*. The publishers are not fools. They know that most of the so-called "mainline" churches are declining in membership, and their clergy are looking for almost any strategy that will reverse the trend. They also know that plenty of eager, independent, entrepreneurial preachers are out there wanting to start and develop new churches. And since almost no pastor would openly admit that their priority is to keep their congregations small, struggling groups that are inhospitable to visitors—almost every church would like to think that it has the potential to grow.

So the books are published, and the continuing education seminars are announced. Like the voice heard by the farmer in the film *Field of Dreams*, the message seems to be "If you print it, they will come."

The apostle Paul started many new churches. But there was no pile of junk mail on his desk telling him how to do it. There were no seminars to help him devise a strategy. His resources were the sense that Christ had called him to preach, the deep convictions of his own faith that the power of the Holy Spirit was leading the church, and the small group of fellow apostles who were engaged in the work of ministry with him. Our text for this morning comes from one of Paul's earliest letters written to the church that he had started in Thessalonica. It may offer the best advice available to any congregation about its growing concerns.

Paul had founded the church during a relatively brief stay in the city. He knew that the congregation was going to face great opposition from other religious and philosophical groups, and that it would have to manage in the midst of many alternative attractions in this busy, prosperous city. He warned them that they would be persecuted simply because they believed in Jesus Christ as Lord. He then arranged for Timothy to visit the Thessalonians and to bring him a report on how they were doing.

In the third chapter of his letter, we learn that Paul has heard encouraging things from Timothy. He wonders if it is possible to thank God enough for the ways that these Thessalonian Christians continue in the faith.

But then he moves beyond these enthusiastic words to tell the Thessalonians and us the fundamental things we need to know about the growing concerns of churches. The principles are remarkably simple: to increase and abound in love for one another and to strive for holy and blameless lives in anticipation that Christ is coming again.

Simple principles. But they are not easy.

First of all, notice that Paul's growing concerns do not mention number of members. As far as he is concerned, the "increase" that the Lord leads the church to experience is an increase in love —for one another and for all persons (vs. 12). Church growth

November 30, 1997
1st Sunday of Advent

may or may not involve a statistical increase in members and attendance, but if it does not involve an increase in self-giving love for those in the fellowship and for those outside of the fellowship, then it is not church growth.

Second, Paul does not mention buildings, budgets, or endowments as growing concerns of the church. Instead, he says Christians should be endowed with holy hearts and blameless lives. Successful, effective, growing congregations are bodies of people whose faithfulness is measured in personal and communal belief-filled behavior. Paul would caution the Thessalonians and us to be indifferent to the sorts of things that catch the attention of secular observers as well as church growth strategists in our day, but to be very focused on the things that concern God. An infinite Lord can look into the hearts and lives of many or few believers—their numbers do not really matter. But when that infinite God looks into the hearts of us believers, will our confession of faith have integrity and will our beliefs be matched with blameless lives?

Some years ago, when the celebrated television preacher Jim Bakker was arrested and facing trial, he stood on the steps of the courthouse and announced publicly, "God has forgiven me, therefore I am innocent." But if, in fact, God had forgiven him, he was not innocent—he was a guilty man who had been pardoned by a gracious God. Forgiveness does not restore us to innocence. Forgiveness is the bestowal of a gift by a loving Lord to bring us back into a relationship with God that we by sin have broken. We are not innocent. We just happen to be the beneficiaries of God's mercy.

Today is the First Sunday of Advent, the beginning of that four-week period of preparation for the coming of Christmas, but more importantly the beginning of that season in the church year when we focus upon Jesus' coming again as our redeemer and our judge. The growing concerns of every congregation rest fundamentally in the fact that our faith and our faithfulness will come face-to-face with the Savior at the end of this age. He may or may not ask what we have done to increase the number of persons who know his name and who call him their Lord. But he *will* ask how we have increased in love for one another, how we have shown overflowing love for those outside the circle of faith, how we exhibited holy hearts, and how we have demonstrated blameless lives as believers in his name.

In the end, the only growing concerns of the church are those that involve our care for one another as God's children.

I have a friend in another state who is not an attorney in private practice. But a number of years ago he took many cases in family court, often as the attorney assigned by a judge to be the advocate for a child in some domestic dispute. When asked why he stopped accepting those assignments, he points to a single case involving a family consisting of a husband and wife and their adopted son.

Early in their marriage, the couple seemed to have had a variety of difficulties with their relationship. Like many couples in troubled marriages, they somehow developed the notion that having a child would alleviate their problems because it would give them someone else upon whom they could focus their attention. However, they were unable to conceive a child, so they sought and secured a three-year-old child through adoption. Five years later, it was obvious that the marriage was hopelessly troubled. The wife decided she could no longer stay in the relationship, and she simply walked out. Through an attorney, she petitioned for a divorce, renounced all claims to the couple's property, and surrendered all rights of custody and visitation for the little boy.

That left the husband with the child, now eight years of age. But for him the little boy was a reminder of the failed marriage. In fact, the little boy had failed in the husband's eyes since they had adopted him to fix their relationship, and it had not worked. So the father petitioned the court to renounce his custody of the child as well. The judge appointed my friend as the attorney to be the advocate and representative of the little boy.

A final court hearing was scheduled in the county courthouse on the morning of December 24, Christmas Eve. The father's request was put before the judge in clear, blunt terms. As attorney for the child, my friend argued that no parent can walk away from his or her responsibilities just because it seems to be inconvenient or unpleasant. In the end, the judge ruled that he agreed with the attorney representing the child regarding parental responsibility, yet he was not going to force that little boy to return to a home where he would be unwanted and unloved.

That was the day my friend decided he could no longer serve in family court. What he remembers of that Christmas Eve is standing in the corridor of the county courthouse with a social worker, each of them holding the hands of an eight-year-old boy, watching a man walk down the hall and out of the building while the child cried, "Daddy, don't leave me! Daddy, don't leave me!"

November 30, 1997
1st Sunday of Advent

Between this first day of the first week of Advent and the Eve of Christmas Day at the close of Advent, we will be thinking a great deal about ways to show our affection for the persons we love. We will buy gifts for family members and friends. We will send cards and letters to people near and far. We will probably see our congregation grow in numbers every time we worship as Christmas draws near. But none of that will matter if there are some of God's children in this congregation and this community who are crying that they need us, and we don't respond.

Because, after all, we were a crying people, too. But a merciful Savior came to us with a gift of hope that is stronger than our guilt. And all we have to do is care for one another in this church and in this world until that Savior comes again. Amen.

—William B. Lawrence
Duke Divinity School
Durham, North Carolina

December 7, 1997

2nd Sunday of Advent

Lessons
Pres/Meth/UCC/Luth	Mal 3:1–4	Phil 1:3–11	Lk 3:1–6
Roman Catholic	Bar 5:1–9	Phil 1:4–6, 8–11	Lk 3:1–6
Episcopal	Bar 5:1–9	Phil 1:1–11	Lk 3:1–6

Introduction to the Lessons
Lesson 1
(1) *Malachi 3:1–4* **(Pres/Meth/UCC/Luth)**
The Israelites held in Babylon as slaves have returned and the temple was rebuilt. Now they look forward to Yahweh's coming to the new temple. His coming will be preceded by a messenger to prepare the people. He will do this by cleansing the priests and their sacrifices. Christians see this messenger in the person of John the Baptizer who prepared the way for Jesus.

(2) *Baruch 5:1–9* **(Pres/Meth/UCC/Luth/RC/Epis)**
While Baruch was a friend and contemporary of Jeremiah, this passage dates from a much later time than theirs. In fact, it probably can be ascribed to the first-century B.C., putting its composition just decades before the birth of Jesus. The content of these verses, however, uses the attitude of returning exiles as background and announces that the time has come to celebrate the dawn of deliverance. Some of the imagery recalls the language of Isaiah's promise concerning the lifting of valleys and the leveling of hills.

Lesson 2
Philippians 1:3–11 **(Pres/Meth/UCC/Luth)**;
Philippians 1:4–6, 8–11 **(RC)**; *Philippians 1:1–11* **(Epis)**
In these opening verses of the imprisoned Paul's letter to the church at Philippi, a Roman colony at an important commercial intersection between east and west, Paul gives thanks for the relationship of mutual affection and mutual prayer in which he and the Philippian Christians are bound together. The salutation includes gratitude for what has marked their relationship in the past, for the way they are held

December 7, 1997
2nd Sunday of Advent

together in the present, and for the promise in which they all trust for the future. Paul notes that he is in prison because of his ministry in the name of Christ, and he affirms his confidence in the final judgment that will occur "in the day of Christ."

Gospel
Luke 3:1–6 (**Pres/Meth/UCC/Luth/RC/Epis**)
Like any good historian, Luke provides a historical framework for the narrative that he continues to build about the life and ministry of Jesus. Yet, accurate historical dating is not nearly so crucial as the theological point that Luke seems to be making. Within a given context of powerful civil government authorities as well as leading clergy, the word of God comes neither to the officers who claim political nor to those who claim priestly grandeur. Rather, the word of God comes to a wilderness preacher of repentance. In the ministry of John, the living word of God and the ancient word of God combine.

Theme
Preparing for Christmas is coincident with, but different from, preparing for Christ.

Thought for the Day
"If Christianity was something we were making up, of course we could make it easier. But it is not. We cannot compete, in simplicity, with people who are inventing religions. How could we? We are dealing with Fact. Of course, anyone can be simple if he has no facts to bother about."
—C. S. Lewis

Prayer of Meditation
O God, we work so hard to be ready for the coming celebration. Let us not neglect to get ready for your coming again. While we prepare our homes, remind us to prepare our hearts. As we wrap gifts, awaken us to the good news we have already received. And when we stand to sing for joy, cause us also to bow in confession, for we are not as prepared as we should be to have you surprise us when you come. Amen.

Call to Worship
Leader: Blessed be the Lord, the God of Israel.
People: For the promise of a redeemer has come.

Leader: By the tender mercy of God,
People: The dawn from on high will break upon us,
Leader: And those who sit in darkness will see a great light!
People: Blessed be the Lord, the God of Israel!

Prayer of Adoration
Lord, we have come to prepare our hearts and lives for the advent of the Savior, and to offer our praise and thanksgiving for the promise of his coming. Grant that our hope will not be hindered by the duties and demands upon us. Grant that our joy will not be blocked by the fears gripping the world around us. Grant that our confidence will not rest in ourselves, but in you, to whom we sing our praises, in Jesus' name. Amen.

Prayer of Confession
Gracious God, whose coming fulfills the promise of the ages, we confess that we may not be prepared to receive you when you come. We may look for a majestic arrival, while you want us to find you in some ordinary manger. We think that the signs of your coming will be clear, but you may enter our world in the darkest of midnights. We may think we have no need of you now, but you know our needs before we understand them. We have so much to do that we suppose we will find peace through our own doings. O Lord, forgive us. Come to us, even though we may not be ready for you. Put us through your cleansing fire. Awaken us to your presence, and to the surprising ways that you will come to us again. In Jesus' name we pray. Amen.

Prayer of Dedication of Gifts and Self
Loving God, who has fashioned the world and all that is in it and who has given us a home in this life and the life to come, we offer our praises to you in words, in songs, in prayers, and in these gifts. Empower your church to use every offering as a means of bearing witness to your redeeming love. And receive these gifts, we pray, as signs that we are prepared to offer more than these tokens of our lives. Inspire us to offer ourselves to you, that we might become your faithful witnesses by our words and our deeds in this world. These things we ask, in laying our gifts before you in the name of Christ Jesus our Savior. Amen.

December 7, 1997
2nd Sunday of Advent

Sermon Summary
All of us at this time of year spend at least some time fretting about our level of readiness for Christmas. But the message of the Scripture for today is that God's work which began among us is going to be brought by God toward a conclusion. It is God's doing, not ours. Readiness for Christmas is not nearly as important as readiness for Christ.

Hymn of the Day
"*Toda la Tierra* (All Earth Is Waiting)." This delightful and very easy hymn has been included in many of the newer hymnals and can be readily found in many collections. Based on the gospel text for this Sunday, the Mexican tune engages us in the sense of celebration that will come with the birth of the Christ child. This is an excellent hymn for children to participate with, perhaps at the lighting of the Advent candles. Printed in both English and Spanish, this hymn is a joy to every nationality.

Children's Object Talk

A Picture Is Worth a Thousand Prayers
Object
   Two photos, one of yourself and one of a family member or friend who was a key figure in your life of faith.
Lesson
   While awaiting the return of Jesus, the family of faith constantly prays for one another.

Do you know who this is? (Show picture of yourself and encourage guesses.) Believe it or not, this is a picture of me taken a long time ago.

And how about this person? (Again, wait for replies.) Who do you think this might be?

This is a person most of you have never met. This is my _____ (friend, grandfather, Sunday school teacher).

When I was a child (or, when as an adult I first began to trust that God loved me) this person taught me many important things about God and God's love. Those are some very important lessons. I'm so grateful I learned about Jesus, and I think God every time I think about this person who helped introduce me to faith.

Long, long ago a very important person named Paul

was in prison. He lived long before cameras were invented so I can't show you his photo. Paul helped many thousands of people learn about Jesus.

Paul was a missionary. That meant he traveled far and wide and found himself in many dangerous situations.

Whenever he was in those lonely or frightening times, he would think about other Christian friends he had met in his many trips. He felt stronger, happier, more at peace whenever he thought about them, and he always thanked God for them.

He says you and I should do that every day, too. Between now and Christmas—during the season of Advent—can you remember to pray every day for friends, or teachers, or family members who have helped teach you about God's love? Let's start now: Thank you, God, for good friends and caring family. They are gifts of love from you. Amen.

—*Jon Temme*

The Sermon

Preparations for the Underprepared

Hymns
Beginning of Worship: "O Come, All Ye Faithful"
Sermon Hymn: "Once in Royal David's City"
End of Worship: "Lo, He Comes with Clouds Descending"

Scripture
Philippians 1:3–11 (For sermon materials on Luke 3:1–6, see the September 1997 and the *1997 May/June Planning Issue* of *The Clergy Journal.*)

Sermon Text
"I am confident of this, that the one who began a good work among you will bring it to completion by the day of Jesus Christ" (vs. 6).

Last year, on the day after Christmas, I stopped at a supermarket to replenish our supply of bread and milk. As I was entering the store, I encountered a friend who was walking out of the store empty-handed. "Did you forget what you came for?" I jokingly asked him. "No," he said, "I always check out the stores after the holiday to see about some bargains on cookies or other things I can freeze for next

December 7, 1997
2nd Sunday of Advent

year. But I couldn't find anything interesting left on the shelves. So I am heading to another store down the street."

I must say that I paused there for a moment, contemplating my guilt about being so underprepared. I had not even planned well enough to have enough bread and milk in the house to last beyond Christmas Day, let alone getting my preparations under way for the cookies that I might need in another twelve months. To say the least, I felt grossly underprepared!

Of course, it is one thing to be underprepared for the coming of Christmas, but what if we are not ready for the coming of Christ?

My suspicion is that the situation of most Christians in the early weeks of December is that our activities look like the preparations of the underprepared. All of us have plenty to do: shopping, baking, decorating, and making travel plans. And beyond all the stuff for the secular seasonal celebration, look at how busy things become in the church—nearly every group schedules a Christmas party, choirs have extra rehearsals, poinsettias have to be ordered and arranged, holiday gift baskets await delivery to the needy, and on and on it goes. Glance at the church calendar and perhaps you will come to the conclusion that I have reached—we have crammed it so full and structured every week so tightly that if Jesus were to come again, he had better pick some other month besides December!

We are too busy to make room for him to surprise us. In fact, most of us prefer structure to surprise in every aspect of our lives.

Within recent decades, we Americans have become accustomed to the way that professional football tends to dominate our Sundays. Many folks who live in or near the home cities of National Football League teams organize their Sunday plans around the eight days that their teams play in their own stadiums. Tens of millions more across the country build their Sundays around the games they can watch on television. Before pro football became a nationally televised spectacle, it had a smaller but equally loyal audience who followed the games on radio. Every Sunday, listeners would plan their afternoons and stay close to their radios, carefully monitoring every play. Then, as now, the listeners did not want any distraction to interrupt their plans.

Fifty-six years ago today, one New York radio station interrupted its broadcast of the Giants game against the Washington Redskins with a news report that the Japanese had bombed Pearl Harbor. Fans bombarded the radio station with telephone calls demanding that the game be put back on the air!

171

It isn't simply that we do not like surprises. It is that, if we can maintain our lives according to the ways we have structured them, then we can go on pretending that there are no such things as surprises. Football fans on December 7, 1941, wanted to maintain the pretense that war had not erupted. And Christians pursue their Christmas preparations hoping to maintain the pretense that Jesus is not coming again. We are quite willing to celebrate his birth. Indeed, we are committed to being very busy in keeping the organized festivities going. But if we can confine the Savior's work to what has occurred in the past and to the traditions we have created for observing it, then we can keep control of Christ and Christmas.

But the apostle Paul, writing to the Philippians, offers another slant. "I am confident of this," Paul says, "that the one who began a good work among you will bring it to completion by the day of Jesus Christ." So the birth of Jesus, the entry of Christ into our world, was simply the start of God's work in our midst. God will yet, at some unknown and unnamed point in the future, bring that work to a conclusion with the return of Christ to the world—maybe before our decorating is done. Maybe before the travel schedule has been finished. Maybe before the anthems are well rehearsed. Maybe before we have confessed our sins, repented of our ways, and turned to him who is coming as our judge.

Well, it is only the second week of Advent. Therefore, it is not too late to see if we can combine our preparations for Christmas with preparing to meet the Christ.

Paul's comments to the Christians in Philippi were written at a time when he was languishing in a Roman prison for the crime of having believed in—and witnessed to—the saving work of Jesus in the world. It certainly would have been possible for anyone who had sacrificed so much to become a preacher of the gospel simply to collapse into despair over what had happened to his plans. Only a small portion of the world's people had become believers. The forces of the world's mightiest power had tried to silence his message. Paul could have looked at this turn of events and decided that the message he preached was not so truthful after all.

But his faith never wavered, though the age was filled with surprises. As a matter of fact, the truth made itself known in every surprising turn. When faced with the surprise of a prison term, Paul used it to celebrate the strength of a mutual link with the Philippians through prayer.

December 7, 1997
2nd Sunday of Advent

When faced with the surprise that his opportunities to preach on each might be coming to an end, Paul saw it as an occasion for love within the Philippian church to overflow even more. When Paul pondered from prison the good work that had been accomplished by the believers in Philippi, he saw that it was just the beginning of what God was going to complete in the world.

I have every confidence that by the time December 25 arrives—*if* it arrives this year—we will have finished all of the necessary preparations for the day. The food will be ready. The gifts will be wrapped. The pageants will have been performed. The parties will have proceeded according to plans.

But if, in addition to all of those things, you and I will spend some time and energy acknowledging that we are underprepared for Christ to come again, we will be even more thoroughly ready for the arrival of the Savior. Because then we will be ready for him to have an affect upon us in the ways we need saving. It may be a matter of his coming to tell us that in order to be saved, we will have to let go of our greed. Or in order to receive the benefits of his coming as a wonderful counselor, we will have to let him heal us of the bitterness we feel toward people of another race. Or in order to recognize him as the prince of peace, we will need to let him lead us to a reconciliation with those from whom our pride has separated us.

Jesus is coming again because the work that he pronounced "finished" on the cross has not yet come to completion in the world. But he will return and complete it. And we, the underprepared, have to get ready. Amen.

—*William B. Lawrence*
Duke Divinity School
Durham, North Carolina

December 14, 1997

3rd Sunday of Advent

Lessons
Pres/Meth/UCC/Luth	Zeph 3:14–20	Phil 4:4–7	Lk 3:7–18
Roman Catholic	Zeph 3:14–18a	Phil 4:4–7	Lk 3:10–18
Episcopal	Zeph 3:14–20	Phil 4:4–7 (8–9)	Lk 3:7–18

Introduction to the Lessons
Lesson 1
Zephaniah 3:14–20 **(Pres/Meth/UCC/Luth/Epis)**;
Zephaniah 3:14–18a **(RC)**

The golden age is presented in poetic images. Judah's enemies will be overcome, and the people's joy will come from the presence of the Lord in their midst. Outcasts will be restored, and those displaced will be brought home.

Lesson 2
Philippians 4:4–7 **(Pres/Meth/UCC/Luth/RC)**;
Philippians 4:4–7 (8–9) **(Epis)**

Very well known, this passage is as much a benediction as an exhortation. *"Rejoice in the Lord always,"* Paul urges. The supreme reward is the peace of God *"which surpasses all understanding,"* and comes as joy in the face of adversity.

Gospel
Luke 3:7–18 **(Pres/Meth/UCC/Luth/Epis)**; *Luke 3:10–18* **(RC)**

The coming judgment calls for repentance, not simply membership in the community. The people's question—*"What, then, should we do?"*—is answered in the simplest terms of daily conduct, for *"the one who is coming"* will baptize with the Holy Spirit and with fire.

Theme
The presence of the Lord is seen most clearly in the transformation of daily life.

December 14, 1997
3rd Sunday of Advent

Thought for the Day

The miracle of God's rule is the integration of hand, mind, and heart. The joy of God's people, renewed through repentance, lies in the transformation of every detail of daily life: deliverance from the fear of disaster, restoration of the lost, shared food, and moral integrity. All is brought about by the baptism of the *"one who is coming,"* which effects a radical change of heart.

Prayer of Meditation

Gracious God, apart from you we are constricted by the darkness of our hearts, and in the world all around us. Let your light shine in the darkness, and open our eyes to see it. Fill us with the peace of Christ, which surpasses all understanding. Transform our living and make us instruments of your will. Make us strong through your Spirit. This we pray in the name of the one who was, the one who is, and the one who is coming, Jesus Christ our Lord. Amen.

Call to Worship

    Leader: Give ear, O Shepherd of Israel,
    People: you who lead Joseph like a flock!
    Leader: You who are enthroned upon the cherubim . . .
    People: Stir up your might, and come to save us!
    Leader: Restore us, O God;
    People: let your face shine, that we may be saved.
    —Psalm 80:1–3

Prayer of Adoration

Gracious God, fill our hearts with true repentance, that we might walk in your light and know the splendor of your presence. Lighten the darkness within us and hear our prayers. Lead us home, O Lord, that we might know the power of Christ's resurrection, the glory of his presence, and the fellowship of his sufferings. Even though we are not worthy to untie the thong of his sandals, help us to stand proudly as forgiven sinners in your presence. All glory and honor are yours, O Lord, now and forever. Amen.

Prayer of Confession

Gracious Lord, your mercy is as wide as the ocean. Yet, we are troubled with the guilt of our sins. We have often surrendered belief for unbelief, hope for despair, and peace for worry. We have often overlooked the need of our neighbor. We have squandered our gifts, wasted our talents, and cheapened our obedience. Forgive us, Lord, for we have sinned before you and our neighbor. Fill our hearts with the peace of your pardon and help to shine with your light, for all the world to see. We pray in Jesus' name. Amen.

Prayer of Dedication of Gifts and Self

Accept these gifts, O Lord, as the offerings of our hearts. Make them into light for the blind, bread for the hungry, hope for the hopeless, and a staff in slippery ways. Fill us, O Lord, with the joy of your saving presence, that all people might see that you are good, and that your mercy endures forever. Use these gifts to make your name renowned in all the earth. For Jesus' sake. Amen.

Sermon Summary

Hope is at the center of all life. Without hope, we die. Despite our deepest fears, Jesus is our best hope.

Hymn of the Day

"People Look East." Continuing with an international selection of Advent hymns, this tune comes from a French folk melody with words by Eleanor Farjeon (1881–1965). This hymn has a lilting, free-flowing tune that draws us ever closer to the time of Jesus' birth, and the words call us to seek the star of love as it rises into the eastern sky. Of particular note is the participation of all nature and creation in the joyful expectation. With four verses, this hymn can be effectively used all four Sundays by adding one verse each time it is sung. You may choose to change the uses of "love" in the last stanza to include "peace," "hope," and "joy."

December 14, 1997
3rd Sunday of Advent

Children's Object Talk

Waiting without Worrying

Object
A large piece of newsprint or flip-chart paper with "Things to Do" written in large letters across the top.

Lesson
There is much to worry about: faith in God turns our worrying into rejoicing.

I need your help this morning. Christmas is coming soon, isn't it? I have so many things to do before Christmas to get ready. I'm worried I might forget something, so would you help me fill out my list?

What are some of the things I need to do to get ready for Christmas? (Prompt as many answers as you can: buy and wrap presents, write Christmas cards, visit friends. Try to write large and fill the paper.)

Look at all that I have to do. I thought making a list would help me worry less, but now I'm even more worried. There's so much to think about.

There sure is a lot to worry about, isn't there? Maybe I should quit my job, and then I'd have enough time to worry all day long. But I'd have to worry about not having any money or food. No, more time for worrying is not the answer.

Do you know what the question is? God has an answer for us whenever we have lots to worry about. The answer is simple. It looks like this. (Fold your hands, bow your head, and pause briefly.)

Yes, God invites us to pray and share all the things that worry us. Some of them are silly worries like rushing around to do little things before Christmas. Some of them are big worries like whether my health will be okay next year or whether children will be safe in my neighborhood. It doesn't matter what's on our "To Do" list. It doesn't matter what "size" the worry is: big or small. We can always talk to God. Let's do it now: "Dear God, thank you for being close when we pray. Teach us to bring our worries to you, especially at busy times like now." Amen.

—*Jon Temme*

The Sermon

What Do You Expect?

Hymns
Beginning of Worship: "Come Down, O Love Divine"
Sermon Hymn: "O God, Our Help in Ages Past"
End of Worship: "Come, Thou Long-Expected Jesus"

Scripture
Philippians 4:4–7 (For sermon materials on Zephaniah 3:14–20, see the September 1997 issue of *The Clergy Journal* and on Luke 3:7–18, see the *1997 May/June Planning Issue* of *The Clergy Journal*.)

Sermon Text
"... The Lord is near. Do not worry about anything..." (vss. 5–6).

Not long ago, a woman who had fought bravely against cancer for several years, entered the hospital for therapy and a round of laboratory procedures. She was responsive to her family and feeling quite energetic. One day, her family visited her, and then left her for a few hours intending to return. When they came back, she had died.

The family was puzzled. I was puzzled. There had been no indication that she was slipping away—there had been no indication that she was even close to death. What had happened?

The story came out later. Her doctor had visited her and had told her that there was nothing more that could be done. In other words, her hope was gone and without the hope that had previously kept her going, she died within hours.

I don't mean to make the doctor the villain. He was practicing good medicine as he saw it. But if I were to quibble, it would be to say that hope is never gone! Our future is not enslaved to statistics and probabilities. We can pray, we can hope, we can trust God, we can cling to life until we're ready to let go, at which point we can cling to God who has promised that in life and in death we are the Lord's. No matter how bad things seem, there is always hope!

Hope has tremendous power to revive us, to sustain us, and sometimes even to heal us of disease. There is nothing more important than hope for making life good, even when we face

December 14, 1997
3rd Sunday of Advent

terrible difficulties. Without hope, life just slips away from us, and we die, little by little.

Today's gospel is about hope. Advent is about hope. Isaiah declares this great truth about hope:

"Surely God is my salvation;
I will trust, and will not be afraid,
for the Lord God is my strength
and my might;
he has become my salvation.

"With joy you will draw water from the wells of salvation. And you will say in that day:
Give thanks to the Lord,
call on his name;
make known his deeds among the nations;
proclaim that his name is exalted"
(Isa 12:2–4).

Advent is a season of the church year with a crystal-clear message: Advent proclaims the hope that God gives us, hope that cannot be quenched by anything in this life, hope that is unshakable, even in the face of life's worst difficulties.

It fascinated me to discover that Luke, in the gospel reading, speaks of the hopes of the people. *"The people were in expectation,"* he writes. They expected that God's promises of a messiah were somehow in the process of being fulfilled.

But I ask you to back up to the subject of expectations themselves. All of us have expectations. Expectations are the same as hopes. The woman I spoke of earlier had hopes for the future: hopes that she might recover from her cancer, hopes that even with her cancer she might have some good times ahead of her. The announcement that nothing more could be done suddenly changed her hopes, her expectations, so that she no longer was able to be hopeful about her future. And without that hope, she died.

As you and I reflect about our lives and our future, we need to be aware of our expectations—our hopes. Depression is an emotional disorder that is common in our society, and especially common during the holidays. Depression is often defined as an overwhelming sense of hopelessness: the sense that the future holds some inevitable catastrophe that is to be dreaded. The papers last week told about a three-year-old boy being treated for depression. He was the son of an antinuclear activist who had so convinced him that the bomb was about to fall that he was filled with a sense of dread about the future. His expectations were salted with a sense of horror, catastrophe, and doom.

What are your expectations for the future? I recently talked with a woman who wakes up in the night gripped with anxious worries about her health. The same week, I talked with a man about to retire from a business career who told me that he is so excited about his retirement that he can hardly wait. Are your expectations, your hopes for the future good? or are they bad?

Paul, in our second lesson, makes reference to his own expectations, his own hopes. He writes:

". . . The Lord is near. Do not worry about anything, but in everything by prayer and supplication with thanksgiving let your requests be made known to God. And the peace of God, which surpasses all understanding, will guard your hearts and your minds in Christ Jesus" (Phil 4:5–7).

Luke's account tells us something else that fascinates me. Luke tells us that all the people *". . . were questioning in their hearts concerning John, whether he might be the Messiah "* (Lk 3:15). I recently saw a TV commercial for an investment program. The ad promised that this program would give the investor peace of mind. I was cynical, because I don't believe that peace of mind is based upon the amount of money one has.

The point is this: when people make promises for the future, we ask questions, and we *need* to ask questions. When people started to think that John was the promised Messiah, their first reaction was to ask questions, and they were right.

But now, let's bring this closer to home. When we hear the message of Advent, God's promise of Christ's coming, and that this is good news to all people including you and me, our first reaction is to ask questions.

We have a lot of questions: How can the future be good for me if nuclear war is on the way? How can the future be good for me if I'm facing health problems? How can the future be good for me if I'm facing financial problems? How can the future be good for me if I'm depressed?

When we hear the promise of Advent, we are filled with questions. And like the people in our text, questioning John, we ask, "Is this the way?"

Luke tells us something else that fascinates us. Regardless of what you're thinking, he says, your greatest hope lies in the future. For *". . . one who is more powerful than I is coming . . . He will baptize you with the Holy Spirit and fire"* (Lk 3:16).

What is our hope? Our hope is in Christ who is coming. Even though he has come, he is coming still in ways that we have not dreamed possible. He is coming still in ways that fly in the face of our deepest fears and our clearest logic. God invites us

December 14, 1997
3rd Sunday of Advent

to trust—to trust with the simple faith of a child.

That is what Paul meant when he said the peace of God that fills our hearts is beyond all human understanding. That is what Luke meant when he wrote that John's preaching was good news to the people. That is what the angels meant when they said, *"Do not be afraid; for see—I am bringing you good news of great joy for all the people"* (Lk 2:10). Our hope is not based upon what we see, what we know, or what we fear. It is beyond all that.

Martin Luther wrote: "I fear death, I fear the judgment of God, I fear the world, I fear hunger, I fear all sorts of thing. But the angel announces a savior who will free us from fear. The angel doesn't say a word about our merits and works, not a word about how we qualify for the gift, but only of the gift we are to receive."

What is the basis for this hope? The angel goes on: *"To you is born this day in the city of David a Savior, who is the Messiah, the Lord"* (Lk 2:11). That's a pretty far-ranging promise, isn't it? So we ask questions. How does it work? How can it be true for me? What about all the problems I face? What about all the problems the world is facing?

Christ is the answer to every problem, every fear, every sorrow, and every pain known to our hearts. Christ is coming. Behold, he is coming soon. Advent is about hope—a hope with the power to transform your life. And the name of this hope is Jesus Christ. May God's Holy Spirit fill your heart with hope.

—*Paul Romstad*
Central Lutheran Church
Minneapolis, Minnesota

December 21, 1997

4th Sunday of Advent

Lessons

Pres/Meth/UCC/Luth	Mic 5:2–5a	Heb 10:5–10	Lk 1:39–45 (46–55)
Roman Catholic	Mic 5:1–4a	Heb 10:5–10	Lk 1:39–45
Episcopal	Mic 5:2–4	Heb 10:5–10	Lk 1:39–49 (50–56)

Introduction to the Lessons
Lesson 1
Micah 5:2–5a **(Pres/Meth/UCC/Luth)**; *Micah 5:1–4a* **(RC)**; *Micah 5:2–4* **(Epis)**
The promised Messiah will come from one of the oldest families to restore the fortunes of Israel and Judah, extending his greatness to the ends of the earth. Like a shepherd, he will establish peace and security for all in his flock.

Lesson 2
Hebrews 10:5–10 **(Pres/Meth/UCC/Luth/RC/Epis)**
Ritual and morality are joined in Christ. Complex analogies establish the connection between ritual sacrifices and moral transformation, accomplished in Christ.

Gospel
Luke 1:39–45 (46–55) **(Pres/Meth/UCC/Luth)**;
Luke 1:39–45 **(RC)**; *Luke 1:39–49 (50–56)* **(Epis)**
John is shown to be a prophet before his birth, and one who points to Jesus. Elizabeth greets Mary as the mother of her Lord, and the child in her womb leaps for joy.

Theme
The long-awaited Messiah comes near, as we witness the meeting of Elizabeth and Mary who celebrate the holy child in Mary's womb.

December 21, 1997
4th Sunday of Advent

Thought for the Day

> Rejoice, then, you sad-hearted,
> Who sit in deepest gloom,
> Who mourn your joys departed
> And tremble at your doom.
> Despair not; he is near you,
> There, standing at the door,
> Who best can help and cheer you
> And bids you weep no more.
>
> —Paul Gerhardt, 1606–1676,
> *The Lutheran Hymnal* (1941), alt.

Prayer of Meditation

Gracious Lord, we pray this day for your clarifying presence that we might connect our deepest hopes and fears with the child who is about to be born. Awaken in us the joy that we see in Elizabeth whose child leaps in her womb at the coming of Mary. Keep us from being so comfortable with holy things, Lord, that we miss the power of your coming. In Jesus' name we pray. Amen.

Call to Worship

Leader: O Lord, my heart is not lifted up,
my eyes are not raised too high;
People: I do not occupy myself with things
too great and too marvelous for me.
Leader: But I have calmed and quieted my soul,
like a weaned child with its mother;
my soul is like the weaned child that is with me.
People: O Israel, hope in the Lord from this time on and forevermore.

—Psalm 131

Prayer of Adoration

Gracious God, as we gather in your presence, fill us with the joy of things to come, children to be born, promises to be fulfilled, and longings to be met. We confess our neediness, Lord. And we cry out to you as the one who has promised to come to us in our needs. Calm our minds, center our thoughts, settle our hearts, open our ears, that your word of promise might strike the center of our being and awaken hope there. In Jesus' name we pray. Amen.

Prayer of Confession

Gracious Lord, we confess that we have so often hoped in our own strength. Help us, Lord, to hope in you, that your glory might be dazzling light to our eyes. Stir our joyless hearts with the joy of your coming. In Jesus' name we pray. Amen.

Prayer of Dedication of Gifts and Self

Gracious Lord, the gifts we offer are not enough. But we pray that you will receive them as the sacrifice of our hearts, and use them for all things good. Bring light to the darkness, Lord. Bring hope to the hopeless, and fullness to the empty of heart. We offer these gifts and prayers in the name of the child who is to be born, Jesus Christ, our Lord. Amen.

Sermon Summary

We are on the verge of Christmas. Our hopes, dreams, and expectations leap up in our hearts like Elizabeth's child who leaped in the womb at the coming of Mary. The promised savior brings hope to a world bogged down in hopelessness.

Hymn of the Day

"My Soul Gives Glory to My God." The Magnificat of Mary is one of the most famous biblical texts ever set to music. This familiar tune is from a book of American hymnody called *Kentucky Harmony* (1816), with a text by poet Miriam Therese Winter. It is a powerful reminder that God does not just come to those with houses, credit cards, and Ford Explorers, but seeks care for the forgotten and lowly, the marginalized and the weak.

Children's Object Talk

A Closer Look Inside

Object

Two boxes: a large gift-wrapped box that contains nothing and a much smaller box, preferably plain or damaged that contains a valuable coin or piece of jewelry.

December 21, 1997
4th Sunday of Advent

Lesson
People and places cannot be judge by outward appearances but inner value.

Have you seen any Christmas presents at your home yet? Maybe at your school? That's fun, isn't it, to look at the wrapping paper and guess what's inside?

I brought along two presents we can open today. But first, let's guess what's inside. Look at this one (fancy, large box). Isn't that beautiful? Someone went to a lot of trouble to make this look nice on the outside. I wonder what might be inside? (engage kids in guessing) Let's see, shall we? Can I have a volunteer open this? Please open it slowly. I don't know what is inside, and it may be very valuable.

Oh no, there's not a thing inside. It looked great on the outside, but it didn't have anything of value inside.

Well, I wonder what might be in this old box then? Anyone want to bother opening it?

(When unwrapped . . .) Wow! Can you believe there was a coin (ring, antique) inside. That's a very valuable gift indeed.

I guess you cannot always assume that big and fancy means important, or that small and plain means unimportant.

That's true of gifts, and people, and places. People assumed that just because Jesus was born in a tiny little town called Bethlehem, he wouldn't mean very much. But Jesus was the Son of God. He brought God's love right down to earth for all people. The most amazing thing that ever happened—Christmas and the birth of Jesus—took place in a plain, tiny town called Bethlehem.

Here is a lesson for us. As we go to school and play this week, let's remember that people, places, and things cannot be judged on how they appear on the outside. What is inside is what is truly important.

—Jon Temme

The Sermon

When Babies Leap in the Womb

Hymns
Beginning of Worship: "Come, Thou Long-Expected Jesus"
Sermon Hymn: "Lo, How a Rose E'er Blooming"
End of Worship: "A Great and Mighty Wonder"

Scripture

Micah 5:2–5a (For sermon materials on Luke 1:39–45 [46–55], see the September 1997 issue of *The Clergy Journal* and on Hebrews 10:5–10, see the *1997 May/June Planning Issue* of *The Clergy Journal*.)

Sermon Text

"But you, O Bethlehem of Ephrathah, who are one of the little clans of Judah, from you shall come forth for me one who is to rule in Israel, whose origin is from of old, from ancient days. Therefore he shall give them up until the time when she who is in labor has brought forth; then the rest of his kindred shall return to the people of Israel. And he shall stand and feed his flock in the strength of the Lord in the majesty of the name of the Lord his God. And they shall live secure, for now he shall be great to the ends of the earth" (vss. 2–4).

Is there really a God? Does God really care about what happens in his world? Does God care about what happens to you and me?

Today, on the Fourth Sunday of Advent, we look at Mary, a person for whom the reality of God burned brightly, someone with the absolute conviction that God cared about this world, that God cared deeply about what happened to her: Mary, the mother of Jesus.

Today on the Fourth Sunday of Advent, we hear the words of Micah, the prophet, who says, *"O Bethlehem ... from you shall come forth for me one who is to rule in Israel, whose origin is from of old ... And he shall stand and feed his flock in the strength of the Lord in the majesty of the name of the Lord his God ..."* (Mic 5:2–4).

In the sixth month of her pregnancy, Mary traveled several days' journey to a little village in the hill country of Judea to visit Elizabeth, her cousin, who was also pregnant—with John the Baptist.

When Mary arrived, Elizabeth, filled with the Holy Spirit, said *"Blessed are you among women, and blessed is the fruit of your womb!"* Mary, after embracing her cousin, also filled with the Holy Spirit, said *"My soul magnifies the Lord, and my spirit rejoices in God my Savior."*

Christmas is very nearly here. I love Christmas. There is no time during the year when I come closer to being able to say and feel what Mary said and felt, *"My soul magnifies the Lord, and my spirit rejoices in God my Savior."*

I am already longing for the first star of Christmas Eve, when the presents are wrapped, the tree is lit, the church is bright with candles, and the dinner is in the oven. I am full of feelings about the beauty of this night. One carol, beautifully sung, can

December 21, 1997
4th Sunday of Advent

move me to tears. The snow on my spruce trees can stir me to thoughts of the goodness of God. And I, too, can say with Mary, *"My soul magnifies the Lord, and my spirit rejoices in God my Savior."* All of that is only days away, and I can hardly wait.

The village where Elizabeth lived still stands high on a hillside just outside of Jerusalem. It is called En Karim today. It looks more a Christmas scene than any place I've seen in Israel. It is heavily wooded with evergreen trees, the wind murmuring in the trees, and the air is heavy with the fragrance of pine.

As I try to visualize the meeting there between Mary and Elizabeth, I hope that the village that day was just like it is today: beautiful, quiet, fragrant. And I hope that the setting helped Mary to be overcome with joy.

Mary's words, *"My soul magnifies the Lord, and my spirit rejoices in God my Savior,"* must have overflowed from a marvelous vision of God deep within her that transformed her living with a warmth, comfort, and a peace that were not of this world, but which came straight from the heart of God.

It is that same marvelous sense with which God overwhelms the heart of his faithful people each Christmas, God's Holy Spirit who comes to the hearts of every one of us today, and in the marvelous days that lie just ahead of us. Mary said, and we say, *"My soul magnifies the Lord, and my spirit rejoices in God my Savior."*

Not long ago, I happened to be wandering through a department store with some time to kill. I found myself in a department that displayed furniture and accessories for babies' rooms. A young couple was there, looking at furniture for the baby who was obviously not far from being born. They were having a wonderful time, both of them radiantly happy, both of them openly excited about the new child for which they were getting ready.

If the world could be as excited about the baby in Bethlehem as this couple was about the baby they were expecting, as excited as Mary was about the baby she was expecting, this world could be transformed. This is God's purpose, after all. And we, the people of God, are again celebrating Advent as we once again go through a time of waiting for the child who is Christ the Lord.

Once again, God is hard at work preparing a place in our hearts for the child who is to be born. Again this year the newspapers are full of the pain and sorrow of people. We grieve for suffering children, we grieve for the victims of plane crashes, auto accidents, and disease. We suffer with needy families, weeping mothers, and the homeless poor in our cities.

But underneath all of this, we are overwhelmed with a joy that is bubbling up in our hearts, the same joy that so overwhelmed Mary that she burst forth in joyful hymn of praise to God. For we, too, will soon hear again the words of the angel who announced to the shepherds and to all people, *"Do not be afraid; for see—I am bringing you good news of great joy for all the people: to you is born this day in the city of David a Savior, who is the Messiah, the Lord"* (Lk 2:10–11). And we, too, will say with Mary, *"My soul magnifies the Lord, and my spirit rejoices in God my Savior."*

We are stirred to the core by the words of Micah, the prophet, who says, *"O Bethlehem . . . from you shall come forth for me one who is to rule in Israel, whose origin is from of old . . . And he shall stand and feed his flock in the strength of the Lord in the majesty of the name of the Lord his God"* (Mic 5: 2–4).

As I was working on this sermon, our disabled daughter came home on the school bus. I had Christmas carols playing on the phonograph, and she burst into the study to show me the Christmas ornament she had made for our tree. She noticed the music and said, "My church? The baby Jesus is coming to my church!" I said, "Yes, he is." Then she said, "Can he come to my house, too? Please? Pretty please?"

It's like the prophet said, *"Out of the mouths of infants and nursing babies you have prepared praise for yourself"* (Mt 21:16). I will give my life savings to anyone who can put it better than our daughter did. "The baby Jesus is coming to my church" she said. "Can he come to my house, too? Please? Pretty please?" That's the best theology of Christmas I've heard for a long, long time.

The baby Jesus is coming soon, to our churches and to our homes. And that's enough to make the angels sing. May God bless your Christmas.

—Paul Romstad
Central Lutheran Church
Minneapolis, Minnesota

December 24, 1997

Christmas Eve

Lessons

Pres/Meth/UCC/Luth	Isa 9:2–7	Titus 2:11–14	Lk 2:1–14 (15–20)
Roman Catholic	Isa 9:1–6	Titus 2:11–14	Lk 2:1–14
Episcopal	Isa 9:2–4, 6–7	Titus 2:11–14	Lk 2:1–14 (15–20)

Introduction to the Lessons

Lesson 1
Isaiah 9:2–7 **(Pres/Meth/UCC/Luth)**; *Isaiah 9:1–6* **(RC)**; *Isaiah 9:2–4, 6–7* **(Epis)**

Israel's message of hope is stated in classic terms. God's covenant with David is revisited with each new king. Now, this hope is realized in the birth of Christ, born to establish justice and righteousness without end.

Lesson 2
Titus 2:11–14 **(Pres/Meth/UCC/Luth/RC/Epis)**

God's revelation inspires us to see the Advent hope fulfilled in the coming of Christ, which promises us deliverance from all impurity and irreligion. Yet, we wait for the fulfillment of this promise, awaiting the final manifestation of God's glory.

Gospel
Luke 2:1–14 (15–20) **(Pres/Meth/UCC/Luth/Epis)**; *Luke 2:1–14* **(RC)**

Luke's narrative of the birth of Jesus places it squarely among the world's poorest, most powerless people. Historic data is linked with God's promise of a Davidic king who fulfills what has been, but promises what is yet to come. This birth transforms all things.

Theme

The birth of Christ brings all things together: the promises of God, and the hopes and expectations of the people. All rejoice, in heaven and on earth.

Thought for the Day

> O dearest Jesus, holy child,
> Prepare a bed, soft, undefiled,
> A holy shrine, within my heart,
> That you and I need never part. —Martin Luther, 1483–1546

Prayer of Meditation

Gracious Lord, you have gathered us around the manger of Bethlehem, standing with the world's poor, with animals, and with those dispossessed by the powers and principalities of this world. Warm us with the love that is here, seen in this child of mystery and promise, Jesus Christ our Lord. Amen.

Call to Worship

Leader: Beloved, let us love one another,
People: because love is from God; everyone who loves is born of God and knows God . . .
Leader: In this is love, not that we loved God but that he loved us and set his Son to be the atoning sacrifice for our sins.
People: Beloved, since God loved us so much, we also ought to love one another.
Leader: So we have known and believe the love that God has for us.
People: God is love and those who abide in love abide in God, and God abides in them.

—1 John 4:7–8, 10–11, 16

Prayer of Adoration

Gracious Lord, you have gathered the whole world around the manger in Bethlehem. Help the light of your love to shine brightly in all that we see, all that we hear, all that we smell, and touch, and taste, and feel that this holy child might transform our hearts into your likeness, made visible in this baby, Jesus Christ our Lord. Amen.

Prayer of Confession

Gracious Lord, the love of this night lays bare the lovelessness in our hearts. We have not loved you, we have not loved each other, we have not loved ourselves. And we have often been blind to our blindness. Fill us with the love of this holy night, that we might become children, women, and men whose love points others to your love given to us in this holy child of Bethlehem. Amen.

December 24, 1997
Christmas Eve

Prayer of Dedication of Gifts and Self

Gracious Lord, your gift in this child reveals the unworthiness of the gifts we offer. Yet, O Lord, you have promised to bless our gifts, making them instruments for your salvation in the world. Use these gifts, Lord; use us to bring the gladness of this holy night to all people everywhere. We pray in Jesus' holy name. Amen.

Sermon Summary

Our sadness, corresponding to the sadness in Mary and Joseph, is suddenly overwhelmed by the message of the angels promising us great joy, despite all things. Luke powerfully tells us the story that has brought hope to the world ever since, *"To you is born this day in the city of David a Savior, who is the Messiah, the Lord."*

Hymn of the Day

"In the Bleak Midwinter." Christina Rossetti set the Christmas story in her native England instead of Jerusalem in her poem of 1872. Later set to its familiar tune by Gustav Holst (1906), the stillness of the night and the depth of God's mystery is conveyed in this very unconventional Christmas hymn. Resisting the urge to grandeur and glory, the author helps us focus on the warmth of parental love, and on the simplicity of offering ourselves in service to the newborn child of God. This hymn is well used for "Blue Christmas" or "Longnight" services for those for whom Christmas brings hard memories or sadness. "In the Bleak Midwinter," like Christ himself, meets us where we are and walks us gently toward the light.

Children's Object Talk

Only a Baby?

Object

Secure two volunteers from the congregation: an infant (with his or her parents) and a tall, strong man or woman. Pictures from a magazine would also work, if you prefer.

Lesson

Jesus, the child of God, is the strength of God on earth.

I want you to look at two people (pictures) and tell me who you think is stronger and more powerful. Is it this newborn baby? Or this big, tall athletic man (woman)? (Allow the kids to giggle or laugh at the question and blurt out the obvious answer.)

Just wait a second. The question may be a little trickier than you think. A small baby can at times be more powerful than an adult.

If there was a room full of people and this baby was brought in, I think everyone would stop what they were doing to look at him (her). They would pinch his cheeks and say how cute he looks. Would they do that for this big, strong person? Of course not.

And if Mr. (Mrs.) _____ was sick, we'd probably say, "Oh, he (she) will get better soon." But if little _____ fusses or cries, people will pay very close attention to what is happening.

God came to earth to be with us in the form of Jesus. God came as a newborn baby. You might think that was silly. What can a baby do? Well, tonight the world is stopping what they are doing and celebrating this baby's birthday. They have done this for 2,000 years, and they'll keep on doing it as long as this world exists. That's how powerful the little baby Jesus is.

Sometimes the world treats you like little kids—not very important, not very powerful. But when you bring the pure and powerful love of Jesus to others in what you do or say, you are as important as anyone in the world.

It is baby Jesus' birthday. Power and joy come in sizes as small as children—even newborn babies! God bless you all this Christmas Eve and every day of your childhood.

—*Jon Temme*

The Sermon

God Steps In

Hymns
Beginning of Worship: "O Come, All Ye Faithful"
Sermon Hymn: "O Little Town of Bethlehem"
End of Worship: "Thy Little Ones, Dear Lord, Are We"

Scripture
Isaiah 9:2–7 (For sermon materials on Luke 2:1–14 [15–20], see the September 1997 issue of *The Clergy Journal* and on Titus 2:11–14, see the *1997 May/June Planning Issue* of *The Clergy Journal*.)

December 24, 1997
Christmas Eve

Sermon Text
"The people who walked in darkness have seen a great light..." (vs. 2).

Before I do anything else, allow me to wish you a merry and joyful Christmas. My own feelings this Christmas are on the painful side. I'm feeling a bit emotional for a white male over fifty. Frankly, I'm feeling sort of down. I'm weary from reading the newspapers: there is trouble in the country and in the world this Christmas. I'm weary from answering my telephone: a number of our church families are experiencing difficulty and tragedy this Christmas.

I'm remembering my father who was a pastor for over forty years. He told me one Christmas some years ago that Christmas was always hard on him because it made the sadness in the world seem even sadder. Last week I preached a Christmas sermon to a group of pastors. Just before we went into the church for the service, one of them said, "don't preach about sadness—we need cheering up this year." My point is that most of us are feeling the sadness in our world this Christmas, and if we aren't, we ought to be.

But if we are sad, this means that we qualify; we qualify for the Christmas message, which is a word of light spoken to a people in darkness: *"The people who walked in darkness have seen a great light,"* declares the prophet. *"... those who lived in a land of deep darkness—on them light has shined"* (vs. 2).

Luke, the author of our gospel tonight, knows how to tell a story. He sets the scene with an episode of governmental intrusion—a nationwide census—which requires Mary and Joseph to travel from Nazareth to Bethlehem, even though they don't have any money, and Mary is near the end of her pregnancy. He continues with a useless search for overnight accommodations. They can't find a room and end up in a stable, which is something like that bus shelter on the corner down the street, not even sealed against the weather. But now, things go from worse to worst: Mary goes into labor and gives birth, and lacking anything better, they put the baby in a manger, the trough used to feed the donkeys and horses. What a scene! Life for Mary and Joseph is about as desperate as life can get.

But now, Luke introduces the action. There were shepherds in the field outside Bethlehem. To understand the story, you need to know about shepherds. Luke tells us they lived in the fields with their sheep, and he means that literally. They were like cowboys in the old West who carried a bedroll and slept under the stars. Shepherds in Palestine were at the bottom of the social order. They weren't even allowed to testify in court because they couldn't be trusted. People thought of them in the same way people in our culture used to think about gypsies. So here were these shepherds, in the middle of the night, who suddenly are terrorized—literally—by angels and light.

The first word of the angel tells everything. In the original Greek, it's slang. The angel says *"phobeisthe,"* which means "settle down," "relax," "get hold of yourself." Our NRSV translators, who tend to be a little bit highbrow, put it this way: *"Do not be afraid; for see—I am bringing you good news of great joy for all the people: to you is born this day in the city of David a Savior, who is the Messiah, the Lord. This will be a sign for you: you will find a child wrapped in bands of cloth and lying in a manger"* (Lk 2:10–12).

At this point, the story seems almost like a Broadway musical, because the action breaks for a song. A chorus of angels sings *"Glory to God in the highest, and on earth peace among whom he favors."* Do you see what I mean about Luke knowing how to get a story told? It's really quite forceful.

But now, something else happens. Suddenly, it's over as quickly as it had begun. The angels are gone, and the shepherds decide to have a discussion. It's like those occasions when my brothers and I were children, and my father would give my mother a knowing look and say, "We need to talk." You remember what happened. They decided to go over to Bethlehem—which wasn't far—to see for themselves.

They left their sheep and arrived at the stable behind the inn. They found things just as the angel had told them they would: Mary, Joseph, and the baby lying in the manger. Luke tells us that they started telling their story to everyone who would listen. I can just imagine them saying, "You're not going to believe this, but . . ." And everyone was amazed. Luke now slips in the observation that Mary hadn't missed a thing—she knew. And finally, the story ends with the shepherds going back to their sheep, praising God, which for them was not exactly in character. But there you have it. Christmas in a nutshell, less than 300 words to tell a story that has given hope to the world ever since.

I started out by talking about sadness: the sadness of the world and my own sadness. And as we read the story, we can see our sadness reflected back to us in the terrible difficulties of Mary and Joseph. If anybody had good reason for sadness, they did. But that was only the beginning, because suddenly, God intervened, just to be sure that the

December 24, 1997
Christmas Eve

world got the message. And what was the message? Simply this: Christ is born this night for you. That's the same message the shepherds got, the same message that Mary and Joseph got, the same message that men, women, and children have gotten in the 2,000 years that have gone by since it happened. Christ is born this night for you: to be light for our darkness, to be hope for our fears, to be strength for our weakness.

Martin Luther, as you know, had a way of putting things that got people's attention. I like his explanation best. He said: "God feeds the whole world through a babe nursing at Mary's breast." And, if I can risk an unlikely connection, I find myself wanting to quote Jackie Gleason here, "How sweet it is."

May God richly bless your Christmas again this year with his gifts of faith, peace, and love.

—*Paul Romstad*
Central Lutheran Church
Minneapolis, Minnesota

December 25, 1997

Christmas Day

Lessons

Pres/Meth/UCC/Luth	Isa 52:7–10	Heb 1:1–4 (5–12)	Jn 1:1–14
Roman Catholic	Isa 52:7–10	Heb 1:1–6	Jn 1:1–18
Episcopal	Isa 52:7–10	Heb 1:1–12	Jn 1:1–14

Introduction to the Lessons

Lesson 1
Isaiah 52:7–10 **(Pres/Meth/UCC/Luth/RC/Epis)**
God's saving act is proclaimed to the world using the imagery of a festal procession, celebrating the return of the Lord to Zion. The people are invited to celebration at the Lord's coming.

Lesson 2
Hebrews 1:1–4 (5–12) **(Pres/Meth/UCC/Luth)**;
Hebrews 1:1–6 **(RC)**; *Hebrews 1:1–12* **(Epis)**
The time of fulfillment has come. Earlier stages of God's revelation were partial, but now God has acted to reveal the new order as Christ is enthroned at God's right hand.

Gospel
John 1:1–14 **(Pres/Meth/UCC/Luth/Epis)**;
John 1:1–18 **(RC)**
Matthew and Luke have begun their accounts of Jesus with his conception and birth, Mark with his baptism, but John goes back to creation. The "word" is a term that is informed by broad use in Hellenistic culture, now brought to clarity in the gospel message of salvation, as all is embodied in Christ. God's salvation is revealed in this holy birth.

Theme
God's central act of redemption has taken place in Christ. The light is shining in the darkness.

December 25, 1997
Christmas Day

Thought for the Day

How silently, how silently
The wondrous gift is giv'n!
So God imparts to human hearts
The blessing of his heav'n.
No ear may hear his coming;
But in this world of sin,
Where meek souls will receive him, still
The dear Christ enters in.
—Phillips Brooks, "O Little Town of Bethlehem"

Prayer of Meditation

Gracious God, through the beauty of this day, point our hearts to the glorious majesty of the holy child who has come to bring life and light to all. We thank you for all the blessings of this day. But above all, we thank you for the word become flesh, to dwell among us, full of grace and truth. Help us to receive him with joy and celebration. Through Jesus Christ our Lord. Amen.

Call to Worship

Leader: I will tell of the decree of the Lord:
People: You are my son; today I have begotten you.
Leader: Ask of me, and I will make the nations your heritage,
People: and the ends of the earth your possession.
Leader: You shall break them with a rod of iron,
People: and dash them in pieces like a potter's vessel.
Leader: Serve the Lord with fear, with trembling.
People: Happy are all who take refuge in him.
—Psalm 2:7–12

Prayer of Adoration

Gracious God, we are overwhelmed this day by the light that shines in the darkness. Enlighten our hearts that we might be full of your praise and make a joyful noise to you. We thank you for the birth of Christ. We thank you for the word of promise that comes to us in this holy child. We thank you for the salvation that you have revealed in the sight of all people. Quiet us, Lord, that we might be a people silenced by your marvelous light, through Jesus, the holy child of Bethlehem. Amen.

Prayer of Confession
Gracious Lord, dispel the busyness and confusion of our hearts that we might be filled with your peace and joy, held close in the beauty of your holiness. We offer to you the things that have blocked your light from shining through us: our greed, our blindness, our hardness of heart. Make us as windowpanes of clear glass that the glorious light of this day might shine also through us. And, above all, make us grateful, for Jesus' sake. Amen.

Prayer of Dedication of Gifts and Self
Lord of all things, we offer these gifts as tokens of the supreme gift you have given us this day. As we return to you what is yours, transform our hearts into beacons of your love that all people everywhere might be warmed by the light of the holy child of Bethlehem. By these gifts, Lord, let the hungry be fed, the lonely be comforted, and the lost be found. We thank you for the gift of this day, through Jesus Christ, our Lord. Amen.

Sermon Summary
Christmas fills us with memories and feelings. But ultimately, our memories are of God's powerful act of salvation in the birth of Christ, which brought hope to the world for us. The birth of Christ kindled a light that shines in the darkness of our hearts, the darkness of the world, and the darkness of human confusion. For unto us a Savior is born. The Lord has returned to Zion, and we are filled with songs of joy and overwhelmed with hope.

Hymn of the Day
"Good Christian Friends, Rejoice!" Also known as *"In Dulci Jubilo,"* the words for this hymn date back to medieval German mystic Heirich Suso (d. 1366), who had a vision of angels singing this carol and who invited him to join their joyful dance. The tune is contemporary with the words and carries all the joy of those angels "tripping round." Not to be sung slowly or timidly, today we sing it out loud and clear that a Savior is born!

December 25, 1997
Christmas Day

Children's Object Talk

An Unbreakable Gift

Object
A toy or game that can be "broken" and then put back together in working order (a toy with batteries, an action figure or truck where a part might be taken off and put back on).

Lesson
Christmas celebrates how God the creator restores the creation forever.

Has everyone opened their gifts yet? I know some of you did last night, and some of you have been up early this morning opening presents. It's great to get gifts, isn't it?

Sometimes gifts can easily break. Look at this truck (toy, doll). It was a nice gift, but now it's broken. The wheel (leg, part) fell off. What are we going to do with this now? (Children may offer suggestions like throw it out, fix it, give it to someone else.)

Some of you might think that all you can do is throw this out. But we can do something else with this gift. We can fix it (do so now). Hey, look! The gift is just as good as new. We know that it can be broken, so we'll have to take extra special care. But we also know that it can be fixed and restored, and that's sure good news.

That's the good news of the gift of Jesus that we celebrate every Christmas. Long before Jesus was born, God created a world of life and love. It was a beautiful gift. But that gift was damaged and destroyed by selfishness and the bad things that people did. People destroyed God's good gift.

What did God do? Throw the gift away? I suppose God could have chosen to do so. But instead, God came to earth to fix it. Jesus is God's son. He came to show people like you and me that we can live in a different way. We can love others, forgive others, and protect God's creation. We aren't perfect "fixer-uppers" of God's world. God is working each day to restore us and our world to be a better place. God even came to earth by sending Jesus. For that Christmas gift we can say only one thing: thank you, God, thank you!

—Jon Temme

The Sermon

Announcing Hope

Hymns
Beginning of Worship: "Love Came Down at Christmas"
Sermon Hymn: "Your Little Ones, Dear Lord, Are We"
End of Worship: "Of the Father's Love Begotten"

Scripture
Isaiah 52:7–10 (For sermon materials on John 1:1–14, see the September 1997 issue of *The Clergy Journal* and on Hebrews 1:1–4 [5–12], see the *1997 May/June Planning Issue* of *The Clergy Journal.*)

Sermon Text
"The Lord has bared his holy arm before the eyes of all the nations; and all the ends of the earth shall see the salvation of our God" (vs. 10).

It's Christmas again, and today, as always, I am filled with feelings. So many of those feelings are tied up with memories.

I'm remembering so many of the people who were part of my childhood Christmases who are no longer with us—my grandmother did Christmas dinners like none in history. Christmas was beautiful on my grandmother's table.

I'm remembering some of the Christmases I spent away from my family home. We'd pile the kids in the car and drive all night to Minneapolis, just to make it home.

I'm remembering the Christmas we spent in the hospital with my dad as one of the most moving Christmases I can remember.

I'm remembering Christmases when our children were small. We had to keep the Christmas tree in a playpen to keep the children from pulling it down.

I'm thinking about the year that our stove went berserk, and the meatballs burned to a crisp while we were in church, and we came home to find the house filled with smoke, our smoke detectors blaring, and our wonderful canary dead of smoke inhalation.

I'm even thinking about the year our kitten climbed the Christmas tree and tipped it over, tempting us to commit felicide.

The point is that Christmas is such a wonderful time, and I suspect that all of us have vivid memories of Christmases past— memories that flood our thoughts every Christmas—memories that give us much to think about.

December 25, 1997
Christmas Day

Christmas, you see, is a time for the heart. Some of the happiest hours of our entire lives—and some of the saddest hours too—are connected with Christmas, for Christmas, more than any other time of the year, activates our hearts. We remember marvelous times with people we've loved; and we are sometimes filled with pain over loved ones we've lost. Most of all, we remember our pure joy and delight as children. Christmas is so very much oriented to the heart, to feelings, to emotions.

But, if we're going to talk about remembering, there's something else, too. Tonight, we remember as a community, a community with a life that goes back nearly 2,000 years (and long before that, actually). Our memories are tied to a story—a story of a mother, a baby, a father, a star, a stable, some angels, some shepherds, some animals, and a lot of surprises.

The prophet who looks forward to this day breaks forth with deep feelings: *"How beautiful upon the mountains are the feet of the messenger who announces peace, who brings good news, who announces salvation"* (Isa 52:7).

One of my friends tells about Christmases when he was a child living on a farm. At 11 P.M., after the family had come home from church and finished dinner, and exchanged gifts, his dad would take all the children—my friend, his brothers, sisters, and cousins — out to the barn and read them the Christmas gospel. To this day, he says, the barn that smells of manure, and hay, and sweaty animals reminds him of Christmas.

There's something so humble—so earthy and ordinary—about the story of Christmas. It isn't something that happened in Palm Springs among the people of the jet set, with live coverage by the TV networks. It isn't something that people bought new clothes to attend; it isn't something that called for valet parking.

It happened, you see, among the poorest of the poor, in a grungy, out-of-the-way village in the west bank, in a dank, humid, manure-scented cave that was used as an animal shelter.

We can't begin to understand until we can get ourselves away from the exotic images of Christmas cards and creches, which so often make Bethlehem look like the Taj Mahal, and make Joseph and Mary look like Ken and Barbie, and make the animals look like stuffed toys—all of which is far, far away from the reality. Joseph and Mary are the commonest of people, totally without privilege, strangers among strangers, and caught in primitive, agonizing poverty.

I walked through the maternity floor at a local hospital

the other day. Let me tell you—that place is really clean. It's like one of those Japanese baths in which you can't bathe until you've first taken a bath—clean!

But the birth of Jesus, in stark contrast to that, took place in an animal shed, with no doctor present, with the baby laid in a feeding trough that was roughly as clean as the dog's dish before it's washed.

We talk about being tired from cooking, shopping, wrapping presents, and partying. After all of this, Joseph and Mary were exhausted.

But at the very center of it all is the story about hope, which—to me at least—is quite astonishing. It is a word of hope addressed to the lowliest of the lowly, the poorest of the poor, the neediest of the needy. A word addressed to every human being; a word addressed to you and to me.

Think of it. The eternal son of God, born in a barn—literally, the word became flesh.

Paul helps us understand: *"God chose what is low and despised in the world . . . to reduce to nothing things that are, so that no one might boast in the presence of God. He is the source of your life in Christ Jesus, who became for us wisdom from God, and righteousness and sanctification and redemption, in order that, as it is written, 'Let the one who boasts, boast in the Lord'"* (1 Cor 1:28–31).

God chose what is low and despised in the world . . . for the world's salvation.

Even the old carol, honored by centuries of use by the church, puts it well:

The heart is tired at Bethlehem,
No human dream unbroken stands,
Yet here the radiant angels fly,
And hope renewed cries out, "Amen."

Somehow, in spite of everything, this is a story about hope, a word about hope addressed to people like you and me who struggle with many things—like Joseph and Mary. Joseph struggled with the meaning of a pregnant fiance; Mary struggled with difficult travel in the last days of her pregnancy; both struggled with an early delivery that couldn't have come at a more inconvenient time. You and I struggle with things too: health, job, marriage, kids, finances, school, and a whole lot of other things.

And yet, the angel said, *"Today in the city of David, is born a savior, who is Christ the Lord. And this shall be a great joy to all the people."* God's promise of hope, announced as good news by the messenger who invites us to break into joyful song.

Ultimately, you see, the miracle of Christmas is realized

December 25, 1997
Christmas Day

in what is born in us: faith—believing God; hope—trusting God for our future; and love—embracing each other with arms of compassion and caring.

Take a moment now for a quick time out. Forget your presents, forget your company, forget your dinner, forget the weather, forget the future, and think of just this one thing: Christ is born this day for you—*your* Savior, *your* hope, *your* strength.

—Paul Romstad
Central Lutheran Church
Minneapolis, Minnesota

December 28, 1997

1st Sunday after Christmas
RC: Feast of the Holy Family—Not listed

Lessons
Pres/Meth/UCC/Luth	1 Sam 2:18–20, 26	Col 3:12–17	Lk 2:41–52
Episcopal	Isa 61:10—62:3	Gal 3:23–25; 4:4–7	Jn 1:1–18

Introduction to the Lessons
Lesson 1
(1) *1 Samuel 2:18–20, 26* **(Pres/Meth/UCC/Luth)**
Samuel, a son born to the faithful woman Hannah, grows before God under the supervision of Eli the priest.

(2) *Isaiah 61:10—62:3* **(Epis)**
The prophet rejoices in the vindication of Jerusalem and the salvation of Zion, following the hardships of the exile in Babylon.

Lesson 2
(1) *Colossians 3:12–17* **(Pres/Meth/UCC/Luth)**
The saints at Colossae are admonished, as God's chosen ones, to clothe themselves in love and to live in peace, guided by the word of Christ.

(2) *Galatians 3:23–25, 4:4–7* **(Epis)**
Paul describes the difference between law and faith, a differentiation made possible by the coming of Christ.

Gospel
(1) *Luke 2:41–52* **(Pres/Meth/UCC/Luth)**
The boy Jesus, at the age of twelve, stays behind in Jerusalem after the festival of Passover and astonishes the teachers in the temple with his wisdom.

(2) *John 1:1–18* **(Epis)**
In this great hymn to the power of the word, John sings the praises of the word made flesh.

December 28, 1997
1st Sunday after Christmas

Theme
Language both defines and creates faith.

Thought for the Day
We are responsible for the words that we use, for our language defines who we are and has the power to redefine who we are in relationship to others.

Prayer of Meditation
Grace-filled and grace-giving parent, our lives have been filled to abundance, if not to confusion, in this holiday season. Help us to focus this day on that most precious gift which is beyond all gifts, Jesus Christ, our Savior and our Lord. Amen.

Call to Worship
> Praise the Lord!
> Praise the Lord from the heavens;
> > praise him in the heights!
> Praise him, all his angels;
> > praise him, all his host!
>
> Praise him, sun and moon;
> > praise him, all you shining stars!
> Praise him, you highest heavens,
> > and you waters above the heavens! —Psalm 148:1–4

Prayer of Adoration
Like the shepherds and wise ones of old, we, too, bow before your throne of straw to worship and adore you. By your simple birth you have transformed all that is common into all that is holy. Transform us as well by the power of your word made flesh, that we, too, may be sanctified. Amen.

Prayer of Confession
How easily we are distracted, how prone to forget, how willing to compromise and to turn from your presence, gracious Lord. Even in this holy season, our hearts and minds are turned from you and from our sisters and brothers, toward that which is ours alone. In this

season of love, forgive us our selfishness, that we might be instruments of your grace to all in and of your creation. Amen.

Prayer of Dedication of Gifts and Self

What can I give him, poor as I am?
If I were a shepherd, I would bring a lamb;
if I were a Wise Man, I would do my part;
yet what I can I give him: give my heart.

—Christina G. Rossetti, 1872,
The United Methodist Hymnal (1989),
#221, stanza 4

Sermon Summary

Words, like all sign-symbols, have both the power to point the way—to give focus and direction, to reveal a greater reality—and the energy to transform and make new. Paul's words to the Colossians contain the potential and promise to form God's people into new creatures in Christ.

Hymn of the Day

"My Life Flows On (How Can I Keep from Singing?)." "How Can I Keep from Singing?" was a popular hymn in many nineteenth-century hymnals, and the original authorship is disputed. Despite this, the tune and text are wonderfully reflective and full of strong praise and assurance, a theme that fits well as we bask in the light of Christmas and prepare for the gospel stories to lead us through the tribulation of Jesus' life and eventually to the cross.

Children's Object Talk

Time to Get Dressed

Object
Protective clothing appropriate to the climate.

Lesson
The Christian is clothed with spiritual values as gifts from God.

Did some of you receive clothes for Christmas gifts? (Allow the children to volunteer answers.) I'll tell you a "not-so-secret" secret.

When I was a child I never liked getting clothes for Christmas. I wanted toys and games.

But let me tell you another

secret. If it weren't for the right kinds of clothes that your family gives you, you could get very sick. Imagine it is freezing cold and snowing, and you do not have a coat, boots, or mittens to wear when you walk to school.

The right kinds of clothes are important, but not just for our bodies. The Bible tells us that God gives us "clothes for our minds and souls" too. These clothes are not like the ones we actually wear, but are things we should "put on" if we are going to live a healthy, happy life.

What are those things? The Bible says we should clothe ourselves in compassion, kindness, humility, meekness, patience, and love.

Some of those are big words. Let's try to find some other words for them. *Compassion* means knowing that if someone is sad or hurting, they could use a kind word or caring action from you. *Humility* is when you don't think only of yourself, you think of others too. *Meekness* means being patient and kind.

If you have those kinds of loving thoughts, then you are dressed in what you need to live a life that pleases God and shows love for others. If we follow Jesus, we will be dressed just right!

—*Jon Temme*

The Sermon

Words of Faith

Hymns
Beginning of Worship: "We Would See Jesus"
Sermon Hymn: "O Little Town of Bethlehem"
End of Worship: "We Meet You, O Christ"

Scripture
Colossians 3:12–17 (For sermon materials on Luke 2:41–52, see the September 1997 issue and on 1 Samuel 2:18–20, 26, see the *1997 May/June Planning Issue* of *The Clergy Journal*.)

Sermon Text
"As God's chosen ones, holy and beloved, clothe yourselves with compassion, kindness, humility, meekness, and patience" (vs. 12).

What if, during the night, a road crew changed all the signs along the interstate, and on your way to worship, you discovered that your exit was now named for a town forty miles away? What if, without notice, your street's name and house number were suddenly, unilaterally changed by the postal service? What if the phone company changed everyone's phone number and would not issue a new directory? What if?

Life would be pretty confusing if such changes did take place. It would be difficult for strangers to find your town, your street, your house, or even to call and indicate they were lost and needed directions. Without such symbols as signs, names, or numbers, life would be most chaotic, indeed.

Sign-symbols are important to our ability to function effectively. They tell us where we are, where to go, and how to get there. But sign-symbols are not all there is. As important as they are, they only point us to that far greater reality which they name or number. Because the sign on the interstate is incorrect does not mean this is no longer your town. Because your street name and number are altered does not mean that you no longer live there. If the sign-symbols are changed, it does not modify who you are. Sign-symbols are important, not only as things in themselves, but in terms of the reality toward which they point. It is very important to know this truth when dealing with our biblical witness and the many sign-symbols that are part of our faith.

On the main road south of the city of Jerusalem, just beyond Rachel's Tomb, there is a sign that has never failed to quicken the spirit, excite the imagination, and heighten expectation. The sign shows a division in the road: Hebron is straight ahead, and to the left is Bethlehem. The sign is so powerful that it has brought tears to my eyes. A mile and a half later, you are standing in Bethlehem's Manger Square, facing the Church of the Holy Nativity.

Having entered the door through the shortened gate, forcing all pilgrims to bow down, you come into a huge and ancient space, dating from the fourth century covering the place where Jesus was born. The guide wants you to look at the mosaics on the floor or the painting on the ceiling above. The Orthodox priest wants to sell you some candles. But you know what you have come to see and to experience. All the signs have pointed in the right direction.

Descending the steps into the grotto below, you come to the sacred place, now covered with a marble floor and a silver star, lit with votive candles, the air ripened with incense. You kneel down, reach to the star, and touch the place where we remember the

December 28, 1997
1st Sunday after Christmas

birth of our Savior. Someone starts singing "O Little Town of Bethlehem." The signs are true; they have pointed the way.

As I stated earlier, sign-symbols point to a reality larger than themselves, but they also have a power of their own. Language is a sign-symbol. Words describe, they point to reveal while at the same time, they have a power all their own. If I say, "I love you," I create something that did not exist before—words have altered our relationship. Our biblical witness says that when God speaks, things happen: creation happens, redemption happens, grace happens.

What shall be our words, our sign-symbols, in this Christmas season; gifts in their own right and gifts that point to a reality larger than themselves or ourselves?

Saint Paul, writing to the Colossians, gives instruction as to the nature, the substance of new life in Christ. The words, the sign-symbols he chooses have both the energy to describe and to create this new state of grace. Hear them, receive them again: compassion, kindness, humility, meekness, patience, forgiveness, and above all, love. Like Ephesians, Colossians is an epistle which is catechetical in its structure and intent, an instrument whereby the faithful are admonished, warned, and formed by the words of faith, as that faith is interpreted to them by their mentor, Paul. An epistle is a kind of public letter meant to be read and shared among the congregation in the firm conviction that in hearing these words, the good news, Jesus Christ might be revealed and in his revelation, the congregation may be formed into his likeness.

If the sign-symbols of our faith become the only language by which we are known by others and by which we know ourselves, then Christmas, the coming of Christ in and through our lives, would be a year-round event.

"As God's chosen ones, holy and beloved, clothe yourselves with compassion, kindness, humility, meekness, and patience."

—John L. Topolewski
Vestal United Methodist Church
Vestal, New York

January 4, 1998

2nd Sunday after Christmas

Lessons
Pres/Meth/UCC/Luth	Jer 31:7–14	Eph 1:3–14	Jn 1:(1–9) 10–18
Episcopal	Jer 31:7–14	Eph 1:3–6, 15–19a	Mt 2:13–15, 19–23

Introduction to the Lessons
Lesson 1
Jeremiah 31:7–14 **(Pres/Meth/UCC/Luth/Epis)**
In spite of Israel's present troubles, the prophet presents God's promise of the restoration of God's people to their homeland.

Lesson 2
Ephesians 1:3–14 **(Pres/Meth/UCC/Luth)**;
Ephesians 1:3–6, 15–19a **(Epis)**
Following a greeting to saints at Ephesus, the author (Paul?) describes the place of Christ in the history of salvation and prays for spiritual wisdom for his readers.

Gospel
(1) *John 1:(1–9) 10–18* **(Pres/Meth/UCC/Luth)**
In this, the prologue of the gospel, John sings the praises of God's word made flesh.

(2) *Matthew 2:13–15, 19–23* **(Epis)**
After the wise men depart from Bethlehem, Joseph is warned in a dream to flee with Mary and the infant Jesus to Egypt, to escape the wrath of Herod. Following Herod's death, the family settles in Galilee.

Theme
We are called to unity in both service and love.

January 4, 1998
2nd Sunday after Christmas

Thought for the Day

Christian unity is not a matter of low priority that can be easily set aside. It is at the heart of our understanding of the gospel. It is the earnest prayer of Jesus and the teaching of Paul. To ignore it, dismiss it, or treat it as a nonessential is to do so at our own peril and risk.

Prayer of Meditation

Focus me, gracious Lord, that I might encounter the word in today's many words, the truth above all that claims self-justification, the Spirit that quickens both heart and life, that I may be made more holy by your grace. Amen.

Call to Worship

> Sing to the Lord with thanksgiving;
> > make melody to our God on the lyre.
> He covers the heavens with clouds,
> > prepares rain for the earth,
> > makes grass grow on the hills.
> ... the Lord takes pleasure in those who fear him,
> > in those who hope in his steadfast love.
> > > —Psalm 147:7–8, 11

Prayer of Adoration

Gracious and loving God, we are bold to stand before your throne, for we know by faith that we are your children, your inheritance, your people of a new covenant. Yet our boldness is not brash, for you alone are God and worthy to be praised. Amen.

Prayer of Confession

You call us to account, O Lord, and no excuse, justification, or equivocation will stand before your judgment. You know us as we are; help us to know you in the same manner, that in the confession of our sin and in the absolution of your grace, we may become what you would have us be: holy. Amen.

Prayer of Dedication of Gifts and Self

We are your people and these are our gifts. Use both to bring honor to your name and vitality to our witness; through Jesus Christ our Lord. Amen.

Sermon Summary
The writer of the Epistle to the Ephesians affirms, in a catechetical, hymnic form, the essential oneness of all people who share the faith of Christ, thereby calling us to account in the present for the divisions within Christendom. Unity in Christ is not an option, but a mandate.

Hymn of the Day
"Go Tell It on the Mountain." Another gem from our African-American Heritage, "Go Tell It on the Mountain" lets us follow the commandment in Jeremiah to "Sing aloud with gladness!" One author notes that this is one of the few spirituals that was sung both inside and outside of the African-American churches (most were not originally sung as hymns, but more often as work or leisure tunes). An adaptable tune, this hymn works especially well with rhythm instruments and enthusiastic accompaniment.

Children's Object Talk

Christmas Every Day

Object
Four small boxes in Christmas gift-wrapping. Inside each box put one message: "Child of God," "Forgiveness of Sins," "Part of God's Plan," "Inheritor of God's Kingdom."

Lesson
As children of God, we daily receive gifts through our relationship with Jesus.

Christmas has come and gone, hasn't it? Soon you will be (or, already are) back to school. I imagine many of you have taken down your Christmas decorations. All the Christmas presents are opened for sure! Right?

Wrong? Yes, wrong. For friends of Jesus, the Christmas never ends. Let me prove it.

Here are some more presents to open. (Distribute the boxes and have the children open them one-by-one as you ask them to in the order below.)

Long ago, a great Christian teacher named Paul reminded his fellow believers of the gifts they could enjoy every day. Do you want to see what they are? Let's open the first gift "Child of God." Thanks to Jesus, we are children of God every day of our lives. That means God always listens to our prayers. We have loving care from our Christians friends like those here in church today and millions more you can't see in churches around the world.

"Forgiveness of Sins." Wow! What a gift—we sure can use it every day. It's the gift of being forgiven for all the bad things we say and do just like we should forgive others who say and do bad things.

"Part of God's Plan." It is sad being left out of family or friends' plans. Paul in the Bible taught us that you and I are always part of God's plan. We count!

"Inheritors of God's Kingdom." That's a really special gift. It means that we will always be with God, when we are alive and when we die.

These things are gifts from God to enjoy every day, not just at Christmas.

—*Jon Temme*

The Sermon

God's Good Pleasure, and Ours

Hymns
Beginning of Worship: "Come, Let Us Join Our Friends Above"
Sermon Hymn: "We Believe in One True God"
End of Worship: "Many Gifts, One Spirit"

Scripture
Ephesians 1:3–14 (For sermon materials on Jeremiah 31:7–14, see the October 1997 and the *1997 May/June Planning Issue* of *The Clergy Journal*.)

Sermon Text
"... *With all wisdom and insight he has made known to us the mystery of his will, according to his good pleasure that he set forth in Christ, as a plan for the fullness of time, to gather all things in him, things in heaven and things on earth*" (vss. 8b–10).

A good friend who teaches English at an area university asks his students at the beginning of each semester to write down the first verse of as many poems as they know within a five-minute time frame. Many simply stare at a blank page, a few know some rhymes, while others have no difficulty at all with the challenge. For this last group, the most common form of poetry recalled is the hymn, the poetry of faith. These students are able to recall and record those verses that serve as both a witness to and a testimony of a people on a journey of faith.

Those of us who stand within the Wesleyan tradition are greatly blessed by a rich hymnody grounded, to a large extent, upon the contributions of John and Charles Wesley. Both brothers were deeply convinced of the use and value of hymns for Christian instruction. In addition to those hymns already in place, John held special regard for his brother's hymns, as they were permeated with Scripture, moved the people, and united Methodists together in both worship and service. In 1780, the first major Methodist hymnbook, *A Collection of Hymns for the Use of the People Called Methodists,* was published. From the very early days of the movement to the present, the Wesleyan tradition has been known for its singing, and John Wesley's "Directions for Singing," first penned in 1761, are reprinted in our *United Methodist Hymnal* today.

Although there is much scholarly debate concerning the authorship of Ephesians, and its primacy over, or dependence upon, Colossians, there is near consensus on the assumption that this epistle is catechetical in form and character. It has been written for instruction's sake. The first three chapters are a thanksgiving, and the last three an admonition. But more focused still is the finding that within chapters one through three, there are four passages (today's lesson included) that are early Christian hymns: 1:3–12 and 20–23; 2:4–10 and 14–18. These are hymns to instruct, hymns to inspire, hymns to unite in service and love.

What is it that the author of Ephesians seeks to teach, in both poetry and prose? What word of instruction, inspiration, and union does he seek to convey? William Barclay summarizes the author's intention this way (I quote this passage without correcting the use of exclusive nouns and pronouns):

"The key thought of Ephesians is the gathering together of all things in Jesus Christ. In nature as it is without Christ there is nothing but disunity and disharmony; it is 'red in tooth and claw.' Man's dominion has broken the social union which should exist between man and the beasts; man is divided from man; class from class; nation from nation; ideology from ideology; Gentile from Jew. What is true of the world of outer nature is true of human nature. In every man there is a tension; every man is a walking civil war, torn between the desire for good and the desire for evil; he hates his sins and loves them at one and the same time. According to both Greek and Jewish thought in the time of Paul, this disharmony extends even to the heavenly places. A cosmic battle is raging between the powers of evil and

January 4, 1998
2nd Sunday after Christmas

the powers of good; between God and the demons. Worst of all there is disharmony between God and man. Man, who was meant to be in fellowship with God, is estranged from him.

"So, then, in this world without Christ, there is nothing but disunity. That disunity is not God's purpose but it can become a unity only when all things are united in Christ . . . The central thought of *Ephesians* is the realization of the disunity in the universe and the conviction that it can become unity only when everything is united in Christ." (William Barclay, *The Letters to the Galatians and Ephesians,* rev. ed. [Philadelphia: The Westminster Press, 1976], p. 66.)

This central theme is joined midway in today's hymn of instruction. *"With all wisdom and insight he has made known to us the mystery of his will, according to his good pleasure that he set forth in Christ, as a plan for the fullness of time, to gather all things in him, things in heaven and things on earth"* (vss. 8–10).

God's good pleasure is that all things shall be gathered in him:

". . . in Christ Jesus you who once were far off have been brought near by the blood of Christ" (Eph 2:13).

". . . in his flesh he has made both groups into one and has broken down the dividing wall, that is, the hostility between us" (Eph 2:14).

". . . you are no longer strangers and aliens, but you are citizens with the saints and also members of the household of God" (Eph 2:19).

". . . the Gentiles have become fellow heirs, members of the same body, and sharers in the promise in Christ Jesus through the gospel" (Eph 3:6).

"There is one body and one Spirit . . . one Lord, one faith, one baptism, one God and Father of all . . ." (Eph 4:4–5).

Such is the witness, the almost creedal affirmation of Ephesians, that in Christ all may be one.

But we are not one, not one as our Lord prayed in the garden, not one in our witness to the faith, not one in the cultural wars that engulf us. Almost from the beginning, starting with Peter and Paul, we have been divided, to say nothing of Constantinople and Rome, or Wittenberg, Geneva, or Oxford. Even in our own time, when so much of the ongoing debate that lingered following the Reformation is no longer vital, we are divided; not just between traditions, but within them, as well. We try to make distinctions between what is essential to the faith, and what is not, but such distinctions are not always possible. It depends on whose essential or ox gets gored.

Martin Marty, in a *M.E.M.O.* column, points out:

"Gary Wills has said that though he is a mainstream Catholic in theology he never gets asked about the Trinity, incarnation and the like. Abortion, birth control, and euthanasia are the obsessive themes of the times. You can't fill a phone both with audiences for discussion of the Trinity or the Two Natures of Christ. You can't find an auditorium big enough for voyeurs of the fight over sex and authority." (*The Christian Century*, October 23, 1996, p. 1023.)

Yet, is it not God's intention that we should be united in the faith? We may not always agree on how that faith comes to expression, but are we not instructed, indeed required, to yearn for and grow toward God's good pleasure to gather all things to Godself? Is not the good news, upon which our various traditions, attitudes, and faith journeys are based, that in Christ we can be one?

What can we say to each other—so long divided, set in our ways, steeped in our traditions, often argumentative if not hostile—in light of the catechetical nature of the epistle whose main point is the unity effected by God's grace in Jesus Christ? How shall we sing the Lord's song in our land, if not in terms of that ancient hymn of the church:

"With all wisdom and insight he has made known to us the mystery of his will, according to his good pleasure that he set forth in Christ, as a plan for the fullness of time, to gather all things in him, things in heaven and on earth" (vss. 8–10).

—*John L. Topolewski*
Vestal United Methodist Church
Vestal, New York

January 6, 1998

Epiphany
RC: Use January 4, 1998

Lessons
Pres/Meth/UCC/Luth	Isa 60:1–6	Eph 3:1–12	Mt 2:1–12
Roman Catholic	Isa 60:1–6	Eph 3:1–3a, 5–6	Mt 2:1–12
Episcopal	Isa 60:1–6, 9	Eph 3:1–12	Mt 2:1–12

Introduction to the Lessons
Lesson 1
Isaiah 60:1–6 **(Pres/Meth/UCC/Luth/RC)**;
Isaiah 60:1–6, 9 **(Epis)**
The prophet sings of the glory of Jerusalem, with the risen Zion welcoming her children home after their long years of exile in Babylon.

Lesson 2
Ephesians 3:1–12 **(Pres/Meth/UCC/Luth/Epis)**;
Ephesians 3:1–3a, 5–6 **(RC)**
The author (Paul?) speaks of his imprisonment and the mystery of Christ, of whose gospel he has become a servant.

Gospel
Matthew 2:1–12 **(Pres/Meth/UCC/Luth/RC/Epis)**
The mission of the Magi and the treachery of King Herod are described by Matthew, as part of his story of the birth of Jesus.

Theme
Do we define the nature of our discipleship as choice or privilege?

Thought for the Day
Sacrifice is not in vogue, as if it ever was! Yet sacrifice, stewardship, self-denial, even obedience are among the core values of our faith. There is much that demands our time and attention, but little, relatively speaking, that requires deep and abiding commitment. Lest we be overworked

and underemployed, it is our responsibility, as individuals and as a community, to sort it all out.

Prayer of Meditation

Help me, Lord of mercy and grace, and those around me, to discover anew who we are and whose we are. If magi can worship, bow down, and present their gifts to Bethlehem's child, help me to know what is required, in Jesus' name and for his sake. Amen.

Call to Worship

> Give the king your justice, O God,
> and your righteousness to a king's son.
> For he delivers the needy when they call,
> the poor and those who have no helper.
> He has pity on the weak and the needy,
> and saves the lives of the needy.
> From oppression and violence he redeems their life;
> and precious is their blood in his sight.
> —Psalm 72:1, 12–14

Prayer of Adoration

At your crib the Magi worshiped, laying themselves at your feet. In such a humble setting, even the mighty are brought low, awed by the magnitude of your presence—the one to save the people. May we too have the wisdom to receive, to worship, and to follow you. Amen.

Prayer of Confession

Too often, most often, we have allowed the holiday season to serve as an excuse for self-indulgence. Forgive us, we pray, and help us to know that it is in serving others, and not ourselves, that we may be renewed by your grace. Amen.

Prayer of Dedication of Gifts and Self

We lay before your throne our gifts, O Lord. May they be to you as gold, frankincense, and myrrh, our tokens of worship and praise. Amen.

January 6, 1998
Epiphany

Sermon Summary
In the third chapter of Ephesians, Paul (setting aside all debate as to the epistle's real authorship) defines the nature of his ministry. In contrast to many of our secularized understandings of vocation, Paul places before his hearers his own self-knowledge concerning his labor.

Hymn of the Day
"Brightest and Best." This special Epiphany hymn was the first ever written by Reginald Heber, a priest in the Church of England in the late eighteenth century who wrote nearly sixty hymns including "Holy! Holy! Holy!" The straightforward imagery in this song of the Magi was long excluded from many hymnals because some felt he was advocating the worship of a star. The phrase "sons of the morning" had its origins in Isaiah 1:4–12 referring to God's angels, but has now variously evolved into either "suns of the morning" or "stars of the morning." Set to a variety of tunes, the words draw us with the question, what can we offer?

Children's Object Talk

Now I Can See

Object
A box containing a piece of paper large enough for all the children to see with the message, "God loves you every day—and forever!"

Lesson
The light of Christ reveals the mystery of faith.

I have a very important message to share with you today on this special day—Epiphany. Here it is (hold up box). Can you read it? You can't? Let me take it out of the box into the light. Now can you see what it says? Yes, it says "God loves you every day—and forever!"

What a great and comforting message that is. When we are sad, that news can cheer us up. When we are happy, it can help us show our thanks and praise to God. When we're scared, it can take away our fear.

But that message would remain a mystery if we didn't have any light to shine upon it. That's what Epiphany is all about. *Epiphany* means revealing or unveiling something hidden. When Jesus came to earth he put a bright light upon the love of

God for us. That love was always there, but we could not see it.

Jesus did and said many things to help us see clearly that God loves us—now and forever.

You can be a light for others to help them see that too. How? Like Jesus, you can show that important message in all you say and do.

—*Jon Temme*

The Sermon

Burden or Gift?

Hymns
Beginning of Worship: "What Child Is This?"
Sermon Hymn: "I Want to Walk as a Child of the Light"
End of Worship: "We Three Kings"

Scripture
Ephesians 3:1–12 (For sermon materials on Isaiah 60:1–6, see the September 1997 issue and on Matthew 2:1–12, see the *1997 May/June Planning Issue* of *The Clergy Journal*.)

Sermon Text
"Of this gospel I have become a servant according to the gift of God's grace that was given to me by the working of his power" (vs. 7).

The interview took a strange turn, and I was both surprised and disappointed. Along with other colleagues, I was on one of our seminary campuses meeting with students who had expressed an interest in our Conference and the possibility of ministry with us.

The interviewee came highly recommended, among the "brightest and best," a second career, focused individual who would be "a great asset to the church." My expectations were high, and, at least initially, well met. But with her response to an inquiry about her call to ministry, our time together began to turn.

Instead of first speaking about what she was moving to, she spoke about what she was moving from and the great costs associated with the decision. Her previous salary, benefits, position, office space, support staff, etc., all became indications of how much she was giving up in order to pursue this new career direction.

January 6, 1998
Epiphany

Then she went on to speak of all she had to offer the church, based upon her prior levels of responsibility and demonstrated effectiveness. Finally, she indicated that if we had a position to match her ability, she might consider ministry among us.

I am not so naive as to think that there were not many dynamics operative in the interview, and that we had both brought different expectations to our encounter. Nevertheless, even with an acknowledgment that many of these interviews can be interpreted as male-dominated power relationships, it was very apparent that arrogance is no respecter of gender.

In contrast, hear some of the words the commentator William Barclay uses to describe Saint Paul, as he is revealed in today's epistle lesson:

"He [Paul] regarded himself as the transmitter of grace. When Paul meets the leaders of the Church to talk over with them his mission to the Gentiles, he talks about the gospel of the uncircumcision being committed to him and of 'the grace that was given to me' (*Galatians* 2:7, 9). When he writes to the Romans, he speaks of 'the grace given to me by God' (*Romans* 15:15). Paul saw his task as that of being a channel of God's grace . . . It is one of the great facts of the Christian life that we have been given the precious things of Christianity in order to share them with others. It is one of the great warnings of the Christian life that if we keep them to ourselves we lose them.

"He regarded himself as having the dignity of service. Paul says that he was made a servant by the free gift of the grace of God. He did not think of his service as a wearisome duty but as a radiant privilege. It is often astonishingly difficult to persuade people to serve the Church. To teach for God, to sing for God, to administer affairs for God, to speak for God, to visit those in poverty and distress for God, to give of our time and our talent and our substance for God, should not be counted a duty to be coerced out of us; it is a privilege which we should be glad to accept." (William Barclay, *The Daily Study Bible Series: The Letters to the Galatians and Ephesians*, rev. ed. [Philadelphia: The Westminster Press, 1976], p. 124.)

There is a large disparity indeed between a new career choice and being a transmitter of grace, a bearer of dignified service, and potentially a sufferer for Christ.

"*Of this gospel I have become a servant according to the gift of God's grace that was given to me by the working of his power*" (Eph 3:7).

There are, of course, others in transition, seeking self-definition and meaningful service, whom we remember on this day, the Feast of the Epiphany. They are the Magi from the east, star-gazers and star-followers who came to worship and share their treasures with a king. We do not know who they were, whence they came or to where they returned. We do not know how many they were or how their encounter with a king born in a manger affected their lives. But we do know this: they were grace-bearers and grace-receivers; their pilgrimage was not a sacrifice, but a privilege; and their long journey was worth the effort in spite of its dangers and difficulties.

What shall define our relationship to the good news of God, the gospel of our Lord Jesus Christ? Is it just one more choice among many, or is it a glory, a privilege, a gift to be shared with others?

—John L. Topolewski
Vestal United Methodist Church
Vestal, New York

January 11, 1998

1st Sunday after Epiphany, The Baptism of Our Lord

Lessons

Pres/Meth/UCC/Luth	Isa 43:1–7	Acts 8:14–17	Lk 3:15–17, 21–22
Roman Catholic	Isa 42:1–4, 6–7	Acts 10:34–38	Lk 3:15–16, 21–22
Episcopal	Isa 42:1–9	Acts 10:34–38	Lk 3:15–16, 21–22

Introductions to the Lessons

Lesson 1

(1) *Isaiah 43:1–7* **(Pres/Meth/UCC/Luth)**
The prophet describes the God of Israel as both creator and redeemer, watching over Israel against hostile forces.

(2) *Isaiah 42:1–4, 6–7* **(RC)**; *Isaiah 42:1–9* **(Epis)**
The servant who will suffer for Israel is presented for the first time as one who will bring justice to the earth. Isaiah then characterizes the Lord as a "light to the nations."

Lesson 2

(1) *Acts 8:14–17* **(Pres/Meth/UCC/Luth)**
Peter and John go to Samaria to baptize the new believers there.

(2) *Acts 10:34–38* **(RC/Epis)**
Peter preaches to the Gentiles at Caesarea, following the conversion of the Roman centurion Cornelius.

Gospel
Luke 3:15–17, 21–22 **(Pres/Meth/UCC/Luth)**;
Luke 3:15–16, 21–22 **(RC/Epis)**
John the Baptist, when questioned about whether he might be the Messiah, tells the people that one mightier than he is coming. Luke then goes on to describe Jesus' baptism by John.

Theme
From baptism's watery grave we have been raised with Christ.

Thought for the Day
One of our most significant rites of passage is that of Christian baptism; it is also the rite that has been most compromised by our culture. "Getting the kid done," not understanding the content or even the context of this sacrament, seems often to be of highest priority. The ongoing renewal of the church could be driven, in part, by reclaiming this ancient rite.

Prayer of Meditation
Quiet me, and help me to focus, gracious God. I have been busy—too busy—and I have not always been productive or effective in all that I do. Help me to attend to matters of spirit, that I might be discerning, and have my labor become transparent to the gospel, the good news of your Son, and my Savior, Jesus Christ the Lord. Amen.

Call to Worship
> Ascribe to the Lord, O heavenly beings,
>> ascribe to the Lord glory and strength.
>
> Ascribe to the Lord the glory of his name;
>> worship the Lord in holy splendor.
>
> May the Lord give strength to his people!
>> May the Lord bless his people with peace!
>
> —Psalm 29:1–2, 11

Prayer of Adoration
You alone are God, creator of time and place, giver of every gift and grace, Father of our Lord Jesus Christ. As we come into your presence, may we do so with songs on our lips and gratitude within our hearts. You alone, O Lord, are worthy. Amen.

Prayer of Confession
We have, at every level, tried to keep our distance from you, O Lord. Our sins are but an expression of our desire to be fully in control, even to be our own god. Forgive us, we pray, and free us for joyful obedience; through Jesus Christ our Lord. Amen.

January 11, 1998
1st Sunday after Epiphany, The Baptism of Our Lord

Prayer of Dedication of Gifts and Self

May these gifts, entrusted to us by your grace and multiplied by our labor, be, along with ourselves, an acceptable offering for the work of the church and the proclamation of your coming kingdom. Amen.

Sermon Summary

If baptism is everything that water is, then baptism can be death by drowning—death in and with Christ, a watery grave from which we shall be raised to live and serve our master.

Hymn of the Day

"When Jesus Came to Jordan." Fred Pratt Green, a noted poet, playwright, and translator, wrote this hymn in 1973 to commemorate the baptism of Jesus. It has quickly won wide acceptance in many of the recent hymnals because of the elegant turn of phrase and wonderful retelling of the gospel story for today. The tune "Complainer" dates back to 1835, but was revamped by Carlton Young in 1988.

Children's Object Talk

A Signpost for Life

Object

A large directional sign with an arrow cut from posterboard that says: "This way to Jesus."

Lesson

Our mission is to point others to Jesus.

What do you want to be when you grow up? Has anyone asked you that question? I'll bet they have. Parents, grandparents, friends all want to know what you think you'd like to be when you grow up. So, tell me: what would you like to be? (Allow time for the children to answer. Be sure to affirm all answers as interesting and good choices.)

Those are all great choices. Not everyone gets a chance to be what they want to be, and sometimes we do things we never thought we would do.

But there is one thing you and I can be all the time—and you don't even have to wait until you're grown up: you can be a signpost!

A signpost? That sounds silly, doesn't it? Signposts are on streets and buildings. People can't be signposts, can they? They can if they are signposts like this. (Display the sign and have a volunteer read it out loud.) Yes, we can all point others to Jesus. That way, they can know about his love and the joy we have in following him.

Today we heard (or will hear) about a person who was a very good signpost to Jesus—John the Baptist. John had quite a few followers. But he also knew that he wasn't nearly as important as was Jesus, the chosen one of God. So John was always careful to say, "The most important thing you can do is to believe that Jesus is your Savior and point others to him."

Why don't you help others find out that Jesus is their friend too? Talk about him with your family and friends this week.

—*Jon Temme*

The Sermon

Death by Drowning

Hymns
Beginning of Worship: "Praise and Thanksgiving Be to God"
Sermon Hymn: "When Jesus Came to Jordan"
End of Worship: "Wash, O God, Our Sons and Daughters"

Scripture
Luke 3:15–17, 21–22 (For additional sermon materials on this passage, see the October 1997 issue and the *1997 May/June Planning Issue* of *The Clergy Journal*.)

Sermon Text
"'I baptize you with water; but one who is more powerful than I is coming... He will baptize you with the Holy Spirit and fire'" (vs. 16).

Remember our last baptism here at the church? Do you recall how bright-eyed and attentive the baby was? How he smiled when I held him up and presented him to the congregation? How proud his parents and sponsors were? It was a time of real joy and celebration, a pleasing time for all of us and a special privilege for me.

I like baptisms, and so, I'm sure, do most of you. But are good feelings the only thing baptism is about, or does it have a darker side, a deeper meaning, and a more complex teaching to

January 11, 1998
1st Sunday after Epiphany, The Baptism of Our Lord

share with us all? Martin Luther, the German reformer, called baptism "death by drowning," and I can recall, from my years of involvement with the Baptist church, the reference to this sacrament as "a watery grave." I'm not sure that any one of us, myself included, had such imagery in mind on that special Sunday just a few weeks ago.

Death by drowning. That aspect of baptism was made very clear to me during my first trip to Israel in the winter of 1992. The site that marks the traditional site of Jesus' baptism, south and east of Jericho, is inaccessible to pilgrims. So, an alternate site, complete with cement steps and ramps into the River Jordan, just below the outlet of the Sea of Galilee, has become the place where Christians remember his baptism as well as their own. It is a lovely spot, shaded by large trees, through which the limestone green-tinted water flows.

In 1992, however, the winter had brought more rain and snow than had fallen in more than two decades. The Jordan was swollen, muddy, and wild. Our group could not get near the steps; they were inundated with the raging torrent. I had so wanted to stand in the Jordan, to scoop up a handful of water, place my wet and dripping hand on my head, and remember that I am baptized. Had I been foolish enough to disregard the clear and present danger of the swollen river, the commemoration of my baptism could, indeed, have been a watery grave.

Removing from baptism the threat and danger that are part of its essence drains the sacrament of its mystery and its power. What the New Testament and the liturgy of the church say about this sacrament cannot be domesticated or made safe. For us, baptism can be no less than death, burial, and resurrection—a mirror of the life of our Lord Jesus Christ.

The gospel lesson from Luke finds us watching John the Baptist, as he stands waist deep in the Jordan, surrounded by people who want to know whether he is the Messiah. John quashes the speculation with words that are hardly comforting:

"'I baptize you with water; but one who is more powerful than I is coming; I am not worthy to untie the thong of his sandals. He will baptize you with the Holy Spirit and with fire. His winnowing fork is in his hand, to clear his threshing floor and to gather the wheat into his granary; but the chaff he will burn with unquenchable fire'" (Lk 3:16b–17).

If you think drowning by water is terrifying, says John, just wait for this more powerful one! The one who baptizes with the Holy Spirit and with fire will clean house from top to bottom and put everything false out to be burned with the trash.

There is a sense in which Jesus' own terror begins in the water of the Jordan. He is baptized, and then he knows that there will be no stopping until the progress of God's events has been fulfilled. The baptismal terror continues into the Garden of Gethsemane, where Jesus is "grieved to death." The cup he drinks, along with his baptism into death, would be the fate of all who share the way with him. Following Jesus is truly death by drowning.

Perhaps the terror of baptism can be compared to having your doctor show you the x-rays and speak the words "cancer," "biopsy," "surgery." Suddenly, everything is charged with new meaning.

My mother-in-law underwent a breast biopsy and has told me that she began to look at everything differently, from the moment the surgeon told her she might have more cancer. She began to take nothing for granted. Things she barely noticed before, like the phone call from a friend to see how she was doing, became a treasured gift. Each day became precious, and she said that even when her biopsy turned out benign, she began to receive the most common things, like a sunny day, with a heightened sense of gratitude. Her best present, she said, was the reprieve she was given from cancer.

Baptism is more than a reprieve. It means resurrection from the dead and a new creation. For those held in the grip of terror comes the voice that speaks with tenderness as well as power:

"'Do not fear, for I have redeemed you.... When you pass through the waters, I will be with you ... when you walk through the fire you shall not be burned...'" (Isa 43:1b–2b).

"'You are my Son, the Beloved; with you I am well pleased'" (Lk 3:22).

Because Jesus went into the Jordan that day, we need have no fear of death-dealing waters or trial by fire. What goes under the water, when we die by the drowning of baptism, is nothing compared to the new self risen with Christ: a self more hopeful, a self more eager to seek God's glory and to look to the needs of our neighbors. The cost of baptism is nothing less than death to our old selves, our old ways of life, and birth into something new, claimed by God to imitate the one of whom it was said, *"'You are my Son, the Beloved; with you I am well pleased.'"*

—*John L. Topolewski*
Vestal United Methodist Church
Vestal, New York

January 18, 1998

2nd Sunday after Epiphany
RC/Pres: 2nd Sunday in Ordinary Time

Lessons
Pres/Meth/UCC/Luth	Isa 62:1–5	1 Cor 12:1–11	Jn 2:1–11
Roman Catholic	Isa 62:1–5	1 Cor 12:4–11	Jn 2:1–11
Episcopal	Isa 62:1–5	1 Cor 12:1–11	Jn 2:1–11

Introduction to the Lessons
Lesson 1
Isaiah 62:1–5 **(Pres/Meth/UCC/Luth/RC/Epis)**
For many years the people of Israel knew of God's silence (Isa 42:14). Now the prophet announces the city's new name because God's silence is broken.

Lesson 2
1 Corinthians 12:1–11 **(Pres/Meth/UCC/Luth/Epis)**;
1 Corinthians 12:4–11 **(RC)**
Paul instructs the Corinthian church on the gifts of the Holy Spirit. It is God, he says, who gives the church of Christ the ability to be the *living word of God*. God's love for the world will not be silenced. Where love and deeds of mercy exist, there Christ's body can be found.

Gospel
John 2:1–11 **(Pres/Meth/UCC/Luth/RC/Epis)**
At the wedding in Cana, Jesus' mother is portrayed as recognizing her son's uniqueness. That is, he has the ability to correct a matter that has gone wrong. Yet this awareness, like Nathanael's insight (Jn 1:50), becomes part of the backdrop. Both of these people, according to John, have become silenced for the sake of the gospel; for the sake of creating faith. At the appropriate time (Jn 2:4b), God breaks all silence to reveal Christ's glory, empowering disciples to faith.

Theme
The obtrusiveness of God's love.

Thought for the Day

"Surely, this commandment that I am commanding you today is not too hard for you, nor is it too far away . . . the word is very near to you; it is in your mouth and in your heart for you to observe."

—Deuteronomy 30:11–14

Prayer of Meditation

In Isaiah 30:15, a promise is given by God. "In returning [to God] and resting [in God, you] shall be saved; in quietness and in trust shall be your strength." Most gracious God, Holy Scripture teaches that our days are complete in you. Still, in the best or the worst of times, we can be caught filling our days with things rather than your love and promise for rest. Quiet us as we seek to study your word and seek to do your will on earth as in heaven. In Jesus' name we pray. Amen.

Call to Worship

Leader: Come, behold the works of the Lord;
see what desolations he has brought on the earth.
People: He makes wars cease to the end of the earth;
he breaks the bow, and shatters the spear;
he burns the shields with fire.
Leader: "Be still, and know that I am God!
I am exalted among the nations,
I am exalted in the earth."
People: The Lord of hosts is with us;
the God of Jacob is our refuge.

—Psalm 46:8–11

Prayer of Adoration

Almighty God, in Christ Jesus good news was declared to us. We give you thanks and praise for the promise of forgiveness of sin, joy to come from mourning, life to follow death, and salvation as you first intended. We pray your blessing upon our lives as we seek to glorify you in both our words and our actions. In Jesus' name we pray. Amen.

Prayer of Confession

In God's presence, we confess that we have sinned against God and each other by what we have done and by what we have left undone. By not loving God with our whole being, we have neglected our neighbors as ourselves. Let us now humbly seek to turn our lives over to God, seeking renewal of mind, body, and soul. (Silence for reflection.)

January 18, 1998
2nd Sunday after Epiphany
RC/Pres: 2nd Sunday in Ordinary Time

Hear the promise of Holy Scripture: there is forgiveness of sin for those found in Christ Jesus; there is life for the baptized; life for those who love God, seek justice, and walk humbly before God. God of light and life, be near us now and forever. We ask this in Jesus' name. Amen.

Prayer of Dedication of Gifts and Self

Almighty God, it is good news to hear that you are constantly after us, seeking to restore us to a life of faith in you. Help us daily to study the Scriptures and hear your word. Strengthen us in tasks that may seem impossible. Lead us through sorrows, turning tears to laughter. Stop us whenever we seek to fill ourselves with nonsense or disbelief. Quiet us, so we may welcome you in our presence, saying and living as Jesus taught: (recite together the Lord's Prayer). Amen.

Hymn of the Day

"Dwelling in Beulah Land." A spirited and popular favorite from C. Austin Miles written in 1939, "Dwelling in Beulah Land" refers to the Hebrew Scripture lesson for today where Isaiah promises that God will wipe away the sins of the people, and the land shall no more be called "forsaken." The people will be given the name "My Delight Is in Her" and the land shall be called "married," or "Beulah" in Hebrew! Sing with delight and gusto.

Children's Object Talk

Better than New

Object
A piece of jewelry that can be hidden in a wastebasket.

Lesson
God promises to restore the faithful as precious jewels in God's own eyes and the eyes of others.

I'm looking for a precious ring (bracelet, brooch). Where do you think I should look? (Elicit answers such as a jewelry store, palace, safe.) Well, those are all good places, but I think I'll look for that piece of precious jewelry right here in a wastebasket.

Do you think I'm crazy? Well, I might be, but let's see. (Make a fuss and sort through the garbage in the wastebasket.)

Look, I've found it. Isn't that a gorgeous piece of jewelry? It must be very valuable.

Finding that was like finding hidden treasure. We certainly did not expect to find it in a wastebasket.

Long ago in Bible times, something very similar happened—not with jewelry but with real people. The people of Israel, because of their sinfulness, were in a very bad situation. Their country and the temple where they worshiped God were destroyed. They were made slaves in a far-off country, and they didn't feel very important. They were being punished for their sinfulness—and rightly so.

But we know that God's love is a forgiving love, so God promised to forgive them and restore them. God sent them back to their own country, let them rebuild the temple, gave them back a life of justice and care for one another.

All at once, these people who looked like junk looked very precious. But really, they were all along. Just because that ring (or whatever) was in the wastebasket didn't make it less valuable. But we had to find it and restore it.

That teaches us a very important lesson. When people do bad things and hurt themselves and others, they are no less valuable as God's children. God can always find the goodness in them, forgive them, and teach them.

—*Jon Temme*

The Sermon

You Can't Shut Up God!

Hymns
Beginning of Worship: "Open Now Thy Gates of Beauty"
Sermon Hymn: "Songs of Thankfulness and Praise"
End of Worship: "Lord, Dismiss Us with Your Blessing"

Scripture
Isaiah 62:1–5 (For sermon materials on 1 Corinthians 12:1–11, see the October 1997 issue of *The Clergy Journal* and on John 2:1–11, see the *1997 May/June Planning Issue* of *The Clergy Journal*.)

Sermon Text
"For Zion's sake I will not keep silent, and for Jerusalem's sake I will not rest" (vs. 1a).

January 18, 1998
2nd Sunday after Epiphany
RC/Pres: 2nd Sunday in Ordinary Time

When I was very young, the word "epiphany" meant nothing to me. However, if I saw a cartoon character with a light bulb over its head, I knew instantly what it meant. The cartoon character had an idea—an epiphany.

I am not striving to set off light bulbs. Instead, I want to explore with you some instances where God has been *loud* around you: loud and noticeable, loud with love for you, loud as a bright light.

In today's Old Testament Scripure, Isaiah is heard telling Israel that God will not keep still. God loves them so much, the silence they've been experiencing is now about to end. That was surely good news for those who longed for God.

The new name over Israel is good news—loud news. Everyone who hears the good news is going to understand immediately what's happened to the people of Israel: *"You shall no more be termed Forsaken, and your land shall no more be termed Desolate; but you shall be called My Delight Is in Her, and your land Married..."* (Isa 62:4).

God will not be quiet, because God desires only to be loud until it is understood who gives God delight, and who God is married to. That is something we see in today's gospel reading as well. It isn't the wedding so much that catches our attention. It's *the hush* from Jesus' own mouth that catches us. Jesus instructs his own mother to ... *hush*. He doesn't even have to say it to mean it. It's written all over his face. Mary is not to be loud. God will be loud at this wedding. When it's the right time, the disciples will walk away with faith. When it is the right time, you will see for yourself. "What concern is it of yours that the wine has given out?" Hush now, my hour has not yet come. Hush.

God can be very loud, even when God is quiet. God has been that way for centuries, both loud and quiet at the same time.

A story passed down to us finds Adam and Eve in a garden. They have done something they shouldn't have. When the leaves of trees are heard rustling, God is also heard—loud, crushing leaves under feet. They start and try to hide, but hear the questionings of God instead: "Why are you hiding? Where are you?"

When Jonah had finished his preaching task with Ninevah, he sat himself down in the hot sun outside the city. His mission was over, but not his complaining. God loved Jonah and blessed him even though he was a grump. As you may remember, God set a bush to grow in his midst so that shade would protect his little complainer. Yet by the time of sunrise the following day, a worm had attacked his gift of grace. So Jonah was found complaining some more.

In the heat of the sun, in the silence of the morning, Jonah hears God loud and clear. "Is it right for you to be angry about the bush? Angry enough to die? You are concerned about the bush, for which you did not labor and which you did not grow; it came into being in a night and perished in a night. And should I not be concerned about Nineveh, that great city, in which there are more than a hundred and twenty thousand persons who do not know their right hand from their left, and also many animals?"

Loud. God can be very loud. God even cares about animals!

With each of us, God has been loud. Yet, even though this is true, many of us could also claim: I have not heard God at all; I don't have the slightest clue as to what God really sounds like. For those who live this way, life must be sad, lonely, and confusing. When we live not hearing God's voice, we most certainly experience isolation, anger, jealousy, envy—envy that others should be so lucky to have God so close to their side.

But isn't that nonsense? Scripture teaches that God—Emmanuel—is always with us. Isn't it more likely that we haven't heard the call to be still—to hush? Aren't we a lot like Jesus' mother sometimes, insistent on knowing when and where God ought to appear, and what God will say to us?

When the Scripture instructs us to be still, as it does in Psalm 46:10—*"Be still, and know that I am God!"*—that is what God wants from us as well. To be totally still. To shut ourselves down. Are we willing to drop all our preconceived ideas of what God is like? Are we willing to shut down and not offer an opinion of why or why not we deserve God's love or wrath? To be still *is* to allow God to crash in on us.

How might God crash in on us? It would be like being found at the communion rail some Sunday morning. There you are, waiting for bread and wine to hit your hand. It is silent where you kneel. Thoughts are spinning in your head, yet you see and hear the minister getting closer. Familiar words are spoken to the person next to you, and then, turning to you and adding, "yes, even you, this bread is given; even for the likes of you." (Pause for moment of silence.)

We are God's delight and we are married to God in Christ Jesus. That is what Scripture is loud about. That is what we are to be loud about with ourselves, with our families, and with our neighborhoods. There is one so close to us, we oftentimes fail to hear or see such brilliance!

How are we to leave this place and share such outrageous news with our neighbors? I don't think it is as simple as saying to

January 18, 1998
2nd Sunday after Epiphany
RC/Pres: 2nd Sunday in Ordinary Time

someone, "Take up some silence and listen for God." Maybe we should begin with ourselves.

Imagine shutting off your television when your favorite program is about to start. Are you kicking and screaming that such silence is too much to bear? If so, ask God to quiet you and hold you in his hand.

Imagine no photographs in *People* magazine. Isn't it refreshing to read again? Ask the question seriously, *Is that why I don't read my Bible; it has no photographs?* Try allowing God to create the images for you instead. Contemplate God's will in your life as you read the Holy Scriptures.

Take it a step further. Imagine no computer screen. Imagine the year 2000, when the Clinton administration wants most of us *netted* together. As powerful and innovative as that might be—bringing the world together like a big fishing net—isn't it possible that God might also be saying to us today: You are shutting me out; all of you are? The whole planet is guilty!

As a pastor, I wonder what the world would be like if we spent as much time with God as we do our computers. Could we live on the planet anymore without our computers? Would we know what to put in its place?

The good news is that God's light is always there, even when we shut God out; even when we are blind; even when we are deaf to our creator.

Loud. God can be very loud.

The good news is the church of Christ can be a lot louder than it is. There's room for more than just growth in Christ's name. There's room for noise, the celebration that is ours, that God gives us a new name. Like the mother who hears it for the first time, standing at the baptismal font with her child.

That silence, loud silence, was there the day you were baptized. That silence, loud silence, was there when Israel received its new name; a name that read like this: "May the Lord bless you and keep you, make his face shine on you and be gracious to you; looking upon you with favor and give you peace." (Period of silence again.) Amen.

—*Peter Rosenkvist*
ELCA pastor
St. Paul, Minnesota

January 25, 1998

3rd Sunday after Epiphany
RC/Pres: 3rd Sunday in Ordinary Time

Lessons

Pres/Meth/UCC/Luth	Neh 8:1–3, 5–6, 8–10	1 Cor 12:12–31a	Lk 4:14–21
Roman Catholic	Neh 8:2–4a, 5–6, 8–10	1 Cor 12:12–30	Lk 1:1–4; 4:14–21
Episcopal	Neh 8:2–10	1 Cor 12:12–27	Lk 4:14–21

Introduction to the Lessons
Lesson 1
Nehemiah 8:1–3, 5–6, 8–10 (**Pres/Meth/UCC/Luth**);
Nehemiah 8:2–4a, 5–6, 8–10 (**RC**); *Nehemiah 8:2–10* (**Epis**)
The Old Testament reading describes a religious ceremony called the Festival of Trumpets. Most contemporary worshipers will not hear or know of the next text in Nehemiah 8:13–18 where the Feast of Tabernacles is described. Side by side these stories uphold the studying of God's law, the Torah. Worship leaders encouraged the people to rejoice and celebrate because freedom would come by keeping the law.

Lesson 2
1 Corinthians 12:12–31a (**Pres/Meth/UCC/Luth**);
1 Corinthians 12:12–30 (**RC**); *1 Corinthians 12:12–27* (**Epis**)
Diversity in religious opinion and practice becomes the excuse for poor missions, poor stewardship, and poor worship habits (see 1 Cor 11:17ff.). Paul reminds the people to uphold the law of Christ, which is to love one another. He conveys this by saying "... *and we were all made to drink of one Spirit*" (vs. 13).

Gospel
Luke 4:14–21 (**Pres/Meth/UCC/Luth/Epis**);
Luke 1:1–4; 4:14–21 (**RC**)
"*The eyes of all in the synagogue were fixed on him*" (Lk 4:20b). Luke is not calling attention to worship etiquette, i.e., that people look to the reader of the Holy Scriptures when the word is proclaimed. Rather, for Luke,

January 25, 1998
3rd Sunday after Epiphany
RC/Pres: 3rd Sunday in Ordinary Time

eyes fixed upon Jesus notes a shift in movement of the salvation story both for himself (Lk 1:3a) and the people of Israel. Jesus doesn't meet our expectations *(Is this not Joseph's son?)*. Yet, those who study and ponder the story of God's salvation behold that God fulfills indeed.

Theme
Beholding a true sense of mission.

Thought for the Day
If you cannot speak like angels, If you cannot preach like Paul,
You can tell the love of Jesus; You can say he died for all.
If you cannot rouse the wicked With the judgment's dread alarms,
You can lead the little children To the Savior's waiting arms.

Let none hear you idly saying, "There is nothing I can do,"
While the multitudes are dying And the master calls for you.
Take the task he gives you gladly; Let his work your pleasure be.
Answer quickly when he calls you, "Here am I. Send me, send me!"
—"Hark, the Voice of Jesus Calling," Daniel March, 1816–1909, alt.

Prayer of Meditation
How lovely is your dwelling place,
   O Lord of hosts!
My soul longs, indeed it faints
   for the courts of the Lord;
my heart and my flesh sing for joy
   to the living God.
Happy are those who live in your house,
   ever singing your praise.
Happy are those whose strength is in you,
   in whose heart are the highways to Zion.

—Psalm 84:1–2, 4–5

Call to Worship
Leader: Stand up and bless the Lord your God from everlasting to everlasting.
People: Blessed by your glorious name, which is exalted above all blessing and praise.

—Nehemiah 9:5b

Prayer of Adoration
Eternal source of joy and love, we come to celebrate your light in our presence. Still, not unlike our ancestors we come: some tired and frail, some with shattered dreams, some sad that prayers go unanswered. There is always darkness in our midst. We pray for the light of Christ to break in upon us this day, so that we may sing praises to you and go out telling the world of your saving work. In Jesus' name we pray. Amen.

Prayer of Confession
Almighty God, we confess to you both as a community of faith, and as a person striving to live within that community. We confess we have not loved you with our whole heart, and we have not loved our neighbors as ourselves. Give us now, we pray, an ability to discern how we may go forth in your grace. Amen.

Prayer of Dedication of Gifts and Self
Dear God, we acknowledge all we have as gifts coming from you: home and family, work and leisure, a sense of mission and a knowledge of forgiveness as seen and witnessed by Christ Jesus. Accept our humble offerings and renew our spirits to dedicate our lives to spreading the good news of Christ Jesus wherever we are living, working, and playing. Amen.

Sermon Summary
For many, the search for God is a constant struggle. For others, sight has been given and the bonds to captivity have been burst apart. The light of Christ made manifest in Nazareth centuries ago is the same light and power shattering darkness in people's lives today. This sermon explores that reality whereby listeners are challenged to make God's mission tangible.

Hymn of the Day
"Many Are the Lightbeams." Perfectly reflecting the Corinthians passage for today, this hymn is based on the ancient writing of an early church bishop, Cyprian of Carthage. It was taken from his 252 C.E. book *De unitate ecclesiae* (Concerning Church Unity). The tune is a simple and stately melodic line that is easy to pick up and sing. This hymn is easily adapted for choir or congregational variations: All sing stanza one, men verse 2, women verse 3, etc. Or individual voices

January 25, 1998
3rd Sunday after Epiphany
RC/Pres: 3rd Sunday in Ordinary Time

may emphasize the theme. A lovely processional piece, the hymn proclaims God's many gifts aptly celebrated in our unity.

Children's Object Talk

Time to Get to Work

Object

A "job jar" filled with notes that say things like: laugh lots, feel great inside, watch others smile, help others enjoy life, etc.

Lesson

Jesus and his followers met their tasks with joy.

I brought along a job jar today. Do any of you have one at home or know what one is? (Allow time for responses, guesses, and dialogue.) Here's my job jar. When I have a lot of chores to do and can't decide which to do first, I put them all in a jar. Then I choose one and do that. When I finish that chore, I choose another. Eventually, I have all the chores done.

Followers of Jesus have something like a job jar, too. Let's see what we have to do. (Have volunteers draw and read tasks. Comment on each as they are chosen. Emphasize that these tasks don't seem like chores at all. They can be fun to do, bring lots of joy, laughter, and smiles and can help family and friends. After all have been chosen and talked about, continue as follows.)

Jesus did many things on earth. He made the poor and lonely know they were precious in God's eyes. He took people who were sad and made them smile. Jesus invites us, his friends and followers, to do the same sorts of things.

Sometimes people think being a Christian is no fun at all. They treat it like a chore: go to church, pray before you eat, do this, don't do that. But we can also see that following Jesus will bring joy, happiness, and laughter to us and others.

Whenever you're bored or confused, wondering what to do, think about Jesus' job jar. Following Jesus will always give you an idea of how you can bring a smile, a song, a laugh, and love to someone else.

—*Jon Temme*

The Sermon

Needed: A Mission

Hymns
Beginning of Worship: "Lord, with Glowing Heart I'd Praise Thee"
Sermon Hymn: "Where Cross the Crowded Ways of Life"
End of Worship: "On Our Way Rejoicing"

Scripture
Luke 4:14–21 (For sermon materials on 1 Corinthians 12:12–31a, see the October 1997 issue of *The Clergy Journal* and on Nehemiah 8:1–3, 5–6, 8–10, see the *1997 May/June Planning Issue* of *The Clergy Journal*.)

Sermon Text
". . . The eyes of all in the synagogue were fixed on him" (vs. 20).

Luke's Gospel is the written record of a number of astonishing incidents that focus on the life of Jesus. One of those incidents is now among us through our hearing and perhaps in our mind's eye, and it is important that we realize that it was and still is astonishing. What if you had been there? What would you have seen and heard?

If you had lived in Nazareth in about the year A.D. 30 perhaps you, too, would have found yourself in the synagogue on the Sabbath. It might have been your habit to meet in the synagogue on the seventh day with relatives and friends in this small Galilean community. Some predictable things would happen. The service would begin with the call, "Hear, O Israel, the Lord your God is One, and you shall love the Lord your God with all your heart, soul, mind, and strength." Prayers and songs would have been included. But at the heart of the service someone would read the Scriptures. Different people would have been honored at significant times in their lives and in being honored, they would read. Itinerant teachers would come through town, and they would read.

But this day was different. Jesus was there. He had been there many times before. He grew up in this congregation. He was Joseph the carpenter's son. He had been away for a while, and almost everyone had heard that he was now a teacher. People were talking about him. Imagine—a local young man, bright

January 25, 1998
3rd Sunday after Epiphany
RC/Pres: 3rd Sunday in Ordinary Time

and capable. He's teaching in the area, and almost everyone is praising him.

He was there, and he was different. There was something about him, something hard to define. He was still Joseph's boy, one of us, but there was something different about how he carried himself.

No one was surprised when the presider gave the scrolls to Jesus to read. What he read was known and familiar. Israel's mission to the world was: *"... good news to the poor ... release to the captives ... sight to the blind ... let the oppressed go free ... proclaim the year of the Lord's favor"* (Lk 4:18–19). It was all families—you know, the kind of stuff we're all supposed to do sometimes. But then it changed. He sat down, not to indicate he was finished, but to inform all that he would now begin to teach about this Scripture. He sat in the chair, rolled up the scroll, looked into the many familiar faces who looked back at him. In fact, you could have heard a pin drop as all eyes were fixed on him. Unblinking, he said, *"... Today this scripture has been fulfilled in your hearing"* (Lk 4:21).

Someday, sometime off in the future, who knows when—that was when this Scripture would be fulfilled. Everyone knew that. But today! That means the Messiah is here! That's impossible! That's preposterous! The Messiah can't be here now. He's not saying that he is, is he?

That was the offense and the scandal of Jesus. He met the fixed gaze of relatives and friends from his hometown in his home church. His time in the wilderness locked in struggle with all the powers of evil and his recent baptism marked by the assuring voice kindled the fire in him and filled his vision with a holy power so that when he said, Today this Scripture is fulfilled, it was not that people disbelieved. They believed him, and that scared them.

That announcement then is not one bit less true now. These words were recorded in the collective memory of the faithful, written in the book, and when read now they have taken on a life of their own. Jesus himself, the unique son of God, no longer walking the earth through Palestinian countryside, is nonetheless alive and in our midst. Bread is broken, water is poured, words are spoken—Jesus is still in our midst declaring the same mission.

We might have entered this building heeding the call of a holy habit, locked into lifestyles where jobs, health, relationships, and worries had taken over, where our attention has been pulled in four directions. But these words have been heard, and they are moving into center stage in our lives. For but a moment that which had most worried us is pushed into the periphery, coaxed into a corner and the mission of Jesus—the mission of the church—is lifted up that we might see it.

Good news, release, sight, freedom—yes, that's it. That's what we need. On the outside we always look like everything is so altogether in our lives, but there have been times when the inner struggle has been so painful we haven't known where to turn. Some have been so filled with darkness that everything has been bad news. Life has felt like a series of constant demands draining energy and life from the very soul, and into that darkness has crept a single word of hope. A song from Sunday school, a hug from a child, a verse from a book, and we have found something to allow us to entertain hope for tomorrow.

Some have been held captive in their mind—filled with doubts and disbelief, unable to comprehend the goodness of God. Questions started and snowballed, destroying any semblance of trust and purpose. There has been blindness to anything that is good, truthful, and full of beauty. A primitive form of slavery existing in the very soul of a human being can eat away and erode the love of every human relationship. People become so entrapped by such powers that they barely realize what's happening.

But that power has been broken by the power of Jesus. Not by magic or superstition. The light of Christ was made manifest in that synagogue in Nazareth centuries ago, and that same light and power shatters the darkness in people's lives today.

I know that many of you have experienced the fulfillment of Jesus' words in your own lives. On the basis of your need you were drawn close to the very heart of God. The love of friends and the comfort of the Scriptures brought healing to your life. The church became important to you.

Now hear this: just as important as that healing light and comfort has been to you, so will it be to others. To be gathered in this house of worship today is to be where the church's mission is proclaimed front and center. What you needed, you received. Now there are many who are still looking for good news, still held captive to despair, still blind to any possibility of hope, still oppressed by darkness in its many forms. Our task is to point to Jesus, the source of that hope. Our mission is to see ourselves as partners in Jesus' mission.

Because life is filled with ambiguity it is not always a matter of *us in here* going with the good news to *those out there*. Life being

January 25, 1998
3rd Sunday after Epiphany
RC/Pres: 3rd Sunday in Ordinary Time

what it is, there are times when it is impossible to tell the rescuers from the rescued. That's probably why the church seldom looks heroic, like a mighty army. The army is bandaged and weary, frail and gaunt, limping but still moving forward in mission. We are most connected to the power of God when we are aware of our own needs. That's why it is seldom a hale and hearty church vigorously in mission. It's a church aware of its needs that seeks to point the way to Jesus.

Elie Wiesel tells a story that illustrates this truth. Wiesel is a living victim of the holocaust. As a teenager he was imprisoned with his family by the Nazis in their final solution to what they called the Jewish problem. He witnessed the death of many family members. But he lived and was rescued by the allied liberation of Auschwitz. He tells of that day when powerful, strong soldiers broke down the fences of the concentration camp to release the prisoners. These prisoners were frail and feeble, near death, victims of horrible crimes. Powerful armed soldiers entered to liberate them. One soldier Wiesel remembers was a strong, Black man who upon seeing the horror of human suffering reflected in the faces of the prisoners was overcome with grief. Sobbing, he was stricken by such sorrow that he slumped to the floor in disbelief. The captives, now liberated, came to comfort their liberator, now debilitated with grief. Sitting beside him with arms about him they offered comfort. (From *Memoirs: All Rivers Run to the Sea*, Elie Wiesel [New York: Alfred Knopf, 1995], p. 97.)

The mission call has been sounded again. We are reminded of our heritage and our future as missionary people: saved and saving. Christ saves us and calls us to join his saving mission. Won't you heed that call?

—*Paul Lundborg*
Grace Lutheran Church
Wenatchee, Washington

February 1, 1998

4th Sunday after Epiphany
RC/Pres: 4th Sunday in Ordinary Time

Lessons

Pres/Meth/UCC/Luth	Jer 1:4–10	1 Cor 13:1–13	Lk 4:21–30
Roman Catholic	Jer 1:4–5, 17–19	1 Cor 12:31–13:13	Lk 4:21–30
Episcopal	Jer 1:4–10	1 Cor 14:12b–20	Lk 4:21–32

Introduction to the Lessons

Lesson 1
Jeremiah 1:4–10 (**Pres/Meth/UCC/Luth/Epis**);
Jeremiah 1:4–5, 17–19 (**RC**)

Jeremiah is called to preach God's message of salvation. Jeremiah knows he will have to convict a great number of people (tear down) in order to convert (build up) the people toward God. God gives Jeremiah all he needs to fulfill his ministry.

Lesson 2
1 Corinthians 13:1–13 (**Pres/Meth/UCC/Luth**);
1 Corinthians 12:31—13:13 (**RC**);
1 Corinthians 14:12b–20 (**Epis**)

Christians lack faith, hope, and love. Paul's vocal inflection would be very different from what is often heard at weddings, i.e., taking poetic license and making this all too sweet. The lections beginning with either 12:31 or 14:12b (RC or Epis) share in common the word "strive." Paul's encouragement is for Christians to strive to live the call worthy of baptism in Christ Jesus.

Gospel
Luke 4:21–30 (**Pres/Meth/UCC/Luth/RC**); *Luke 4:21–32* (**Epis**)

Jesus has declared his mission in his hometown synagogue by proclaiming the text for the day as being *fulfilled* in their hearing. Luke says Jesus continued with disclosing the fact that God does love Gentiles. The result of his authentic preaching (vs. 32) filled the people with both amazement and rage.

February 1, 1998
4th Sunday after Epiphany
RC/Pres: 4th Sunday in Ordinary Time

Theme
Familiarity to the gospel isn't what Jesus wants from you.

Thought for the Day
Jesus prays that his disciples might know him and not just know about him. *"And this is eternal life, that they may know you, the only true God, and Jesus Christ whom you have sent"* (Jn 17:3).

Prayer of Meditation
> How very good and pleasant it is
> > when kindred live together in unity!
>
> It is like the precious oil on the head,
> > running down upon the beard,
>
> on the beard of Aaron,
> > running down over the collar of his robes.
>
> It is like the dew of Hermon,
> > which falls on the mountains of Zion.
>
> For there the Lord ordained his blessing,
> > life forevermore. —Psalm 133

Call to Worship
> Leader: May the glory of the Lord endure forever;
> People: May the Lord rejoice in His works—
> Leader: who looks on the earth and it trembles,
> People: who touches the mountains and they smoke.
> Leader: I will sing to the Lord as long as I live;
> People: I will sing praise to my God while I have being.
> Leader: May my meditation be pleasing to him,
> People: for I rejoice in the Lord. Amen.
> > —Psalm 104:31–33

Prayer of Adoration
Eternal God, source of our life and breath, we give you thanks and priase for your saving work in our lives. It is the news of Christ that draws us together. It is the news of Christ that gives voice to our songs. It is the news of Christ that frees us for service in the world. Bless our worship with your presence, and lead us in ways to bear faithful witness to your son, Jesus Christ our Lord. Amen.

Prayer of Confession
Almighty God, we cannot withstand the dangers that come from sin. Strengthen us in body, mind, and spirit to overcome the weaknesses that our sin has brought upon us and all the world. In Jesus' name we confess our sin against you and those we've been entrusted to care for: children, parents, stranger, and neighbor. (Silence for reflection, whereupon the pastor gives a word of absolution, followed with:) Give us now, we pray, an ability to discern how we may go forth in your grace. Amen.

Prayer of Dedication of Gifts and Self
Dear God, accept our humble offerings and renew our spirits to dedicate our lives to spreading the good news of Christ Jesus wherever we are living, working, and playing. Amen.

Sermon Summary
Luke's Gospel considers the challenges of knowing Jesus too well. Familiarity to someone or something can move us to apathy and indifference. Jesus said his own people would be challenged by such familiarity. Can we also get too close to Jesus? In his day, his friends found his messianic identification untrustworthy. What aren't we seeing or laying claim to?

Hymn of the Day
"Love Divine, All Loves Excelling." The epistle speaks of the nature of love's transforming power and certainly inspired Charles Wesley's famous hymn when it first appeared in 1747. His words suggest that Christ's love can transform us all into children of God, and that through him we may be made pure. This notion proved too radical, however, for many including his brother John Wesley who altered "pure and sinless" to "pure and spotless" in the fourth verse and omitted the second verse altogether to avoid suggesting that Christians could achieve a sinless perfection in this life. There are many good tunes to choose from for this hymn, the most popular being "Hyfrydol" and "Beecher." Try "Hymn to Joy," "Holy Manna," or *"In Babilone"* for some welcome variety.

February 1, 1998
4th Sunday after Epiphany
RC/Pres: 4th Sunday in Ordinary Time

Children's Object Talk

No Good Reason

Object
None.

Lesson
Awe turns to anger against Jesus when selfish human expectations are not met.

During the last few weeks we've been hearing about how Jesus brings joy and laughter to people. You would think that everybody loved Jesus. But sadly, that was not true. Lots of people in Bible times were angry at Jesus.

But why would people be mad at Jesus? They knew Jesus was a powerful individual. Many believed what we know to be true—that Jesus was the Messiah, the chosen one of God. But they wanted Jesus to do and say things that were what they wanted to hear or have happen. It's as if they wanted Jesus to fulfill all their selfish wants.

Now we may think we're not going to act like that, and I hope we never will. But we must always be careful that we don't think we can turn our love for Jesus into some magic that gets us whatever we want. Let's remember that Jesus is Lord of all, not slave to a few.

—*Jon Temme*

The Sermon

Jesus and His Own People

Hymns
Beginning of Worship: "Let the Whole Creation Cry"
Sermon Hymn: "Jesus, Thy Boundless Love to Me"
End of Worship: "On What Has Now Been Sown"

Scripture
Luke 4:21–30 (For sermon materials on 1 Corinthians 13:1–13, see the October 1997 issue and on Jeremiah 1:4–10, see the *1997 May/June Planning Issue* of *The Clergy Journal*.)

Sermon Text
"And he said, 'Truly I tell you, no prophet is accepted in the prophet's hometown" (vs. 24).

A popular song in an earlier decade carried the title, "He's Not Heavy; He's My Brother." The visual images accompanying the music often displayed children who were refugees of war taking turns carrying each other over a rugged, mountainous trail. Adults offered assistance and were willing to carry a child, but the independent elder brother dismissed them with a wave of his hand with the words, "He's not heavy; he's my brother."

That is a picture of family devotion and high ideals that brings tears to the eyes and a warmth to the belly.

Perhaps the more common image in family life might be found in the phrase, "Him? That's just my brother." Or, "Her? She's only my sister." It's an opposite perspective, but likely more realistic. Brothers and sisters often fail to appreciate each other unless they have gone through a common crisis or until they have reached a certain age. Growing up as the youngest of four children, I learned years later that my older siblings took turns riding the family bicycle one day and taking care of me the next. No wonder they didn't appreciate me at that time in their life!

Very often we fail to appreciate the things or people with whom we are very familiar. It is far more exciting to meet a famous person, a media personality. The first "famous" person I met is an unknown by today's standards, but I will never forget meeting Ordell Braase, a professional football player. I had the honor of introducing him to a student-body gathering when I was a college student, and I was awestruck. His size caused me to marvel and feel downright puny in contrast, and the fact that he was famous impressed me immensely. I suspect, however, that his family didn't get that excited when they saw him.

Eating homemade lemon meringue pie (or whatever your favorite food) is a wonderful treat, but it would cease being a treat if you ate it all the time.

Visiting a far-off, mysterious place is exciting, but living there might take away some of the glamor.

We can generate a lot of enthusiasm about the prospect of hearing a famous person speak, but that excitement would wane after sitting and listening for a week.

What would it be like to hear about Jesus for the very first time? Can you imagine beginning to grasp the realities of love and forgiveness and salvation for the first time? But many of us are familiar with the message—even overly familiar. And our response is often less than enthusiastic. Enthusiasm can give way to boredom because of familiarity. A pastor friend of mine will never

February 1, 1998
4th Sunday after Epiphany
RC/Pres: 4th Sunday in Ordinary Time

forget the parishioner who came to complain about his preaching. This took place back in the early 1970s, when American culture was feeling the tension of the Vietnam War, and my friend had encouraged the congregation to not abandon the fruit of the spirit. She entered the pastor's study shouting in a most angry voice, "Love, joy, peace. Love, joy, peace. I am so sick of hearing about love, joy, peace." Enthusiasm can even turn to cynicism.

We seldom appreciate those things with which we are most familiar. Remember the energy and excitement of the newly converted? The newly married? The first-year student? The new person at work? Most often they possess a unique degree of enthusiasm. We love to see the shiny new sports car and seldom appreciate the old clunker with 70,000 miles on it.

Jesus came to people of his hometown, the ones who knew him, those who were familiar with him and his family, and he said to them, *"No prophet is accepted in the prophet's hometown"* (Lk 4:24). He made the point that they understood—people seldom appreciate the persons they see every day. And they fulfilled his truth, for they could not accept his greatness. They could not believe he was the promised Messiah. Their eyes were covered by the blindness of familiarity. They wondered, "How can someone we know be that important?" Then they proved their blindness by trying to push him off a steep cliff for speaking such blasphemy in their ears.

Jesus was Jewish. The people of Israel were his own family. His roots went back to Abraham, Isaac, and Jacob. The nation of Israel knew the Messiah would come from them to save them. Their destiny was to save the world. They had fed on those promises for centuries. But at this moment in time the Messiah was among them, and they didn't recognize him. He spoke to them, and they rejected him. They looked beyond him. Because they rejected him, Jesus implied that God would reject them.

There's a message here for us, for you and me—the church—those who believe in Jesus today. We, the church, are the new Israel, the inheritors of the promise. We are God's means of bringing this message of salvation to the world. We are the ones who know Jesus, the ones who are most familiar with him. The words he spoke then are directed to us now. He was right. It is difficult for a prophet to speak to the people who are too familiar with him.

We have heard enough to be overly familiar, and our senses have been dulled. And when we fail to hear his promises, we hear his judgment. If we reject him, then he rejects us.

Being too familiar and thus being bored with Jesus is not good. Apathy and indifference are powers that can corrode our collective soul. Jesus said, *"I wish that you were either cold or hot. So, because you are lukewarm, and neither cold nor hot, I am about to spit you out of my mouth"* (Rev 3:15b–16). Iced tea is refreshing, and hot tea is soothing, but the first-aid books recommend lukewarm tea to make a person vomit.

Is there apathy, boredom, and an overly developed kind of familiarity with the holy among us? Many of us who are of northern European background are never too excited. Sometimes that's a virtue, but when it comes to the big issues of life, like our relationship to God and loved ones, it is all right to share some excitement.

What can we do? How can we avoid overfamiliarity, boredom, indifference, and apathy toward Jesus and toward the important relationships in our lives?

You can't manufacture enthusiasm—it is a gift. But you can remove barriers to the gift. We can stop stifling the excitement when it happens. We can give permission to one another to share the enthusiasm when it's there. We can allow the warmth of gentle humor and a calm demeanor to drive out the gloominess of complaining. We can express appreciation for the gift of life and pass on encouraging words when we hear them. We can allow joy to flow through to us. Let it happen! Enjoy it! Don't put it down! We are to let go and be free to enjoy what God has given us.

Maybe the best way to do this is to go beyond the surface with each other. When we live only on a superficial level with each other, we get picky about little things and neglect the big things. We see people's faults more frequently than we see their gifts. We focus on mistakes instead of on strengths. Jesus' death and resurrection, his victory over death and the devil, his gift of salvation—these are strengths. My relationship with you, love and forgiveness, the spirit's gifts for the common good—these are strengths. Potential friendships with conversations about hopes and dreams, fears and worries, joys and victories—these are strengths.

To beat the traps of boredom and familiarity we have to go beyond the surface; first with ourselves, and then with each other. When we plunge the depths, we discover the power.

Those who were in a position to know and love Jesus turned on him. They rejected his claims. Let us not do the same.

—*Paul Lundborg*
Grace Lutheran Church
Wenatchee, Washington

February 8, 1998

5th Sunday after Epiphany
RC/Pres: 5th Sunday in Ordinary Time

Lessons

Pres/Meth/UCC/Luth	Isa 6:1–8 (9–13)	1 Cor 15:1–11	Lk 5:1–11
Roman Catholic	Isa 6:1–2a, 3–8	1 Cor 15:1–11	Lk 5:1–11
Episcopal	Jud 6:11–24a	1 Cor 15:1–11	Lk 5:1–11

Introduction to the Lessons by John R. Brokhoff
Lesson 1
(1) *Isaiah 6:1–8 (9–13)* **(Pres/Meth/UCC/Luth)**;
Isaiah 6:1–2a, 3–8 **(RC)**
In the year 740 B.C., when King Uzziah of Judah died, Isaiah received his call to be a prophet. He was worshiping in the temple when he had a vision of the holiness of God. Isaiah confessed his sin, was forgiven, and then responded, "Here am I! Send me."

(2) *Judges 6:11–24a* **(Epis)**
The Israelites were oppressed by the Midianites in the time of the Judges. An angel came to Gideon and called upon him to free Israel from their enemy. Gideon begged off saying that he and his clan were the weakest in Israel. But Yahweh assured him that he would be with him and give him victory over the Midianites.

Lesson 2
*1 Corinthians 15:1–11***(Pres/Meth/UCC/Luth/RC/Epis)**
What is the gospel? Paul sums it up: Christ died for our sins, was buried, and rose from the dead. Since this letter was written about A.D. 50, it is the earliest written account of the resurrection. Paul enumerates the times when the risen Christ was seen. He was one of those who saw him even though he at first persecuted the church.

Gospel
Luke 5:1–11 **(Pres/Meth/UCC/Luth/RC/Epis)**
Peter becomes a disciple of Jesus. It happened at the Sea of Galilee where Peter and friends were fishing. Since they had caught nothing

all night, Jesus told Peter to cast out his nets, and behold, the net was filled with fish! Peter fell down at Jesus' feet, confessing his sin. Then Peter and his partners abandoned their business to follow Jesus full time.
—John R. Brokhoff, *Introductions to the Lessons,* Austin, TX: Church Management, Inc., 1992, p. 154

Theme
Called to be vulnerable with God.

Thought for the Day
In the first letter of John, the author calls believers to live deeply in God's love. Repeatedly, throughout the text, the author instructs Christians to *abide* in God and his love, and to do it in active ways. One way the author seems to do this is by living a very childlike life before God and before others. Consider 1 John 2:14, 18, 24–27; 3:1–3. Consider the ways you abide with God and mark that in your Bible.

Prayer of Meditation
Gracious God, I offer you these brief moments of my attention. Anytime I would turn to you, there are many distractions. I so easily turn away from you; instead I turn to my worries. I long for you, but my mind wanders. Quiet me so I may hear your voice; so I may hear your call again, your invitation to trust, to follow, to serve. Thank you, God, for knowing and loving me and calling me to be your child. In Jesus' name. Amen.
—From a pastor's desk

Call to Worship
> Leader: O Lord, my heart is not lifted up,
> my eyes are not raised too high;
> People: I do not occupy myself with things
> too great and too marvelous for me.
> Leader: But I have calmed and quieted my soul
> People: my soul is like a weaned child with its mother;
> like the weaned child that is within me.
> Leader: O children of Christ, abide in the Lord
> People: from this time on and forevermore. Amen.

—Adapted from Psalm 131

February 8, 1998
5th Sunday after Epiphany
RC/Pres: 5th Sunday in Ordinary Time

Prayer of Adoration

Almighty God, as children we are struck by the night sky. It is enormous. Later in life other big things catch our attention: grocery bills, new babies, earthquakes, storms of disaster, family arguments. When we look lower along the earth's surface, we see beauty but more often than not, we are caught up in daily worries. Grace our worship with your presence, and though we are less than divine, help us to see how you continue to sustain your handiwork. In Jesus' name we pray. Amen.

Prayer of Confession

Almighty God, we know we sin against you in thought, word, and deed. We confess that much of our energies are directed at how much we need, or what we lack. We recognize we live in a culture that tempts us to spend enormous amounts of time comparing ourselves to others rather than to Jesus. Forgive us when we are selfish like this. Help us to look for you and to see you dwelling deep within and around us. This and whatever else you know we need, we ask in Jesus' name. Amen.

Prayer of Dedication of Gifts and Self

Lord God, you call us to go deeper, to open ourselves to your love, and to share that love with others. Bless the works of our hands so that in serving others we might show your grace and justice in all the world. Amen.

Sermon Summary

Peter hears Jesus' invitation to "go deeper." This invitation was not confined to the fishing experience, but to his own life of discipleship as well. We, too, are called to open our small worlds to the grace of God.

Hymn of the Day

"Jesus Calls Us o'er the Tumult." What better tune than "Galilee" to accompany the call of the fisherman written especially for these words by organist William Jude in 1887? The words themselves are from Ireland, contained in a poem by Cecil Alexander (1852) to help young catechists remember St. Andrew's Day. The words are especially relevant in our society where distraction from the gospel is a constant concern. The poem reminds us that Jesus still calls us, no matter the ease or chaos of our current situation.

Children's Object Talk

Fishing for People

Object
A fishing rod with a bare hook. Also needed are several pictures from magazines of people smiling, laughing, enjoying being together with others, and helping each other.

Lesson
The gifts of the community of faith can be used to fish for people.

It's the middle of winter, but I was thinking about going fishing. I've brought along my fishing rod, but was wondering what sort of bait to put on the hook. Do you have any ideas? (Have fun with the responses and draw out some the children might not expect.) Sure, we can use worms or minnows. Some fish even like things you might think are gross like leeches, cheese, and liver—even grasshoppers!

Long ago, when Jesus lived on earth, he had several close followers called disciples who fished for a living. Once, Jesus asked them to think about inviting others to follow him. He said they could be "fishers of people."

That sounds strange, but Jesus was saying we can always invite others to follow Jesus. But what do you suppose we could use for bait? I brought along a few examples.

Here's a picture of people laughing and smiling. Let's put that on the hook. When people follow Jesus, they smile a lot. Why? Because they know they are loved. They know they are forgiven. They have hope and peace.

We could also use this picture for bait. Here's a big group of people. When people follow Jesus, they become part of the family of God in a special way. They have new friends who are like loving brothers and sisters to them. There's always something to do and someone to do it with in the kingdom of God.

Finally, we might use this for bait. Here's a picture of . . . (Describe the actual situation. For example, people helping rescue others from a flood.) When people follow Jesus, they know they will be rescued from many problems, and they know they can be part of a team that helps rescue others when problems come.

There are many things you could use as bait to catch fish. In the same way, there are many things we can share with others about the family of God. You and I can do what Jesus asked of his very first followers: become fishers of people for Jesus' sake.

—*Jon Temme*

February 8, 1998
5th Sunday after Epiphany
RC/Pres: 5th Sunday in Ordinary Time

The Sermon

Go Out Where It's Deep

Hymns
Beginning of Worship: "Amazing Grace"
Sermon Hymn: "Let Us Ever Walk with Jesus"
End of Worship: "Hark, the Voice of Jesus Calling"

Scripture
Luke 5:1–11 (For additional sermon materials on this passage, see the *1997 May/June Planning Issue* and on 1 Corinthians 15:1–11, see the October 1997 issue of *The Clergy Journal*.)

Sermon Text
"When he had finished speaking, he said to Simon, 'Put out into the deep water and let down your nets for a catch'" (vs. 4).

The reading from Luke 5:1–11 is what some would name a "calling story." It's the story of how Jesus specifically called persons to trust him and become his followers. I have heard similar calling stories from some of you. Probably your stories might not have had such dramatic content, a net full of fish or "left everything to follow him," but your stories have been equally moving to hear. Stories like: brought up in the faith, drifted away, but I married this person and he/she took me to church; or met this person whose life and qualities I admired, and they invited me to church; or came to this point in life where I had to face these questions and I started coming to church.

Rare indeed are the people for whom there is a "once-and-for-all-ness," a finished quality about their life of faith. As I read the Bible and listen to your stories, I realize that Jesus is always calling, inviting, summoning; and occasionally, we hear and are changed.

The name of Simon Peter is familiar to many who know some Christian history. His is an important name, and he was a colorful character. All of that rich history and colorful personality had an original point of contact with Jesus, and the reading from Luke told the story of that beginning. I wonder if, while I reflect on Peter's call to believe in and follow Jesus, you will hear that same invitation today?

According to Luke, Simon Peter must have met Jesus once

earlier. It is said in the previous chapter that Jesus came to the home of Peter's mother-in-law and healed her of her fever. In this story, however, Jesus' early focus is on the crowds. Jesus found it necessary to get into the boat to address the crowds lining the shore. Imagine a small lake in a bleak landscape, and you will be seeing Lake Genesaret, also called the Sea of Galilee. Jesus' pulpit was the boat, and the pews consisted of the shoreline. The crowds were curious as word concerning Jesus' authority was spreading. What did he say to the crowds? We don't know because Luke, the storyteller, doesn't tell us. Luke wants to tell us about Peter.

After Jesus finished speaking to the crowds, he must have said to Peter, "Let's do some fishing!" This wasn't a "grab your pole and some worms" kind of invitation because Peter fished for a living. He was in a partnership with James and John. They had nets and big boats. Fishing was work. Fishing was the means of caring for their families, putting bread on the table. Most likely, their fathers and grandfathers had fished. This was serious business at the center of their lives. In fact, they had fished all night and caught nothing. They had been minding their own business, fixing their nets and cleaning their boats when Jesus had come along seeking relief from the crowds, and it was mere politeness that had Peter serving as the guide for Jesus. Now that the speech was finished, I suspect Peter was eager to get his guest back on the shore so that the work of net-mending and boat-cleaning might be completed before going home for some bread and rest.

But this was not to be. Playfully, Jesus said, "Let's go out deeper and try our luck." Peter's polite weariness came through in his response, "Sir, we fished all night and had no luck." What do you imagine inspired Peter's further response? "But at your word, I'll put the nets out." Jesus gave no command. This was not an order. It was a suggestion—an invitation is offered. He sounded gentle and playful. "Let's try it." And Peter does it.

So often we are heavy-handed in our description of God and how God deals with people. The vocabulary of law/command, duty, responsibility: all those weighty words come to mind. But in this account, Jesus suggests and Peter says okay. Do you suppose this is the invitation? Peter, with brief protests including, "Well, we tried all night and I don't know what you're talking about, but I'll give it a try," says "yes"? His life was forever changed.

The full net is no surprise to us. As listeners to the story, we probably saw it coming or

February 8, 1998
5th Sunday after Epiphany
RC/Pres: 5th Sunday in Ordinary Time

remembered it from hearing it earlier. But the dialogue between Peter and Jesus is the surprise. There's no longer restrained politeness on Peter's side. Now he bares his soul. "Jesus, get away from me, for I am a sinful man." Another translation reads, "I'm a sinner and I can't handle this holiness." The miracle is too much for him. It's overwhelming. God's power and might sent him reeling. It's sometimes scary to brush up against that which is of God. If all Peter was ever looking for was fish, he would have been overjoyed! This should have been the culminating moment of his workaday career. If his life's quest had been a full net, he had now arrived. But in the midst of his world, he must have been hungry for God, and now it dawned on him why he had even gone along with this foolish request to go deeper. The ever-abiding emptiness and heart weariness that caused him to long for God with all his being had just exploded to the surface and met the Messiah face to face! Peter's life had been transformed with the simple, gentle request, "Let's go a little deeper."

Jesus loved Peter and wanted him to know God. Jesus wanted Peter to join him in bringing this message of God's love for all the world. Lovingly, Jesus responded to Peter's fear. Isn't that what Peter was expressing with his "get away from me" speech? Wasn't it fear? As much as any one of us might long for God, aren't we also afraid that when God gets close to us we might be changed? And even though there are moments of self-loathing and disgust in our lives—times when we are desperate for change—it's still scary to think of being changed.

Jesus didn't argue with Peter. No condescending platitudes. No pious gibberish. A wink, I suspect, and a riddle. He probably scooped up a few fish alongside Peter and said, "from now on, Peter, these fish won't occupy your attention. You'll be catching people." Now what in the world did that mean? What kind of riddle was this?

Peter's life was his work. His job was catching fish. Now he will catch people? Lovingly, gently, playfully Jesus had changed Peter's life. Jesus had met Peter at the very center of his existence, the place that meant the most to him—his job! And the message imparted to Peter was this: "Life is more than your job! Here you are with all the fish you had ever hoped for, and now you know that there is more to life than fish. Come with me. You will be throwing our nets to catch people to draw them close to God. Your future includes letting others know what you are experiencing right now of God's deep and abiding love for them. Help people come close to this love."

I'm so impressed with Jesus' gentle touch with Peter. Later events in the ongoing story reveal that Peter was impulsive, passionate, maybe even volatile. He was headstrong, independent, and rebellious. Jesus did not overpower him. He charmed, coaxed, wooed. Some among us, perhaps the most independent, look for God's presence in a different manner. Speak of God and some anticipate a godly hammer, a fist, or rock perhaps, and steel themselves against it. Jesus comes with a breath, a touch, a riddle, even a tear and gets closer. He gently entered Peter's world of fishing and turned it upside down. With an arm on his shoulder he said, "Don't be afraid. Join me to catch people." The concluding line to this touching story is that Peter, James, and John "left everything and followed him." Is this not a calling story?

I hear a clear voice in this story. "Go deeper." Get into the deeper waters of life. If you hunger for a word from God, a calling to trust and obey, a reason to follow, don't linger in the shallows. The daily news and the talk shows, the world of the superficial and mean-spirited will not satisfy. Jesus will ask you to go deeper. Overwork and busyness will rob you of your soul. Complaints and anger will betray your emptiness.

Go into the deep. Go deep into God's word. Pray from the depths. Cry out to God. Fall into the loving arms of Jesus. Still your competitiveness, cease your envy. Quit worrying about what others think. You are loved. There is hope. Mercy abounds. All this can be found in the deep places of life, the depths of God's presence. Be done with self-pity; open your small world to the grace of God. Jesus wants you to be with him sharing this love. Listen. Go into the deep and put down where he tells you. Abundance of grace and compassion will be yours. Could this be the start of your new calling story?

—*Paul Lundborg*
Grace Lutheran Church
Wenatchee, Washington

February 15, 1998

6th Sunday after Epiphany
RC/Pres: 6th Sunday in Ordinary Time

Lessons
Pres/Meth/UCC/Luth	Jer 17:5–10	1 Cor 15:12–20	Lk 6:17–26
Roman Catholic	Jer 17:5–8	1 Cor 15:12, 16–20	Lk 6:17, 20–26
Episcopal	Jer 17:5–10	1 Cor 15:12–20	Lk 6:17–26

Introduction to the Lessons
Lesson 1
Jeremiah 17:5–10 (**Pres/Meth/UCC/Luth/Epis**);
Jeremiah 17:5–8 (**RC**)

Jeremiah employs a psalm that echoes Psalm 1 to warn the Hebrews of the consequences of trusting in humankind rather than God. Those who trust in humans alone will become spiritually barren; those who trust in God will bear fruit despite drought. God blesses or curses humankind according to its deeds.

Lesson 2
1 Corinthians 15:12–20 (**Pres/Meth/UCC/Luth/Epis**);
1 Corinthians 15:12, 16–20 (**RC**)

Some Corinthian Christians denied the resurrection of the dead. Paul argues if there is no resurrection of the dead, then Christ was not raised, and if Christ was not raised, our "faith is futile." But Christ *is* raised, Paul rejoices, and Christians are heirs to eternal life.

Gospel
Luke 6:17–26 (**Pres/Meth/UCC/Luth/Epis**);
Luke 6:17, 20–26 (**RC**)

The disciples are the main target for Christ's "sermon on the plain." After healing members of the capacity crowd, Jesus outlines the "blessings" of discipleship (poverty, hunger, sorrow, and rejection) and the "curses" of a self-serving life (wealth, ample food, laughter, and status). Christ's reversals set out common understanding of "blessing" on its ear.

Theme
Christ's sermon offers the *advanced* course in discipleship and Christian life.

Thought for the Day
>His words rang out across the plain, a call to servant bliss,
>For those who leave their wealth behind, no matter what is missed;
>He said that lives of comfort, might hinder love's perfection
>But joy in Christ will rest on those who serve despite rejection.

Prayer of Meditation
Too often, Lord, we consider our material blessings—our homes, our food, our status in the community—as signs of your favor. Your sermon on the plain suggests that our comfort and ease may be the source of our deepest woe. Help us to learn, servant God, that our spiritual contentment—our blessings—comes as we answer the call to the simple life of servanthood. For Christ's sake we pray. Amen.

Call to Worship
>Leader: Blessed are you who are poor,
>People: For yours is the kingdom of God.
>Leader: Blessed are you who are hungry now,
>People: For you will be filled.
>Leader: Blessed are you who weep now,
>People: For you will laugh.
>Leader: God turns our curses into blessings,
>People: And our sorrow into elation.
>
>—Luke 6:20b–21

Prayer of Adoration
O come let us worship and bow down to the God who upends human understanding. We seek status, you made yourself nothing. You fasted, we fill our plates. You embraced rejection, we crave approval. We lift our hearts in humble gratitude, O God, for this model of Christian perfection. Make us willing to divest ourselves of all material blessings, that we might be filled with your richest treasures. In the name of the servant Jesus, we pray. Amen.

February 15, 1998
6th Sunday after Epiphany
RC/Pres: 6th Sunday in Ordinary Time

Prayer of Confession
Have mercy on us, O God, and forgive us for thinking your plan for our lives should be easy. We realize that many who lived faithful lives endured hardships, rejection, even death for your sake. We see the stresses Moses bore to liberate your people. We know the stories of the prophets, seldom revered, often reviled. We honor Christ's mother, Mary, who set aside the joys of maidenhood to mother the savior of all. And Jesus, the faithful perfector of our faith, chose the hard path that led to his death. We know the path of blessing can be dark and barren, yet we seek the blacktop roads with all of life's amenities. Move us back on the path of blessing, O Lord, even if it winds away from human comfort. In Jesus' name we pray. Amen.

Prayer of Dedication of Gifts and Self
The lessons we learn from the sermon on the plain invite us to walk the high road. We thank you for blessing us with gifts of body and spirit. Take back from us this day these tokens of our gratitude. Walk with us on the journey of faith wherever it may lead. May all we learn from you advance us on the road to eternal peace. In Christ we travel, through Christ we pray. Amen.

Sermon Summary
When Jesus delivers his sermon on the plain, he outlines the heart of Christian discipleship. It is not a lesson in what Christians should do for Christ, but a description of who they are in Christ. Christian discipleship means abandoning our self-interest to become servants of the poor. This is the path of true blessing.

Hymn of the Day
"There Is a Balm in Gilead." Simple and moving, this spiritual conveys the burdens we each carry. As we remember the healing power of Jesus on this Sunday, this hymn reminds us that Jesus' words, both kind and harsh, are shaped out of love. A slow tune, this hymn makes an excellent prayer response, or a prelude to reading the gospel.

Children's Object Talk

Fair's Fair

Object
Three similar glasses or containers: one filled with rice, the second half-full, and the third empty.

Lesson
God fills the poor and needy with good things.

Did you bring your imaginations with you today? I hope so because we have to imagine or pretend something for a few minutes. I have brought along three glasses. I want you to pretend these glasses are people, and if your imaginations are really sharp, you can pretend they are people's stomachs.

One of these stomachs (empty glass) is completely empty. I'll bet if you put this glass to your ear you might, if you're a world-class pretender, hear that tummy growl! Another stomach (half-full glass) has some rice to eat. And the third stomach (full glass) is full.

It's not really fair that one is completely empty. Why don't we fill it up. (Take the half-full glass and pour it into the empty one.) There! The empty one now has something to eat. (Wait for a reaction to see if anyone notices that a new empty glass results.) Now we've got another problem. We still have an empty glass. It's a different one, but it is still empty.

Maybe we can share a little. (Divide the half-full into the empty so that both are one-quarter full.) That seems to work, but those two stomachs don't look like they have very much and the other is so full. I'm not even sure that little bit of rice is going to keep them alive.

What are we going to do? (By now, the obvious solution should be suggested by someone.) Yes, you're right. This full stomach is going to have to share. The only way the poor glass will be treated fairly is if the rich glass gives up some of what it has (pour out until all three are equal).

Jesus once talked about treating the poor fairly. He said God wants them to be filled. But if that's going to happen, the rich will have to share what they have. That might make them angry. The more selfish they are, the angrier they will become. But you and I can see that it's the only way that all God's creation can have a chance to enjoy God's goodness.

—*Jon Temme*

February 15, 1998
6th Sunday after Epiphany
RC/Pres: 6th Sunday in Ordinary Time

The Sermon

Advanced Lessons

Hymns
Beginning of Worship: "You Servants of God"
Sermon Hymn: "'Take up Your Cross,' the Savior Said"
End of Worship: "O Master, Let Me Walk with You"

Scripture
Luke 6:17–26 (For sermon materials on 1 Corinthians 15:12–20, see the November/December 1997 issue of *The Clergy Journal* and on Jeremiah 17:5–10, see the *1997 May/June Planning Issue* of *The Clergy Journal*.)

Sermon Text
"'But woe to you who are rich, for you have received your consolation'" (vs. 24).

My friend Bill was surfing the Internet recently when he came across this humorous piece called "The Lesson" on the Rainier United Methodist Church Home Page. It goes like this:

"Then Jesus took his disciples up the mountain and gathering them around him, he taught them saying,
    Blessed are the poor in spirit, for theirs is the kingdom of heaven
    Blessed are the meek . . .
    Blessed are they that mourn . . .
    Blessed are the merciful . . .
    Blessed are you when persecuted . . .
"Then Simon Peter said, 'Do we have to write this down?'
"And Andrew said, 'Are we supposed to know this?'
"And James said, 'Will we have a test on it?'
"And John said, 'The other disciples didn't have to learn this.'
"And Judas said, 'What does this have to do with real life?'
"Then one of the Pharisees present asked to see Jesus' lesson plan and inquired of Jesus his terminal objectives in the cognitive domain.
"And Jesus wept . . ."

Anyone who has ever taught students knows how resistant they can be to their lessons, especially to the material that really challenges their intellects. So we smile knowingly at the idea of the

Lord's disciples resisting the hard lesson Jesus taught on the Judean plain. And it was a tough lesson, the advanced lesson if you will, in true discipleship.

In his gospel, Luke places this sermon immediately after his account of the naming of the twelve apostles. Perhaps Jesus had observed the newly chosen twelve feeling quite full of themselves and their prestigious appointments, and felt moved to outline just what "blessings" their new assignments would bring: poverty, hunger, weeping, hatred, exclusion, insults, and rejection. Surely this was not what they signed on for when hearing their names called to be the Lord's apostles, their chests puffed out and their heads swelled with pride. Maybe they thought it would be easier at the top, less demanding, thought they could delegate the grunt work of the ministry to the disciples beneath them in the pecking order.

But, no, the advanced lesson made it perfectly clear that the path to a blessed life would not be paved with riches and comfort, status or prestige, but with humility, sacrifice, and the willingness to lose everything to gain everlasting life.

Not long ago I attended the ordination of a new minister. At a point in the ceremony, all the ordained ministers and elders were invited to lay hands on the ordinand. There were at least fifty hands pressing down on my friend as the celebrant offered the ordination prayer. Later, the celebrant explained that the many hands pressing down on the ordinand symbolize the burden of ministry, the burden of Christian discipleship.

Yet Jesus, in his advanced lesson, offers the great paradox of Christian discipleship: the greater the burden, the greater the blessing. The greater the loss, the greater the gain. The greater the risk, the greater the reward, *But whoever loses his life for my sake and for the gospel will save it"* (Mk 8:35, NIV).

Every cell in my body resists this paradox of burden being blessing. I want to believe that Christian discipleship can be a *little* bit of burden and a *lot* of blessing. Deep down, though, I know love is more demanding than that. Love doesn't stop until the last tear is dried, the last slave freed, the last wrong righted, the last sinner saved.

When I was in seminary, I often ate lunch with another student I'll call Jim. Jim and I were on very different career tracks. I was headed for a comfortable parish in a small town; Jim was headed for ministry with the poorest of the poor. While I fretted over what video I should show my youth group on Friday night, Jim

February 15, 1998
6th Sunday after Epiphany
RC/Pres: 6th Sunday in Ordinary Time

wondered how he could be with an illegal immigrant during a court appearance and still attend a peace rally set for the same day. And Jim didn't just help the poor. He dressed simply, ate simply, and lived simply.

One day I asked, "Jim, what motivates you to live with such dedication to the poor?" He thought for a minute and answered quietly, "Because for me, that's what discipleship is . . . it's the only way I find peace."

Today I understand that Jim was living the paradox. In his poverty, he had discovered the riches of the kingdom. In his hunger, he had become full. The burden of discipleship had become his peace. All outward appearances to the contrary, my friend Jim was blessed.

This word *blessed* is important. Some biblical scholars say it means "happy." Others suggest the translation comes closer to "congratulations," as in "congratulations, you who are poor, for yours is the kingdom of God." Now Jesus was not congratulating the followers who would achieve the high standards for discipleship laid out in the sermon on the plain. He was congratulating any who would discover the secret of love hidden beneath the external requirements.

The secret is this: The sermon on the plain does not simply outline *what we should do;* it describes *who we are* as children of the Most High. If we are truly in touch with who we are and allow the Holy Spirit to direct our lives, we will spend our days answering the call of love. As long as there are poor people, we stand in solidarity with them. As long as there are hungry people, we are hungry, too. If one weeps, we all weep. We will endure whatever hatred and persecution comes our way as we seek justice for those who are still oppressed.

In his articles, *Beatitude Stories,* Charles Minifie retells a bit of the story of Anne Frank, the young Jewish girl who, after weeks of hiding from the Nazi troops, was captured and taken to a concentration camp where she and her family died.

While in hiding, Anne lived for weeks in cramped quarters with little food or water and with terror as her constant companion. Yet days before her arrest, Minifie reminds us, she refused to abandon her ideals continuing to uphold her belief in the essential goodness of humankind. "I still believe that people are really good at heart," she wrote in her journal just weeks before a gas chamber took her life.

How I admire people like Anne Frank and my seminarian buddy Jim who have managed to uncover the utter simplicity of Christ's advanced course in discipleship. Our blessings, they learned, will not be found at mega malls, in the never-ending quest for status and self-importance, or even on our "food-shelf Sundays," which may restock the food pantries but still leave us feeling hungry. Christ's advanced lesson teaches us that we will only feel full when we empty ourselves of self-interest and become servants of the poor and the persecuted.

Like Peter, and James, and Bartholomew in *The Lesson*, I keep asking God, "Do I have to learn this?" or "Are we gonna have a test on it?" or "Do I have to turn this in?" But people like Anne and Jim are good teachers and every day I am feeling more ready to take the "advanced lesson." They tell me it can be a real blessing.

—Theresa M. Roos
First Presbyterian Church
South St. Paul, Minnesota

February 22, 1998

Transfiguration
RC: 7th Sunday in Ordinary Time

Lessons

Pres/Meth/UCC/Luth	Ex 34:29–35	2 Cor 3:12—4:2	Lk 9:28–36 (37–43)
Roman Catholic	1 Sam 26:2, 7–9, 12–13, 22–23	1 Cor 15:45–49	Lk 6:27–38
Episcopal	Ex 34:29–35	1 Cor 12:27—13:13	Lk 9:28–36

Introduction to the Lessons
Lesson 1
(1) *Exodus 34:29–35* **(Pres/Meth/UCC/Luth/Epis)**
After receiving the tablets of law from Yahweh, Moses returns from Sinai, his face radiating God's glory. Overcoming their fear of his appearance, the Israelites draw near to Moses to hear God's law. Each time Moses communes with God, he returns with a radiant face. Later he covers his face with a veil so the people will not see the radiance fading.

(2) *1 Samuel 26:2, 7–9, 12–13, 22–23* **(RC)**
David and his nephew, Abishai, find King Saul (who has hunted David) encamped with his troops. They have the chance to kill the king while he sleeps in his tent. Wishing to bring no harm to God's anointed king, David spares Saul's life taking Saul's spear and water jug from the tent to prove his good intentions. Learning that David spared his life, Saul blesses young David.

Lesson 2
(1) *2 Corinthians 3:12—4:2* **(Pres/Meth/UCC/Luth)**
Interpreting Exodus 34:29–35, Paul suggests that Moses covered his face to keep the people from seeing the limits of the law to reflect God's *abiding* glory. Before Christ, the hearts and minds of the people were veiled and prevented from seeing and reflecting God's glory. Christ revealed the fullness of God's glory and through him, Christians are able to reflect God's glory by ever-increasing degrees.

(2) *1 Corinthians 15:45–49* **(RC)**
Paul reflects on the relationship between the first Adam who signifies the physical reality of humankind, and the new Adam, Christ, who represents the spiritual reality of humankind. Just as the physical bodies of humankind will return to dust as was the case with Adam, so will the spiritual bodies of humankind be raised to eternal life, as was the case with Christ.

(3) *1 Corinthians 12:27—13:13* **(Epis)**
Outlining the need for different forms of service in the Christian community, Paul insists each function, though different, is crucial to the work of Christ's body on earth. What equalizes all forms of Christian service is the presence of God's love. The forms and functions of servanthood will end; love will never end. Humans can see only a dim reflection of Christ's glory. Eventually, we will see the fullness of God's glorious love.

Gospel
(1) *Luke 9:28–36 (37–43)* **(Pres/Meth/UCC/Luth);**
Luke 9:28–36 **(Epis)**
On a mountaintop, Peter, John, and James see the praying Jesus transfigured to a dazzling radiance. They also see Moses and Elijah, in all *their* glory, conversing with Jesus about his impending departure from earth. Peter wishes to preserve this glorious moment, but instead the brilliant scene is cast in shadows by a dark cloud and a voice saying: "This is my Son, my Chosen; listen to him!" The following day, off the mountain and back among the needy, Jesus casts a demon from a young boy whom the disciples were unable to heal. Impatient, Jesus rebukes human faithlessness and warns of his immanent betrayal. The disciples don't understand his warning, but are too afraid to ask for its meaning.

(2) *Luke 6:27–38* **(RC)**
Luke continues his record of the "sermon on the plain," further outlining the demands of love. We are to love our enemies, those who hate and abuse us; we are to give even more than is asked of us. Summarizing the precepts, Jesus calls us to "do to others as you would have them do to you." The full rewards of Christian love will be given to those who love unreservedly, expecting nothing in return.

Theme
Fidelity to God on the mundane days will often lead to glory days.

February 22, 1998
Transfiguration

Thought for the Day

How good, Lord, to be here!
Yet we may not remain;
But since you bid us leave the mount,
Come with us to the plain. —Joseph A. Robinson

Prayer of Meditation

There are days, faithful God, when to serve you is sweet bliss. Our minds are filled with prayer, our hearts are filled with compassion, our work feels blessed and fruitful. There are also days when serving you feels dry as desert sand. Our minds are filled with complaints, our hearts filled with cynicism, our work barren and fruitless. Keep us faithful through it all, O God, and perhaps some dreary day when we least expect it, your glory will lift us from the mundane and place us on the mountaintop. In Christ we pray. Amen.

Call to Worship

Leader: I will praise you, O Lord, among the nations;
People: I will sing of you among the peoples.
Leader: For great is your love, higher than the heavens;
People: Your faithfulness reaches to the skies.
Leader: Be exalted, O God, above the heavens,
People: And let your glory be over all the earth.
—Psalm 108, NIV

Prayer of Adoration

O God, the light of your glory pierces all darkness. The warmth of your radiance softens the hardest heart. The presence of your glory breathes life into creation. Because you cannot bear to see your people in despair, you blanket the earth with color. Because you cannot bear to see your people downcast, you send giggling babies and hands of friendship. Because you cannot stand to see your people in sin, you sent us Jesus, the redeemer who guides us into the realms of your glory. Thanks be to you, O God. Amen.

Prayer of Confession

We confess, liberating God, we sometimes choose to be stuck in our routines. They are safe and predictable even if they lack excitement. We like adventure, but we don't like risk. We like comfort, not hardship.

We like a challenge, but not if it's too tough. Forgive us for not trusting you to lead us to mountaintops. We are afraid the terrain will be too rough, the food scarce, the leisure at a premium. Give us the courage to travel the high roads with you. That may take courage, but it may also lead to your glory. In the name of Jesus, we pray. Amen.

Prayer of Dedication of Gifts and Self

How blessed we are, great giver, to live in such abundance. Forbid us, Lord, for taking even one day for granted. Each minute can hold a prayer, each hour the possibility of love and compassion. Today, as we dedicate these gifts, we surrender our time to you, too. O Lord, may we spend each moment in joy no matter what we must face. Help us see your glory in every living thing. Through the grace of Jesus Christ. Amen.

Sermon Summary

Most people have experienced "glory days," mountaintop days when all impediments to experiencing the glory of God temporarily disappear. Those days inevitably fade, leaving only the memory of their joy. When we begin to *see* the world with open, unencumbered and perceptive eyes we begin to see God's glory each day in the little signs all around us.

Hymn of the Day

"I'm Pressing on the Upward Way (Higher Ground)." The disciples are given a brief glimpse of the glory of God when they ascend the mountain with Jesus. Like them, we still seek the path back to the holy ground of height and light. Johnson Oatman Jr. wrote this one of his more than 5,000 gospel songs to express that desire while selling insurance in Mount Holly, New Jersey.

Children's Object Talk

The End of the Road

Object
> A handcrafted object that takes a long time to complete such as a model airplane, or a needlecraft or woodworking project.

Lesson
> The transfigured Jesus confirms that the way of the cross is the way of ultimate glory.

I brought something today that I'm pretty proud of. It took a long time to finish it. It was hard work and sometimes I wondered why I even started working on it.

But I had a picture of what this was going to look like when finished. That picture really looked good and was what started me on this project in the first place. Whenever I felt like giving up, I would just look at the picture and keep on going.

Something like that happened for three special disciples of Jesus who followed him. Their names were Peter, John, and James. They had seen Jesus do many wonderful things. Jesus had healed the sick, turned water into wine, and even raised people from the dead. They believed Jesus was someone special, someone holy and divine.

But they also saw that Jesus made many people angry. Lately, we've been talking about why. Jesus showed people that they were selfish, and that they needed forgiveness. Many people didn't want to hear that. It wasn't always easy for Peter, James, and John to follow Jesus and see that anger.

So one day, Jesus and the three disciples went away to a high mountain. There, before their eyes, Jesus was transfigured. That's a fancy word that means the disciples saw Jesus in all his glory—Jesus, the true God. Following Jesus was hard work and brought many challenges. But at the end of that road was glory, even if the path was hard work.

—*Jon Temme*

The Sermon

Glory Days

Hymns
Beginning of Worship: "O, for a Thousand Tongues to Sing"
Sermon Hymn: "Oh, Wondrous Type! Oh, Vision Fair"
End of Worship: "In the Cross of Christ I Glory"

Scripture
Luke 9:28-36 (37-43) (For additional sermon materials on this passage, see the November/December 1997 and the *1997 May/June Planning Issue* of *The Clergy Journal*.)

Sermon Text
"Now Peter and his companions were weighed down with sleep; but since they had stayed awake, they saw his glory..." (vs. 32).

In the 1970s Bruce Springstein wrote the song *Glory Days* that tells the story of a group of his friends who can't stop reminiscing about the glory days of high school when they were great athletes, lovers, and beauties. In the chorus he sings:

> Glory days, well they'll pass you by
> Glory days, in the wink of a young girl's eyes,
> Glory days, glory days.

Thirty years later, I still can recapture one of my glory days. I was a new elementary teacher in Detroit, Michigan, and my second-grade students and I had decided to put together a Christmas concert for their parents. Using construction paper "capes" for our choir robes, the children sang five songs accompanied by 45-rpm records played on an ancient record player I'd scrounged from the school's audiovisual room.

The "choir," which was made up of around thirty children, half White, half African American, sounded fantastic that day despite our primitive equipment. When they finished the "concert," their parents, grandparents, aunts, and cousins broke into thunderous applause (as thunderous as a group of twenty-two adults can be). The kids were positively radiant from the attention . . . and so was their teacher that day.

Years later, I can still see the faces of those children and remember the incredible pride we felt at our accomplishment. On many a dark day in my life, when I was lower than a snake's belly in a wagon wheel rut, I could conjure up that "glory day" and be renewed.

The day of Christ's transfiguration on the mountaintop must have been that kind of "glory day" for Peter, John, and James. They probably thought, as they made their ascent, that they were just getting away from it all so Jesus could pray. Surely, they never expected to see Jesus in all *his* glory, much less see the great prophets, Moses and Elijah, or hear the voice of God. In fact, it was such a high moment that Peter wanted to hold on to it forever by building three dwellings where Jesus and the prophets could live permanently.

But there's no stopping glory days. They come, they move us, and then they pass, leaving behind only a faint whiff of the joy we felt while we lived them. "Glory days, well they'll pass you by, glory days, in the wink of a young girl's eyes, glory days, glory days."

Unless, of course, we begin to see the glory hidden in every day. Unless, of course, we are brave enough to let go of yesterday's glory so we can see the glory God is revealing today.

February 22, 1998
Transfiguration

How we experience God's glory each day depends, I believe, on just how well we can "see." On the day of the transfiguration, for instance, Luke tells us that *"Peter and his companions were weighed down with sleep; but since they had stayed awake, they saw his glory"* (Lk 9:32). I wonder what kind of eyes the disciples needed, and what kind of eyes we need, to really see God's glory?

For starters, our eyes need to be *open*. The disciples' eyes were tired; perhaps the Lord's transfiguration was too much for their eyes to take, so they were fighting against sleep. By the grace of God, though, they managed to stay awake and saw the miracle unfold before them.

Isn't it amazing how much of life we miss by being asleep . . . even when we're awake? There are times when I feel I have sleepwalked through an entire day. I work at breakneck pace, never looking up to see the weary face of a co-worker, or the loneliness in a parishioner's eyes, or the gloveless hands of the homeless man I pass on a downtown street.

I want to stay awake, but I fill my days so full of activity that I become numb and stop feeling the emotions each day brings. It becomes easier to focus on the glory days gone by than to slow down enough to catch a glimpse of the glory that is unfolding today.

Recently, I created an overview of the Bible on a long piece of bright yellow shelf-paper. Using pictures and key words, I lifted up for my confirmation students the highlights and lowlights of our religious history. At one point in the presentation, one of the students who had been in Sunday school for years asked, "Why didn't we ever hear about any of this before?"

Of course, he *had heard* it all before. But that morning, when he heard our faith story, he was awake, or the story awakened him, and he saw it with new eyes. If we want to see God's glory, our eyes must be open.

Our eyes must also be *unencumbered*. Luke tells us that on the day of the Lord's transfiguration, Peter, John, and James were "weighed down with sleep." How often are we kept from experiencing God's glory each day because we are so encumbered, so "weighed down" by our worries and cares.

These days, massage is often used as a vehicle for getting people in touch with their senses. Massage therapists know that the stress caused by our problems often lodges in our musculature. Those tense muscles can impede our ability to experience the full richness offered up by our senses. The masseuse understands that the more relaxed we are, the more we are able to take in the glorious experiences God sets before us each day.

We may not have a masseuse available every time our muscles tighten. But we do have available a Savior who once said, "Come unto me all you who labor and I will give you rest." It is often when we are restful, unencumbered by our cares, that we enter a glory moment or have a glory day. If we want to see God's glory, our eyes must be unencumbered.

Our eyes, finally, must be *perceptive*. The root word of perceptive means "taking it in." When we really *see* something, when we *take it in*, we understand it at a deeper, more profound level.

Experiencing God's glory each day requires us to look beyond the superficialities of the people and things around us so we can take them in at a deeper level. Some time ago, I read a column in the *St. Paul* (Minnesota) *Pioneer Press* by James Lileks called "Goodbye, Mom, we'll miss you." In his stunning memorial, the author recounts his final meetings with his mother who was dying from cancer, and his reflections on the impact she had on his life. Watching her die, Lileks *saw* his mother for the first time . . . and what he saw was glorious. He writes:

"The ordinary now has its true face: miraculous. Growing up under her hand, her gaze, her heart was a miracle, unbelievable luck . . . We take the miraculous as commonplace because it happens every day." (James Lileks, "Goodbye, Mom, we'll miss you" [*St. Paul Pioneer Press*, November 6, 1996].)

James Lileks had learned what we all must learn, that to see God's glory each and every day, our eyes must be perceptive.

Are the "glory days" behind us as they were for the group in Springstein's song? Or are they before us, stretched out like so many miracles leading us to the heart of God? They are before us, I believe, if by the grace of God our eyes can remain open, unencumbered and perceptive. Then we'll see God's glory all around us, and how radiant it will be.

—Theresa M. Roos
First Presbyterian Church
South St. Paul, Minnesota

February 25, 1998

Ash Wednesday

Lessons

Pres/Meth/UCC/Luth	Joel 2:1–2, 12–17	2 Cor 5:20b –6:10	Mt 6:1–6, 16–21
Roman Catholic	Joel 2:12–18	2 Cor 5:20 –6:2	Mt 6:1–6, 16–18
Episcopal	Joel 2:1–2, 12–17	2 Cor 5:20b –6:10	Mt 6:1–6, 16–21

Introduction to the Lessons

Lesson 1
Joel 2:1–2, 12–17 **(Pres/Meth/UCC/Luth/Epis)**;
Joel 2:12–18 **(RC)**

The prophet sounds an alarm to Israel: the day of the Lord, the day of God's judgment, is at hand. He calls them to repentance through fasting, sorrow for sin, worship, and prayerful supplication for God's forgiveness. If Israel returns to her religious disciplines and turns from her sins, God's harsh judgment may be averted, for ours is a compassionate God.

Lesson 2
2 Corinthians 5:20b—6:10 **(Pres/Meth/UCC/Luth/Epis)**;
2 Corinthians 5:20—6:2 **(RC)**

Paul appeals to the Corinthian Christians to be reconciled to God, for "now is the day of our salvation." Defending the apostolic validity of his ministry, Paul cites the authority of God, the hardships he has endured, and the righteousness he has demonstrated to prove that his ministry is genuine. People may judge him based on outward experiences; the Spirit will judge the purity of his heart.

Gospel
Matthew 6:1–6, 16–21 **(Pres/Meth/UCC/Luth/Epis)**;
Matthew 6:1–6, 16–18 **(RC)**

The prophet Joel calls for the "sound of the trumpet" to bring God's people to repentance. Jesus warns the people to give alms, offer prayers, and fast without "tooting their own horns." If they practice the spiritual disciplines for everyone to see, that will be their reward. It is better to receive God's secret rewards by practicing the disciplines in private.

Theme
Reconciliation to God requires a change in heart, not just a change in external appearances.

Thought for the Day
> The world may judge my gifts and skills
> And give me highest marks
> But God surveys my inner soul
> And grades my depth of heart.

Prayer of Meditation
Holy God, on this Ash Wednesday we come to you seeking the day of our salvation. Our days speed by in a blur of activity, leaving little time for spiritual self-assessment or the practice of spiritual disciplines. Yet we know our souls are restless until they rest in thee. Come, Holy Spirit, and reorganize our priorities so that we may focus our attentions on the things you value most and not on those things most valued by this world. Save us for thy sake, O Lord. Amen.

Call to Worship
> Leader: I acknowledged my sin to you,
> People: And I did not hide my iniquity;
> Leader: I said, "I will confess my transgressions to the Lord,"
> People: And you forgave the guilt of my sin.
> Leader: Happy are those whose transgression is forgiven,
> People: Whose sin is covered. —Adapted from Psalm 32

Prayer of Adoration
In quiet moments when we reflect upon the gift of Jesus Christ, we are rendered speechless by the enormity of his great sacrifice. Perhaps you are most praised at those moments, loving God, when words fail us and we can only wipe away our tears and stand before you in humble gratitude. As we enter this Lenten season, help us to carve out time each day to reexperience Christ's redeeming grace and recommit our lives to you. Only through such fellowship will we find our hope and satisfy our deepest longings. We praise you, saving God. Amen.

February 25, 1998
Ash Wednesday

Prayer of Confession

We do not like to be reminded of the fleeting nature of life, O God. We prefer to live in denial, pretending our lives on earth will never end. The ashes of this day force us to consider the brevity of our lives. We confess to you, God of our days, that we have kept our eyes focused on ourselves while averting our eyes from you. Are we afraid to see your holiness? Afraid of its demands? Forgive us, Lord, for trying to escape your gaze with too many distractions, too many plans. Gently turn our eyes toward you so that we might spend the rest of our days in sight of our salvation. Amen.

Prayer of Dedication of Gifts and Self

We bring our gifts to you as a sign of our penitence. We promise in the days ahead to seek you in quiet prayer, in confession, in repentance and renewed zeal for your word. You have held nothing back from us in your effort to free us from self-centeredness and sin. You gave your own son. Help us to give the best of ourselves. For Christ's sake, we ask it. Amen.

Sermon Summary

The phoenix, a beautiful bird from Greek mythology, was believed to rise from the ashes of her predecessor. When Christians seek reconciliation with God, ourselves, and others we also find new life springing from the ashes of broken relationships.

Hymn of the Day

"Jesus, Keep Me Near the Cross." Ash Wednesday begins the walk with Jesus to Jerusalem and the crucifixion. The hymn for today preserves both reality of that saving act of Christ so long ago, but also the reality of ourselves living in the shadow of that grace and sacrifice. The tune is simple and meditative, with a refrain that will help those who are unfamiliar with it to feel the mood it sets for Lent. Fanny Crosby sent this and 8,000 other hymns winging around the world under various false names. Blind from birth, she worked frequently with lay composer William Doane, who wrote the line for her hymn in 1869.

Children's Object Talk

Anytime Is Forgiveness Time

Object
Several large three-ring binders full of papers.

Lesson
Anytime is the right time to receive forgiveness and rejoice in God's grace.

Today is a special day. Normally we worship on Sunday, but this is Wednesday. Yes, it's Ash Wednesday. For hundreds of years, Christians have worshiped on this day to begin to get ready for Easter celebrations. Do you know what Easter is? (wait for responses) It's when we remember that Jesus died for our sins and rose again from the dead.

But today on Ash Wednesday, people around the world will think about something sad. They'll think about how they have sinned and not done what God wants them to do. Hopefully they'll think about the good news that God forgives our sin. Because of that we can forgive ourselves and others also.

But we don't have to have just one day a year when we think about the bad things we have done. That would mean we'd have to keep a record of all the things we've done wrong and save them up. For people like you and me, that would start to add up to a lot of paper (bring out the three-ring binders). It is easy to be disobedient, stubborn, selfish, or hurtful. If forgiveness came only once a year, we would have to organize our sins to remember them all. We would need binders, dividers, and tabs, and lots and lots of paper.

But thank God that when we know we have sinned and want to be forgiven, God is ready to listen and forgive right away. Whether it's first thing in the morning, at lunch in the middle of the day, or late at night, we can always confess our sins to God and be assured that we are forgiven.

It is important to have a few special times during the year like today, Ash Wednesday, to think about our need for forgiveness. But don't forget: anytime is the right time to say "I'm sorry, God. Please forgive me."

—*Jon Temme*

February 25, 1998
Ash Wednesday

The Sermon

Phoenix from the Ashes

Hymns
Beginning of Worship: "Forgive Our Sins as We Forgive"
Sermon Hymn: "Great God, Your Love Has Called Us Here"
End of Worship: "What Wondrous Love Is This?"

Scripture
2 Corinthians 5:20b—6:10 (For sermon materials on Joel 2:1–2, 12–17, see the November/December 1997 issue of *The Clergy Journal* and on Matthew 6:1–6, 16–21, see the *1997 May/June Planning Issue* of *The Clergy Journal*.)

Sermon Text
"... *we entreat you on behalf of Christ, be reconciled to God*" (vs. 20b).

Greek mythology tells the story of a magnificent bird, plumed in purples, golds, reds, and blues, that was known as the phoenix. According to the myth, the phoenix lived for 500 years, and at its life's end would build a nest high in the trees and line it with richly scented spices and herbs. There the phoenix rested until the sun ignited the nest, and the fire consumed both nest and bird. The miracle came when a new phoenix would rise from the ashes of its predecessor, new life springing from the sacrifice of the old.

Is there anything as lifeless as a pile of cold ashes? I think of the many fires my husband built on our camping trips out West. How warm and cozy those fires were on crisp Montana nights. How cold and uninviting the ashes were the next morning. It is hard to imagine any life springing from cold, dry ashes.

The power of the myth of the phoenix rising from the ashes is that while it does not deny the inevitable death of living things, still it points beyond to the ultimate power life has over death. And that is the power of Ash Wednesday, too. The cross formed from ashes on the foreheads of Christian people reminds us and the world around us that death is inevitable. But the ashes also point beyond to the possibility of new life arising from the cold, hard reality of death.

In her book, *To Dance with God*, Gertrude Mueller Nelson describes an Italian custom that takes place just as the season of Epiphany gives way to Lent. All the townspeople sort through and discard everything they collected during the previous year. They pile up the stuff—old clothes, box springs, cast-off chairs—and they burn everything in a huge bonfire. This is their way of clearing out the old to make way for the new. It is a way of reducing to ashes the chaff of their lives to make way for what will be new.

Lent is like that for Christians. It is our annual rite of passage, our time in the wilderness between the hope of Christmas and Easter's endless joy. During this in-between time we remember Christ's passion for all people, his commitment to God's life-giving word, his willingness to go as far as obedience required to remain faithful to God's call. Lent is our time to remember.

Lent is also a time for reconciliation, a time when we let go of the accumulated debris that keeps us from experiencing intimacy with ourselves, with others, and with God. The root definition of *reconciliation* is "bringing back together again." Being reconciled means breaking down any barriers that keep us from being authentic and close. When people are reconciled to one another the tension between them gives way to gentle ease. They let down their guard and talk without fear of offending the other. Once reconciled, laughter and tears flow more easily, for peace is restored.

Ash Wednesday, with its reminder of death and its promise of new life, invites Christians into a time of fence-mending when, once relationships are restored, hearts can love openly and souls can soar freely, unburdened now by sin and alienation. *"We entreat you on behalf of Christ,"* Paul said, *"be reconciled to God."*

Being reconciled to God often starts with being reconciled to ourselves. My life has taught me that our capacity for intimacy with God and others is directly proportionate to our capacity to love ourselves.

When I entered into friendship with God, I was only half myself. I was hurt in childhood, so my heart had a lot of emotional scar tissue that needed to be removed before I could feel God's love. There were times when it felt like God was using a pumice stone to smooth my hardened heart. In God's skillful hands, the scars on my heart were reduced to a powder which God blew gently to the wind. Finally I was at peace, reconciled to myself and open to receiving God's grace.

Not long ago I read an excerpt from a book by Syl Jones, a writer from Excelsior, Minnesota, called *Rescuing Little Roundhead*. As a child, Syl was sexually molested by an older boy in a

February 25, 1998
Ash Wednesday

men's room in a neighborhood park. Though there were people around who could have protected him, no one came to his rescue. After he described the abuse to his parents, his father criticized him for not preventing the attack. Syl was eight years old.

The molestation cut deep scars into Syl's spirit. He became hard, tough, and defensive. Filled with despair, he decided to end his life. Preparing to jump from the roof of his own house, a voice within kept him from suicide saying, "You have something to do." That voice pushed open the door to Syl's reconciliation with himself, and from the ashes of his self-hatred a writer was born.

Being reconciled to God also means being reconciled with one another. As a minister I have had the holy privilege of spending time with dying men and women. After the shock of the initial diagnosis abates, most people are not afraid to die. What they fear most is dying without being fully reconciled to the people they've hurt.

My dear friend, Bea, spent the last months of her life writing letters to people she loved. In each letter she thanked the person for the good times they had shared and asked forgiveness for any wrong she might have done to them. When she died, Bea was totally reconciled to everyone she knew. Bea's death was radiant; from the ashes of her dying grew a life of eternal peace.

Peace, in the end, is why God calls us to reconciliation. Speaking for God, Isaiah sounds the call: "Let them make peace with me, yes, let them make peace with me." It is a call to honesty, to introspection, to confession and especially to repentance—a changed life.

Not long ago I watched the movie *Dead Man Walking*, the story of a hardened murderer on death row who is befriended by a nun, Sister Helen Prejean. Throughout the movie, Matthew Poncelet denies his participation in the brutal murders of two teenage lovers.

When all appeals for clemency are exhausted, the date of Matthew's execution is set. During the hours before his death, Poncelet finally confesses the murders to Sister Helen and in a highly emotional scene they pray and weep. Just before the lethal injection is administered, Matthew asks forgiveness of the parents of the victims and dies with prayer on his lips.

"Dead man walking," the executioner calls out as Matthew is led to his death. But he is not a dead man. He is alive . . . alive in Christ because in a moment of grace he was reconciled to God through Jesus Christ—just like a phoenix rising from the cold, lifeless ashes.

—*Theresa M. Roos*
First Presbyterian Church
South St. Paul, Minnesota

March 1, 1998

1st Sunday in Lent

Lessons

Pres/Meth/UCC/Luth	Deut 26:1–11	Rom 10:8b–13	Lk 4:1–13
Roman Catholic	Deut 26:4–10	Rom 10:8–13	Lk 4:1–13
Episcopal	Deut 26:(1–4) 5–11	Rom 10:(5–8a) 8b–13	Lk 4:1–13

Introduction to the Lessons

Lesson 1
Deuteronomy 26:1–11 (**Pres/Meth/UCC/Luth**);
Deuteronomy 26:4–10 (**RC**);
Deuteronomy 26:(1–4) 5–11 (**Epis**)

After reciting the law of Israel, Moses outlines the ritual for bringing the first fruits of the land to the Lord's sanctuary. Handing the basket of produce to the priest, each head of household recites the story of his liberation from Eygptian oppression and God's provision of fertile land. The presentation of first fruits commences a communal celebration of the people.

Lesson 2
Romans 10:8b–13 (**Pres/Meth/UCC/Luth**);
Romans 10:8–13 (**RC**); *Romans 10:(5–8a) 8b–13* (**Epis**)

Unlike the Hebrew people who sought righteousness through observance of Torah (Israel's polity), followers of Christ find righteousness through confession of and belief in Christ alone. Whether Jew or Greek matters not; all who call "on the name of Christ will be saved." Justification is not earned; it is God's gift to all who believe.

Gospel
Luke 4:1–13 (**Pres/Meth/UCC/Luth/RC/Epis**)

Following his baptism, Jesus is driven by the Holy Spirit into the wilderness where he fasts for forty days. Famished, he is visited by the devil who tempts him with promises of food, power, glory, and miraculous protection from harm. Jesus rebuts each temptation with Scripture, standing firm against the urge to employ his divine power for personal use. Thwarted, Satan gives up—for the time being.

March 1, 1998
1st Sunday in Lent

Theme
Telling our faith stories gives language to our hearts and a path to spread the gospel of Christ.

Thought for the Day
When touched by grace, the heart wells up
With gratitude and joy;
To speak its truth for all to hear,
The heart must speech employ.

Prayer of Meditation
The signs of your grace are all around us, God of ceaseless love. Each new morning, each free breath we take, bears witness to the life we find in you. Because of Christ, sin has loosened its grip on our souls. Because of Christ, though trouble may attach, it no longer defeats. Give us, God of the word, a language to tell our stories of faith, so that we may speak of your saving presence and your great healing heart. Amen.

Call to Worship
Leader: I will also praise you with the harp
People: For your faithfulness, O my God;
Leader: My lips will shout for joy
People: When I sing praises to you—
Leader: My tongue will tell of your righteous acts
People: All the day long.
—Adapted from Psalm 71

Prayer of Adoration
What a wonderful gift is your holy word, O God. Each page of the Scriptures reveals a glimpse of your goodness, a whisper of your grace, a hint of your love. Truly we are, by your mercy, a "people of the book." May we never devalue your word, O God. May we never use your word as a weapon to prove a theological point or promote a religious position. May it be for us and others simply a "lamp to our feet and a light for our path." In Jesus' name we pray. Amen.

Prayer of Confession

Pardon us, dearest Lord, for the ways our words have wounded others this week. Surely nothing cuts the human heart deeper than the unkind word. Yet we often use our words to criticize, judge, and put others down. Gossip is a national sport, our way of building ourselves up at the expense of others. Fill our hearts with your words, O God, that we might build your kingdom of love . . . one word at a time. In joy we ask it. Amen.

Prayer of Dedication of Gifts and Self

These gifts tell a story, Lord. They are the language of our grateful hearts. They offer our thanks for the many who, in telling their stories of faith, have brought us in contact with you. They express our desire to keep the story going so that in the end "every tongue will confess that Jesus Christ is Lord." In whose name we pray. Amen.

Hymn of the Day

"Forty Days and Forty Nights." Minor tunes were very much the staple of hymnody for centuries, but are now largely an anomaly. During Lent, however, they are more appropriate than ever. Using them through the season will allow the celebration of resurrection to resound in even greater contrast. *"Heinlein"* is one such tune attributed to Martin Herbst in 1676, but the text was written much later (1856) when it appeared in a short collection by George Smyttan, the son of a British doctor in Bombay.

Children's Object Talk

One for All

Object
Some small treat, preferably not candy, for those children who are present.

Lesson
God's grace is for all people.

I have a little present for all of you today. Or at least I think I do. I'm not sure I have enough to go around. Maybe we should divide up into two groups.

Could I have everyone who has clothing with the color red in it to sit over here. Everyone who is not wearing clothing with red can sit over there. (Modify the

March 1, 1998
1st Sunday in Lent

selection to fit your own circumstances, but *do not* use age or gender as the factor.)

Great, now we have two groups. I guess I should tell you that I don't like the color red, so I'll pass out the gifts to those who are not wearing red. Does that seem fair? (Wait for a reply, and then engage the children in a discussion of what is not fair about it. Try to elicit feelings they have about being discriminated against in this arbitrary way.)

You know, you are absolutely right. This was not fair. Please all sit together again. I assure you I have enough gifts to go around and will give them to you in a few minutes.

What I just did has a long word to describe it. It's called *discrimination*. Selfish people, and that can be you and me at times, sometimes think that certain people are better than others. Many times they think that way because of foolish reasons. Maybe it's the color of one's skin or how poor or rich someone is, or how old they are.

I'll tell you a fact that you should always remember. God wants us to treat all people equally. Jesus lived, died, and rose again for everyone. God created and loves all people, and all who call Jesus their friend and Savior are part of the kingdom of God.

—*Jon Temme*

The Sermon

Winning Words

Hymns
Beginning of Worship: "Come, Christians, Join to Sing"
Sermon Hymn: "I Love to Tell the Story"
End of Worship: "O Word of God Incarnate"

Scripture
Romans 10:5–13 (For sermon materials on Deuteronomy 26:1–11, see the November/December 1997 issue of *The Clergy Journal* and on Luke 4:1–13, see the *1997 May/June Planning Issue* of *The Clergy Journal.*)

Sermon Text
"For it is with your heart that you believe and are justified, and it is with your mouth that you confess and are saved" (vs. 10, NIV).

Did you hear the one about Ole and Lena? Lena says to Ole, "Ole, you never tell me you love me anymore!" And Ole says, "I told you I loved you on the day that we got married. If I change my mind, I'll let you know."

I guess Ole hasn't read any of the research studies that show just how important people find those three little words, "I love you." Of course, the words have to be backed up with loving actions, but still, there's nothing quite as uplifting to a tired spirit than to hear those three gentle words.

When I provide marriage counseling to young couples, I always ask them to describe how they tell one another of their love. Often the women will say, "I tell him I love him all the time; I wish he would say it more." The men more often describe the things they do to demonstrate their love, telling me of flowers they've brought home, or cars they've repaired, or bathrooms they've cleaned—without having to be asked.

Allowing for the differences between men and women, I still tell couples, especially the fellows, that saying words of love each day is crucial to sustaining intimacy, especially after the first fires of passion have dimmed. I know of what I speak. My husband has healed and renewed me each day of our marriage with his words of love and support.

It's amazing how powerful words are. They can lift people up or bring them down. They push people forward or hold them back. Words can be toxic, or they can be tonic for the soul. Words can woo people, wound people, win people.

Winning people is what Christianity is most about and words are one of the important vehicles for communicating the gospel of love. "One *believes with the heart* and so is justified, and one *confesses with the mouth* and so is saved," Paul says in today's text. Faith, it seems, is a two-step process.

Faith begins in the heart like a tiny flame which, when fanned, spreads like wildfire to the whole of one's being. I think back to the weeks and months before I knew that Jesus was and would always be my Savior.

I was raised in a pious Christian home, but by the time I reached college I had fallen away from the faith. I stayed away from the church and from God for more than a decade, though, of course, God never strayed from me. When I married, my new husband and I began attending a little church on the prairie.

The minister of that church was not a great preacher, but he was a great Christian. He loved the Bible and took very seriously the commission to make disciples of all nations. Sunday after

March 1, 1998
1st Sunday in Lent

Sunday he preached sermons about the need for salvation. And for the most part, he was preaching to the converted.

But sitting in the middle of the congregation, there was one young woman who had not heard the good news preached in many years. One Sunday, it was late in the Lenten season, the minister suggested to his flock that telling the good news was like throwing a life preserver to a drowning man. "You can throw that life preserver right next to that drowning soul," he said in his high-pitched voice, "but unless that person is willing to grab on, that life preserver won't do him any good."

The concept was so simple as were his words, but his sermon hit the mark and the mark was my heart. For I was drowning. I looked okay from the outside, no one would have suspected I was in any danger. But inside, my soul was sinking in despair.

I thought of that sermon all week. It was Holy Week. Spring was beginning to warm the air and green the trees. It took all week, but our pastor's words finally melted my heart. Sitting in my room looking out at a newly budded tree, I caught hold of that life preserver and knew in my heart I was saved. It was Good Friday, a very good day indeed.

For weeks, I kept my conversion hidden in my heart. It was, I thought, a secret I shared with God. One day, though, I was with our pastor and he admitted to me that as he neared retirement, he wondered sometimes if his ministry had counted for anything.

I could not keep silent. "You remember that message you preached about the gospel and the life preserver?" I asked. "Yes," he said, turning slowly toward me. "Well, I really needed that life preserver and if you hadn't thrown it out to me, I might never have found Christ's peace." I am sure I've never seen a smile as radiant as his was that day.

The day I told my faith story to our pastor, I completed step two of the faith process. I had already believed the truth about Christ in my heart. Telling the story to my pastor became my first confession of faith. I think Paul was right: belief and profession belong together. The gospel was never meant to be a private affair; it is meant to be proclaimed.

In our age, though, it can be hard to confess our faith. We are afraid we might embarrass ourselves by talking about where God is present in our lives. Even in the church, in casual conversations, people often avoid talking about their faith. Yet, most of us are Christians today because people had the courage to talk about their faith in Christ.

During our church's adult education time, a seminary professor spoke with gratitude about the Sunday school teacher he had as a high school student. Week after week this dedicated teacher challenged her students to think about the faith, talk about their doubts, affirm what they believed. She took Christianity seriously and created an open, intellectually stimulating environment in which her students could safely discuss their faith.

Where would we be if others had never confessed their faith? If our ancient foremothers and forefathers hadn't wondered about God around campfires, at town wells, and in synagogues? If Mary and Martha, Peter and Paul hadn't told their stories of faith?

After my conversion in that little midwestern church, I devoured books about the faith. C. S. Lewis challenged my intellect; Peter Marshall stirred my soul; Marjorie Holmes showed me Christ in everyday life; Thomas Merton led me to solitude. More recently, Kathleen Norris, in her books *Dakota* and *The Cloister Walk*, has reminded me of what God can do in a person's life when she willingly steps onto the path of faith.

In the end, we are all preachers leading souls to Christ. I once visited a fourth grade Sunday school class where the teacher was reading a book about giving. Each time she asked a question, even before the question was out, a little boy in the back shouted, "Jesus." Every answer he offered to her questions was "Jesus." Some might think this little boy was missing the point of the lesson, but I knew he wasn't. Deep in his heart, he'd already gotten the point. For Christians, the answer is Jesus. Jesus the teacher. Jesus the prophet. Jesus the healer. Jesus the crucified. Jesus the risen. Jesus the life preserver.

That little guy had gotten faith in his heart, and he kept right on confessing it. He had heard God's gospel of "I love you," and wanted to keep on saying it.

—*Theresa M. Roos*
First Presbyterian Church
South St. Paul, Minnesota

March 8, 1998

2nd Sunday in Lent

Lessons

Pres/Meth/UCC/Luth	Gen 15:1–12, 17–18	Phil 3:17—4:1	Lk 13:31–35
Roman Catholic	Gen 15:5–12, 17–18	Phil 3:17—4:1	Lk 9:28b–36
Episcopal	Gen 15:1–12, 17–18	Phil 3:17—4:1	Lk 13:(22–30) 31–35

Introduction to the Lessons

Lesson 1
Genesis 15:1–12, 17–18 (**Pres/Meth/UCC/Luth/Epis**);
Genesis 15:5–12, 17–18 (**RC**)
This exchange between Abram and God discloses God's promise of land and descendants. As commanded, Abram offers a sacrifice, and God responds by making a covenant, promising to give the land spanning from the Nile to the Euphrates Rivers to Abram's descendants.

Lesson 2
Philippians 3:17—4:1 (**Pres/Meth/UCC/Luth/RC/Epis**)
Paul implores the Christians at Philippi to follow his example and condemns the practice of those who seem to be consumed with earthly and physical pursuits. He raises the imagery of the heavenly citizenship of the faithful who will be transformed in the coming glory of Christ.

Gospel
(1) *Luke 13:31–35* (**Pres/Meth/UCC/Luth**);
Luke 13:(22–30) 31–35 (**Epis**)
Warned to flee from Herod, Jesus vows to continue his mission and declares his intention to go to Jerusalem. He concludes with a lament over Jerusalem, noting the city's refusal to respond to God's prophets.

(2) *Luke 9:28b–36* (**RC**)
This is Luke's account of the transfiguration, with Jesus' physical appearance changing dramatically in the midst of his praying upon

the mountain. His disciples see him talk with Moses and Elijah while a voice from above declares his sonship.

Theme
Grace is not given for the sake of exploitation.

Thought for the Day
Karl Barth once observed that grace always demands to be answered with gratitude. Gratitude should be the echo that follows the shout, the thunder that follows the lightning.

Prayer of Meditation
Not one of us here has been made to be a copy of anyone else, O God, and your love for each of us is as if we were the only child you have. Your acts of creating are ever unique and undertaken with a care that we can scarcely imagine. Help us to see that as we have been created with such care to guard our individuality, so you have called us to respond with an appreciation of the value of our personal relationship with you. As you have loved us in particular ways, so let us return that love out of our distinct and different being. Amen.

Call to Worship
You are the salt of the earth. You are the light of the world. Let us gather to be renewed as the body of Christ that in our life and witness we might give flavor and shed light on the world in which we live.

Prayer of Adoration
Loving God, we marvel at your countless expressions of that love. Though we have turned from you more times than we can remember, you have never responded in kind. To know you has been to be undergirded by a steady, constant grace. In our experiences of lostness, you have searched us out. In our moments of confusion, you have supplied orientation and order. In our rebellions and restlessness, you have been ever-patient. If it seems that your love has been lost on us, we say that we have taken notice of how our ties have endured. Thanks be to you, dear God, for holding us safely and securely. Amen.

March 8, 1998
2nd Sunday in Lent

Prayer of Confession

Too much we have exploited faith, dear God. We have accepted forgiveness without having ever faced our sins. We have harbored too many expectations in our faith and shied away from sacrifices. Too many prayers have centered on our wants and too few have been offered for the needs of others. We have been content to be served instead of moving forward to serve others. Blessed with the gifts of intellect and reason, we have used those gifts to plot and connive and seek advantage. Save us from ourselves that your grace may not become a stumbling point. Give us the clarity of faith in this moment to pray rightly. Give us a measure of Christ's heart and refresh our memories that while he was rich, he became poor for our sakes. In his spirit we strive to pray. Amen.

Prayer of Dedication of Gifts and Self

Help us to see the sacramental quality of our giving, dear God—outward signs of inward graces. Help us to see how each act of stewardship demonstrates how you are at work within the life of the giver. Help us to see evidence of your loving presence in the tithes and offerings that we now place upon the altar and dedicate to the continuing ministry we carry in the name of Christ. And finally, dear God, consecrate these gifts and guide their usage so that this congregation may indeed become the blessing to others that you intend us to be as the body of Christ in whose name we pray. Amen.

Sermon Summary

Paul is forced to confront those who have perverted the major theme of his preaching by declaring that grace has liberated believers from the need to attend to the righteousness of their personal lives. Paul declares that grace frees people for and not from ethical life.

Hymn for the Day

"O Love, How Deep, How Broad, How High." This is an unusual tune, and not for the timid organist or congregation! It is, nevertheless, a hymn of great power recounting the life of Christ that is well worth the time to learn. The melody is in a punctuated Gallic rhythm that will bear careful attention: it is thrillingly done with strength, deadly when done too slowly or without strong leadership from the organ or a singer. The tune *"Deo Gracias"* dates back to the conquest of France by Henry V of England around 1415. To the song recounting the battle it is said that he requested the words, *Deo Gracias* (Glory to God), to be added in thanks for the victory. The words are from an anonymous Latin text of the same period. Though harder than average, this tune could be part of a congregational Lenten discipline: adding a verse each Sunday as the life of Christ unfolds.

Children's Object Talk

Dual Citizenship

Object
A passport and a baptismal certificate.

Lesson
As "heavenly" citizens, we owe allegiance to and claim a place within the kingdom of God.

I want to show you a very important document. Does anyone know what this is? (Wait for responses.) It is a very official-looking document, isn't it? It has a few government stamps on it and my photo, too. It serves a very important purpose. It tells others that I am a Canadian (or American).

When I travel outside of Canada, this shows I belong to a country. If I have any problems when I travel, I can phone the Canadian embassy for help.

Whenever I carry my passport, I think about how glad I am to live in a country like Canada. There are many great countries to live in, but Canada is my home. I'm proud of that. I hope that when people look at me they think good things about my country based upon my actions.

We are citizens of _____. But you and I are also citizens of another kind of home or family—the family of God. We don't have a passport for that family. But we do have a special document. If you have been baptized you have a baptismal certificate. Ask your dad or mom to show it to you. Maybe they even could have it framed and hang it on your bedroom wall.

Your baptismal certificate is like a passport. It can remind you that you are protected by God wherever you go. It reminds you that you always have a place to call home.

As a citizen of a heavenly family, you also have special responsibilities. People should look at what you do and say and think good things about the family of God. And you should think often about the blessings and benefits you enjoy as part of God's family, a citizen of God's kingdom.

—*Jon Temme*

March 8, 1998
2nd Sunday in Lent

The Sermon

Some Are Enemies of the Cross

Hymns
Beginning of Worship: "All Hail the Power of Jesus' Name"
Sermon Hymn: "In the Cross of Christ I Glory"
End of Worship: "Stand Up, Stand Up for Jesus"

Scripture
Philippians 3:17—4:1 (For sermon materials on Genesis 15:1-12, 17-18, see the November/December 1997 issue of *The Clergy Journal* and on Luke 13:31-35, see the *1997 May/June Planning Issue* of *The Clergy Journal.*)

Sermon Text
"For many live as enemies of the cross of Christ; I have often told you of them, and now I tell you even with tears" (vs. 18).

Paul would probably be stunned to hear that the words he wrote to particular Christians and particular churches were ever brought together as sacred Scripture to be applied to universal circumstances. His letters were not treatises and theological works with a general audience in mind.

This morning's text is a continuation of a rather passionate outburst begun earlier in his letter, but it seems that the object of his scorn has shifted. No longer does he seem to be speaking to foes who are asserting that grace is not sufficient to make Christians right with God. Now, he seems to be speaking to another group who have been sympathetic to what he has preached ... indeed, more than sympathetic. These are men and women who have rejected the law as a means of righteousness and with an absolute reliance upon grace have declared that no behavior is forbidden. Since they had been claimed on a spiritual level, nothing done at the physical level was any longer of consequence.

Likely, Paul is especially incensed by this perversion of his preaching, and he fires off some angry words telling these folks that their behavior will bring them destruction and he calls them "enemies of the cross." This curious phrase is Paul's way of saying that they are abusing the victory that was won in Christ's death and sacrifice. Instead of being freed from sin, they have seized an opportunity to sin.

Anyone who has ever preached or sought to articulate the faith in any form has been misunderstood from time to time. A statement intended to say one thing is heard to say quite another. Sometimes it is a lack of precision by the speaker and other times circumstances within the listener have interfered with the transmission. It is understandable and manageable.

Of course, there is another dynamic that occurs from time to time when the misunderstanding is not as innocent. Sometimes the listener sifts for particular hints and evidence. The proclamation is twisted to serve the whims of the hearer. The listening is only to direct the sermon, and that is when preachers get angry. The anger does not pour out of a candid disagreement. To admit that we see things differently is to stay in bounds; no preacher has a lock on the truth of the gospel. On the other hand, to try to preach faithfully all the while an audience is twisting words to serve another agenda is to provoke a kind of righteous anger. That is, I imagine, what is behind Paul's outburst. His own words are being used to promote a perversion of the gospel of grace he was preaching.

Paul's anger begins to subside, leading him to close out this section of his Philippian letter, and he does this in a most interesting way. He tells the Philippians that we are "citizens of heaven." Perhaps a more faithful rendering would be that we are "a colony of heaven" and if that is so, then Paul's words would have struck a proud and familiar chord in the hearts and minds of the folks at Philippi. It was a Roman colony, after all—on the edge of Asia Minor and Greece. It was a long way from Rome, but it was a colony nonetheless. People acted Roman. They spoke Latin, dressed in Roman garb, and attended courts and commercial pursuits that had been modeled after Rome. Paul is writing to people who understood what it meant to be a citizen of a colony, so he reminds them that they are citizens of a different empire. Their community is an extension of heaven, he tells them. So act like it, he says. "Stand firm in the Lord, my beloved."

Yes, he says, we are made righteous by God's actions and not our own. But if you have been touched—really touched by grace—then you know that you belong to another kingdom. In the same way that Roman citizenship requires a certain kind of behavior, so to be a citizen of heaven requires that people act in one. It is not

March 8, 1998
2nd Sunday in Lent

Roman clothing and language and currency that makes one a Roman citizen. Citizenship is bestowed from beyond both in the case of Rome and heaven. Grace comes from beyond, and it is not what we do that makes it happen. Once that grace takes hold of us, however, and we are enfolded by the healing presence of God, how can one try to twist faith to serve selfish purposes.

With this, Paul concludes his words. Perhaps the Philippians needed to be dressed down for their abuses. I suppose we all could stand to be scolded from time to time.

—Gary L. Walling
Heights Christian Church
Shaker Heights, Ohio

March 15, 1998

3rd Sunday in Lent

Lessons

Pres/Meth/UCC/Luth	Isa 55:1–9	1 Cor 10:1–13	Lk 13:1–9
Roman Catholic	Ex 3:1–8a, 13–15	1 Cor 10:1–6, 10–12	Lk 13:1–9
Episcopal	Ex 3:1–15	1 Cor 10:1–13	Lk 13:1–9

Introduction to the Lessons

Lesson 1

(1) *Isaiah 55:1–9* **(Pres/Meth/UCC/Luth)**
The prophet opens with a wonderfully gracious call for the people to come and receive wine, milk, and bread despite a lack of money. The promise of a covenant is declared that will make the nation great. The passage concludes with a call for repentance, noting that the ways of God are always higher than the ways of people.

(2) *Exodus 3:1–8a, 13–15* **(RC)**; *Exodus 3:1–15* **(Epis)**
While tending flocks, Moses encounters God in a burning bush. God declares that he has seen the sufferings of the Hebrews enslaved in Egypt and is commissioning Moses to return to the land of the Nile to liberate the people. God directs Moses to worship upon the mountain on which he is standing when he returns with the people.

Lesson 2
1 Corinthians 10:1–13 **(Pres/Meth/UCC/Luth/Epis)**;
1 Corinthians 10:1–6, 10–12 **(RC)**
In demanding that the Christians in Corinth live faithful and exemplary lives, Paul utilizes historical memories. He suggests that God's displeasure with their ancestors who had escaped from Egypt led to them being struck down in the wilderness.

Gospel
Luke 13:1–9 **(Pres/Meth/UCC/Luth/RC/Epis)**
In response to a question about some people slaughtered by Pilate, Jesus replies that their demise was not evidence of their sin. Nevertheless,

March 15, 1998
3rd Sunday in Lent

people must repent or face punishment. He offers the parable of the barren fig tree to demonstrate the destruction of that which is worthless.

Theme
The life of faith is filled with demands.

Thought for the Day
The assurance of faith is not that we shall be spared all pain and evil, but that even when we walk through the valley of the shadows, we shall not be alone.

Prayer of Meditation
Let our faces be reflections of your kindness. Let our hands be reflections of your passion for your children. Let our hearts be reflections of your love. We pray, dear God, that our lives may provide evidence of your life in us and among us. Amen.

Call to Worship
God has showed us what is good, and what the Lord requires of us: to do justice, to love kindness, and to walk humbly with our God.

Prayer of Adoration
You have created our world and set it into motion. You have set time in place to govern life and paced its flow by the turning of the seasons. Though the cold of the season lingers, there is something in the air . . . hints of new life about to break out. We give thanks for the completeness of your design: for the fallow times that prompt us to pause and consider and for the stimulating times of growth and celebration. Because in you we know what it means to be whole and good, we draw close, O God. Receive us now. Amen.

Prayer of Confession
Where you have given the gifts of purpose, O God, we have substituted unbridled ambition. Where you have given us dominion over creation, we have come to value things over people. Where you have opened before us a vision of life in the kingdom, we have been content with the life we have known. Where you have shed light upon

your world, we have preferred the darkness. Forgive our obstinacy and short-sightedness. Forgive us our failures and open before us one more time the way of the one who came that we might have life and have it in all of its intended fullness. In his name we pray. Amen.

Prayer of Dedication of Gifts and Self

As we bring these offerings before you, O God, we recall the lives of those men and women who have preceded us: those who have built this sanctuary and worshiped here; those who have been nurtured within these walls; those to whom the faith has been passed with love; those who have proclaimed the gospel; those who have been baptized, married, and memorialized; and those who have moved from this place to live the gospel of Jesus the Christ. Surrounded by this cloud of witnesses, we have found our place here. As they have given out of their abundance, so we now give out of ours. Receive and bless these gifts. Receive and bless us to your continuing service. Amen.

Sermon Summary

Memories of the past often give reason for hope and confidence. Memories of failures, however, also serve us as we measure flaws and resolve to live with integrity.

Hymn of the Day

"We Walk by Faith and Not by Sight." The path to repentance is never an easy one. As Jesus points out in the gospel lesson for today, most of us are more concerned with how much guiltier our neighbor is than we. In Henry Alford's 1844 hymn is the recognition that we in our time don't have the actual person of Christ to confront us, and so must move by faith beyond our doubt, apathy, and bad habits. The third verse is of particular relation to the lessons for today.

March 15, 1998
3rd Sunday in Lent

Children's Object Talk

A Fair Test

Object
A baseball and a bat.

Lesson
God never tests our faith unfairly.

In Florida and Arizona right now, baseball players are in the middle of spring training. Hundreds of ballplayers are trying to get jobs playing major league ball. On every team, coaches and managers are testing how good these ballplayers are.

Some of those tests are really hard. This little ball (show the ball) is not so easy to hit when it's thrown by a major league ballplayer. How fast do they throw it, do you know? (Elicit answers before describing how fast that is.) Yes, many major league pitchers can throw this about 90 miles per hour. A car on a highway is usually allowed to travel only 55 miles per hour. So you can imagine how fast that ball is coming right at you when a major league pitcher throws it.

Do you think it would be fair to ask someone who has never lifted a bat before to hit a major league fastball? No, that wouldn't be a fair test at all. You'd need lots of practice and lots of teaching to be ready for the major leagues.

It's a little like that being a follower of Jesus. Jesus asked his followers to do some very hard things: put other people first, love your enemies, be willing to love all people. Those can be hard things to do.

It wouldn't be fair for God to expect that new followers of Jesus would be perfect in all those things right from the start. Being a Christian involves learning what it means to follow Jesus. We will learn from our mistakes. We will learn from experience. We will learn from the example of others. We learn from good, and solid Christians just like young ballplayers learn so much from watching veteran ballplayers.

We all have more we can learn each day about loving God, others, and our own self more and more. God puts challenges and little tests before us to see what we have learned. But it is important to know that God never puts us to an unfair test.

—*Jon Temme*

The Sermon

Examples from the Past

Hymns
Beginning of Worship: "I Am Thine, O Lord"
Sermon Hymn: "Were You There When They Crucified My Lord?"
End of Worship: "Take My Life and Let It Be"

Scripture
1 Corinthians 10:1–13 (For sermon materials on Luke 13:1–9, see the November/December 1997 issue and the *1997 May/June Planning Issue* of *The Clergy Journal.*)

Sermon Text
"Now these things occurred as examples for us, so that we might not desire evil as they did" (vs. 6).

Today we begin with the apostle Paul invoking a memory. It is an ancient memory spanning more than fifteen hundred years, and as such it is not so much a personal recollection as a memory of the community.

Paul reminds the church at Corinth of the trials and tribulations of the Hebrews who, having escaped from slavery in Egypt, languished in the wilderness for a generation. Part of Israel's painful memory of their ancestors' escape was the forging of a bull-calf from gold and the worship of this idol accompanied by feasting and revelry. Paul calls to mind another transgression that occurred at Shittim where Israelite men took up relationships with Moabite women and joined in the pagan worship of another God. Moses ordered the execution of those who had broken God's law. Paul tells the Corinthians that he wishes to remind them of these horrors from the past because they serve as reminders of not to let their hearts stray toward the pull of idolatry and evil.

This theme is taken up elsewhere in this week's set of readings. The gospel lection echoes this theme of the correlation between sin and punishment, even if the lesson is a bit confused. Asked about the fate of some people who had been slaughtered by order of Pilate, Jesus declares that their deaths were not a result of sin. He continues, however, to

March 15, 1998
3rd Sunday in Lent

say that if his listeners do not repent of their evil, they will face a similar destruction.

For all of us who have ever attended the funeral of a person who died in the prime of life and asked, "Why?," this matter of cause and effect is disconcerting. Illness, financial reversal, job losses, and so many other seemingly undeserved occasions for suffering leave us uneasy with explanations that suggest that what we are experiencing or observing is divine punishment being meted out. There is, of course, ample evidence in some cases of the relationship between choices and endings. I have presided over funerals of people whose lives ended early because they were overweight, smoked, or drank to excess. I have buried others before their time, however, with no apparent explanation or at least under circumstances that had not been of their choosing: congenital birth defects, rare diseases, and automobile accidents in which they were not at fault. In any of these cases, talk about punishment has never struck a chord in me.

If we are willing to accept Scripture as having symbolic and literary qualities, however, it may be that there is a truth to be discerned and embraced in the text before us today. Even where we may have lingering questions about the direct cause and effect pattern of sin and death proposed by Paul's use of the Hebrew Scriptures, there is a warning in his words that is valid and troubling in the most authentic way. There is a truth being spoken that has the power to stop us in our tracks and force us to consider what we are making of our lives. This truth is the declaration that what we are doing affects our future and the future of all those around us.

I am thinking of the values that we transmit—with or without intention—to our children. Some years ago, Harry Chapin wrote a song about a father whose pursuit of his career led to the neglect of his son. Years later in his retirement when he turned to his son for companionship, his son had adopted his pattern and was too busy to spend time with his father. Many of us give lip service to the excessive consumption reflected in our culture, but we find it exceedingly difficult to say "no" to our children. Why do we turn around and wonder about how commercial our celebration of Christmas has become? Why do we wonder about the confused values of the younger generation? We ought to know them well, for we have seen them in the mirror.

I am thinking about recent elections that have spawned unprecedented negative campaigning tactics. The electorate has become increasingly cynical and apathetic, and voter turnout is on the decline.

I am thinking about truthfulness and fidelity. I am thinking about compassion and regard for the well-being of others. I am thinking of what becomes of us when we do not attend to the higher callings that have been placed upon us. I am thinking about . . . well, perhaps what really matters is what *you* are thinking about. The matters of lust, and idolatry, and the power that they come to have over us to shape us in highly destructive ways is exactly what Paul is trying to impress upon the ancient and the modern community by evoking the ancient memory of a people who were destroyed by the lives they chose.

My wife once told me about visiting an elderly woman who spent the entire conversation complaining and voicing her mistrust of the people around her. She declared, "I hope I don't end up like that when I get old," only to have a friend observe, "People don't get like that because of age . . . at most, you get more like you already are." He was right, I think. We too often do a misservice to the elderly by assuming that they have any more tendency to take on negative traits than any of the rest of us. What is true is that every one of us spends our days fashioning what we will be. The future is neither arbitrary nor inevitable. What we create today we will inherit tomorrow. It is worth considering.

Set your hearts on what is right and good.

—*Gary L. Walling*
Heights Christian Church
Shaker Heights, Ohio

March 22, 1998

4th Sunday in Lent

Lessons

Pres/Meth/UCC/Luth	Josh 5:9–12	2 Cor 5:16–21	Lk 15:1–3, 11b–32
Roman Catholic	Josh 5:9a, 10–12	2 Cor 5:17–21	Lk 15:1–3, 11–32
Episcopal	Josh (4:19–24) 5:9–12	2 Cor 5:17–21	Lk 15:11–32

Introduction to the Lessons

Lesson 1
Joshua 5:9–12 **(Pres/Meth/UCC/Luth)**;
Joshua 5:9a, 10–12 **(RC)**; *Joshua (4:19–24) 5:9–12* **(Epis)**
The Israelites observe the Passover while camped at Gilgal. On the day after the Passover, they ate produce from the land of Canaan, thus ending the need for God's gift of manna.

Lesson 2
2 Corinthians 5:16–21 **(Pres/Meth/UCC/Luth)**;
2 Corinthians 5:17–21 **(RC/Epis)**
This is Paul's remarkable call for Christians to engage in the ministry of reconciliation, noting that we no longer look at others from a human perspective. People in Christ have become new creations, and we have all been entrusted as ambassadors of Christ to be about the ministry of reconciliation.

Gospel
Luke 15:1–3, 11b–32 **(Pres/Meth/UCC/Luth)**;
Luke 15:1–3, 11–32 **(RC)**; *Luke 15:11–32* **(Epis)**
This is the familiar parable of the Prodigal Son. A younger son takes his inheritance early and spends it in wild and lavish living. He returns home to a bitter brother but a reconciling father.

Theme
God's trust in the men and women of faith is evidenced in the gift of the ministry of reconciliation entrusted to them.

Thought for the Day
The way to the unity of God's children is through the embracing of the brokenness of Christ. Disciples of Jesus become witnesses to the unifying power of God's love through the proclamation of the theology of the cross.

Prayer of Meditation
Dear God, when we look at the people with whom we share life, we do not see all nor do we understand every pain and burden that they carry. It is to see each person as your valued child to whom we have been called to offer ourselves to be the warmth and strength of your care.

Call to Worship
"How very good and pleasant it is when kindred live together in unity" (Ps 133:1). Gather together that we might be made one in God's everlasting love.

Prayer of Adoration
In our words of thanksgiving, dear God, hear our united witness that in the broken body of our Lord Jesus, we are made one. We offer testimony to the difference that love has made in our world. We can tell of a hurting world, but how much more can we tell of a world healed and made whole by a reconciling love. We praise your name for the forgiveness that has marked our sins and then washed them away, for the strength that has lifted those who are one the margins of life and brought them to the center of life, and for the call that has taken alienated people and shaped them into one great family. Thanks be to you, O God. Amen.

Prayer of Confession
We know too much about brokenness, dear God. We know about having feet of clay and hearts that have strayed. We have spoken words we ought not have uttered and been silent when circumstances have demanded a faithful word. We have turned away from those in

March 22, 1998
4th Sunday in Lent

need and neglected to carry burdens that we might have lifted to make the load lighter for others. We have stood to the side and watched the Lord carry not only his cross but ours as well. Forgive all in us that needs forgiving. Where we have known the power of the world to break us, let us know now your power to break our lives apart that they might be refashioned in the way of the one whose life and death is before us now. Whatever we have been and failed to be, we would be more like him in love and sacrifice and devotion to your will. Amen.

Prayer of Dedication of Gifts and Self

When we consider your nature as giver, O God, we discover how you intend for us to emerge in like manner. What value are the blessings that come our way if they are not shared with others? In this season in which we contemplate the gift of your son, so hear our resolve to be among those who add to the world's resources rather than diminishing them. Let these gifts mark our efforts, however meager, to return a portion of our blessings to your service. Use these tithes and offerings that in seeing this community of faith, the world might say, "As they have been blessed, so they have become a blessing." Amen.

Sermon Summary

The gospel calls us to look at one another from a different point of view. We are expected to see one another through the eyes of Christ.

Hymn of the Day

"Jesus, Lover of My Soul." Another of Charles Wesley's hymns, the words connect meaningfully with the text of both the epistle where Paul encourages the people to become reconciled to God and with the gospel in the parable of the two sons, relating the abiding and saving love of God to both the son who feels wronged and the one who has gone astray. This is an early hymn by Wesley (ca. 1739–1740), full of the wonder of God's grace after his conversion and baptism.

Children's Object Talk

Appealing, Not Repelling

Object
   Two large magnets and paper clips.
Lesson
   In Christ we are reconciled to God and others.

Does anyone know what these are? They're magnets. I love playing with magnets, even though I'm not sure how they work.

You can do neat things with magnets—and magnets can do neat things with other magnets. Let me show you.

Each end of a magnet is charged with energy in a certain way. You can use the charged ends of magnets to pick up metal things. (Demonstrate with paper clips.) But because the ends are charged, it's very different when two magnets are brought close together. Sometimes, the charges around the ends of the magnets push them far apart. (Demonstrate with the magnets and allow children to feel the "push" of the repulsion.)

But if you turn the ends around (demonstrate as above), the magnets are pulled right together! Then you have twice the force to pick up things.

People are a little bit like magnets. We all have strong feelings, likes, and dislikes. When some people get near others, those strong feelings might push people apart (demonstrate again with magnets).

But Jesus came to turn us around. First, Jesus turns us around to draw us closer to God. What a joy it is to be close to God. After we're close to God, we can be closer to others. God promises that people who couldn't get along before and were enemies can be friends (demonstrate with magnets). It doesn't happen by magic, but by being drawn close to Jesus first. As more and more people are drawn closer to Jesus, there's more and more energy to love others.

—*Jon Temme*

March 22, 1998
4th Sunday in Lent

The Sermon

No Longer from a Human Point of View

Hymns
Beginning of Worship: "For the Healing of the Nations"
Sermon Hymn: "Help Us Accept Each Other"
End of Worship: "Let There Be Peace on Earth"

Scripture
2 Corinthians 5:16–21 (For sermon materials on Joshua 5:9–12, see the November/December 1997 issue of *The Clergy Journal* and on Luke 15:1–3, 11b–32, see the *1997 May/June Planning Issue* of *The Clergy Journal*.)

Sermon Text
"From now on, therefore, we regard no one from a human point of view; even though we once knew Christ from a human point of view, we know him no longer in that way" (vs. 16).

Recent years have been characterized as an Age of Narcissism, recalling the Greek myth of the lad that fell in love with his own reflection. Indeed, much that we see in the country today reinforces this claim. Increased and often aimless leisure time, greater material wealth, and a general decline in social concerns combine to make this a description that seems to fit quite well.

Sometimes the answer to this pervasive sense of self-infatuation has been to call for repentance. It is a helpful warning when it has not been simplistic or extreme, but often the call to turn from self has not taken the time to understand and address the root causes of this preoccupation with self, leaving only the resulting sense of guilt and shame. The more disturbing response has been the suggestion that self-promotion is the right order of things. It is like the documentary I saw some years ago about a preacher who declared that possessions are good and are a sign that God wants us to "have it all." The commentator spoke for many of us in referring to this movement as the "Gospel according to Southern California."

In extreme forms, we note the dangers of both suggestions, but their more moderate forms often strike us as well-reasoned and caring. That is, who would propose self-alienation as a cure to self-love, and who would want to defend the proposition that the life of faith is designed to impoverish?

Nevertheless, I am convinced that the community of faith must make a more helpful contribution to this matter of our absorption with ourselves, and we may if we are able to discern that self-love is not the reality but the facade that we face. We begin by questioning the very characterization of our society as in love with itself. I once heard it proposed that the root of sin is not self-love at all but self-hate. Insofar as this is true, it is possible to suggest that we are far from standing over a pool of water entranced by our own images. Perhaps it is more helpful to strain to see how we end up covering with more and more cosmetics the pervasive feeling that something is wrong at our very core. It is time to ask whether our indulgences are truly a result of self-infatuation or whether we seek bright lights and fast action because we dare not slow down enough to look inside hearts and souls.

I have this suspicion that self-hate may well be the real enemy. Could it be that the number of people who are uneasy with their lives actually outnumber by far the people who are genuinely blind to their shortcomings? The remarkable thing may well be that many of those who are held to be the "beautiful people" in truth are as insecure as anyone else. Have you ever seen some unbearable bore whom you suspected of masking loneliness? Have you ever discovered how arrogance can be put on to mask insecurity and how boasting can hide fear? Do you know a workaholic who has no sense of personal value beyond a career? It is a discerning eye that can see reality lying beyond the facade. Not that self-doubt exists only in excess. We might be able to speak about the milder conditions of being separated from ourselves—of not liking who we are, of being embarrassed about what we do not have, of being confused over where we've been and where we hope to go. To know these things is to know something of the uneasiness our age feels about itself.

I think Paul was addressing this concern in the text read earlier. When he says we no longer know Christ from a human point of view, he is not speaking about metaphysics. Rather, he is talking about what and how we come to know. Paul is repudiating the human value system that places all of us on trial. What is at stake is whether we will judge the one from Nazareth on the basis of his lowly birth and humble social position, on the basis of his doubtful associations and his

March 22, 1998
4th Sunday in Lent

appeal to the oppressed, on the basis of his disregard of the law, or whether we will judge him as the crucified Messiah, Lord of history. What is at stake is whether we will be judged from a point of human standards, or whether we will be judged by a new knowledge revealed in Christ which is the knowledge of life with God. Paul calls us to a new world of relationships rooted in God's grace and redemption. In Christ, we are new creations, no longer subject to the judgments of the world but subject to the justification of God.

We cannot afford, however, to become sentimental about Paul's sermon. Simply recognizing the new standard of valuing human life does not change the environment. The human point of view persists—it does not disappear at Paul's words. So, we find ourselves living in the midst of the old creation but challenged by our faith to live according to a new creation. This is more than clever jargon; it is something other than theological doubletalk. Though we live in the midst of an old creation, we can allow ourselves no longer to be judged by earthly standards, nor can we put these standards to others.

We have been entrusted with the ministry of reconciliation which means that we have been called to undergird the esteem of every one of God's children in order that each might see themselves to be the creation of God.

To this end, Paul speaks resolutely, "Therefore, if anyone is in Christ, he is a new creation . . . all this is from God, who through Christ reconciled us to himself."

—Gary L. Walling
Heights Christian Church
Shaker Heights, Ohio

March 29, 1998

5th Sunday in Lent

Lessons
Pres/Meth/UCC/Luth	Isa 43:16–21	Phil 3:4b–14	Jn 12:1–8
Roman Catholic	Isa 43:16–21	Phil 3:8–14	Jn 8:1–11
Episcopal	Isa 43:16–21	Phil 3:8–14	Lk 20:9–19

Introduction to the Lessons
Lesson 1
Isaiah 43:16–21 **(Pres/Meth/UCC/Luth/RC/Epis)**
God speaks, calling to mind the miraculous defeat of the Egyptian army at the Red Sea crossing. But do not be lost in the past, for God is about to do a new thing. A way will be made in the wilderness and the desert.

Lesson 2
Philippians 3:4b–14 **(Pres/Meth/UCC/Luth)**;
Philippians 3:8–14 **(RC/Epis)**
Paul recites a list of impressive Hebrew credentials, but declares that these mean nothing in comparison with what he has gained in knowing Christ. His sole desire in life is to draw close to Christ in order to share in his experience of death and resurrection.

Gospel
(1) *John 12:1–8* **(Pres/Meth/UCC/Luth)**
Jesus dines in the home of Lazarus and his sisters. Mary anointed Jesus' feet with a very costly perfume, prompting the criticism of Judas. Jesus rises to her defense and declares that the perfume is for his burial.

(2) *John 8:1–11* **(RC)**
The scribes and authorities bring a woman charged with adultery and ask Jesus to pass sentence. He instructs whoever is sinless to throw the first stone, and the crowd disperses. Turning to the woman, he releases her and charges her not to sin again.

March 29, 1998
5th Sunday in Lent

(3) *Luke 20:9–19* **(Epis)**
The parable of the vineyard foreshadows Jesus' death by telling of a group of tenants who refuse to pay for their use of a vineyard. They go so far as to kill the son of the owner, who then returns and destroys the tenants.

Theme
The past and the future intersect in the present moment.

Thought for the Day
One measure of the vitality of our faith is the conviction that the God of the good old days is also the God of the good new days. We recall God's great acts of old in anticipation of God's continued movement in our world and in our lives.

Prayer of Meditation
O God, give us strength to see us through the whole day. Give us strength to rise with the dawn when life is fresh and vital. Give us strength to move into the world and play the roles that have been entrusted to us. Give us strength to gather with those we love and make our homes once more as the day moves to its conclusion. Give us strength when the shadows lengthen and the night comes to lay our bodies down in trust of your love and your eternity. Amen.

Call to Worship
"In the beginning was the Word, and the Word was with God, and the Word was God" (Jn 1:1). So we remember, but we cannot remember a time when God was not with us. So we gather with the assurance that God is in our midst even now.

Prayer of Adoration
Even as the storm clouds gather, we would offer our words of praise, dear God. Even as the forces of evil are marshalled against the Messiah, we would sing our songs of his greatness. Even as the crowds fall away and then reassemble to shout against him, we would shout his name. Even as he is crucified, we would draw close to him. And even when our courage wanes and terror overwhelms us, our hearts

cannot allow us to forget him. Forgive us when we fail, and tune our hearts once more to sing his praise. In his name we pray. Amen.

Prayer of Confession

Too many of our prayers have been halfhearted, O God. We have settled for petitions that have asked too much of you and offered too little of ourselves. Our minds have been too much upon reward and too little upon discipleship. When the cross has come too close, we have moved to another place to begin our prayers. We have assumed that in Christ your will has been accomplished, and failed to ask what is demanded of us. Give us the energy and integrity that is required of authentic prayer, lest our meek words grow wearisome to you and to us. Enter our lives and empower us with the example and spirit of Christ Jesus such that our living rather than our words become our true prayer. Amen.

Prayer of Dedication of Gifts and Self

As you have laid claim upon our lives, so let us now lay claim upon your life with us. As you have made yourself known to us as parent, so let us see ourselves as your beloved children. As we have reveled in your gifts to us, so revel now in our gifts for you. As we have turned to you in our moments of need, so turn to us to be your arms and legs, your heart, and your love in our world. Amen.

Sermon Summary

The promise of the gospel is the promise of new life. While the past may instruct us, it is not the essence of faith. We are called to look forward to embrace the God who is always doing a new thing.

Hymn of the Day

"What Wondrous Love Is This." One of the most important hymns of the American Appalachian tradition, this hymn was first published in *Mercer's Cluster* of 1836. The extravagant gift of perfume that Mary lavishes on Jesus in the gospel lesson is echoed in the even more extravagant gift Christ makes of his life. Erroneously sung slowly, this tune is traditionally sung at a moderate to quick tempo as the words and tune shout together in thanks for Jesus' sacrifice.

March 29, 1998
5th Sunday in Lent

Children's Object Talk

Good as New? No, Better than New!

Object
An object that has been repaired and made stronger (eyeglasses with a new bow, a chair with a stronger leg, a book with a new binding).

Lesson
God not only forgives and restores us, but makes us stronger in the process.

It is no fun when things break whether it's a toy, or a car, or a part of the body. It doesn't matter how big or small the item is. We don't like it when things break.

But sometimes when they do break and need to be repaired, something very wonderful happens. Let me show you. About two years ago, my glasses broke. What a pain. I couldn't see very well for a few days. I couldn't drive my car. I got headaches when I tried to read.

I took my glasses to a person called an optician. He not only fixed the broken part here, but he put on a stronger piece. I used to have glasses that were weak and wobbly. Thanks to the repair, my glasses are not as good as new—they are even better than new.

Remember, I said earlier that lots of things break and need fixing. People are like that. Churches and communities are like that. Even marriages and friendships can be like that. Sin can hurt, damage, and destroy friendships and people. Fortunately, God has a remedy for sin. It's called forgiveness.

When God forgives sin we are restored and can be made stronger or healthier than ever. How? We learn from our sin and mistakes. When God puts us back together in a way that's right and pleasing, we are usually wiser, stronger, more loving and more lovable.

It's more than being just like we were before. We're new, stronger, and better than ever. God loves to take what is old and broken and make it new. When we believe that, then some of the sadness we feel when things and relationships are broken will disappear. Thank you, God.

—*Jon Temme*

The Minister's Annual Manual

The Sermon

New Things

Hymns
Beginning of Worship: "Lift High the Cross"
Sermon Hymn: "Beneath the Cross of Jesus"
End of Worship: "O Sacred Head Now Wounded"

Scripture
Isaiah 43:16–21 (For sermon materials on John 12:1–8, see the January 1998 issue of *The Clergy Journal* and on Philippians 3:4b–14, see the *1997 May/June Planning Issue* of *The Clergy Journal.*)

Sermon Text
"I am about to do a new thing; now it springs forth, do you not perceive it?" (vs. 19a).

I was looking through some photograph albums the other day. Maybe I was just in a melancholy mood, but I was struck by the images of people who are now absent from my life. There was the picture of my grandfather beaming while holding me at the age of one on the seat of his tractor—he died of cancer perhaps a year later. There is another picture of my brother and me with our other grandfather. We are standing in an oil field in West Texas and all three of us are decked out in protective helmets.

There was the photo of my little league baseball team. I was the shortstop, standing beside my best friend, the catcher. Pat's family moved to Missouri and in time we lost touch with one another. Another snapshot shows me with my girlfriend at a college dance. It was several years later that I got word of Cheryl's death. Another photograph was taken when I was a youth minister—the young people in that setting are scattered across several states. They are grown and married with children of their own. There were pictures of family gatherings that included loved ones married to siblings and now divorced.

As I say, it was a sad hour in many ways, yet it evoked so many memories of good times and dear ones whose lives have been a great blessing to me.

The temptation to look into

March 29, 1998
5th Sunday in Lent

the past to find life is appealing, and we are well into a season in which the days that have passed take a strong hold upon us. That is why if we have truly allowed ourselves to enter into the Lenten season, we may be startled by the text we have open before us this morning: *"I am about to do a new thing."* What lies ahead is unsure, even frightening. The urge is to return to what had been, not to press ahead. Jesus' declaration that he must go to Jerusalem is no assu-rance to his band of disciples. It is terrifying.

Faith is always in a struggle with time zones. The past and the future each has something to offer, though what will be is seldom as comforting as what has been. Even when we pursue the religious life with vigor, it often takes the form of an attempt to fashion faith in the form of the past. What is often lost is the portrait of Jesus as one who regularly broke out of the existing forms of religion.

The most regular charges leveled against Jesus were allegations that he was not adhering to the faith of the past. He was not observant of the Sabbath, for example, and offended righteous people with the declaration that the Sabbath was created for people instead of the reverse. Our inclination at our most religious point is often to try to lock down the words of Christ that may cause us to miss his spirit. That is to say that the model of Jesus is a willingness to release the past in favor of a radical openness to the future. "I am about to do a new thing," says Isaiah, and to believe these words in the depths of one's heart is to open oneself to what shall be.

The words I remember most from my ordination came from the pen of the Dutch theologian and writer on spirituality, Henri Nouwen. He wrote that the imitation of Christ is not fulfilled in an attempt to copy the life that Jesus lived. The endeavor to follow in his footsteps bears no fruit, for though the past can provide direction and sustenance, it cannot be recreated. No, wrote Nouwen, the imitation of Christ is something else. It depends upon capturing the spirit of Jesus so that we learn to live our lives with the same authenticity out of which he lived his. The spirit of Jesus then requires less a preoccupation with the minutia of religion and more of the spirit of boldness that embraces the gift of life which God has given, but more importantly, which God continues to give.

The text invites us to take up that same boldness, that same openness to what God may yet do. We are not called to see yet. We are not required to believe yet. We are just required to be willing to see and believe when

315

the moment comes. We are just asked to be willing to release our grip on the past enough to take in the signs of something else—a future that is about to open before us.

Oh yes! One more thing! I went back to the photograph albums a few days later. Perhaps I was in a better mood or the company was more pleasant. Whatever it was, I was struck by something that I had not noticed before. I thought about all of the people who were missing from those photographs but who are now present in my life. My wife, for one, was not in any of those pictures from my childhood. My daughter and my son were missing from all of the snapshots of my college years. The circle of friends that make my life rich and whole have largely entered my life since the years represented in those old albums.

While I cannot recover what I was thinking in the days each of these old photographs was taken, I know that I could never have imagined what my life would come to be and how richly I have been blessed with God's new gifts.

I confess that there is a temptation to try to lock down all of these people who are filling the pages of this year's albums, but that is neither possible nor desirable. What is possible is to strive to be as open to what shall be as I am to what has been.

God says, *"I am about to do a new thing..."* It is an old, old story. And a new one.

—*Gary L. Walling*
Heights Christian Church
Shaker Heights, Ohio

April 5, 1998

Passion/Palm Sunday

Lessons

Pres/Meth/UCC/Luth	Isa 50:4–9a	Phil 2:5–11	Lk 22:14—23:56
Roman Catholic	Isa 50:4–7	Phil 2:6–11	Lk 22:14—23:56
Episcopal	Isa 45:21–25	Phil 2:5–11	Lk (22:39–71) 23:1–49 (50–56)

Introduction to the Lessons
Lesson 1
(1) *Isaiah 50:4–9a* **(Pres/Meth/UCC/Luth)**; *Isaiah 50:4–7* **(RC)**; *Isaiah 45:21–25* **(Epis)**

The verses from Isaiah 50 contain one of the suffering servant poems from which Christians have drawn instruction and inspiration for understanding the passion of Jesus on the cross.

(2) *Philippians 2:5–11* **(Pres/Meth/UCC/Luth/Epis)**; *Philippians 2:6–11* **(RC)**

In this passage Paul reminds his readers that it is in the passion of Jesus Christ, on the cross, that all who believe in him are made righteous by the free gift of God's grace.

Gospel
Luke 22:14—23:56 **(Pres/Meth/UCC/Luth/RC)**; *Luke (22:39–71) 23:1–49 (50–56)* **(Epis)**

These passages contain Luke's version of the passion narrative, the story of Jesus' last hours of earthly ministry. It begins with the Upper Room and concludes with the crucifixion.

Scholars believe that these gospel passion narratives were among the first extended stories that were incorporated in the gospel texts.

Theme
A suffering servant ministry is a teaching ministry.

Thought for the Day

We are to learn from Jesus, as we study the events surrounding his last days on earth and his suffering on the cross, the meaning of a servant ministry in the world. Isaiah's poem on the suffering servant as teacher aids us in that instruction, and guides the present church in its teaching ministry.

Prayer of Meditation

We turn to you in prayer at the beginning of our worship, gracious and loving God, asking that the guidance of your Holy Spirit may be in our midst when we sing, when we pray, in all our speaking and thinking, so that our teaching ministry may become clearer to us. We ask it in Christ's name. Amen.

Call to Worship

> I love you, O Lord, my strength.
> The Lord is my rock in whom I take refuge,
> my shield, and the horn of my salvation, my stronghold.
> I call upon the Lord, who is worthy to be praised,
> So shall I be saved from my enemies.
>
> —Psalm 18:1–3

Prayer of Adoration

All praise, honor, and glory be to you, God Almighty. You call the worlds into being, create and sustain all living things, and enter into covenant with our humanity, created in your image. Your glory fills the heavens, the earth, and our lives. In the midst of all that distracts our attention, that diminishes our wonder, as we ponder your holy power and being, open us afresh to that wonder. Empower us to attend to you and your amazing life in the midst of us. We pray in Christ's name. Amen.

Prayer of Confession

We confess to you, merciful and gracious God, that we have followed your will for us when it seemed the easy and popular way, when the crowds shouted, "Hosanna." We confess that our service to you and to our neighbor has been limited by our desire to enjoy that service, not

April 5, 1998
Passion/Palm Sunday

to suffer, not to take an unpopular stand. We confess that while we know that serving you is the way of the cross, we have tried to make it a way of convenience. Have mercy on us, forgive, and restore us, by inspiring us to follow the Christ to the cross and the tomb, not just in the midst of the cheering crowds. We trust in your forgiving love freely poured out. Make us grateful and renew our discipleship. We ask these things in Christ's name.

Prayer of Dedication of Gifts and Self
Receive these gifts, we pray, with our lives, rededicated to serving you where there is any human need or suffering. Let our lives, the stewardship of all that we have and all that we are, be a blessing in the church and throughout the whole world. We pray in the name of Jesus Christ. Amen.

Sermon Summary
To be a Christian believer and to be a Christian community means following Jesus Christ as a suffering servant in the ministry of teaching. Like all teaching there are obstacles to face and overcome. But we have a message to be taught, and a method, or way of teaching, that will keep us faithful in this sacred calling.

Hymn of the Day
"All Glory, Laud, and Honor." A great processional hymn, the words are actually taken from a Latin text written by the imprisoned bishop of Orleans, Theodulph, in 818 C.E. Theodulph was brought to France by Charlemagne but was suspected of treason by Louis I, one of Charlemagne's successors who had him thrown in jail. It was during this time that he wrote "All Glory, Laud and Honor." The original ran to thirty-nine verses to accommodate the long Palm Sunday processionals held in and around the cathedrals of Europe. When Louis I heard Theodulph sing this from his prison window, he was so moved that he ordered the bishop's immediate release.

Children's Object Talk

Ears to Hear

Object
Your own ears and mouth.
Lesson
We hear God's good news with our ears and share it with our voices.

Today I would like you to answer a few questions for me. The first question is "What part of our bodies do we hear with?" The second question is "What part do we talk with?" (wait for responses) That is right. We hear with our ears and talk with our mouths and tongues.

Please place your hands tightly over your ears when I do and then take them away when I take mine away. (Cover your own ears as you continue talking.) God sent Jesus to love and save us. (Now uncover your ears and encourage the children to do so.) Did you hear what I said when your ears were covered? Why not? That's right, when our ears are covered we cannot hear. But when our ears are uncovered we can hear.

In the Bible, the prophet Isaiah talks about how important it is to use our ears to listen to what God says and teaches. When your ears were covered this is what I said: "God sent Jesus to love and save us." That's very good news. We hear it from the Bible. We hear it in Sunday school. We also hear it from other people like parents and pastors.

When we hear such good news we want to share it. Maybe we can shout "Hosanna! Hosanna!" and wave palm branches like people did so long ago for Jesus in Jerusalem. Or, maybe we will tell someone that God loves them.

Remember to use your ears to listen to God and the good news of Jesus' love, and then be sure to use your voice to tell someone else about it.

—*Jeanette Strandjord*

April 5, 1998
Passion/Palm Sunday

The Sermon

The Suffering Servant as Teacher

Hymns
Beginning of Worship: "Ride on in Majesty"
Sermon Hymn: "When I Survey the Wondrous Cross"
End of Worship: "All Glory, Laud, and Honor"

Scripture
Isaiah 50:4–9a (For sermon materials on Luke 22:14—23:56, see the January 1998 issue of *The Clergy Journal* and on Philippians 2:5-11, see the *1997 May/June Planning Issue* of *The Clergy Journal*.)

Sermon Text
"The Lord God has given me the tongue of a teacher, that I may know how to sustain the weary with a word" (vs. 4a).

Have you ever been a teacher? Are you a teacher now? If so, you will know both the satisfactions and the terrors that go with teaching.

The satisfactions are many, but we don't talk about the downside of teaching so much, and we may even think things will improve (think again!). As we meditate on the suffering servant as teacher, we should think more about the terrors of teaching.

There are many kinds of teaching anxieties. First, there's the apprehension of not knowing enough, not being well prepared, the consternation of the student who knows more about the subject than you do, or who will ask a question you can't answer. Time, age, and experience ease these anxieties, but they never go away.

A second kind of terror felt by the teacher is the fear of handling the behavioral and relationship problems afflicting students. Some will be bored or apathetic while others may be angry and resistant. Others may try to become the teacher's favorite friend. Students will develop problems with one another—arguments and fights will break out. And these days, in some schools and neighborhoods, students may be carrying weapons. Experience helps, but human beings are unpredictable. You just never know what they are going to do.

Third, the teacher feels apprehensive about the degree of influence and power he or she gains over the lives of students. This involves not just the power and consequences of grades, but also how the teacher affects the very fabric of the student's life, the student's beliefs and values, the student's emerging identity. It's a heady realization. If you're not careful, you can use this power to your own advantage, not the student's. You can play to the audience. You can turn on the charm and wit. You can cultivate a cadre of disciples. You can even enjoy your disciples' disparaging remarks about their other teachers.

Finally, a fourth terror of the teacher is the temptation to succumb to cynicism and despair, what with poor pay and long hours, lack of administrative support, low prestige in society, or being blamed by politicians and candidates for the failures of the schools. Seminary teachers sometimes hear it said that they have to teach because they could not succeed in the ministry; they could not preach weekly, care for people, administer an organization, raise money, and all the other things that go along with the parish ministry. "Those who can, do; those who can't, teach," is what they say.

I dwell on these often unspoken terrors of teaching because in the Scripture lesson from the prophet Isaiah, the servant is identified as a teacher. This is one of the "servant" poems. We study these passages when the church pays particular attention to Jesus Christ: Advent, Lent, Holy Week. Why? Because Christians have always read these servant poems as references to the coming Christ. Isaiah speaks in these poems of a suffering servant who will come to restore Israel. Christians in ancient times and down through history have confessed that Jesus Christ is that servant.

In the servant poem that begins in chapter 50, verse 4a, the servant says, *"The Lord God has given me the tongue of a teacher, that I may know how to sustain the weary with a word."* What a wonderful way to state the vocation of a teacher: *"to sustain the weary with a word."*

Other servant poems in Isaiah depict the servant as a shepherd leading and feeding his flock, as a light to the nations who will bring justice on earth, as one who opens the eyes of the blind and releases prisoners, as the one who will restore the nation of Israel, as a suffering servant who will take on the sins of the people, and who will preach good news to the oppressed, bringing justice and compassion. In this poem the servant is depicted as a teacher, as one who will know how *"to sustain the weary with a word."*

April 5, 1998
Passion/Palm Sunday

It is easy to see how the earliest Christians saw Jesus Christ in these poems. We cannot be sure, say Old Testament scholars, who precisely the author had in mind. Perhaps it was a coming messiah, an individual. But the servant could also be the whole community of Israel, brought back from exile, with a new vocation of suffering service for all the nations.

These unanswered questions about the ancient Jewish meaning of these poems have never kept Christians from confidently declaring that the servant foretold is Jesus Christ. And so this logical sequence unfolds from that conviction: Since the church is the community of Jesus' followers, Jesus' disciples on earth, and since Jesus' followers are to follow in his steps, that means that the church, yes, the very congregations where we belong, and each member of every congregation, are to be teachers in this world, to sustain the weary with a word, and in turn to be instructed by Jesus Christ, our teaching mentor, each day in our teaching ministry. Teachers to the world! Yes, that is who we are. And as such we will experience all the satisfactions and terrors of the teacher.

What is it we are to teach? We are to teach the world the good news of the gospel, of God's love in Jesus Christ, saving us from our brokenness and aimlessness, and of the presence and power of the Holy Spirit.

That is the content of our teaching. But this content must be clothed in personal experience, so that part of what you teach to the world is the story of your own faith experience, your own faith pilgrimage, your own pathway by which you came to your most cherished convictions. In the experience of hearing your story, others will be encouraged to explore and tell their own stories of faith.

I ask you to think about this question: when is the last time you told anyone about your personal story of faith? Perhaps you have let yourself be overwhelmed by terror number one, the terror of not feeling well enough prepared. There is no quick fix, but study and practice will help. Not everyone is comfortable with words, especially words about deep matters. But everyone can find a good way to tell your story of faith. Practice teaching: that's a good way to begin to overcome the terrors of the teacher.

As a community of teachers and as individual teachers, we also need to pay attention to *how* we teach, not just *what* we teach. We teach not just by telling the story of faith, but also by living the story of faith. In the church's communal witness to the world and in our individual storytelling, we live the good news of a gospel we can trust; of a love we can share with others; of a justice we can work for in our personal lives, our families, our communities, our nation, and the world community; of a divine compassion that embraces all who suffer; of a hope that will not fail. It is these attitudes, these dispositions, this kind of character that shape the "how" of our teaching.

But there will be opposition to such teaching. Why? Because the Christian world of the United States is dominated these days by two movements we must fearlessly critique and reject in our teaching: the mega-church movement, which represents consumer and media values, not the gospel; and the so-called Christian right, which is an ultraconservative social and political movement thinly disguised with Christian rhetoric. In these struggles we will often feel besieged. But we can trust in the power of the Holy Spirit.

Well, there you are, another terror of the teacher. Makes you want to quit and move to a cabin in the woods. That may be Christ's calling for a few special individuals. But Christ's calling to the church, and to each one of us, is to the teaching vocation, with low pay, long hours, stress, misunderstanding, opposition, and all those terrors.

But not to worry! It is a vocation woven out of the fabric of love and hope. It is a spiritual vocation—the Spirit comes to our aid. We will find the words, the courage, the strength to persevere, trusting in that Spirit.

So I urge you to become more conscious of your teaching vocation and more actively engaged in it. You will be a blessing to a weary world. And you will be guided and blessed in your teaching.

—Clyde J. Steckel
United Theological Seminary
New Brighton, Minnesota

April 9, 1998

Maundy Thursday

Lessons

Pres/Meth/UCC/Luth	Ex 12:1-4 (5-10), 11-14	1 Cor 11:23-26	Jn 13:1-17 31b-35
Roman Catholic	Ex 12:1-8, 11-14	1 Cor 11:23-26	Jn 13:1-15
Episcopal	Ex 12:1-14a	1 Cor 11:23-26 (17-32)	Jn 13:1-15

Introduction to the Lessons
Lesson 1
(1) *Exodus 12:1-4 (5-10), 11-14* **(Pres/Meth/UCC/Luth)**;
Exodus 12:1-8, 11-14 **(RC)**; *Exodus 12:1-14a* **(Epis)**
God's institution of the Passover meal, as a way of marking and saving the chosen people of Israel on their night of liberation, creates an ancient narrative framework for Jesus' last supper with his disciples, which then becomes the Christian sacrament of the Lord's Supper.

(2) *1 Corinthians 11:23-26* **(Pres/Meth/UCC/Luth/RC)**;
1 Corinthians 11:23-26 (17-32) **(Epis)**
Paul summarizes the narrative of the last supper of Jesus with his disciples, using Jesus' own words of institution from the gospel narrative, but then adds the affirmation that the supper is also a proclamation the church makes to the whole world until the Christ returns in glory.

Gospel
John 13:1-17, 31b-35 **(Pres/Meth/UCC/Luth)**;
John 13:1-15 **(RC/Epis)**
Jesus washes the feet of the disciples, something done at that time only by a servant or slave, showing that his ministry, and the ministries of his followers, must be servant ministries, not the kind of overlord ministries familiar in his time.

Theme
Passover and the Lord's Supper incorporate us into a life-giving story.

Thought for the Day
Remembering Jesus on Maundy Thursday is an act of being "re-membered" by him and by God, connected by the power of God's Holy Spirit to the true source of our life's meaning and purpose.

Prayer of Meditation
As we prepare to sit at table with you, loving Savior, and claim our own place among your disciples, help us to listen to your teaching with eager humility, so that we do not play out bit parts in a familiar drama, but rather find our lives being continually transformed after the model of the teacher who is our host and our friend. In his name we pray. Amen.

Call to Worship
> You prepare a table before me
> > in the presence of my enemies;
> you anoint my head with oil;
> > my cup overflows.
> Surely goodness and mercy shall follow me
> > all the days of my life,
> and I shall dwell in the house of the Lord
> > my whole life long.
>
> —Psalm 23:5–6

Prayer of Adoration
We praise and adore you, God of mighty wonders, for calling people out of slavery into freedom, to be your servant people in the world. As you called out ancient Israel from bondage, so free us from the bonds that keep us enslaved, that we may indeed sing your songs in freedom, declaring your marvelous glory throughout the universe. We pray in Christ's name. Amen.

April 9, 1998
Maundy Thursday

Prayer of Confession

Gather us about your table, merciful God, enabling us to confess freely that like Jesus' disciples at that first holy meal, we do not understand what this means, why he is doing this, what his teachings signify, what part we will have in his heavenly realm. Enable us to confess these confusions, and our stumbling, halting efforts to follow him, so that we may be forgiven and restored by your mercy, and may both claim and celebrate Jesus Christ's friendship with us, bringing love and peace. We pray in the name of that same Jesus Christ who is both our host at the table and also our nourishment. Amen.

Prayer of Dedication of Gifts and Self

We give you these offerings, God of all our gifts and graces, in response to the life-giving food of the loaf and the cup which bear for us and in us the true body of Christ, that we may give ourselves to the world as loaf and cup. We pray in Christ's name. Amen.

Sermon Summary

Remembering Passover and remembering Jesus' last supper with his disciples is more than an act of historical recollection. As we gather at the table Jesus Christ is truly present in our midst, as the host of divine hospitality and as the food we need to be truly nourished. Remembering thus becomes "re-membering," have ourselves put back together, a new and renewed people.

Hymn of the Day

"When Jesus Wept." William Billings, who wrote this tune, was a self-taught choir master at Boston's Old South Congregational Church. He was considered particularly skilled at contriving harmony parts for altos and tenors in a countermelody fashion that lent depth and richness to his hymns. This simple tune is a canon that can be repeated several times.

Children's Object Talk

Remember and Celebrate

Object
A picture of a birthday cake.

Lesson
We celebrate that Jesus gave his life for us and promises to be with us.

I would like us to think for a while about celebrations. When I say *celebration*, I am talking about a special time or party. A birthday party would be a special celebration. (Hold up the picture of the birthday cake.) Have all of you been to a birthday party or had one? (Wait for and acknowledge their responses.) A party is fun, and it is a time to tell someone that they are special.

In the Bible we have a story about a very special celebration. It is called Passover. God told the people to celebrate Passover as a special occasion, a celebration because God was saving the people from slavery in Egypt. God was leading the people out of Egypt into a new and good land to live.

This is Maundy Thursday. On this day we remember that long ago Jesus had his last supper with his disciples. After this supper, Jesus would die on the cross, and then be raised again on Easter morning.

Today is a special time to remember Jesus and his love for us. Jesus is the special person we honor. Because of Jesus and all he did for us, we have the good news that he loves us and will always be with us.

—*Jeanette Strandjord*

April 9, 1998
Maundy Thursday

The Sermon

A Day to Remember

Hymns
Beginning of Worship: "O Sacred Head Now Wounded"
Sermon Hymn: "Be Known to Us in Breaking Bread"
End of Worship: "Ah, Holy Jesus"

Scripture
Exodus 12:1–4 (5–10), 11–14 (For sermon materials on John 13:1–17, 31b–35, see the January 1998 issue of *The Clergy Journal* and on 1 Corinthians 11:23–26, see the *1997 May/June Planning Issue* of *The Clergy Journal*.)

Sermon Text
"This day shall be a day of remembrance for you" (vs. 14a).

What makes a day, any day, a day to remember? Surely it must be a day when something so vivid, so life changing takes place that the details of the day are forever etched in memory. The very first day of school, the day of graduation, the day when you realize you have fallen in love, the day when you said "Yes" to God and to a life of faith in a new and decisive way, a day of failure or success, the day a loved one dies. All these become days to remember.

Speaking of remembering, do you remember the news items and photographs several years ago about the churches that were staging Leonardo Da Vinci's painting of the Last Supper on Maundy Thursday? Some of them had gone all out—professional set designers, lighting technicians, costumers, makeup artists, actors. Other performances were strictly amateur. But they all came to a dramatic climax: the house lights were turned out, the actors took their places, and then a sudden burst of stage illumination revealed a living portrait of the Last Supper. People gasped in awe and wonder at the spectacle.

Why go to all that bother and expense? Why not just use a traditional liturgy for Maundy Thursday? Each church would have to explain why it decided to stage such a spectacle on Maundy Thursday. Somewhere in those explanations I'd bet you would hear about the power of dramatic spectacle, especially the power of a familiar visual image, to make people feel engaged, that "they are there"—present at the founding Last Supper.

When you think back to the last meal Jesus had with his disciples in that upper room, it too was a reenactment, a restaging of that most holy Jewish event of liberation, the Passover, celebrating that night when God freed Israel from slavery in Egypt.

Whether it was actually on Passover (Matthew, Mark, and Luke) or just before Passover (John), the stories of that last meal Jesus ate with his disciples are filled with Passover imagery: Jesus as the spotless sacrificial lamb, the lamb's body to be roasted and eaten until nothing is left, his shed blood securing the rescue of his people from their bondage, and the promise that his people were now to live in a community of freedom, loyal to their liberating God.

It is no accident that the Passover narrative in Exodus 12 has deeply touched the lives of enslaved, oppressed, hopeless people wherever the story has been told. Surely it was Israel's story first and foremost, and now is the defining narrative and ritual of the Jewish religion. But many others have seen their own struggle and despair, their own longing for liberation set forth in the Passover story.

As a movement among Jews led by a rabbi, primitive Christianity also saw its own bondage and liberation set forth in the Passover narrative, and therefore framed its own memories and written narratives of that last supper with Jesus as a new Passover.

My, what rich memories come flooding back when we remember Jesus at the table with his twelve disciples on that first holy Maundy Thursday! It is truly a day to remember. We have many of those in the Christian year: Easter, the day of resurrection, and the way each Sunday is a remembering of that first Easter; Pentecost, when the Holy Spirit descended upon them; Good Friday, when Jesus was crucified; Christmas, when we celebrate Christ's birth, the incarnation.

But, Maundy Thursday is a special day to remember. Why? Because when Jesus asked his followers to do these things *"in remembrance of me"* (Lk 22:19; 1 Cor 11:24), he was not only asking them to recall the founding supper, he was also offering the gift of "re-membering," the promise that when we gather to share the bread and the cup, we are re-connected, "re-membered." Like a structure that has suffered

April 9, 1998
Maundy Thursday

destruction and scattering, with its parts here and there in a disarray that seems impossible to repair, we are nevertheless gathered and reassembled, more beautiful than before.

Throughout Europe in those difficult years right after World War II, people from cities and towns and parishes of every persuasion sifted through the rubble of their bombed churches and synagogues wondering whether enough pieces could be located, enough money and workers found to rebuild. Not all of them could be reconstructed, but many of them were, mixes of old and new material. And now they stand as proud reminders that the broken and scattered can be "re-membered."

It is the same when we read and ponder the Passover narrative in Exodus, or when we are invited to a Seder in a Jewish temple or home. We are invited not just to recall an ancient event of liberation, but also to have our broken lives "re-membered," reconnected through that reenactment, to let that liberation happen in us, here and now.

It is the same when we gather as a Christian community on Maundy Thursday to reenact Jesus' last supper with his disciples. By remembering him at the table, he "re-members" us, reconnects us to that true source of our life's purpose and hope, to that loving God who created us and who, in Jesus Christ, redeems us from the broken, scattered, fragmented, misshapen lives we either make for ourselves or have imposed upon us. What a day to remember!

So perhaps we should not too quickly look down our liturgical and theological noses at those among us who want to stage the Last Supper, with Leonardo da Vinci's painting as the model. They've got the right idea: it's not just an ancient liturgy, it is indeed a reenactment, with all the drama and color and pizzazz that a good stage play should have. Let's turn off our critical batteries and let ourselves gasp, be wowed when the lights come up. Suddenly we are there. We remember, and are re-membered!

—*Clyde J. Steckel*
United Theological Seminary
New Brighton, Minnesota

April 10, 1998

Good Friday

Lessons

Pres/Meth/UCC/Luth	Isa 52:13—53:12	Heb 10:16–25	Jn 18:1 –19:42
Roman Catholic	Isa 52:13—53:12	Heb 4:14–16; 5:7–9	Jn 18:1 –19:42
Episcopal	Isa 52:13—53:12	Heb 10:1–25	Jn (18:1–40) 19:1–37

Introduction to the Lessons

Lesson 1
(1) *Isaiah 52:13—53:12* **(Pres/Meth/UCC/Luth/RC/Epis)**
In this passage, one of the servant poems in this second section of Isaiah, the servant is poetically depicted as an obedient sacrificial lamb suffering for the sins of the people. Though he had no blemish, he bore the sins of all, and they, along with him, will be glorified by God.

(2) *Hebrews 10:16–25* **(Pres/Meth/UCC/Luth)**;
Hebrews 4:14–16; 5:7–9 **(RC)**; *Hebrews 10:1–25* **(Epis)**
In the Hebrews 10 passage, the writer summarizes the new covenant in Jesus Christ, whose sacrifice once and for all has obtained reconciliation with God, something the older priestly system could only achieve temporarily. The verses from chapters 4 and 5 describe the high priestly office of Jesus Christ, and the way his appointment to that office led him through a sacrificial death.

(3) *John 18:1—19:42* **(Pres/Meth/UCC/Luth/RC)**;
John (18:1–40) 19:1–37 **(Epis)**
These two chapters from the Fourth Gospel contain the writer's narrative of Jesus' betrayal and arrest, his trial, Peter's denial, Jesus before Pilate, Jesus' death sentence and crucifixion, his words from the cross, and his death and burial. Through these chapters the question of Jesus' true identity runs as a connecting theme. Is he a king, and if so, in what way? Why do both the religious and secular authorities fear his power? Why do his own disciples betray and deny him?

April 10, 1998
Good Friday

Theme
God's love for all creation, and for all those made in the divine image, is so great that it is a suffering and sacrificial love.

Thought for the Day
Since God's love for us is so profoundly sacrificial, our love for God and neighbor, for the whole of creation, should manifest that same sacrificial spirit, even though it goes against the grain of our human desires.

Prayer of Meditation
Enfold us in your love that knows and understands us fully, loving God. Let the power of that sacrificial love displayed in the cross of Jesus open ourselves, including those hidden depths we want to protect or deny, so that we can be continually transformed by that same power to be your loving and sacrificial ministry community in this world. We pray in the name of the crucified one, Jesus Christ. Amen.

Call to Worship
> My God, my God, why have you forsaken me?
> Why are you so far from helping me, from the words
>   of my groaning?
> O my God, I cry by day, but you do not answer;
> and by night, but find no rest.
> Yet you are holy, enthroned on the praises of Israel.
> In you our ancestors trusted; they trusted, and you
>   delivered them.
> To you they cried, and were saved;
> in you they trusted, and were not put to shame.
> —Psalm 22:1–5

Prayer of Adoration
All praise and glory to you, Lord God of the universe, and our loving God, for you have come to us in human flesh, in Jesus Christ, not counting the cost of suffering and sacrifice and shameful death on a cross, to show us how much you love us and how we are to love in return.

Enable us to praise you for this astonishing gift not only with our words but also with our lives. We pray in the name of the Christ. Amen.

Prayer of Confession
We unite in confessing to you, merciful and forgiving God, that too often we are those who, hearing your word, turn away sadly; that all too often we are those who, seeing your love incarnate in our midst, betray and deny that love; that all too often we are among those who stand by the cross of Christ, shaking our heads, wondering what went wrong. Help us to admit our sin, to turn and repent, and to experience that miraculous renewal that comes when your sacrificial love takes root in us. We pray in the name of the merciful Christ. Amen.

Prayer of Dedication of Gifts and Self
What can we give you, God of all gifts and graces, except that which you have already given us? So we pray, as we return these gifts for your service in the world that you will bless all those good works they enable, and bless our giving too, in the name of Jesus Christ. Amen.

Sermon Summary
The kind of sacrificial love depicted in Isaiah's servant poem and the narrative of Jesus' trial and crucifixion face serious obstacles in our modern world. Our misconstrued preoccupations with self-esteem, assertiveness, wealth, power, and violence must all be confronted if we are to truly hear and receive the message of the cross. Nevertheless, the power of God's Holy Spirit is at work to do that in us. We can trust that Spirit.

Hymn of the Day
"My Song Is Love Unknown." This is a gifted hymn by a writer who probably never heard it sung. The author was Samuel Crossman, who composed a small book of verse published in 1664, but this work doesn't appear as a hymn until well into the latter 1800s. Particularly meaningful in the text is the way in which the singer is placed into the story as an active witness. "What has my Lord done?" is the cry in verse four as the events of Good Friday are recounted not in chronology, but in the feelings that the actions evoke in our hearts.

April 10, 1998
Good Friday

Children's Object Talk

Suffering Servant

Object
A picture of Jesus on the cross.
Lesson
Jesus suffered and died for us as God's servant.

There is a word in our Bible reading from Isaiah that is very important. It is the word *servant*. Can anyone tell me what a servant does? (Wait for responses, which may include such words as *helps, works,* and *serves*.) Yes, servants do many things and our Bible reading tells us about some more of them. In this passage, the servant doesn't have a very easy life. This servant was sent by God to us. He was a good person and tried to help people. He didn't harm anyone, but still people didn't like him. In fact, the people hurt the servant and finally killed him.

We Christians believe that these words from the Bible tell us about Jesus who is God's servant. God sent Jesus to us to teach us and help us. Jesus didn't harm anyone, but people did hurt him (show picture). They hung him up on this wooden cross because they said he was a troublemaker—but he wasn't.

Today is Good Friday. It is a special day when we remember that Jesus died on the cross. He truly was God's servant because he helped people who were sick and troubled. He worked to tell others about God, and he was willing to give his life to serve God. He loved God and us so much that he was willing to even die for us. On Good Friday, we talk about this and remember it. We can also say thank you to God for sending Jesus, and thank you to Jesus for being such a loving servant.

—*Jeanette Strandjord*

The Sermon

He Was Wounded for Our Transgressions

Hymns
Beginning of Worship: "In the Cross of Christ I Glory"
Sermon Hymn: "What Wondrous Love Is This?"
End of Worship: "Were You There When They Crucified My Lord?"

Scripture
Isaiah 52:13—53:12 (For sermon materials on John 18:1—19:42, see the January 1998 issue of *The Clergy Journal* and on Hebrews 10:16-25, see the *1997 May/June Planning Issue* of *The Clergy Journal*.)

Sermon Text
"But he was wounded for our transgressions, crushed for our iniquities; upon him was the punishment that made us whole, and by his bruises we are healed" (vs. 5).

Why is the cross the preeminent Christian symbol? Why not the empty tomb of the resurrection, or the tongues of flame of Pentecost? Why not a tree from the garden of creation or the ship of the church?

Good Friday answers those questions. On that most holy and dreadful day, Jesus Christ was executed on a cross, with two thieves. The one who walked among us, coming from the very heart of God's love, affronted the religious and political establishments of his day. He showed that divine love is the true power of the universe. The principalities and powers of his day did not tolerate such sedition. So he was led away and crucified.

On this Good Friday we need to remember again that God's incarnation, God's being with us, is a love that moves in us and with us through sacrificial love, through truth telling, through healing and exorcising the demons, and finally, through suffering and death itself. That divine love is no stranger to any of our human triumphs and tragedies. That divine love is in us and with us at every human extremity, in death itself, overcoming the power of death.

These are days when a message of sacrificial love, a love that takes us to the cross, is not gladly received. In a society that prizes self-esteem, sacrifice seems too

April 10, 1998
Good Friday

self-negating. In a society that prizes appropriate assertiveness, sacrificial love seems too passive, too reactive. In a society that prizes enterprise, sacrifice could be taken for sloth, or a fear of competing. In a society that prizes riches and possessions, sacrifice seems too spiritual, too otherworldly. In a society trying to stop child abuse, the thought of a heavenly father willing the death of his beloved son on a cross is troubling and disturbing. In a society that tolerates violence, where some crave violence, where the threat of violence is a normal exercise of power, sacrifice seems hopelessly weak, impotent.

These are immense obstacles to confront, not just on Good Friday! For the core message of the gospel is Jesus Christ crucified. The cross remains the preeminent Christian symbol. We cannot be faithful to the gospel message without holding fast to that cross, without confronting those obstacles.

The servant poem in Isaiah 52:13—53:12 is rich with images that have nourished Christian believers in struggling with the mystery of the cross. Scholars do not agree on the identity of the servant in these poems, some arguing for a restored community of Israel, some arguing for a future messianic figure. In spite of these interpretive difficulties, Christians throughout the centuries have believed that the prophet depicted, in anticipation, God's incarnation in Jesus Christ. The servant had nothing unusual to commend him. He was despised and rejected by people. He bore our infirmities. He was crushed for our iniquities. He took the punishment that makes us whole. In a perversion of justice, he was led away like a lamb to slaughter. And yet, out of his anguish, out of his righteousness, many are made righteous. Therefore he will be allotted a portion with the great.

The parallels between the images contained in this servant poem and the gospel narratives of the meaning of Jesus' crucifixion are so striking that readers of the Scriptures, preachers, and theologians down through the centuries have made the connections even if we can never be precisely sure of the author's intentions.

Their precedent can serve us on this Good Friday, as we ponder the great mystery of the crucifixion and as we confront the severe obstacles to the message of the cross in the modern world.

To take up the obstacles one by one, self-esteem should never be viewed as the opposite of sacrificial love. True self-esteem, the kind grounded in God's gracious love freely given, enables one to give freely of oneself, sacrificially, not counting the cost, because one's selfhood is never spent or lost that way. Rather, one's selfhood is enhanced through sacrificial love in the knowledge that as one shares a love freely received, more than that amount of love is returned from the limitless reservoir of divine love.

Appropriate assertiveness seems set against sacrificial love, but that's a false opposition also. Assertiveness mean's claiming one's right as a beloved child of God, not trying to assert one's own claims against those of others. When we are secure in that divine love, we are not passive doormats, enjoying being put down under the guise of Christian sacrifice. We are, rather, active, assertive bearers of the divine love that is within us, and that we know is the true power present in the whole universe. Truly sacrificial love asserts vigorously its right to give and to love on and on, against all that is set against such love.

Enterprise, that great engine of our political economy, would seem clearly threatened by a message of sacrificial love. After all, it is competition that drives the entrepreneur to provide better goods and services than those of competitors, and so to succeed not only in serving social needs but also in creating wealth. Surely a message of sacrificial love would, if taken seriously, undermine such enterprise. Not necessarily. Sacrificial love is also enterprising, energetic, though the growth such love seeks is not wealth in itself, but growth in a just social and economic order where the needs of all people are met. That kind of loving, just goal does stand against, indeed *must* stand against any doctrine holding that enterprise is inherently good. Sacrificial love insists that enterprise is good if it aids the common good, if it builds up the realm of God's loving justice, not if enterprise benefits a few at the expense of many.

The pursuit of riches, amassing possessions, so dear to our acquisitive society, must surely be at odds with sacrificial love. If the pursuit of wealth, if the joys of acquiring and consuming become dominant, yes, indeed, there is a serious conflict. Sacrificial love employs riches and possessions to enhance the well-being of others, to bring them joy, to enable them to express gratitude to the God who is the ultimate giver of everything we have. As with enterprise, the measure is not in the activity itself, but what we do with its results. God's gifts are always meant to be shared. We call it stewardship. There is nothing wrong with riches, with possessions, if they are employed in meeting human need, in building up a positive and just society.

Can sacrificial love ever be an excuse for child abuse, for

April 10, 1998
Good Friday

spouse abuse, for any kind of abuse? Such a suggestion seems utterly abhorrent, at first blush. But here is the argument: the story of God's test of Abraham's faith by commanding Abraham to sacrifice his son, Isaac, and the way in which Christian piety has described God's sacrifice of his beloved Son on the cross—*"Yet it was the will of the Lord to crush him with pain"* (Isa 53:10a)—have been used, so the argument goes, to legitimate child abuse, to sanction human sacrifice. If that is so, surely those are examples of the abuse of Scripture and tradition, not of any abusive quality inherent in the texts or traditions. The God we know in Jesus Christ loves sacrificially with the aim of calling all things into a redemptive and transforming relationship, not into victimization. It is the great reality and mystery of the cross that such love is set before us in the suffering of the one who died there, not because he was God's victim, but because he chose the pathway of suffering sacrifice, in order to make it clear that such is God's way with us.

That leads to the last obstacle, violence. Surely sacrificial love stands impotent before the specter of violence, or so it would seem. The power of violence to destroy and kill, the threat of violence to coerce the timid seem compelling objections to any claim of power held by sacrificial love. But we should not rush to judgment. The power of such great persons of sacrificial love as Mahatma Ghandi or Martin Luther King Jr. shows that even when violence gets its way, it cannot kill the longing for freedom and hope, and that love can grow and thrive even in a hostile climate.

On this Good Friday, when the death of Jesus weighs heavily on our hearts, we should honestly acknowledge that the pathway of sacrificial love that he trod is a difficult path to follow, however serious our intentions. We should honestly acknowledge that the obstacles to such love in ourselves and in our society are truly overwhelming. But we should also honestly acknowledge that, as we meditate on the suffering servant poem from Isaiah, there is finally no other pathway to take, on the way to life. Other pathways abound, but they lead to death, not life. They avoid the cross, deny the cross. And so they miss life. Jesus' way to the cross leads to the empty tomb, and through death to life eternal.

—*Clyde J. Steckel*
United Theological Seminary
New Brighton, Minnesota

April 12, 1998

Easter Day

Lessons

Pres/Meth/UCC/Luth	Acts 10:34–43	1 Cor 15:19–26	Jn 20:1–18
Roman Catholic	Acts 10:34a, 37–43	Col 3:1–4	Jn 20:1–9
Episcopal	Acts 10:34–43	Col 3:1–4	Lk 24:1–10

Introduction to the Lessons
Lesson 1
(1) *Acts 10:34–43* **(Pres/Meth/UCC/Luth/Epis)**;
  Acts 10:34a, 37–43 **(RC)**

This passage from Acts tells the story of Peter's call to the household of Cornelius, where he has a dream disclosing God's love for all, not just those who observe the proper ceremonial customs. Peter understands that God means for the gospel message to be preached to Gentiles as well as Jews. So Peter baptizes Cornelius and preaches a resurrection sermon intended for the whole world.

(2) *1 Corinthians 15:19–26* **(Pres/Meth/UCC/Luth)**;
  Colossians 3:1–4 **(RC/Epis)**

Paul's conviction about the centrality of the resurrection is set forth in both these passages. The Corinthians passage addresses the question of the implications of the view that there is no resurrection of the dead, and he explains that Christ gives life to Adam's descendants, whose legacy was death. In Colossians, Paul outlines the resurrection life we have here on earth and the life to come in heaven.

(3) *John 20:1–18* **(Pres/Meth/UCC/Luth)**;
  John 20:1–9 **(RC)**; *Luke 24:1–10* **(Epis)**

In these passages from John, the writer tells the story of the empty tomb, first discovered by Mary Magdalene, then Peter and one other disciple. Also narrated is the conversation between the risen Jesus and Mary Magdalene. Luke's version of the same events appears in 24:1–10, where two other women, Joanna and Mary the mother of James, are with Mary Magdalene when she discovers the empty tomb. Only later does Peter visit the tomb.

April 12, 1998
Easter Day

Theme
The resurrection message contains the fullness of God's action in creation and human history to bring reconciliation, justice, and peace.

Thought for the Day
When we sing our jubilant "alleluias!" on Easter, we are declaring God's mighty victory over all that is opposed to the divine gift of redeeming love.

Prayer of Meditation
As we prepare our hearts and minds to hear the good news of Christ's resurrection, keep us mindful of all those ways you have brought new life into the midst of our own suffering and dying, bringing confidence in your saving power both in this world and in the world to come. We pray in the name of the risen Christ. Amen.

Call to Worship
>Alleluia! Alleluia! Alleluia!
>O sons and daughters, let us sing
>the flower of heaven, alive as spring,
>o'er death today rose triumphing,
>Alleluia! Alleluia!

Prayer of Adoration
We adore and praise you, resurrection God, bringing victory over death, new life in the place of old, hope in the place of despair, glimpses of your peace and justice in our lives in the place of violence and oppression. Give us astonished and grateful hearts as we receive this miracle. We pray in the name of our risen Savior, Jesus Christ.

Prayer of Confession
We confess to you, merciful and reconciling God, that as we stand before the great, incomprehensible miracle of the empty tomb, we are too often doubtful, skeptical, unbelieving, and go away not in joy but in despair. Free us to delight, give thanks, give praise for your triumph

over death in Jesus Christ. Forgive and restore us and believing disciples, those who have seen the risen Lord and received him into their lives. And enable us to live in that renewing mercy. We pray for the sake of the risen one, Jesus Christ our Lord. Amen.

Prayer of Dedication of Gifts and Self
Take these gifts we present on this holy Easter day, gracious God, and take our lives as well, as expressions of deep gratitude for your victory over death and for the promise of eternal life. Let our gifts extend that witness into the whole world. In Christ's name we pray. Amen.

Sermon Summary
The Easter message, as Peter summarized it at the household of Cornelius, is much more than the empty tomb. It includes the whole history of God's creating and reconciling work in creation and human history, and the promise of the age to come. Especially on Easter we need to keep that whole message before us, and live out of its profound truth.

Hymn of the Day
"Halle–Halle–Halleluja!" This simple song contains no other words, and yet with its infectious Caribbean melody and beat, it says all that is needed. It is meant to be repeated over and over and can be begun by one singer who then adds the choir, then some instruments, and finally the whole congregation. It makes a wonderful processional, recessional, or gospel acclamation. Celebrate, for Christ is risen!

April 12, 1998
Easter Day

Children's Object Talk

Jesus Is Lord!

Object
　A posterboard sign with "Jesus Is Lord!" written on it in large letters.

Lesson
　Jesus is Lord.

Today is the most important day in the whole church year. It is Easter. This is the day when we celebrate that Jesus came alive again after being killed on the cross.

A long time ago when many people were telling the good news of Jesus being made alive again on Easter, Christians would get together. When they gathered, something like we are doing here today in church, there was one important sentence they would say: "Jesus Is Lord!" Please say it with me now. (Hold up posterboard and lead children.) Now, let's ask the rest of the people here today to say it with us. (Again hold up posterboard and include whole congregation.)

The disciple Peter says this about Jesus in our Bible reading from Acts. Let's think about what Peter meant, and what we mean when we say "Jesus Is Lord." Our reading from Acts helps us. For Jesus to be Lord means he has great power. Jesus can help and heal sick people. Jesus can love us and forgive us. He can even live again after being killed. That is great news!

Jesus is able to help us, forgive us, and even one day, bring us to heaven to live with God. This is what we celebrate on Easter Sunday.

Let's celebrate it once more by saying together "Jesus Is Lord!"

—Jeanette Strandjord

The Sermon

The Resurrection Message

Hymns
Beginning of Worship: "Christ the Lord Is Risen Today"
Sermon Hymn: "Thine Is the Glory, Risen Conquering Son"
End of Worship: "I Greet You, Sure Redeemer"

Scripture
Acts 10:34–43 (For additional sermon materials on this passage, see the January 1998 and the *1997 May/June Planning Issue* of *The Clergy Journal*.)

Sermon Text
"... God raised him on the third day and allowed him to appear, not to all the people but to us who were chosen by God as witnesses, and who ate and drank with him after he rose from the dead" (vss. 40–41).

Alleluia! Jesus Christ is risen today. Alleluia!

Such poetic, liturgical exclamations may be the best response we can make to the amazing mystery of Christ's resurrection. A miracle like that defies rational explanation, or even the limits of prose narrative.

But there is also a resurrection message. At Easter we are called to meditate on that entire message, not just to bask in the joy of new life coming out of death.

There are many places in Christian Scripture where this entire resurrection message appears. Scholars believe that these were early sermons, hymns, or communal confessions of faith, which the writers incorporated into their texts.

One of these entire resurrection messages is found in Acts 10:34–43. This is Peter's sermon to those gathered in the household of Cornelius, "a centurion, an upright and God-fearing man, who is well spoken of by the whole Jewish nation" (Acts 10:22). Peter's sermon comes after his vision of the sheet being lowered from heaven, filled with all kinds of creatures, some of which were illegal as food for Jews.

"Get up, Peter; kill and eat," says the voice. But Peter protests. He has never eaten anything that

April 12, 1998
Easter Day

is profane or unclean. "What God has made clean, you must not call profane," says the voice.

This story is often used to document the universal promise of the gospel message. It is a message for Gentiles as well as Jews. The Christian movement can no longer be viewed as a Jewish sect. The book of Acts and Paul's letters, particularly Galatians and Romans, abundantly illustrate the importance of this shift in outlook taking place in the early Christian movement.

Too often, though, as we review this affirmation of Christian universality in Luke 10, we neglect Peter's concluding sermon. Once we have been inspired by his conversion, we pass quickly over his remarks.

Especially on Easter we need to read and ponder his sermon as well. And what do we find? It is an amazingly compact and powerful statement of the entire resurrection message. Would that all of us who preach could always be so focused and clear!

Peter begins with two essential affirmations: God accepts anyone in any nation who fears God and does what is right. And Jesus Christ, the one who brings peace, is Lord of all. There it is in two sentences: the core of the gospel message!

But Peter does not stop with that much. He goes on to tell the essential details of the entire resurrection message: John's preaching of baptism; Jesus' anointing by the Holy Spirit with power; Jesus' ministry of healing and good deeds; his execution on the cross; his resurrection on the third day; his appearances, not to everyone, but to those chosen to be his witnesses; his eating and drinking with the disciples after his resurrection; his command that all his followers are to preach the good news that Jesus Christ is the one ordained to judge the living and the dead; and the promise that everyone who believes in him receives forgiveness of sins.

There it all is, in one tiny but powerful sermon—the entire resurrection message. How urgently we need to reflect on that entire message, and not only the resurrection event, on this most holy day of Easter! How quickly we merge the empty tomb with images of new life coming to birth in the warmth of spring (at least in the northern hemisphere!). How our leaf buds and flowers and balloons and eggs distract us, for all the good feelings they inspire, from the entire resurrection message on Easter. Flowers and eggs do not seem to leave much room for execution on a cross, for mysterious appearances, for stern commands to witness.

Well, you say, let's just enjoy the springtime and the rebirth of beauty and the rebirth of hope in our Easter celebrations. There are plenty of Sundays for the other things. What's wrong with just having one big celebration on Easter?

Nothing is wrong with that, so long as the entire resurrection message is not muted or lost altogether. How do we keep that from happening? One way is through the various creeds we say or sing in our worship services. Did you notice how closely Peter's sermon parallels those early creeds, like the Apostles' Creed or the Nicene Creed? In the churches that use creeds in worship, ancient or modern creeds, one purpose is to keep the entire resurrection message before us. Our praying, our singing, our preaching may wander this way and that, depending on our moods, the circumstances of our lives, or the lectionary texts for that day. But when we say the creeds, the entire resurrection message is not only set before us, but it also works its way through our minds and bodies as we say or sing the words.

You may object that familiar words and phrases allow our minds to drift. They become routine. But not always! Those great phrases of that resurrection message, rising from the voices of a community of worship, make a magic of their own. The Holy Spirit dwells among us as we tell the saving story.

On this Easter, as we reflect on a story from Scripture not frequently associated with this holy day, let us resolve to make our individual and communal observance of Easter one that is faithful to the entire resurrection message, one that remembers the baptism of Jesus, how he was empowered by the Holy Spirit, how he taught and healed and drove out demons, how he came to be executed on a cross of suffering, how he was raised by God's own power and appeared to his disciples, how he commanded them to be his witnesses to the world, how all of this is great and good news for a world often mired in bad news, without hope.

If we can do that, the peace and healing of God's reconciling message will fill all our being, and we will be on the way to becoming people of the entire resurrection message each day we live. Easter is the special celebration of that reality. But each day can be an Easter if the entire resurrection message fills our souls.

—*Clyde J. Steckel*
United Theological Seminary
New Brighton, Minnesota

April 19, 1998

2nd Sunday of Easter

Lessons

Pres/Meth/UCC/Luth	Acts 5:27–32	Rev 1:4–8	Jn 20:19–31
Roman Catholic	Acts 5:12–16	Rev 1:9–11a, 12–13, 17–19	Jn 20:19–31
Episcopal	Acts 5:12a, 17–22, 25–29	Rev 1:(1–8) 9–19	Jn 20:19–31

Introduction to the Lessons

Lesson 1

(1) *Acts 5:27–32* **(Pres/Meth/UCC/Luth)**
Deemed incorrigible by the authorities who seek unsuccessfully to stifle their almost compulsive preaching, Peter and the other apostles witness not to a compulsion but to the compelling cause for their spirited and enthusiastic witness, the crucified but now exalted Jesus, agent of Israel's salvation.

(2) *Acts 5:12–16* **(RC)**
This passage is a witness to the effective transfer of power, and life, and healing from Jesus to his apostles. The celebrity of Peter and the others, and the esteem with which they are regarded, is the result of an effective and evangelical healing ministry.

(3) *Acts 5:12a, 17–22, 25–29* **(Epis)**
The apostles' devotion to their vocation renders them subordinate to God's authority at work in their ministries, an authority that easily takes precedence over human authority including the attending systems (like prison) invoked to buttress and enforce it.

Lesson 2

(1) *Revelation 1:4–8* **(Pres/Meth/UCC/Luth)**
The seer of Patmos greets his audience churches on behalf of the risen and exalted Lord, summarizing the resurrection faith and pointing toward the still-to-come event of Christ's return and recompense.

(2) *Revelation 1:9–11a, 12–13, 17–19* **(RC);**
Revelation 1:(1–8) 9–19 **(Epis)**
This opening section from the author of Revelation establishes him in the long line of prophets who have received and relayed their experiences and encounters of the Holy One. The awesome image that is conjured up and that corresponds to visions of other apocalyptic prophets (Ezekiel, Daniel, Zechariah) is, at the same time, a commanding and sometimes reassuring presence in the midst of the congregations whom the author is addressing.

Gospel
John 20:19–31 **(Pres/Meth/UCC/Luth/RC/Epis)**
Thomas demonstrates how, for some, faith must have a tangible, practical, even tactile dimension, as if these things provide a surer foothold or handhold for the great mysteries of death and resurrection. Without putting him down, Jesus accommodates Thomas' need, while at the same time affirms those whose five senses are not the only access to a believing heart.

Theme
Faith and doubt can complement each other.

Thought for the Day
Ways people have of believing are as complex as people themselves. What manages to prompt the faith response of one person can prompt questions on the part of others. Inquiries and questions, though, are not necessarily obstructions to faith; they can be avenues to faith.

Prayer of Meditation
God of Easter and of all our days, we approach you with a kind of awe appropriate to this season. Some come joyfully to embrace your resurrection promises and others come reluctantly. Some are faith-filled and some are fearful. Some approach with certitude of conviction, while others bring curiosities and questions. Help us to know that, in love and understanding, you meet and receive us as we are. Amen.

Call to Worship
    Leader: Sing to God, O people!
    People: God has indeed done excellent things!

April 19, 1998
2nd Sunday of Easter

Leader: Sing to God, O people!
People: For God, in mercy, has comforted us.
Leader: Thanks be to God.
People: For God has given us the victory through our Savior, Jesus Christ.

Prayer of Adoration

Mighty God, you who were pleased to be made known and available to us through Jesus the Christ, we praise you for accepting and blessing us, even when our faith is imperfect or incomplete. Overcome and outlast the barriers that tend to separate us from you. Come into all the shut places of our lives: the fears, the narrow prejudices, the cloistered hearts. Open doors that have long since been closed against you, that in our need to apprehend you, we might be grasped by your presence in our very midst and touched by your Spirit upon our own flesh. Amen.

Prayer of Confession

Gracious God, we acknowledge before you the times when we have stood tentative and timid before the claims of faith. At the same time we ask forgiveness for when, in certitude or in covering up our own misgivings, we have stifled others' questions. We sometimes behave as if having hard and fast answers is more important than sustaining a faithful search for wisdom and truth. Whatever it is we know and don't know, whatever we believe and what we doubt, grant that it leads us to a deeper faith and further acquaintance with you, through Jesus Christ our Savior. Amen.

Prayer of Dedication of Gifts and Self

O God, receive from our hands and hearts these gifts. In receiving them, transform them, just as you promise to transform us, into joyful expressions of your love. Grant us the grace of life made new and abundant, through Jesus Christ our Savior. Amen.

Sermon Summary

Just as many can identify with the father who exclaims, "I believe; help my unbelief!" Many believers as well as nonbelievers can identify with Thomas. There are moments when we beg our human frailty and fragility, needing unambiguous confirmation of Christ's presence alive and well among us. Jesus and the disciples seem to honor Thomas and his conditions to belief, allowing doubt in the same room where faith holds sway.

Hymn of the Day

"Come, Ye Faithful, Raise the Strain." This exultant celebratory hymn reminds us that Easter is not a day, but a whole season. Appropriately, the fourth verse references the risen Christ among the disciples as the gospel lesson for today recounts. The original text comes from the seventh-century author, Saint John of Damascus, of whom almost nothing is known. In contrast, many will be surprised to know that the composer of the tune is Arthur Sullivan of Gilbert and Sullivan operatic fame. By setting Saint John's words to this tune, he proves he is the very model of a modern martyr-music maker.

Children's Object Talk

Gather Together

Object
A Bible.
Lesson
It is good for us to gather together and listen to Jesus.

I am so happy that all of you are here today! You can help us sing our songs today. You can pray with us. You can listen to the Bible being read (hold up Bible) and hear about Jesus. We do all these things when we meet together for worship. It is so good that you came today.

One of the stories in the Bible is about someone who wasn't always good at meeting with other followers of Jesus. His name is Thomas. Long ago when Jesus came to see all of the disciples after Easter, Thomas wasn't there. The other disciples met together, but Thomas missed the meeting. Because Thomas wasn't there, he didn't see Jesus and had a hard time believing that Jesus was really alive again.

About a week later, all of Jesus' friends got together again and this time Thomas came too. It's a good thing he did because Jesus was there. Jesus showed Thomas his hands and his side where he had been hurt on the cross. Jesus helped Thomas to believe that Jesus was really alive again.

When I hear the story about Thomas and Jesus, I think of how important it is for all of us to make sure we come together like we are in church today. When we come together, we can hear Jesus' words in the Bible. Jesus talks to us through the Bible. We can also sing, pray, and talk to each other. When we do these things, Jesus is with us and helps us to believe in him, just like he helped Thomas.

—*Jeanette Strandjord*

The Sermon

The Benefit of a Doubt

Hymns
Beginning of Worship: "Come, Ye Faithful, Raise the Strain"
Sermon Hymn: "These Things Did Thomas Count"
End of Worship: "Yours Is the Glory, Resurrected One!"

Scripture
John 20:19–31 (For additional sermon materials on this passage, see the January 1998 issue and the *1997 May/June Planning Issue* of *The Clergy Journal*.)

Sermon Text
"... *Jesus came and stood among them and said, 'Peace be with you.' Then he said to Thomas, 'Put your finger here and see my hands. Reach out your hand and put it in my side...' Thomas answered him, 'My Lord and my God!'"* (vss. 26–28).

There's an unofficial but long-standing tradition that accompanies this Sunday after Easter. Preachers sometimes focus whole sermons on it, or sometimes we slip unconsciously into it. One way or another, the phenomenon manifests itself and I'm talking about the subtle bantering or not-so-subtle bashing of those folks who filled these pews last week, but today are out and about, doing their usual Sunday routine.

I confess that I myself have succumbed on occasion to such critical musings and verbal whippings. But I also have to confess a soft spot in my heart for those folks who show up this one time a year. Think about it. Easter is unashamedly glorious! The full choir, the beautiful and flower-bedecked cross, the special music, the instrumentalists that punctuate the already impressive songs of resurrection faith with octaves of bells and trumpet blasts. There's a jolt of triumph and certain exclamation that charges through this space on Easter Sunday morning, as it should, as we declare our confidence in God's mightiest deed of resurrection.

The soft spot I have on Easter is for those folks who end up here, curious perhaps, or otherwise drawn to Easter's mystery but whose faces nevertheless visibly register shades of doubt and no little bewilderment at the apparent faith of everyone else. They look to the right and left and see others singing their hearts out on this high and holy day that "Christ the Lord is risen today, Allelujah!" Given that, it is hard for these folks, if one receives the news of a loved one's dying, to declare Easter's resounding assurance that "Death is swallowed up in victory." It's hard, that very next Monday, to pick up the newspaper, read of the continuing violence all around them, the wanton murders in our own cities, or to receive the lab report that unfortunately, the tests were positive. It's hard to do that and still sing with Easter morning's gusto "The strife is o'er, the battle won." The Monday after Easter Sunday can sometimes drop like a heavy curtain after the high moment of standing ovation is past.

The fact is that all of us—not just Easter visitors—have to wake up on the Monday after Easter and face a seemingly unchanged world. And if, in all honesty, we admit along with them to even the slightest reservation or doubt, I want us to know that it's all right. The Bible itself assures us that we are in plenty of good company.

On this second Sunday of Easter, the lectionary (wisely, I think) commends to us the story of the disciple, Thomas. He has come to be branded "doubting Thomas" because he will not take this news of Jesus' resurrection lightly, nor on hearsay. Actually, Thomas' doubting is not an isolated incident. When you read through the Easter stories, you find in every gospel that one of the reactions of the disciples to the good news of Easter is doubt.

In Matthew, we're told that the eleven disciples meet the risen Lord in Galilee. They worship him, it says, but it adds that some also doubted. And in Mark, in that later section that was tacked on, we're told that after two separate incidents are reported, independently confirming Jesus' being alive, the reaction of the disciples was not the "Hallelujah Chorus" but disbelief, a douse of cold water—not a torch of fiery faith.

In our lesson for today, Thomas insists upon seeing for himself the risen Christ and touching the mortal wounds. While some fault Thomas and use him as a whipping boy, his

April 19, 1998
2nd Sunday of Easter

story offers us some precious insights into the value of doubt and its relationship to faith.

First, this story of Thomas introduces questioning and doubt not as *enemies to faith, but avenues to faith*. Doubts are not deadends but sometimes circuitous, even difficult ways to truth. In our judicial system we place great value on doubt. The benefit of doubt can sway an entire jury's decision in such weighty matters as life and death. Faith that is grounded and growing also honors the value of doubt. Thomas comes to his expression of faith only after expressing his misgivings. Faith rarely comes without questioning and doubt. In fact, it usually comes *through* questioning and doubt.

While I'm a so-called "senior pastor," I like working directly with young people, from teaching Vacation Bible School to three- and four-year-olds to teaching confirmation to high school students. I like young people because they are so unreservedly honest about what they believe and about what they can't or don't yet believe. They seem so capable of a kind of humble, honest, and healthy questioning that expresses the integrity of their faith but also the integrity of their uncertainty.

What I like most to do is not just preach the faith to them, but practice the faith with them by giving them opportunities for "hands-on faith" like serving in a soup kitchen or working in an inner-city food distribution center. I think about Thomas wanting to touch Jesus' wounds, needing a hands-on kind of faith. When we work for others, that's our way of touching the wounds in society and bringing the love of Jesus. That's the way we have of being Christ's presence and embodying the resurrection.

At the end of today's story, Thomas is moved to proclaim at last "My Lord and my God!" But only after his doubting does it happen. Thomas never made such a celebrated confession of faith earlier. Only here does a full disclosure of faith come and from the same lips that earlier had risked ostracism and raised piercing questions.

Thomas and the other disciples are to be credited for not letting doubt or insufficient faith determine who's in or who's out of the company of Christ's people. Thomas is never excluded from the others. No one drives him away, telling him he can't come back until he's memorized the Apostles' Creed. Nor is Thomas hostile in his questioning. He doesn't go out and start his own church, "The Saint Thomas Doubter's Society." Verse 26 picks up with these words:

"A week later his disciples were again in the house, and Thomas was with them. Although the doors were shut, Jesus came and stood among them and said, 'Peace be with you.' Then he said to Thomas, 'Put your finger here and see my hands. Reach out your hand and put it in my side . . .' Thomas answered him, 'My Lord and my God!'"

To the end, Thomas is included in the circle despite his questioning. Belief and doubt live together. Not just opposites, doubt and belief spark each other. Frederick Buechner says that doubts are the "ants in the pants" of faith. Both faith and doubt witness to the unbelievable good news of resurrection; both faith and doubt respect the great mystery of Easter and testify to its power and magnitude to embrace both.

For many of us regulars and once-a-year visitors alike, Easter can be both a drawing card and a stumbling block of faith. In these ongoing days of Easter season, we're called by this text to keep company and faith with one another, honor one another's questions and answers, and let Easter's great consuming mystery have its way with us until we—perhaps because then beyond the benefit of a doubt—will be able to blurt out, with doubting/ believing Thomas, "My Lord and my God!"

—*Steven L. Davis*
Shepherd of the Hills UCC
Phoenix, Arizona

April 26, 1998

3rd Sunday of Easter

Lessons

Pres/Meth/UCC/Luth	Acts 9:1–6 (7–20)	Rev 5:11–14	Jn 21:1–19
Roman Catholic	Acts 5:27b–32, 40b–41	Rev 5:11–14	Jn 21:1–19
Episcopal	Acts 9:1–19a	Rev 5:6–14	Jn 21:1–14

Introduction to the Lessons

Lesson 1
(1) *Acts 9:1–6 (7–20)* **(Pres/Meth/UCC/Luth)**;
Acts 9:1–19a **(Epis)**

Saul, the stalker of disciples of Jesus, becomes the one who is caught. The hunter becomes the hunted. Saul's conversation speaks to that amazing grace that makes us lost when we think we're found and makes us blind when we think we see. It is quite a journey Saul makes from "breathing threats and murder" against Jesus to proclaiming him as the Son of God.

(2) *Acts 5:27b–32, 40b–41* **(RC)**

Deemed incorrigible by the authorities who seek unsuccessfully to stifle their almost compulsive preaching, Peter and the other apostles witness not to a compulsion but to the compelling cause of their spirited and enthusiastic witness, the crucified but now exalted Jesus, agent of Israel's salvation.

Lesson 2
(1) *Revelation 5:11–14* **(Pres/Meth/UCC/Luth/RC)**;
Revelation 5:6–14 **(Epis)**

A worshipful context is suggested by the images of both heavenly and earthly creatures bowing down and acknowledging the slain lamb. It is the lamb's sacrificial actions that are honored and held high in praise. Meanwhile the lamb enjoys divine access and authority, obviously sharing in God's sovereignty.

Gospel
John 21:1–19 (**Pres/Meth/UCC/Luth/RC**); *John 21:1–14* (**Epis**)
The author of this gospel appears to have appropriated what seems originally like a "call" story and placed it in a post-resurrection setting. It is part of the genius of this theologically astute gospel writer to know the depths of human grief, joy, and confusion. Jesus appears to the disciples who try to "lose" themselves in their work, and gently but firmly recalls them and reminds them (epitomized in Peter) that their new vocation likewise consists in finding, fishing, netting, and feeding those who are hungry for the good news.

Theme
The new life we're called to is to do what love requires.

Thought for the Day
In stunned grief over the crucifixion and confusion/joy over seeing Jesus again, it only makes sense that the disciples do what so many of us do: they get busy with routine tasks, almost mindless things, that permit them some relief from the stress of days that have been emotion-filled and trauma-laden.

Prayer of Meditation
God of Easter and of all our days, we ask that Christ approach us as he did the disciples in resurrection power. Let us not return too easily to busy ourselves with the usual tasks and resume old habits casually taking up things as they were. On this side of new life, help us keep senses and souls open to the call to do what love requires on behalf of Christ and all those who are led to meet Christ through us. Amen.

Call to Worship
Leader: People of God, Christ is risen!
People: Christ is risen, indeed!
Leader: Have you seen him?
People: Sometimes he slips into our thoughts and our dreams.
Leader: Sometimes he takes us by surprise when we least expect it.
People: We feel his insistent pull toward the love of others.
Leader: We sense his continuous call toward those in need.
People: Christ is risen! Christ is risen, indeed!

April 26, 1998
3rd Sunday of Easter

Prayer of Adoration

O God, in Christ you are pleased to follow us and find us, even as you would have us find and follow you. You are patient and loving to cajole us from the easy distractions of a compulsive world. Your calls faintly filter through, reminding us to share with those who need it most the power of your love and the promise of your resurrection. You have christened us for a mission that carries us far and wide, but keep us, O God, ever in range of your centering, saving word. May we have ears to hear and the heart to reply. Amen.

Prayer of Confession

God, whose gift of new life is ours to lavish upon others; there have been moments, sad to say, when we have been unseeing, unhearing, and inattentive to the requirements of love in our daily rounds. We have not prepared ourselves well for the feeding and loving of those whom we encounter. We confess our empty-handedness at times, and our empty-headedness at times. Forgive us and keep us mindful of the mercies we are called to embody, the ministries we are privileged to perform, in Christ's name. Amen.

Prayer of Dedication of Gifts and Self

Accept, gracious God, these gifts as expressions of our gratitude for your Easter promise and presence. Though it be a curious and uneasy peace that we know, we are thankful that you do not give up on us, that your Spirit continues to comfort us in the search for truth, encourages us to live the truth we find, and guides us to seek the truth yet to be revealed. Thank you, in Christ's name. Amen.

Sermon Summary

Immediately upon the heels of their grief, the disciples are overwhelmed and overcome by an awareness of Jesus among them still. While, for a brief time, the crucifixion cancels everything, it is the resurrection life that changes everything. It reintroduces and reinforces all Jesus' teachings and promises, and it once again presents to would-be disciples the call to follow, to feed, and to love.

Hymn of the Day

"He Lives." Words and music for this gospel classic were composed by Alfred Ackley in 1933. The acclamation of Christ's continuing presence recalls the joy and surprise that disciples must have felt after Jesus appeared to them following the resurrection. A good intergenerational hymn, the chorus has easy parts for children so they can join in.

Children's Object Talk

Work Together

Object

A sack or pillowcase filled with something heavy.

Lesson

The church works together to do God's will.

I have a very heavy sack over there, and it is hard for me to lift it all by myself. I'd like to bring it over here, and I think I could do it with your help today. Will you help me? I know that if we work together, we can do it! (Lead children to sack and carry it together back to where you were.) Great! Thank you all so much. I couldn't have done this all by myself.

We can get a lot done when we work together. It's that way for all people who follow Jesus. A story in the Bible tells us about that. After Easter, Jesus talked to his disciples about the work they needed to do to tell everyone about Jesus. Jesus asked Peter and the other disciples to go and tell people about him. That meant they would travel to lots of different places around the world. They would heal sick people, preach about Jesus, and help build new churches. That was a big job, just like it was a big job to carry this heavy sack over here. But the disciples did it because everyone was willing to work.

Today, Jesus still wants you and me to tell other people about him. We can invite other children to church and Sunday school. We can collect food for hungry people. We can sing about Jesus and pray for other people. We can give our Sunday school and church offering to help others build new churches. That's a big job, isn't it? How are we going to do it? (wait for responses)

We'll do our big job of spreading the news about Jesus like the disciples did it. We'll all join in the work. And Jesus will help us do it all just like he helped his disciples a long time ago.

—*Jeanette Strandjord*

April 26, 1998
3rd Sunday of Easter

The Sermon

A Curious, Uneasy Peace

Hymns
Beginning of Worship: "Jesus Calls Us, o'er the Tumult"
Sermon Hymn: "They Cast Their Nets in Galilee"
End of Worship: "Listen to Your Savior Call"

Scripture
John 21:1–19 (For additional sermon materials on this passage, see the January 1998 issue of *The Clergy Journal* and on Revelation 5:11–14, see the *1997 May/June Planning Issue* of *The Clergy Journal*.)

Sermon Text
"Simon Peter said to them, 'I am going fishing.' They said to him, 'We will go with you'" (vs. 3).

"Easter is over," she said in a tone that conveyed polite annoyance. "Why are we still singing about it?" This woman, I suspect, is not alone in wondering why Easter has to be drawn out into a season. It is as if there is an anticlimax to these post-Easter days. Or, maybe it's a matter of wanting to get on with life as usual. We have a near inexhaustible capacity for relativizing everything. Even something as unusual as resurrection, which has no frame of reference, is subject to our need to relegate everything to its reasonable and proper place.

Perhaps that is why, for many of us, Easter's eventfulness and meaning slip into the past with a remarkable ease and once-and-for-allness. Easter celebrations fade quickly. In the northern climes, minds are prompted to shift to other new-life rituals: the garden that needs planting, the lawn that needs seeding, the summer vacation that needs planning. We settle ourselves in what is left of Easter's trailing wake and head for summer with its longed-for leisure of enjoyable weather and relaxed schedules.

If any of this feels even a little familiar in your experience, you are not too unlike Peter, Thomas, Nathaniel, and the others. We can imagine it to have been a becalmed and serene evening when they gathered their nets and set out from the shores of the Sea of Tiberias, a common experience on a seemingly ordinary evening. John's story follows them through to the end of their outing, early morning. All-night fishing had met with little success, and as they returned in understandable disappointment, they looked to shore and came to recognize a familiar figure and voice.

Now, for the overly pious, this story poses some problems. Less than a week has passed since the forlorn trauma of Jesus' death, followed so soon by the unspeakable joy of the Easter sightings. Yet, where are the disciples? On corner soapboxes in Jerusalem? In the temple praising God? Planning an empirewide evangelistic mission to "win others to Christ"? None of the above. They are found fishing, performing their daily and familiar tasks just as they had before Jesus' intrusion into their lives.

It's hard to understand. We cannot ride the roller coaster of our highest and deepest emotions too long, especially when grief is part of what we have to assimilate into our lives as survivors. What do we do? We endure shock, of course, disbelief, even anger. Then we hold fast to the promise of eternal surprises and new life. But there's always the voice inside or someone around to tell us to keep busy, to fill our days and nights with the details and distractions of getting on with life as best we can.

You notice how similar this story in John is to other accounts in other gospels of the disciples' original calling. So striking is the similarity that this story appears to be the same one, only adapted and situated at the conclusion of this gospel. Obviously, Jesus' calling of Peter and his command to Peter and the others to follow him belong at the beginning of Jesus' ministry, not at the end or after the fact. Still, the author of this Fourth Gospel deliberately positions the story in the aftermath of the resurrection. It revisits the original commitments and punctuates the ongoing nature of a resurrection faith.

Imagine the awkward excitement of that early morning. A distant but familiar voice beckons them to try fishing the other side of the boat. When the nets are filled to bursting, so is their excitement in realizing who it is who has called to them. Simon Peter is so overcome that he jumps ship and impulsively swims to shore in an obvious display of rekindled dedication.

I cannot help but think that second thoughts and some apprehension might have accompanied his excited strokes toward shore. For Peter and the others had weathered the ups and downs of the past few years, the last week especially haven taken its toll. The empty tomb was a vindicating and victorious climax

April 26, 1998
3rd Sunday of Easter

to the challenge that had shaken their world, changed their lives, and made them alien to their own households. Now it was over. Now they could go home.

In the wake of that glorious event, the turbulence was behind them. They could be husbands again to their wives, fathers to their children. They could bury their dead, put their hands to the plow, and look back as often as they pleased. They could return to their boats and resume fishing, buoyant that their immediate past had been well spent and had a happy ending that they could cherish forever. As fisher-types are wont to do, they could spin this tale out to their children and to their children's children well into retirement and grandparenthood. Or could they?

I remember reading an account of a young Nazi officer who had been part of the conquest of France. He watched in disdain as the vanquished French soldiers paraded before him in defeat and disgrace. They stretched on for miles. But then a discordant note forced itself into his mind. These men were going home. It was a road of defeat, but it was taking them back to their families, friends, and local bistros. But where was he going? What lay ahead for him and his army? They were the victors, but he could only shudder at the prospects of the burning sands of Africa or the white wilderness of the Russian winter.

Swimming to shore and pulling up the boat, Peter and the others must have sensed a similar kind of unresting future ahead of them. Their brief respite and return to normalcy was to be short-lived in light of a victorious and risen Lord who summons them with the same haunting words that had compelled their allegiance initially: "Do you love me? Then feed my lambs. Come, and follow me."

The hymn "They Cast Their Nets in Galilee" says it so well:

They cast their nets in Galilee,
    just off the hills of brown;
Such happy, simple fisherfolk,
    Before the Lord came down.
Contented, peaceful fishermen,
    Before they ever knew
The peace of God that filled their hearts
    Brimful, and broke them too,
The peace of God, it is no peace,
    But strife closed in the sod.
Yet, let us pray for but one
    thing:
    The marvelous peace of God.
(William A. Percy)

The "peace of God" is a curious and uneasy peace for would-be disciples; the resurrection is a curious and uneasy victory for those called to follow a risen and relentless Lord. Christ stands as a familiar one at the edge of all of our post-Easter days as we fill them with both mindful and mindless activity. Those who are serious disciples cannot ignore forever or screen the persistent question: "Yes," we need to gird our souls for the familiar summons that we know is to surely come: "Feed my lambs. Love one another. Follow me."

The peace of God: it is a curious, uneasy peace for Easter people. And the resurrection: it is a curious and uneasy victory. Christ is ever before us, appearing to us and summoning to us in every person and decision and condition demanding our care and attention. Such is the quality of the new life we're given.

May the curious, uneasy peace of God be with you, now and always.

—*Steven L. Davis*
Shepherd of the Hills UCC
Phoenix, Arizona

May 3, 1998

4th Sunday of Easter

Lessons

Pres/Meth/UCC/Luth	Acts 9:36–43	Rev 7:9–17	Jn 10:22–30
Roman Catholic	Acts 13:14, 43–52	Rev 7:9, 14b–17	Jn 10:27–30
Episcopal	Acts 13:15–16, 26–33 (34–39)	Rev 7:9–17	Jn 10:22–30

Introduction to the Lessons

Lesson 1

(1) *Acts 9:36–43* **(Pres/Meth/UCC/Luth)**
The death of the disciple, Tabitha (Dorcas, in Greek), occasions the summoning of Peter from a town nearby. Peter is curiously asked to come "without delay," which he does. Upon arrival he enters the company of mourners who are around the deceased. Such an occasion is not new to Peter. According to the writer of Luke–Acts, Peter was among the privileged, skeptical, and astounded few who were with Jesus at the raising of Jairus' daughter (Lk 8:49–56). Peter's raising of Tabitha punctuates that Jesus' presence and power are now available through the faith of his followers.

(2) *Acts 13:14, 43–52* **(RC)**; *Acts 13:15–16, 26–33 (34–39)* **(Epis)**
The appearance of Paul and Barnabas in the synagogue on the Sabbath and the invitation to them to speak results in Paul's reciting the salvation history of the people Israel. This promise of history is fulfilled, Paul proclaims, in the raising of Jesus, and through it, the forgiveness of sins and freedom from the law. Upon being heard with interest, they are urged to speak again the following Sabbath. When contradicted by strict advocates of traditional Jewish faith and practice, Paul and Barnabas welcome Gentiles into the promise. After being cast out by the authorities and the leading citizens, Paul and Barnabas then move on to extend the promise and invitation to all who will receive in joy the good news they preach.

Lesson 2
Revelation 7:9–17 **(Pres/Meth/UCC/Luth/Epis)**;
Revelation 7:9, 14b–17 **(RC)**

The community of those who are heirs of God's promises and others adopted into God's salvation history is diverse and full of praise and thanksgiving. The vision is that of a great and grateful throng, gathered in the presence and power of God.

Gospel
John 10:22–30 **(Pres/Meth/UCC/Luth/Epis)**;
John 10:27–30 **(RC)**

In suspense and/or vexation, those who intercept Jesus and interrogate him insist upon a clear answer as to who he is. Jesus says little about his identity; rather, he speaks to his identification with God (the Father), in effect, letting them deduce for themselves who he is and decide whether they number among those fortunate enough to be his flock and to know him as their shepherd.

Theme
Those whom God loves are entrusted to Jesus, the good shepherd.

Thought for the Day
That God's people are entrusted into the hands of Jesus is occasion for both comfort and challenge. We are comforted if we number among those who acknowledge ourselves to be in such good hands. We are likewise challenged to extend God's loving reach and caring grasp through that of our own in loving one another.

Prayer of Meditation
Gracious God, grant us the assurance that we are—in body and soul, in sin and righteousness, in life and death and beyond—always in your loving reach. May we trust well and follow closely the one whose grasp is sure, whose touch is tender, and whose beat of heart and strength of hands are yours, Jesus, the good shepherd. Amen.

Call to Worship
> Leader: Make a joyful noise to the Lord, all the earth.
> People: Worship the Lord with gladness; come into God's presence with singing.

May 3, 1998
4th Sunday of Easter

Leader: Know that the Lord is God . . .
People: We are God's people, the sheep of God's hand . . .
Leader: The Lord is good; God's steadfast love endures forever;
People: God's faithfulness extends to all generations.
—Adapted from Psalm 100

Prayer of Adoration

We bless you, Holy One, and give you thanks for the ways you gather us in love, seek and secure us in strength, and build us up in hope that we ourselves might be a source of inspiration to the world that you so love. All this we are privileged to enjoy and extend to others because of Jesus Christ. He who lives beyond the bounds of death gives us new life; he who is one with you makes us all one in the Spirit. We praise you for the good shepherd in whom we see you and in whose fold we are blessed forevermore. Amen.

Prayer of Confession

O God, whose will and welcome is known to us through the shepherd of the sheep, Jesus Christ; we confess the downside of our sheep-likeness all too often: the stupid ways we behave, sometimes causing injury and insult; the stubborn behavior of which we are so capable, impervious to the amendments of reason; the wandering we do from truth and compassion, usually in the oblivious quest of satisfying some hidden hunger or selfish desire. We regret and confess all these things now that we are in your presence. Call us back by the voice we know, that we might be more trusting, trustworthy, and true to our calling, through Jesus Christ our Savior. Amen.

Prayer of Dedication of Gifts and Self

Accept, O God, these gifts from our hands. We appreciate that all of who we are and have is because of the strong but gentle hold of your hands upon us. Keep us in your care always, and may the gifts we give and the lives we lead witness gratefully to your faithfulness in Jesus the Christ. Amen.

Hymn of the Day

"The Lord's My Shepherd (Brother James' Air)." Of the many settings of the Twenty-third Psalm, one of the most interesting is "Brother James' Air" composed by James Leith Macbeth Bain in nineteenth-century Scotland. This setting to the Scottish Psalter of 1650 is no somnolent funeral dirge. It is a triumphant tune acclaiming God's saving power. The tune dances with the life of the shepherd and should be sung at a lilting tempo. It is easily accompanied by flute, recorder, or trumpet.

Children's Object Talk

Jesus Loves Me

Object
Red paper hearts (on a string necklace or with tape backing).
Lesson
Nothing separates us from Jesus' love.

I have a heart that I would like each one of you to wear. I'll put them on you as I talk to you. (Begin distributing the hearts among the children. Get a helper if you have a large group.)

A heart can be a way of saying "I love you." Today this heart tells you that Jesus loves you. And Jesus does love you just like he loved his disciples so long ago. That's what our Bible story talks about today.

In the story, Jesus is telling some people that he loves his followers and will always help them. No one can ever take them away from Jesus. Jesus' love is forever.

Sometimes we might forget that. There are times when we make mistakes or do bad things. Maybe you can think of some times like that: times when we lose our temper and hit somebody or when we are mad and we yell and fight. Maybe we call someone a bad name or word. After we do things like that, we might wonder if God still loves us.

We might wonder if God still loves us when someone gets very sick or maybe someone dies. We feel all alone and sad then. We wonder whether Jesus is still with us and loves us. The answer is "Yes!" Jesus has promised to love us and be with us forever.

—*Jeanette Strandjord*

May 3, 1998
4th Sunday of Easter

The Sermon

In Good Hands

Hymns
Beginning of Worship: "I Greet You, Sure Redeemer"
Sermon Hymn: "Savior, Like a Shepherd Lead Us"
End of Worship: "Such Perfect Love My Shepherd Shows"

Scripture
John 10:22–30 (For additional sermon materials on this passage, see the February 1998 issue of *The Clergy Journal* and on Revelation 7:9–17, see the *1997 May/June Planning Issue* of *The Clergy Journal*.)

Sermon Text
"'What my Father has given me is greater than all else, and no one can snatch it out of the Father's hand'" (vs. 29).

In what seems like several lifetimes ago, I ran track for my high school varsity team. The coach was a perfectionist, and his penchant for flawless performance took a particular form when it came to those of us who ran relays. Hours were dedicated each week to our practicing the mile and half-mile events.

The thing was, he seldom took out the stopwatch to clock our times; rather, he focused his attention on what he considered the critical aspect of such relays, where he claimed races were won and lost—in the hand-off exchanges of the baton. "It's in the hands," he would insist. "Good hands are more important than fast feet!" An inexpert or bumbled exchange, particularly a dropped baton, meant a race run in vain, no matter how fast we were. His satisfaction came and went with how well our strides were in sync, our legs pumping with the same rhythm, our hands reaching with the same grace, almost as if, at the instant of exchange, we were indistinguishable from one another—running as one.

In today's lesson, the writer of John's Gospel revisits the theme of the identical, indistinguishable ways and works of Jesus and of God. Other images are reinforced as well, such as the mention of Jesus' followers being the sheep who belong to him and his being the good shepherd. The security and safety of this special relationship is strengthened by the reassuring promise, *"No one will snatch them out of my hand. What my Father has given me is greater than all else, and no one can snatch it out of the Father's hand. The Father and I are one"* (Jn 10:28b–30).

What John wants to convey to would-be followers, to those who would be of the sheepfold, is that there is no more sure grasp we could be in than that of the good shepherd who receives us into his care as if from God's own hand. It is a sure exchange, we are told, for in his works and words, Jesus is so indistinguishable from—so identical with God—that we are not to worry about being dropped, or left behind. A more care-filled, smooth, expert handling could not be imagined, even by my coach, I suspect.

The question, then, for us would-be people of God, who would be, or who are followers of Jesus, is why so much worry? How do we manage to consume ourselves with such fretting over this and that and forego what is confidently described as our ultimate security?

I suspect that it has to do with what Jesus' interrogators say at the beginning of this lesson. They gather around him, we are told, and ask, "How long will you keep us in suspense?" Another way of saying it is, "Why do you vex us so? Just come out and tell us!" Supposedly, they want a straightforward answer to who he is. Is he the Messiah at last, the promised one finally come in whose hands they are to entrust themselves, their fortunes, and their future? They are not sure about the advisability of letting go of their securities (fortunes, designs on future, etc.) in order to grasp and be grasped by what it is that Jesus offers them.

So it is with us. There is always a ripple of suspense, sometimes a hint of vexation to this faith business. What is it that will fully convince us that we are in God's hands, no matter what? What will get us to reach out, to loosen our white-knuckle grasp on the things that we've come to clutch so closely: things like control, acquisition, and status? Jesus seems to indicate that it is only by being grasped by him and believing in him that we can know we are secure. Belief is not the same as cognitive certainty. Nor is it strictly doctrinal assent, as when we are able to sit comfortably in a pew and read or recite the Apostles' Creed.

The word *belief* in this context hinges more upon the meaning suggested by its Anglo-Saxon origin: *by lief,* "by life," or "that which we live by." In this sense, of course, our relationship to Jesus is not one simply of cognitive assent based on what we say we think or know. Rather, its basis is on how we behave, the assumptions and actions by which we proceed in the course of a typical day. This is what constitutes "following" the good

May 3, 1998
4th Sunday of Easter

shepherd: not knowing with certainty but trusting, and trust by definition always allows for an element of suspense. It is when we acknowledge whatever suspense we have but nevertheless proceed that we actually live by, follow, trust, and put ourselves in the hands of God.

There is a difference between trusting with the heart and believing with the head. Trust is measured by demonstration, by doing, by following. Even in the greatest trust there can be a flutter of "what if?" Even in the surest, most practiced of baton exchanges, there is the split-second letting loose and letting go that has to risk a bumbled exchange and lost race. With the most disciplined highwire artists there is still always a suspended and suspenseful moment, lending literal meaning to what it means to take a "leap of faith."

To put ourselves in sure hands takes demonstrable trust in God's singular, indistinguishable purpose. What is just as exacting as our living by such trust is that the good hands we are in enlist us in the exchange, the passing on, the extending of God's purpose to still others. What might that be, that purpose that we are to receive and pass on, to grasp and to be grasped by? We have it spelled out for us at almost every sporting event: track and field, football, hockey, baseball. Almost every stadium has had it painted on a sheet and raise behind a goalpost or home plate: "John 3:16." Simply, that God so loved the world that God's Son is entrusted to us for our believing in him, our behaving by him, our following him.

"I give you a new commandment," Jesus says in our lesson for next week, *"that you love one another. Just as I have loved you, you also shall love one another. By this everyone will know that you are my disciples, if you have love for one another"* (Jn 13:34–35). That is quite a baton to handle. And, as we all know, the loving one another that we're supposed to do involves some perilous exchanges. Not only are we to entrust ourselves to the hands of God, we are ourselves enlisted in this race of faith, this relay of trust, this oneness and belonging we are to know with God and one another through Jesus Christ.

If my high school track coach were in charge of all this, everything would be based on perfect performance, flawless exchanges, and the adage that practice makes perfect. Thank God that the one we're coached and encouraged by is the good shepherd in whose good hands we are enfolded despite moments of suspense or when we stumble or bumble our way through—the reachable and incredible love of God.

—*Steven L. Davis*
Shepherd of the Hills UCC
Phoenix, Arizona

May 10, 1998

5th Sunday of Easter

Lessons

Pres/Meth/UCC/Luth	Acts 11:1–18	Rev 21:1–6	Jn 13:31–35
Roman Catholic	Acts 14:21b–27	Rev 21:1–5a	Jn 13:31–33a, 34–35
Episcopal	Acts 13:44–52	Rev 19:1, 4–9	Jn 13:31–35

Introduction to the Lessons
Lesson 1
(1) *Acts 11:1–18* (Pres/Meth/UCC/Luth)
To his critics in Jerusalem who require an explanation for his fraternizing with Gentiles, Peter tells the story of her conversion. Beginning with his dream/vision in Joppa, Peter relates the revelation made to him, how none of God's creatures are to be profaned or labeled unclean. He then bears witness to the coming upon a gentile household of the Holy Spirit, just as the Spirit had visited him, showing no partiality. Peter's conversion moves his critics to praise for God's gift of life to all.

(2) *Acts 14:21b–27* (RC)
Despite persecution by rabble-rousing detractors from Antioch and Iconium, Paul and Barnabas continue their missionary work among the Gentiles. Paul's efforts and successes at establishing new communities are commended by the church upon his return to Antioch.

(3) *Acts 13:44–52* (Epis)
When Paul and Barnabas proclaim the gospel to Gentiles in Antioch of Pisidia, certain Jews of the city become jealous. Paul makes clear that the gospel of Christ he was given to preach shows no favorites but extends to both Jews and Gentiles alike.

Lesson 2
(1) *Revelation 21:1–6* (Pres/Meth/UCC/Luth);
***Revelation 21:1–5a* (RC)**
The seer of Patmos relates a vision of a new heaven and new earth, where a heavenly Jerusalem will be joined to a transformed earth, where sadness and sorrow shall be no more and all things will be made new.

May 10, 1998
5th Sunday of Easter

(2) *Revelation 19:1, 4–9* **(Epis)**
A vision is described of great praise and doxology. Elders, servants, and a "great multitude" join in and celebrate the marriage of Lamb and the bride (church) who is made presentable and ready for this union by the righteous deeds of the saints.

Gospel
John 13:31–35 **(Pres/Meth/UCC/Luth/Epis)**;
John 13:31–33a, 34–35 **(RC)**
As part of his farewell discourse to his disciples, Jesus gives them a new commandment: that they "love one another," thereby imitating his love for them and identifying themselves to others as Jesus' own.

Theme
Jesus' farewell bequest to his disciples is a new commandment.

Thought for the Day
Those who love as Jesus loves practice a kind of self-giving posture, taking pleasure not in denial of self but finding in their caring dispositions toward others true fulfillment of who they desire to be in Christ Jesus.

Prayer of Meditation
O God, grant us the wisdom and wherewithal to receive the bequest of Christ's new commandment as a gift and not merely a challenge. May our love for one another be manifest in the worship we share, the joys, concerns, and greetings we exchange, and whatever kindnesses we embark upon today and every day in your name. Amen.

Call to Worship
This is the day the Lord has made. Let us rejoice and be glad in it. Rejoice we can, and be glad, for in the making of this day there come occasions for us to live out Jesus' command that we love one another. For this day, this challenge, this opportunity, this gift, we say, "Thanks be to God."

Prayer of Adoration
O God of Easter and giver of new life, we praise you for your love. We see it at the heart of your law and commandments, we experience

it in the person of Jesus the Christ, and we are to embody it in our own love for one another. Thank you for new commandments that remind us not only of what you will for us, but also of who we have it in us to be, through the example and power of your resurrected one. Amen.

Prayer of Confession
In your presence, O God, our defenses fall away, and we are faced with our shortfalls and oversights, our faults and our failings. We confess we ignore your commandments. We do not love you with all our heart, mind, and strength; we do not love neighbor as self; we do not love our enemies, and we fail to love one another as Jesus has loved us. Forgive us, we pray, that we may try again and live anew, through our Savior Jesus Christ. Amen.

Prayer of Dedication of Gifts and Self
In gratitude, O God, for your gifts of life and love, we return but a portion of the blessings we have known. Transform them and dedicate us, we pray, to renewed love of others in your name. May we enrich the lives of those around us and extend the reach of your care to all who need Christ's presence and power in their lives. It is in his name that we ask it. Amen.

Sermon Summary
The words with which Jesus says farewell to his disciples center around a new commandment, that the disciples are to love one another as Jesus has loved them. What he commands is both burden and blessing. While it challenges his followers, it also confirms who it is they are and whose they are.

Hymn of the Day
"To God Be the Glory." From Psalm 148 comes the exhortation to praise God for all the mighty deeds of the Lord. From the prolific hand of Fanny Crosby and William Doane (see Transfiguration Sunday) comes this hymn with its joyous chorus. Very easy to sing either as a psalm replacement or accompaniment, the praise of God for wonders also complements the Festival of the Christian Home and Mother's Day celebrated in many churches this Sunday

May 10, 1998
5th Sunday of Easter

Children's Object Talk

Love One Another

Object
A large cross drawn on tagboard.

Lesson
As Jesus loves us, so we love one another.

Today in our Bible story from John's Gospel, Jesus tells us something very important. He tells us to love each other like he has loved us. Let's think about that for a minute.

First, let's think of all the ways Jesus has helped us and loved us. Please help me make a list. (Wait for responses such as healed, taught, forgave, and fed. You might briefly recall Bible stories that illustrate these.) Yes, Jesus did lots of loving things for people, and the most loving thing he did was to die on the cross for us. I've brought a drawing of the cross with me (show picture). The cross reminds us that Jesus died for us.

See how the cross has two parts (point to drawing). The long part points up to heaven and down to earth. That reminds us of how God sent Jesus to be with us and even die for us. The second, shorter part of the cross points outward both ways. That can make us think of how Jesus wants his love to spread outward to others. So, God's love came down in Jesus to us (gesture to the long, vertical bar) and then Jesus wants us to pass this love around to others (gesture to the horizontal bar). Every time you see a cross, I want you to think of this and of how Jesus tells us to love each other (point to the horizontal bar) as he loved us (point to the vertical bar). God was loving and kind to us. We can be loving and kind to each other. We can share with others. Help others. Be friends with others. There are lots of good ways to show love, just like Jesus did.

—Jeanette Strandjord

The Sermon

What's Love Got to Do with It?

Hymns
Beginning of Worship: "*Un Mandamiento Nuevo* (A New Commandment)"
Sermon Hymn: "Where Charity and Love Prevail"
End of Worship: "We Plant a Grain of Mustard Seed"

Scripture
John 13:31–35 (For additional sermon materials on this passage, see the February 1998 issue of *The Clergy Journal* and on Revelation 21:1–6, see the *1997 May/June Planning Issue* of *The Clergy Journal*.)

Sermon Text
"'I give you a new commandment, that you love one another. Just as I have loved you, you also should love one another'" (vs. 34).

In her popular song by the same title, Tina Turner asks,

> What's love got to do,
>   got to do with it?
> What's love but a sweet,
>   old-fashioned notion?

The inquiry of what love has to do with anything is not one that any self-respecting contemporary or colleague would have asked Jesus. When, at one point in the Gospel of Mark, the question is put to him about which is the greatest commandment, Jesus responds with the textbook answer: that we are to love God with all our heart, mind, and strength, and our neighbor as ourselves. This was not news.

Every rabbi knew that love has to do with everything It is the heart of Torah. The love of God is the greatest law to fulfill—not always the easiest, but the greatest. How wise of those ancient ones not to talk of fearing God or serving God or pleasing God—but loving God, for in love all these others are included and supersede: the respecting, the serving, and the pleasing.

And how right of Jesus to remember the love of neighbor in the very next breath; for as the Gospel of John later says, "How can you love God whom you have not seen if you do not love your neighbor, whom you have seen?"

In our lesson for today from John's thirteenth chapter, Jesus

May 10, 1998
5th Sunday of Easter

issues the one and only explicit command in this gospel. It comes in the middle of a farewell discourse to his disciples. This is a particular literary genre that the author strategically employs to heighten the significance of what is happening and being said. We are to appreciate the drama of this scene, akin to other episodes both in biblical history and recorded in ancient Mediterranean literature where followers or family or friends gather around a celebrated figure for a final goodbye. The suspense builds through the announcement of one's imminent dying or departure and by whatever blessing or benediction or last testament the central figure is about to pronounce.

Jesus and the disciples have gathered for the Passover, what is to be his last supper with them. This is the setting for Jesus' farewell. He has made veiled predictions of the events that are to occur shortly, now that his "hour has come for him to depart this world." In leaving the disciples, what he gives them is a new commandment: that they love one another. *"Just as I have loved you, you also should love one another. By this everyone will know that you are my disciples, if you have love for one another"* (Jn 13:34–35). As we said, there is nothing new about love or the command to love. We are to love God, our neighbor, even our enemies. So we might wonder, "what's all the fuss?" What is new and fussworthy and often missed for its radical nature is that the love the followers of Jesus are to exhibit for one another is the same kind that Jesus shows for them. It is a matter of identification, a badge of belonging, the love that Jesus displays and now bestows.

With all due respect to Tina Turner and other recording artists who sing of love as a "sweet old-fashioned notion," or a compelling physical attraction, or a sentimental feeling, the kind of love Jesus is talking about is far different. It is nothing less than the expression of the whole person: the involvement of heart, soul, and mind, one's entire life. It is self-giving rather than self-centered. Others have gone so far as to call Jesus' love self-denying or self-sacrificial, but since denial and "sacrifice" have come to acquire such negative and even masochistic connotations, we need to be careful how we use such references.

First of all, we must remember that self-giving love is really self-fulfilling, not self-denying. Even in dying, Jesus is not giving up his life and denying himself. Rather, he is living and giving his life to the will and work of God, ultimately fulfilling who he is and what he is about. Such love is the consummate expression of who we are. It is not something forced on us but something we choose, we desire. It does not deplete or deny us, but completes and confirms us. Anyone who has truly loved knows that sense of wanting above all else the well-being and fulfillment of the other person.

Another new dimension of the kind of love Jesus commands is that it is also mutual. As we give, we also receive. As we reach out to others, so we are to graciously receive those who reach out to us. Love is not an independent, individual act, but a shared covenant, a rhythm of giving and receiving. It is the element and expoxy that defines the community of Jesus' followers and binds them to one another.

It may seem easy at first, this kind of love for like-minded folks who, alongside us, are followers of the same Jesus. Surely, it is harder to love one's loosely defined neighbor or even one's enemy. But have you noticed how church conflicts can be the worst conflicts? Have you noticed, from the days beginning right after Jesus' life, death, and resurrection, how disputes among followers became epidemic, sometimes even lethal? It is not always our enemies or outsiders who vex us the most, but rather those with whom we share common goals and ground. Father John Powell quotes a verse:

> Oh, to live above with the saints we love,
> That would be the highest glory
> But to live here below with the saints we know
> Is quite another story.

Church fights are like family fights. Instead of occasioning creative and constructive approaches to conflict, they can quickly deteriorate and have the potential to bring out the worst in everyone. Those who know and love us best can also hurt us most.

Jesus has been with his disciples long enough to know there's nothing easy about the love he is prescribing for them. The author of the gospel too has been around the early Christian movement long enough to appreciate the pressures from outside, but also the pressures from within the rank and file. Still, the spirit with which this parting, new commandment is offered is not just an in-your-face challenge but a to-your-heart gift. To love in the manner Jesus prescribes, we become new persons. We become more and more imaged in God. We become more and more identified with Jesus and the one whose love for us and the world he so embodies.

What's love got to do with it? John's answer is "everything." Loving in the manner Jesus commands broadens us, enriches us, and makes us new. And as Jesus' last bequest to us, it opens the door to God's great Easter mystery: *"We know that we have passed from death to life, because we love one another"* (1 Jn 3:14).

—*Steven L. Davis*
Shepherd of the Hills UCC
Phoenix, Arizona

May 17, 1998

6th Sunday of Easter

Lessons

Pres/Meth/UCC/Luth	Acts 16:9–15	Rev 21:10, 22—22:5	Jn 14:23–29
Roman Catholic	Acts 15:1–2, 22–29	Rev 21:10–14, 22–23	Jn 14:23–29
Episcopal	Acts 14:8–18	Rev 21:22—22:5	Jn 14:23–29

Introduction to the Lessons

(1) *Acts 16:9–15* **(Pres/Meth/UCC/Luth)**
Paul, having entered Europe for the first time, stays in Philippi, a Roman colony, founded to provide land for military veterans. In the absence of a synagogue, for which ten Jewish males are needed, Paul finds a place of Jewish prayer by the river, and there he converts a businesswoman named Lydia, baptizing her and her household, and staying at her home. She is Paul's first convert in Europe (though Lydia herself is from Thyatira in Asia).

(2) *Acts 15:1–2, 22–29* **(RC)**
Some unspecified Judeans trouble the Antioch church, insisting that gentile converts be circumcised. Paul, Barnabas, and others are appointed to go to Jerusalem to discuss this issue with the apostles and the elders. Their visit results in the Apostolic Decree, which apparently forbids certain types of marriage ("abstain from fornication") and lays down certain food laws ("abstain from what has been sacrificed to idols and from blood and from what is strangled"), so as to facilitate gentile and Jewish fellowship in Christ.

(3) *Acts 14:8–18* **(Epis)**
In Lystra, Paul, having discerned that a crippled man "had faith to be healed," tells him to stand, and the man does. This causes adoring crowds to worship Paul and Barnabas, worship which the apostles reject (cf. 10:26). Paul's ensuing sermon, his first to a pagan audience, differs from his previous preaching in synagogues, in its stress on God as creator (cf. 17:22ff.).

Lesson 2
Revelation 21:10, 22—22:5 **(Pres/Meth/UCC/Luth)**;
Revelation 21:10-14, 22-23 **(RC)**;
Revelation 21:22—22:5 **(Epis)**

John describes the eschatological Jerusalem, full of God's presence and glory (so it has no need of temple nor created light), its residents enjoying absolute safety (thus there is no need to shut the gates) and everlasting life ("water of life," "tree of life"). John stresses that "unclean," "accursed" persons will not be found therein.

Gospel
John 14:23-29 **(Pres/Meth/UCC/Luth/RC/Epis)**

Jesus and his Father will come and make their home with those who love Jesus and obey his words. To guide these believers in their understanding of his words, Jesus promises the Holy Spirit. Jesus through the Spirit (cf. 20:21-22; Gal 5:22) gives peace, but "not as the world gives." Jesus gives *his* peace, and he gives it *effectually*, establishing in the hearts of the recipients of this peace the very security, joy, and strength he himself experienced on the way to the cross.

Theme
Jesus makes his home with us.

Thought for the Day
Christians today are better off spiritually than the eyewitnesses of Jesus' earthly ministry. We are better off because through the Holy Spirit Jesus lives among us and in us continuously. We tend to think of being at home with Jesus as something we will experience in the future, when we die or at his Second Coming (cf. 14:2). But we should reflect at least as much if not more so on what it means to have Christ at home with us now in this life (14:23).

Prayer of Meditation
Almighty God, in this time of worship, still the restlessness within us, and let us rest in you. Give us an expectant faith that hears your word, an obedient love that allows you to come and live with us, an abiding hope in the final fulfillment of all your promises. Throughout this hour, day, and week, guide us into good paths of praise, service, and sacrifice. In Jesus' name. Amen.

May 17, 1998
6th Sunday of Easter

Call to Worship
Leader: See, the home of God is among mortals.
People: He will dwell with them as their God;
Leader: They will be his peoples, and God himself will be with them;
People: He will wipe every tear from their eyes.
Leader: Let us worship God!
—Revelation 21:3–5

Prayer of Adoration
Almighty God, source of all love, grace, and wisdom, you sent us Jesus in whom we have seen your love practiced, your grace evidenced, your wisdom revealed. Turn our hearts and thoughts anew to the contemplation of your goodness. May our worship in this hour be acceptable in your sight; through the same Jesus Christ our Lord. Amen.

Prayer of Confession
Lord Jesus, you revealed your truth to us; you called us to follow you; you promised the help of your Holy Spirit. But too often our willfulness has kept us from recognizing your saving work in the world, and sharing in it. Too often our selfishness has kept us from noticing the needs of suffering people, and helping them. Have mercy on us; forgive us; renew us. Open our eyes anew to see what we should do for you, and unlock our hardened hearts to care for others in your name. Amen.

Prayer of Dedication of Gifts and Self
O God of grace, we thank you for the many blessings you have so freely given us in Jesus: acceptance and forgiveness; meaning and peace; strength for today, and hope for tomorrow. In dedicating these gifts to the work of your church, we dedicate also ourselves, and pledge that we will live this week in the service of Christ, and in the strength of the help the Holy Spirit gives us. In Jesus' name. Amen.

Sermon Summary
Christ comes to make his home with those who love him and keep his words. Our genuine efforts to love and serve our Lord allow him to live with us. As he lives with us we grow and mature in the Christian faith, and then we know more and more the blessings of salvation in Christ's promised, imparted "peace."

Hymn of the Day

"Shall We Gather at the River." Another striking image of healing and grace from the book of Revelation, the river of life flows through Robert Lowry's 1864 tune. The inspiration for the hymn came to him when contemplating the epidemic raging through Brooklyn at the time. He composed the words in a quarter of an hour, and then set about making a tune that became instantly popular, being "part brass band music" with a march movement. The Scripture upon which it is based ranks with those of Isaiah for its moving vision of peace and healing.

Children's Object Talk

Keep Learning

Object
A Spanish-English dictionary (or other language).
Lesson
We learn about Jesus through the Bible, teachers, parents, and others.

Today I have a book that is helping me learn a new language (hold up dictionary). When I look up the word "hello" it tells me that in Spanish I would say *hola*. Can you say that? Great, you just learned some Spanish. Now try the word for goodbye, *adios*. Great, you are good learners.

We could learn these two words because we had this book to help us and also because I could help teach you. If you were learning Spanish in school you would have a special teacher to help you. To learn something, we need help. We need books, teachers, time, and practice.

The same is true in learning about Jesus. If we want to keep learning about Jesus we need to read our Bibles, listen to our Sunday school teachers and parents, and take time to come to God's house, the church. Jesus told us that in all these ways, God will help us learn about him. God promises to use his power to tell us about Jesus.

You can always be learning no matter what age you are. Maybe you can think of ways you can help others learn about Jesus. When you learn to read you could read a Bible story to a brother or sister. When you are older, maybe you'll be a Sunday school teacher or a pastor. We can be both learners and teachers. God can work through us in both of these ways.

—*Jeanette Strandjord*

May 17, 1998
6th Sunday of Easter

The Sermon

Christ at Home

Hymns
Beginning of Worship: "O for a Heart to Praise My God"
Sermon Hymn: "Thou Didst Leave Thy Throne"
End of Worship: "Be Thou My Vision"

Scripture
John 14:23–29 (For additional sermon materials on this passage, see the February 1998 issue of *The Clergy Journal* and on Revelation 21:10, 22—22:5, see the *1997 May/June Planning Issue* of *The Clergy Journal*.)

Sermon Text
"Jesus answered him, 'Those who love me will keep my word, and my Father will love them, and we will come to them and make our home with them'" (vs. 23).

An oft-iterated theme of some traditional children's hymns is the desire to be transported back in time to see and to be with Jesus in the Holy Land. In "Tell Me the Stories of Jesus," as the singing child imagines herself with little ones gathered around Jesus' knee, she can "fancy his blessing resting on me."

In "I Think When I Read That Sweet Story of Old" the singing child wishes that he had felt Jesus' gentle touch and "seen his kind look" when Jesus invited the children to come to him.

Today's Scripture stands dead-set against such wistful romanticism. Our gospel text proclaims instead that you and I today, in late twentieth-century America, can know and love Jesus far more fully and effectively than any eyewitness to his earthly life ever could. Christ does not just pass us by on a street, or speak to us from a particular hillside. Christ does not just place his hand upon us briefly, or call us to follow him for a year or two. No, Christ comes to us permanently. Christ stays with us continuously. Jesus, who during his earthly ministry "ha[d] nowhere to lay his head" (Mt 8:20), has come to make his home with us through his Holy Spirit. The poet Robert Bridges was right:

Not ev'n the Apostles in the days
   They walked with Christ,
     lov'd him so well
As we may now.

Christ makes his home with us. Perhaps as we reflect upon how we live in our own homes, we can best understand some of the serious implications and wonderful consequences of Christ's coming to live with us. Let's consider three things today.

First, we clean up our own homes. Perhaps like me you live alone, and perhaps like me you are not the best housekeeper in the world. I find that it is when I have invited students, friends, or family over to my apartment that I am most ready and willing to give it a good cleaning. I cannot imagine having them over with dirty dishes in the sink, bits of fuzz on the carpeting, or a half-read newspaper on the couch.

Will Jesus come and stay in an ill-kept heart? He says in our Scripture that he comes and lives not with the world, but only with those who love him and keep his words. To live with Jesus we have to love him with a love that issues forth in obedience to his teaching.

Not that Christ expects perfection. When we invite people over to our homes we sometimes pile things in a closet or hide them under a bed in an effort to make our homes more presentable. If Jesus is to live with us through his Holy Spirit, we have to make an effort to make ourselves presentable. We have to try to forgive the person toward whom we feel vengeful. We have to try to stop indulging in the behavior we know full well is hurtful to others and harmful for us. God in Christ preaches an exacting ethic, but God honors a good try.

Second, we grow up in our homes. Many homes have pencil marks in a kitchen or a basement where the height of the children living in it has been measured and remembered. In our Scripture, after saying that he will make his home with us, Jesus adds that the Holy Spirit will *"teach [us] everything"* (vs. 26). Jesus thus reveals that being at home with him entails progressing in our knowledge of his truth, and maturing in our witness to his goodness. As John Calvin observes in his commentary, those with whom Jesus lives "will daily increase more and more in the gifts of God." If to become a believer in Jesus is to be *born* again, it follows that to remain a believer in Jesus is to *grow* in faith, hope, and love.

Finally, we feel "at home" in our homes. After a demanding day at work, we look forward to the comparative quiet of our homes, where we can change into something comfortable, where we can relax. Even if the telephone rings, even if the children act up, we still feel so much more at ease, so much less stressed when we are home. That home is best is a recurrent theme in popular poetry

May 17, 1998
6th Sunday of Easter

and song. There is no place like our home because our home is a place of peace. Some of us hang on our walls framed calligraphy or embroidery proclaiming the peace of our homes.

On the night before his death Jesus takes leave of his disciples, saying, "Peace." On the day of his resurrection Jesus greets his disciples, saying, "Peace." "Peace" was a customary word of departure and of greeting among the ancient Jews. Only they often uttered it without conviction, much as we do today when we say, "goodbye." We don't necessarily mean "God be with you," of which "goodbye" is a contraction. We usually just mean that we're off. But when Jesus says, "Peace," Jesus really means, "Peace."

Jesus does not say "Peace" as a mere formality. He *gives* peace as an actual possession. Jesus gives *his* peace. Jesus is about to be betrayed, forsaken, tried, crucified, but he still has peace to give. The peace Jesus has to give is the peace that comes from his trust in God, even in the face of awful death—a trust in God that we too can experience through the Holy Spirit.

On Easter evening Jesus says to his disciples, "Peace be with you," and, "Receive the Holy Spirit." Earlier Jesus had said of the Holy Spirit: "he will take what is mine and declare it to you." The Holy Spirit takes Christ's peace and imparts it to others. The Holy Spirit takes Christ's peace and implants it in us. We, like the first disciples, can receive Christ's peace through the Holy Spirit. We, like they, can have a sure trust in God's abiding and eternal love for us. The peace we receive from Christ enables us to know for sure that nothing at all can ever "*. . . separate us from the love of God in Jesus Christ our Lord*" (Rom 8:39).

In conclusion, we experience our own material homes as places of peace, as places of growth, as places that we take care of, clean. Jesus makes his spiritual home with us. He makes his home with us as we try to do his will, as we grow in discipleship, and especially as we trust God's saving love in all and even the worst circumstances of life.

—*Steven D. MacArthur*
Lyon College
Batesville, Arkansas

May 21, 1998

Ascension Day

Lessons
Pres/Meth/UCC/Luth	Acts 1:1–11	Eph 1:15–23	Lk 24:44–53
Roman Catholic	Acts 1:1–11	Eph 1:17–23	Lk 24:46–53
Episcopal	Acts 1:1–11	Eph 1:15–23	Lk 24:49–53

Introduction to the Lessons
Lesson 1
Acts 1:1–11 **(Pres/Meth/UCC/Luth/RC/Epis)**

After a brief summation of his gospel, Luke tells of Christ's convincing appearances to his disciples in his resurrected body during forty days. Teaching them about his kingdom, Christ instructs them to stay in Jerusalem where they will be empowered with the Holy Spirit to be his witnesses to all the earth. Rising into a cloud, Christ makes it plain to them that the time of his visible bodily presence with them has come to an end. Two angels then affirm that Christ will return just as surely, suddenly, and mysteriously as he has departed.

Lesson 2
Ephesians 1:15–23 **(Pres/Meth/UCC/Luth/Epis)**;
Ephesians 1:17–23 **(RC)**

Thankful for his readers' faith and love, Paul assures them of his constant prayers for their spiritual welfare, and exults over the glory of their inheritance and the greatness of God's saving work in Christ who exercises authority over "all things for the church."

Gospel
Luke 24:44–53 **(Pres/Meth/UCC/Luth)**; *Luke 24:46–53* **(RC)**;
Luke 24:49–53 **(Epis)**

The risen Jesus speaks of the testimony of the Old Testament Scriptures to him as the Christ and of the necessity of proclaiming to all nations the salvation he brings. His disciples must stay in Jerusalem until they receive power to proclaim this salvation. At Bethany, Christ blesses them and then withdraws from their sight. The disciples return with great joy to Jerusalem where they continuously worship God in the temple.

May 21, 1998
Ascension Day

Theme
Christ is sovereign over all; Christ's church is central in all.

Thought for the Day
The ascension means that Christ is Lord over all of life and should be served in every aspect of our lives. The ascension means as well that the church is indispensable for every person's faith in and obedience to Christ.

Prayer of Meditation
Almighty God, bless us we pray with quietness of spirit, humbleness of mind, and openness of heart, as we come into your presence now. Speak to us your word, reveal to us your will, and give to us your Spirit. Through the time we spend together now in worship, may we be cleansed of sin, renewed in love, and strengthened for service; through our Lord Jesus Christ. Amen.

Call to Worship
> Leader: But God, who is rich in mercy, out of the great love with which he loved us even when we were dead through our trespasses, made us alive together with Christ—
> People: By grace you have been saved—
> Leader: and raised us up with him and seated us with him in the heavenly places in Christ Jesus, so that . . . he might show the immeasurable riches of his grace . . .
> People: For by grace you have been saved through faith, and this is not your own doing; it is the gift of God—
> Leader: Let us worship God!
> —Ephesians 2:4–9

Prayer of Adoration
O most gracious God, your son ascended "far above all the heavens, so that he might fill all things." Fill our sanctuary with the presence of Christ. Fill our hearts with his love. Fill our very lives with the grace and truth of Christ our Lord. In his name we pray. Amen.

Prayer of Confession
Most Holy God, we confess that we have resisted living under the lordship of Christ. His claim upon us is complete, but in too many

parts of our lives we have been undisciplined and indifferent in our service of him; selfish and hardhearted; unfair to family, and unkind to strangers. Have mercy upon us, and forgive us our sins. Confirm us in the high resolve to live as Christ's disciples, speaking his truth and showing his love. In his name we pray. Amen.

Prayer of Dedication of Gifts and Self
We ask, heavenly Father, that we may wisely use all that you have given, all that you are giving, and all that you have yet to give us. We dedicate these tokens of all that we have received from you to the work of your church. May its corporate witness and may our own personal lives reveal to men and women your saving love in Jesus Christ our Lord. Amen.

Sermon Summary
In our Scripture Paul celebrates three key implications of Christ's ascension: (1) Christ now rules without exception over every sphere of life; (2) the reality of Christ's rule can only be known in and through the church; (3) Christ's absolute rule removes angels to the margins of Christian faith.

Hymn of the Day
"Crown Him with Many Crowns." This stirring tune suits perfectly the close of the Easter season and the birth of the church at Pentecost. The hymn recounts the events of the resurrection and provides a liturgical "bookend" for worship accompanied by George Elvey's majestic and driving tune. The tune *"Diademata"* was written for these words and the name is from the Greek word for "crowns."

Children's Object Talk

Watch Jesus

Object
 A lantern.
Lessons
 Christ is the head of the church, and we keep our eyes on him.

When I go camping, I like to have one of these along. Can you tell me what it is? And what do we use it for? (allow responses) Yes, this is a camping lantern that helps me see at night at my campsite.

May 21, 1998
Ascension Day

There is a time when this lantern is especially helpful to me. When I'm camping by a lake, I like to take a boat out on the water when it is nighttime and very dark. I can see so many beautiful stars that way. But one problem is finding my way back to my campsite.

In the dark on a lake, it isn't easy to see the shoreline. So this is what I do. I put my lighted lantern on the shore right by my campsite. When I want to steer my boat back to the right place, I look for the light of this lantern. When I see the light, I know I'm headed in the right direction.

Lanterns are one thing that help us go in the right direction. We also use signs and maps. As Christians we have a way to help us, too. It's a person. It is Jesus Christ. Sometimes we wonder what to do when we have a problem or a hard choice to make. God sent Jesus to help us. Jesus is the one to watch and listen to. He is "the head over all things for the church." Like this lantern, he is the one to watch so we go in the right direction.

—*Jeanette Strandjord*

The Sermon

Christ, His Church, and the Angels

Hymns
Beginning of Worship: "Crown Him with Many Crowns"
Sermon Hymn: "O Where Are Kings and Empires Now"
End of Worship: "All Hail the Power of Jesus' Name"

Scripture
Ephesians 1:15–23 (For sermon materials on Acts 1:1–11, see the February 1998 issue of *The Clergy Journal* and on Luke 24:44–53, see the *1997 May/June Planning Issue* of *The Clergy Journal*.)

Sermon Text
"And he has put all things under his feet and has made him the head over all things for the church" (vs. 22).

There is a story about a minister who resolutely preached meticulously researched, carefully written sermons on the doctrine of the ascension of Christ year after year on Ascension Day. After the sixth or seventh such sermon, a lifelong parishioner met the minister at the door and said, "That was a particularly good try."

The story illustrates the difficulty of the doctrine of the ascension. The Scottish scholar William Barclay is of this opinion:

"The Ascension is far and away the most difficult incident in the life of Jesus either to visualize or to understand . . . No one has ever succeeded in painting a picture of the Ascension which was anything other than grotesque and ridiculous. In films of the life of Christ, if the Ascension is portrayed, the whole matter descends into sheer bathos."
(William Barclay, *The Apostles' Creed for Everyman* [New York: Harper & Row, 1967], p. 162.)

The ascension is difficult because, of all Christian doctrines, it is perhaps the one most susceptible to trivialization. The New Testament speaks of Christ being *"taken up to heaven"* (Acts 1:2), *"carried up into heaven"* (Lk 24:51), *"gone into heaven"* (1 Pet 3:22), and we too easily tend to take literally these figurative statements of spiritual truth.

Oddly, we seem more inclined to bring literal-mindedness to bear upon biblical language than we do upon everyday secular language. We speak of highways, for instance, not implying that they are far above sea level, but heavily traversed. We speak of high churches, not meaning that they are particularly tall, but that they use elaborate liturgies. We teach and take upper-level classes that can be taught on the first floor of buildings, and even in the basement. We commonly employ expressions of physical elevation in an analogical way.

Our untroubled use of such ordinary spatial metaphors should guard us against conceiving of the ascension as some sort of mysterious passage through "atmospheric astronomic space" (Karl Barth) to a place called heaven. Our verses in Ephesians, in fact, by speaking of Christ in *"heavenly places"* as being *"far above"* anything we can imagine in this life or the next (vs. 21), invite us to eschew spatial categories in our apprehension of the ascension. The verses represent Christ as having ascended to a different condition or position, not a different place.

Our verses focus on three key implications of Christ's ascension for faith and life: Christ is over all, the church is at the center, and angels are at the periphery.

Christ Is over All
Christ has ascended to God's right hand. Being at someone's right hand is an easily recognized metaphor for delegated authority and responsibility. There is a clear allusion here to Psalm 110, *"The Lord says to my lord, 'Sit at my right hand . . .'"* (vs. 1). The early Christians discerned in this verse a

May 21, 1998
Ascension Day

prophecy of Christ's ascension to a position of power at God's right hand. Indeed, the New Testament writers cite or intimate this verse far more often than any other Old Testament verse. This suggests very strongly that the focus of the faith of the first Christians was on the fact of Christ's lordship over all of life and every aspect of their own lives.

The doctrine of the ascension means that Christ is in charge. Christ is "in charge of running the universe, everything from galaxies to governments," as Eugene H. Peterson expresses it in *The Message: The New Testament in Contemporary Language*. "Everything" here includes everything about us. Everything from our labor to our leisure, from our volunteering for something to our voting for someone. There is no circle of life, no type of activity, however secular, however worldly, in which Christ is not supreme, in which Christians need not seek to know and to do this will. The *"all in all"* of verse 23 applies as much to my own life, to your own life, as it does to the universe.

The Church Is at the Center

Christ's exaltation as head of everything has been accomplished *"for the church, which is his body"* (vss. 22–23). Nothing on earth but the church is filled *"with all the fullness of God"* (3:19). The church is the one created reality *"which is being constantly and totally filled"* (as F. F. Bruce translates) with Christ's surpassing love and power.

This means, as Peterson puts it, that "the church . . . is not peripheral to the world; the world is peripheral to the church" *(The Message)*. The church, insofar as it lives in a vital connectedness with its energizing head, guided and sustained by Christ, is the most momentous thing on earth.

Christ is no talking head. Christ is an embodied head. Christ as head is connected to and encountered through his body the church. The world knows Christ's love and power only in and through the church. The church is central, indispensable in God's saving purposes toward women and men.

Angels Are at the Periphery

Christ's significance for our lives far exceeds the significance of any other spiritual beings. God has *"seated"* Christ *"far above all rule and authority and power and domination"* (vs. 22). Christ's preeminence makes any Christian angelology profoundly unimportant. Billy Graham's all-time best-selling book, *Angels*, is by our text suggested to be at least consequential.

Angels is Billy Graham's most popular book (more than three million copies have been sold since 1975) because our culture has become enamored with angels. We encounter angels on Broadway and in popular songs, on television and at the movies. There are angels-only seminars, magazines, shops, and sections of bookstores. Angels have their own line of Hallmark greeting cards.

Newsweek speaks of an "angel subculture," the *New York Times* of "angelmania" in contemporary American society. But John Calvin in his commentary on Ephesians claims that excessive attention to angels pulls people away from "the true Mediator." And our text asserts that Christ's ascension has relegated angels to "the edge, not the center, of Christian faith," as Gabriel Fackre phrases it in *Theology Today* (October 1994); angels might appropriately appear "in the stained-glass windows but not on the altar."

In conclusion, our text invites each of us to recognize Christ's absolute lordship over all of our life, to see the church as essential in our life with Christ, and to regard angels as peripheral.

—*Steven D. MacArthur*
Lyon College
Batesville, Arkansas

May 24, 1998

7th Sunday of Easter

Lessons

Pres/Meth/UCC/Luth	Acts 16:16–34	Rev 22:12–14, 16–17, 20–21	Jn 17:20–26
Roman Catholic	Acts 7:55–60	Rev 22:12–14, 16–17, 20	Jn 17:20–26
Episcopal	Acts 16:16–34	Rev 22:12–14, 16–17, 20	Jn 17:20–26

Introduction to the Lessons
Lesson 1
(1) *Acts 16:16–34* **(Pres/Meth/UCC/Luth/Epis)**
Paul, with Silas in Philippi, exorcises from a slave girl a spirit of divination. When her owners see that they can no longer make money from her fortune telling, they arouse a marketplace crowd and prevail upon the Roman authorities to have the apostles first beaten with rods (cf. 2 Cor 11:25) and then fixed in painful stocks in the most loathsome part of the city's prison. The only other persecution of apostles by Gentiles in the Acts also occurs for economic reasons (cf. 19:23ff.).

(2) *Acts 7:55–60* **(RC)**
Stephen ends the speech he began in verse 2 by denouncing his hearers for opposing God. As they become "enraged" and cut his speech short, Stephen himself is "filled with the Holy Spirit." Stephen's martyrdom by stoning is accompanied by a vision of the ascended Jesus. Stephen offers two prayers, one for Jesus' reception of Stephen's own "spirit" and another for the forgiveness of Stephen's executioners, both prayers reminiscent of Jesus' last words on the cross (cf. Lk 23:34 [lacking in some manuscripts], 46). Stephen's death is attended by "a young man named Saul."

Lesson 2
Revelation 22:12–14, 16–17, 20–21 **(Pres/Meth/UCC/Luth)**;
Revelation 22:12–14, 16–17, 20 **(RC/Epis)**
Final statements of the Lord Jesus place his authority firmly behind the revelation John has shared with his readers and emphasize his

imminent advent as judge. Earlier imagery is reprised (cf. 1:8; 2:28; 5:5; 7:14). An unmitigated denunciation of wrongdoers (vs. 15) and a dire warning against tampering with the words of the book (vss. 18–19) have been left out of the lectionaries. This has the effect of stressing God's invitation to salvation ("Come!"). Believers "come" (vs. 17) to the "coming" (vss. 12 and 19) Christ.

Gospel
John 17:20-26 **(Pres/Meth/UCC/Luth/RC/Epis)**
Jesus prays that all who believe in him may be united, sharing the glory and love of the Father and the Son so convincingly, that the whole world may know salvation.

Theme
Christians should celebrate and exhibit oneness in loving diversity.

Thought for the Day
The seemingly paradoxical oneness of three persons in the Trinity is a differentiated unity of self-giving love. The three persons in the Trinity who indwell one another dwell among us. Our participation in their love will convince the world that God sent Jesus.

Prayer of Meditation
Almighty God, you have created the marvelous variety in the universe. You have called us to live in love with others in your church. Use this hour of worship to renew both our love of nature and our ties to other Christians in our own congregation and throughout the world. In Jesus' name. Amen.

Call to Worship
> Leader: Great and amazing are your deeds, Lord God the Almighty!
> People: Just and true are your ways, King of the nations!
> Leader: Lord, who will not fear and glorify your name?
> People: For you alone are holy.
> Leader: Let us worship God!
> —Adapted from Revelation 15:3–4

May 24, 1998
7th Sunday of Easter

Prayer of Adoration
Almighty God, you made a world full of infinitely diverse wonders, and you called it good. You sent Jesus as Savior and Lord, and he called us into one family, your church. Destroy among us harmful divisions that make any one person seem less worthwhile than any other. Create among us wonderful differences that help us to realize that each one of us is an unrepeatable person in whom you delight. Do this for us through the power of your Spirit working in us. In Jesus' name. Amen.

Prayer of Confession
Gracious God, we confess that we have been judgmental, unsympathetic, and self-obsessed. We have looked down at the less successful, looked the other way when confronted with injustices, looked upon ourselves as centers of reality around whom others are in orbit. Forgive us, renew us, and so fill us with your Spirit that we may see with your eyes so as to love the unloved, help the troubled, and affirm every person's essential dignity; through Jesus Christ our Lord. Amen.

Prayer of Dedication of Gifts and Self
Loving God, you give us even more than we ask, and much more than we deserve. Help us to show a like generosity in all that we do for you and for other people. May the gifts we give and the lives we live be ways in which you bless others. In Jesus' name. Amen.

Sermon Summary
Our verses oppose ecclesiastical uniformity and celebrate a higher Christian diversified unity in love that is like the love among the three persons of the Trinity.

Hymn of the Day
"Where Cross the Crowded Ways of Life." This hymn carries the author's deep commitment to social justice in the cities. It was written for the 1905 Methodist hymnal. Compassion is the main theme expressed in the lyrics, especially Jesus' compassion for the least cared for in human societies. Though some of the verses relate to the text from Revelation, the prayer in verse 5 harkens to Jesus' prayer in John's Gospel that all may be united with God and in God's love.

Children's Object Talk

Jesus Makes Us One

Object
Name tags saying "Jesus Is in Me."
Lesson
It is Jesus' love in us that unites us.

Let's take some time today to talk about what some of our favorite things are. I would like each one of you to think about your favorite color, favorite toy, or favorite food to eat. Now would anyone like to tell me some of their favorites? (Allow time for children to respond. You may have to be the first to volunteer.)

Thank you for telling me some of your favorites. Some of us had the same favorites, and some of us named different things. We are not all alike, are we? We can tell that just by looking around at each other. We don't have the same color hair or eyes. We aren't all the same height or weight. Wow! We really are different from one another.

In the Bible, Jesus says something surprising. He says that he wants us all to be one. He asks God to make us work together and be together. I wonder how that can happen when we're all so different?

Jesus tells us how. He says that he will be in us. That means his love is in each of us helping us to be together and work together.

I'd like each of you to wear this tag that says, "Jesus Is in Me" to remind you that Jesus is with each one of you (put tag on each child). That's how we are alike and that's why we can be together and work together.

—*Jeanette Strandjord*

The Sermon

That They May Become Completely One

Hymns
Beginning of Worship: "I Love Thy Kingdom, Lord"
Sermon Hymn: "Blest Be the Tie That Binds"
End of Worship: "They'll Know We Are Christians by Our Love"

May 24, 1998
7th Sunday of Easter

Scripture

John 17:20-26 (For additional sermon materials on this passage, see the February 1998 issue of *The Clergy Journal* and on Revelation 22:12-14, 16-17, 20-21, see the *1997 May/June Planning Issue* of *The Clergy Journal.*)

Sermon Text

"'I in them and you in me, that they may become completely one, so that the world may know that you have sent me and have loved them even as you have loved me'" (vs. 23).

On the last night of his earthly life, Jesus Christ prayed for you. He prayed for you, and me, and all who would believe in him. He prayed for our unity as Christians.

You might expect that what Jesus prayed for, God would give! The most recent *Handbook of Denominations in the United States,* however, describes more than two hundred fifty separately organized churches in this country alone. Has Jesus' prayer for Christian unity not been heard by God? Or has the sinfulness of Christians thwarted Christ's intention for his church?

William Barclay tells of a Japanese Christian leader, Kagawa, who used to like to call attention to the fact that his pronunciation of "denomination" sounded rather like "damnation"—quite so, as he figured they were pretty much the same thing! Barclay suggests that "the sin of denominationalism" may be "the greatest sin of the modern church."

Is denominationalism a great sin? Does it contradict Christ's desire for our Christian lives? Is it somehow wrong to be Lutheran, Methodist, Presbyterian? If so, we seem to have become of late more deeply steeped in this sin. Efforts toward the unification of mainstream American denominations no longer make the news. The modern ecumenical movement to merge churches has come to something of a screechless halt. Albert Outler, who describes himself as "a grizzled ecumaniac with a wealth of golden memories," recently declared that "official ecumenism seems to be dead in the water."

On the last night of his life, Jesus prayed for Christian unity. He prayed "that they may become completely one." How should we understand the Christian oneness of which our Lord prayed?

First of all, it is a oneness that comes from God, and is not simply the product of human efforts. This is clear enough from the fact that Jesus prays for it.

It is even more evident when we notice that Jesus prays for this unity so that the world may believe God has sent him. A supernaturally empowered Christian unity proves to the world that God loves the world in Christ.

Second, this Christian oneness is like the oneness of Christ and God, like the oneness of the Father and the Son. Jesus prays "that they may be one, as we are one." He prays for a unity among human believers that will be like the unity among divine persons in the Trinity: the Father, the Son, and the Holy Spirit.

Some dismiss the Christian doctrine of the Trinity (three persons in one God) as hopelessly esoteric and unnecessary. Yet, it provides the key to the interpretation of our verses in John, for the Scriptures suggest that it is love that both binds together and keeps distinct Father, Son, and Holy Spirit in triune unity.

The Scriptures stress the self-denying love of Father, Son, and Holy Spirit for one another. The Scriptures insist that God creates all things in and for the Son (Col 1:16), that the Son does the will and work of the Father (Jn 4:34), that the Spirit takes what is Christ's and declares it to Christians (Jn 16:15). The Scriptures represent the oneness of the Trinity as a oneness of self-giving love. Such unselfish loving, as Diogenes Allen observes in *Finding Our Father*, enables the three persons of the Trinity to be at one and the same time profoundly united and yet "irreducible to one another." Within the absolute oneness of divine trinitarian love, there is an ineluctable distinctiveness. There must be. "Difference," declares Daniel Migliore in *The Power of God*, "is the necessary condition of genuine love."

So, in our verses when Christ prays to the Father that *"the love with which you have loved me may be in them"* (vs. 26), he prays that we Christians might share and show the world a Trinity-like love united in diversity, a love that overturns barriers dividing Christians while preserving an intrinsic distinctiveness among Christians. It is the oneness amid differences of this love that can convince the world.

In Christian love, we strive to respect various ways of worship and witness—of Quakers and Catholics, prophets and scholars, charismatic and liturgical Christians. Such a unified diversity appears so novel a phenomenon, so unlike the uniformity the world tends to expect of persons, that those who behold it consider our religion heaven-sent. Our very differences as Christians, if we love one another in them, can convince the world that God sent Jesus.

In his letter to the Galatians, Paul refers to the church as

May 24, 1998
7th Sunday of Easter

"our family in the faith" (6:10, Today's English Version). As Lesslie Newbigin comments in *The Light Has Come,* "Children of one Father [God] should live together as one family." We all know human families with siblings so different they seem to come from different parents, even different planets. Brothers and sisters develop distinct personalities, express opposing points of view, pursue unlike vocations. Yet, each is loved equally by mother and father and learns as well to love very different sisters and brothers. Life in the church should be like that, lived in just the same sort of dissimilar oneness of love.

In his commentary on our verses, a turn-of-the-century Scottish scholar, Marcus Dods, writes:

"This text is often cited by those who seek to promote the union of churches. But we find it belongs to a very different category and a much higher region. That all churches should be under similar government, . . . should use the same forms of worship . . . is not supremely desirable . . . Christ's will is all-embracing; the purposes of God are wide as the universe, and can be fulfilled only by endless varieties of dispositions, functions, organizations, labours. We must expect that, as time goes on, men [and women], so far from being contracted into a narrow and monotonous uniformity, will exhibit increasing diversities of thought and of method, and will be more and more differentiated in outward respects."

This need not lead to rivalry and conflict, if we take to heart the model of love revealed to us in the Trinity. Our very diversity as Christians can most vividly and effectually exhibit our unity in love.

In conclusion, it is a oneness of love, like that of the Trinity, to which Christ calls us, a love that obliterates the uncaring barriers that divide us at the same time as it celebrates the marvelous diversities that distinguish us. It is this wonderful oneness of love that our Lord prayed we would exhibit as Christians, so that the world might believe that God sent him.

—*Steven D. MacArthur*
Lyon College
Batesville, Arkansas

May 31, 1998

Day of Pentecost

Lessons

Pres/Meth/UCC/Luth	Acts 2:1–21	Rom 8:14–17	Jn 14:8–17, 25–27
Roman Catholic	Acts 2:1–11	1 Cor 12:3b–7, 12–13	Jn 20:19–23
Episcopal	Acts 2:1–11	1 Cor 12:4–13	Jn 20:19–23

Introduction to the Lessons
Lesson 1
Acts 2:1–21 **(Pres/Meth/UCC/Luth)**; *Acts 2:1–11* **(RC/Epis)**
The Spirit comes with power upon *all* the earliest believers in Jesus gathered in the Upper Room (cf. 1:13–14). They speak in other languages so that devout Jews from every nation under heaven hear them proclaiming God's deeds of power. The prophecy Peter cites from Joel underscores that the Spirit is being poured out now upon sons, daughters, young men, old men, slaves, both men and women—everyone. The "tongues of fire" remind us of the prophecy of the Baptist (Lk 3:16) who preached to crowds, even tax collectors and soldiers (Lk 3:10–14)—everyone.

Lesson 2
(1) *Romans 8:14–17* **(Pres/Meth/UCC/Luth)**
Because we have received the Holy Spirit, we are children of God and heirs of salvation with the Son if we suffer with him. Like Christ (Mk 14:36) in Gethsemane, we approach God in prayer as "Abba" (cf. Gal 4:6), and we accept suffering in God's service.

(2) *1 Corinthians 12:3b–7, 12–13* **(RC)**;
1 Corinthians 12:4–13 **(Epis)**
Anyone who confesses Christ as Lord has been spiritually blessed and empowered by one and the same Spirit of God. All believers contribute in various needful ways to the common good. Every believer is an equally valuable participant in the life of the church.

May 31, 1998
Day of Pentecost

Gospel
(1) *John 14:8–17, 25–27* **(Pres/Meth/UCC/Luth)**
The apostle Philip wants to know God. Jesus directs him to Jesus' own words, works, and person. All we really know about God, we know through Jesus. Disciples will continue and even expand upon Jesus' saving work in the world, as they pray in his name, obey his commandments, and have the Holy Spirit as their advocate.

(2) *John 20:19–23* **(RC/Epis)**
Appearing to his fearful disciples, Jesus gives them peace by imparting the Holy Spirit. He breathes on them the Spirit as God breathed on Adam "the breath of life" (Gen 1:7). The risen Christ thus creates them anew. He sends disciples who have been hiding in a locked room out into the world to continue his saving work.

Theme
We must listen in love to one another.

Thought for the Day
Pentecost celebrates variety among human beings. Luke's account of Pentecost does not state that people are speaking the same language, but that people who speak various languages are really hearing one another. As Christians we need to have ears to hear, we need to truly listen (Mk 4:9) to the reality of other people, as well as to the reality of God's word in Christ.

Prayer of Meditation
O God, to the first Christians at Pentecost you came in the Spirit as wind and fire. Let the wind of your Spirit drive out of me tendencies to disbelieve and temptations to disobey. Let the fire of your Spirit ignite within me a real desire to know and to do your will. In the name of Jesus. Amen.

Call to Worship
> Leader: I will pour out my Spirit on all flesh.
> People: Then everyone who calls on the name of the Lord shall be saved.
> Leader: Let us worship God!
> —Adapted from Acts 2:17b, 21

Prayer of Adoration

Almighty God, you mysteriously move among us, leading us out of our locked-in selfishness, leading us into relationships of love. You have created and saved, guided and befriended us. You have given yourself to us in Jesus your Son. Today we celebrate the gift of your Holy Spirit dwelling in and among us. Yours is the praise and the glory, forever and ever; through Jesus Christ our Lord. Amen.

Prayer of Confession

O God, Creator, Savior, Spirit, we confess that we try to hide from you, that we tend to live for ourselves, that we turn away from our neighbors in need. In your never-ending mercy, forgive us. Free us from selfishness, and raise us to newness of life, through Jesus Christ our Lord. Amen.

Prayer of Dedication of Gifts and Self

O holy and loving God, we praise you, for you create love, give guidance, provide comfort, and give peace. You deliver us from difficulties, alert us to new insights, lead us into fresh adventures, arouse in us powerful longings for all that you intend for us to enjoy by faith in Christ and to share in the service of Christ. You give us everything in Christ Jesus. Let this offering be a sign that in return we want to give to you all that we are and all that we have. In Jesus' name. Amen.

Sermon Summary

At Babel, sin culminates in a diversity that divides humanity and impedes love. At Pentecost, the Spirit creates a diversity that unifies persons and enables love. This new unity amid diversity makes its appearance by a miracle of hearing. The text calls us to listen in love to one another.

Hymn of the Day

"Like the Murmur of the Dove's Song." This hymn is a gentle and unusually engaging contemporary Pentecost hymn. The rushing wind of the Acts passage is here evoked by a rich and elegant imagery. The words were composed especially for this tune and appeared first in *The Hymnal 1982* (Episcopal). Jewish Midrash suggests that the dove was made God's messenger of peace because it never stops murmuring, always speaking of both blessing and persistence to God's people.

May 31, 1998
Day of Pentecost

Children's Object Talk

Celebrate and Tell the News

Object
A world globe.

Lesson
God calls the church to spread the good news of Jesus.

Today we celebrate the birthday of the church. Birthdays are special days. Each of you has a birthday, and you probably celebrate it with cake and candles. The church has a birthday, too.

In the Bible, we read the story about the church's birth or beginning. Long ago many people were meeting together several weeks after Easter. As they came together, God sent the Holy Spirit to them and suddenly they could speak in many languages. People were speaking the languages of many different nations and peoples. The Bible lists many of them. They were the languages of the Parthians, Medes, Elamites, and people who lived in Asia, Egypt, Libya, and even more places. That is a lot of languages.

God had a reason for doing this. God wanted people all over the world to hear about Jesus and all that God has done.

I have a globe here today. Can someone find where we are on this global map? (let volunteer help) Here we are, but look how much more of the world there is. We have a big country, but there are certainly many more countries besides ours. There are lots of places for you and me to tell about Jesus.

A good way to celebrate the birthday of the church would be for you and me and all of us here to think of someone to tell about Jesus. God wants us to tell others. You don't even have to speak another language. You can tell a friend at school or a neighbor right on your own street. God will help us do that just like God helped Christians a long time ago.

—Jeanette Strandjord

The Sermon

A Festival of Listening

Hymns
Beginning of Worship: "On Pentecost They Gathered"
Sermon Hymn: "Spirit of God, Descend upon My Heart"
End of Worship: "Where Cross the Crowded Ways of Life"

Scripture
Acts 2:1–21 (For additional sermon materials on this passage, see the February 1998 and the *1997 May/June Planning Issue* of *The Clergy Journal*.)

Sermon Text
"'And how is it that we hear, each of us, in our own native language?'" (vs. 8).

At the beginning of the Old Testament narrative of the tower of Babel, *"Now the whole earth had one language and the same words . . . And they said to one another, 'Come, let us make bricks . . .' . . . Then they said, 'Come, let us build . . .' . . . And the Lord said, '. . . Come, let us go down, and confuse their language . . . so that they will not understand one another's speech.' So the Lord scattered them abroad from there over the face of the earth, and they left off building the city"* (Gen 11:1–9).

The narrative commences with the monotony of a single language in one location. It ends in a babble of multiple tongues all over the earth. And God transforms this erstwhile uniformity into multiplicity.

God's dispersal of persons at Babel is entirely consistent with what the book of Genesis has already told us about what God intends for humanity. God at the creation tells men and women to *"fill the earth"* (1:28; 9:1), and God after the flood wants humanity to *"spread abroad on the earth"* (10:32), because God desires variety in his vast creation. The God who sees that *"everything he had made . . . was very good"* (1:31) abhors conformance and sameness. God our creator delights in differentiation.

So when the Lord brings to an end the building of the Tower of Babel, we should be able, on the basis of what we have read before, to discern that this action expresses God's opposition to all the hegemonic towers of cultural or social, religious or political conformity that men and women try to construct. The Babel narrative protests against every human effort to achieve unity through uniformity.

When Luke wrote his account in the Acts of the Apostles of the gift of the Spirit at Pentecost, he had the narrative of the Tower of Babel in mind, and he wanted his readers to remember it too. There are lots of linkages between the two narratives. In both, people have gathered together *"in one place"* (Acts 2:1). In both, divine intervention *"from heaven"* transforms the circumstances of those who have gathered (Acts 2:2). Moreover, in an ancient Jewish writing earlier than the New Testament, we encounter a tradition that *"the Lord sent a great wind upon the tower [of Babel] and overthrew it"* (Jubilees 10:26), and at Pentecost the sound of the coming Spirit is *"like the rush of a violent wind"* (Acts 2:2). And, of course, the main similarity between the two narratives is that they both focus on language and stress listening.

The two narratives are meant to be read as a diptych, which is an altarpiece consisting of two separate but related depictions. Just before he calls Abraham, God judges uniformity among human persons at Babel. Just after he raises Jesus, God blesses diversity among human persons at Pentecost. The two narratives belong together; they elucidate each other.

God intervenes in the Old Testament narrative so that the builders of Babel *"will not understand one another's speech"* (Gen 11:7). The Hebrew word here translated "understand" has the basic meaning of "hear" or "listen." God confuses their language so that they might not "listen" to one another. Like other early sections of Genesis, the Babel narrative describes human existence as it *is* but should *not* be. Just as the account of the fall from grace in the Garden of Eden tells of pain, toil, and death, so the Babel narrative says that men and women who live in sin and alienation from God do not *listen* to one another. This, like sorrow and suffering, like the pain of childbearing and the toil of farming, is not the way God intended human life to be.

God intervenes in Luke's Pentecost narrative so that people will understand one another's speech. The giving of the Spirit entails a miracle of *listening*. The emphasis throughout is on *hearing*. *"Each one heard them speaking in the native language..."* (Acts 2:6). *"And how is it that we hear, each of us, in our own native language?"* (Acts 2:8). *"In our own languages we hear them speaking about God's deeds of power"* (Acts 2:11). The miracle of Pentecost, the gift of the Spirit, creates *"a fresh capacity to listen,"* as Walter Brueggemann observes in his book *Genesis*, a new pneumatic capacity to hear and to respond to persons who are different than we are. Luke presents Pentecost as a veritable festival of listening involving diverse persons from every corner of the known world.

Some years ago, a brokerage firm had an ad campaign that centered on the refrain, "When E. F. Hutton talks, people listen." The implicit assumption behind the slogan was that ordinarily when someone talks, people don't really listen. Theodore Reik, an American psychologist, made this the theme of his helpful book, *Listening with the Third Ear*. Really hearing what other people are saying to us requires special effort and sensitivity, Reik wrote. In *Life Together*, Dietrich Bonhoeffer castigates a common "kind of listening with half an ear that presumes already to know what the other has to say . . . an impatient, inattentive listening, that despises the [other] and is only waiting for a chance to speak and thus get rid of the other person."

At Pentecost we celebrate the gift of God's Spirit that creates in Christians a fresh capacity to listen. In the Spirit, the continuous din of our own concerns need not keep us from really hearing and responding to the cries and sighs of other women and men. In the Spirit the loud certainty of our own convictions need not keep us from really hearing and considering the ideas and perspectives of other persons. In the Spirit we are brought out of the locked-door mentality of natural self-centeredness into lives of genuine encounter with diverse persons, just as the first fearful disciples were driven from an upper room with locked doors into Jerusalem streets teeming with visitors from all over the world.

In the Spirit when we hear that every minute eighteen children die of malnutrition, we can listen to this statistic, sense the pain they endure, and try to respond. In the Spirit, when others share their burdens with us, we can listen to these persons, sense the weight they carry, and try to help.

Luke's report of Pentecost holds up before us both the necessity of our listening to, and the reality of our connectedness with people unlike us, near to and far from us. Many of these other people suffer so much more than we can even imagine. But by God's Holy Spirit, we can reach out to any of them in love, and we can thereby begin to bring about in our own lives that unified diversity, that differentiated oneness for which God created us, and for the sake of which God sent his Spirit into the world.

—*Steven D. MacArthur*
Lyon College
Batesville, Arkansas

June 7, 1998

Trinity Sunday

Lessons

Pres/Meth/UCC/Luth	Prov 8:1–4, 22–31	Rom 5:1–5	Jn 16:12–15
Roman Catholic	Prov 8:22–31	Rom 5:1–5	Jn 16:12–15
Episcopal	Isa 6:1–8	Rev 4:1–11	Jn 16:(5–11) 12–15

Introduction to the Lessons
Lesson 1
(1) *Proverbs 8:1–4, 22–31* **(Pres/Meth/UCC/Luth)**;
Proverbs 8:22–31 **(RC)**
Wisdom, personified in these verses as a woman preaching to simple youth, introduces herself. God created her "before the beginning of the earth," and she worked beside God "as a master worker": when God created the heavens and the earth. She rejoiced in the inhabited world and delighted in the human race.

(2) *Isaiah 6:1–8* **(Epis)**
Isaiah includes in his memoirs an account of his call. Isaiah is an observer of God's heavenly council and must undergo a purification rite to be in God's presence. Isaiah then hears God's request that someone speak for God and immediately volunteers, "Send me!"

Lesson 2
(1) *Romans 5:1–5* **(Pres/Meth/UCC/Luth/RC)**
This passage from the longest of the apostle Paul's letters to young churches leads us to the pinnacle of God's plan of salvation. Life in Christ means having peace with God, sharing the glory of God, and enjoying God's love poured into us by the Holy Spirit.

(2) *Revelation 4:1–11* **(Epis)**
Using highly symbolic language typical of apocalyptic literature, literature dealing with the end times, John offers a detailed look at the heavenly throne room. His description is similar to various Old Testament conceptions of heaven.

Gospel
John 16:12–15 (**Pres/Meth/UCC/Luth/RC**);
John 16:(5–11) 12–15 (**Epis**)

Jesus has washed his disciples' feet, eaten his Last Supper with them, and given them a new commandment, to love one another. This passage, about the work of the Spirit, is from Jesus' farewell address to his followers.

Theme
The doctrine of the Trinity expresses our experience of God.

Thought for the Day
The entire Bible talks about God and has been written to reveal God to people. It does not indulge in abstract speculation about God. Instead, it tells the stories of people who have experienced God.
—From *Evangelical Catechism: Christian Faith in the World Today*, American Edition, Minneapolis: Augsburg Publishing House, 1982, p. 69

Prayer of Meditation
You show yourself to us, holy and triune God, as Father, Son, and Holy Spirit. We enjoy the wonder of creation, which the Father brought into being—earth and sky, land and sea, plants and animals, birds and fish. Thank you, Father, for these gifts. We hear your word in Jesus Christ, God made flesh, living among us. Thank you, Jesus, for speaking to us. We enter into fellowship with you and your whole church by the life-giving power of the Holy Spirit. Thank you, Spirit, for entering our hearts. Amen.

Call to Worship
> Leader: Creator God,
> People: By your word breathed into the chaos, the foundations of the earth were laid.
> Leader: Light of the world,
> People: You were nailed to a cross and gave up your breath that we might have life.
> Leader: Perfect Spirit,
> People: Fill us with your life-giving breath, that we might worship the holy God.

June 7, 1998
Trinity Sunday

Prayer of Adoration

O Lord our God, creator, redeemer, and sanctifier, your power and glory are great, yet sometimes you make yourself small enough that we can see you. You show yourself to us through Jesus who came to be one of us and walked, and ate—and died—with us and who rose from the dead that we too might rise to eternal life. You come to us also through your word, and through water and bread and wine. For these great revelations and for all the other ways you reach out to us, we thank you, God. In Jesus' name. Amen.

Prayer of Confession

Throughout the ages, O God, your servants have come before you in deepest humility. We know that when Moses heard your voice out of the burning bush, he hid his face because he was afraid to look at you. When Isaiah saw you in the temple, he cried out with amazement, "Woe is me!" because he had seen you. When Paul encountered you on the road to Damascus, he was blinded by your presence. We, too, are overwhelmed by you because you are holy. Cleanse our hearts, gracious God. Wipe away every sin that we might come to you without fear. Heal all brokenness that we might come into your presence with rejoicing. In the name of Jesus who died and rose again to overcome sin and reconcile all creation. Amen.

Prayer of Dedication of Gifts and Self

Thank you, Father, for the gift of creation. Thank you, Jesus, for the gift of your life. Thank you, Spirit, for the gift of faith. Thank you, God, Father, Son, and Holy Spirit for sustaining us, healing us, and making us holy. Receive these gifts from our hands, tokens of the wealth you have showered on us. Use these gifts in the service of your work on earth. Use each of us, your people, to feed the hungry, welcome the stranger, clothe the naked, and visit the sick and imprisoned. We pray in Jesus' name. Amen.

Sermon Summary

The doctrine of the Trinity is implicit, rather than explicit in Scripture, but it is not a mysterious formula or a perplexing and complicated dogma. It is an expression of our experience of God, particularly as we pray and celebrate the sacraments.

Hymn of the Day

"Come, Thou Almighty King." Though the author of this hymn is anonymous, he or she has left us with three enduring images of God for Trinity Sunday: Almighty God, Incarnate Word, and Holy Comforter. The words to this hymn were first published in a George Whitefield collection dated 1747. The tune was composed by a famous violinist of the day, Felice de Giardini, who named it "Italian Hymn" after his homeland.

Children's Object Talk

Lots Left to Learn

Object
   A Bible and a dictionary.

Lesson
   Jesus teaches us through the Bible.

Does anyone know what this big book is? (Hold up dictionary and wait for responses.) Yes, it is a dictionary, and it can teach us lots of words. Here's an interesting word, "cavy" (ka'vi). Does anyone know what that is? Neither did I until I read about it in this book. It is a guinea pig from South America.

We can learn lots of things from books. I've got another big book here (hold up the Bible). The Bible is a very special book. It is special because it tells us about God and God's love for us and the whole world. It's in the Bible that we learn about Jesus, God's son.

This Bible is such a big book that we could read it all day long and still not finish it. There's a lot to learn about Jesus and God's love. That's what Jesus was talking about when he said to his disciples, "I still have many things to say to you, but you cannot bear them now." Jesus has a lot to teach us, but we can't learn it all at once.

The good news is that Jesus will keep on teaching us every day. Jesus is a good and patient teacher. He will teach us as we read the Bible. He will teach us when others talk about the Bible with us. Every time we open up this book (open the Bible), Jesus helps us learn about him and God's love. This is the one book that will last you your whole life.

—*Jeanette Strandjord*

June 7, 1998
Trinity Sunday

The Sermon

The Doctrine of the Trinity

Hymns
Beginning of Worship: "All People That on Earth Do Dwell"
Sermon Hymn: "All Glory to God on High"
End of Worship: "Holy God, We Praise Your Name"

Scripture
John 16:12–15 (For additional sermon materials on this passage, see the February 1998 and the *1997 May/June Planning Issue* of *The Clergy Journal*.)

Sermon Text
"When the Spirit of truth comes, he will guide you into all the truth..." (vs. 13).

For centuries the doctrine of the Trinity—the belief that God is three "persons," Father, Son, and Holy Spirit—has been thought by the church's greatest teachers to express the deepest truth of our faith. It is probably also the most perplexing teaching of the Christian church, and over the years, you have probably heard various illustrations designed to uncover its mystery.

Supposedly Saint Patrick once showed a student a stalk of three-leaf clover to demonstrate the three-in-one nature of God. You may also have heard it said that the Trinity is like water—sometimes we see it as a liquid, sometimes a solid, and sometimes a vapor. If you do not think you have a good grasp of the Trinity, take heart. During the early centuries of the church's existence, the Trinity was one of the main things church leaders argued about, and two great councils were held in the fourth century to debate and establish key teachings on the subject.

At least one of the reasons people have had so much difficulty with the doctrine of the Trinity is that the idea is implicit, rather than explicit in Scripture. We can point to the Great Commission in which Jesus commands his disciples to baptize all nations *"in the name of the Father and of the Son and of the Holy Spirit"* (Mt 28:19). Paul closes his second letter to the Corinthians with the salutation, *"The grace of our Lord Jesus Christ, the love of God, and the communion of the Holy Spirit be with all of you"* (2 Cor 13:13). But nowhere in the Bible does it say,

"God is triune, and here's what that means."

Still, the Trinity is not a mysterious formula or a perplexing and complicated dogma. It is actually a very earthy and practical teaching. It is an expression of our experience of God. We know God as creator and sustainer of light and life and as the Father of Jesus Christ. We know God as the Son, as one who became like us, even to the point of dying. And we know God as the Holy Spirit, the one who opens our hearts and minds in faith. Yet it is the same God, one God, who does all these things.

The Apostles' Creed grew out of early baptismal formulas, the words that were said as a person being baptized was immersed in a pool of water. The Creed has three "articles," each one describing an expression of our experience of God—Father, Son, and Holy Spirit. The great sixteenth-century teacher Martin Luther in *The Small Catechism* wrote explanations of these three parts of the Creed that help remind us of the ways we experience God. Of God the Father, Luther says:

"God has given me and still preserves my body and soul . . . God daily and abundantly provides . . . all the necessities and nourishment for this body and life. God protects me against all danger and shields and preserves me from all evil." (*A Contemporary Translation of Luther's Small Catechism*, Study Edition, Timothy J. Wengert, trans. [Minneapolis: Augsburg Fortress, 1994], p. 25.)

For his explanation of the Second Article of the Creed, which deals with Jesus, Luther turns to the biblical stories, the record and interpretation of the experiences of the people who knew Jesus when he walked on this earth two thousand years ago: Jesus was born of the virgin Mary, redeemed us with his precious blood, and is risen from the dead, all so that we may belong to him and live eternally in God's realm.

The explanation to the Third Article again describes experiences that even we twentieth-century people know firsthand:

"The Holy Spirit has called me through the gospel, enlightened me with his gifts, made me holy, and kept me in the true faith, just as he calls, gathers, enlightens, and makes holy the whole Christian church on earth . . . The Holy Spirit abundantly forgives all sins—mine and those of all believers . . ." (Ibid., p. 29.)

People outside the church who have a sense that there is a God probably have an image and experience of God that is most

June 7, 1998
Trinity Sunday

like what Christians describe as God the Father. Many Christians, on the other hand, tend to focus most of their attention on the second person of the Trinity, on Jesus. In our gospel lesson for today, however, Jesus is most interested in the Spirit. He says to his disciples, *"When the Spirit of truth comes, he will guide you into all the truth"* (Jn 16:13). The Spirit will take God's self-revelation—as Father, Son, and Holy Spirit—and make that revelation meaningful to each generation of Christians.

How does the Spirit do this work? The Spirit works through a variety of tools. God has specifically promised to be present to us in at least three ways. First, God comes to us through the living word, through Scripture and God's spoken word. God also comes to us through the waters of baptism, and through the bread and wine of Holy Communion.

Throughout the ages, though, Christians have experienced the work of the Spirit in other ways. Jesus said, "Where two or three are gathered, there am I." God came to the prophet Elijah in a still, small voice. The woman caught in adultery experienced God through Jesus' words of forgiveness.

We are called by the Spirit to participate in a rich life. In this Spirit-led life, we encounter God as creator of our world. We also meet God in the word—in the saving action of Jesus Christ. And it is God the Spirit who enables us to respond in faith to Jesus and to join with others in Christian fellowship. We can describe all the work of God by using sentences and paragraphs and perhaps even by writing whole books. Or we can describe God quite simply—as Father, Son, and Holy Spirit.

—Beth Ann Gaede
ELCA pastor, editor, and writer
Minneapolis, Minnesota

June 14, 1998

2nd Sunday after Pentecost (Proper 6)
Pres: 11th Sunday in Ordinary Time
RC: Body and Blood of Christ—Not listed

Lessons

Pres/Meth/UCC	1 Kings 21:1–10 (11–14), 15–21a	Gal 2:15–21	Lk 7:36—8:3
Episcopal	2 Sam 11:26—12:10, 13–15	Gal 2:11–21	Lk 7:36–50
Lutheran	2 Sam 11:26—12:10, 13–15	Gal 2:15–21	Lk 7:36—8:3

Introduction to the Lessons
Lesson 1
(1) *1 Kings 21:1–10 (11–14), 15–21a* **(Pres/Meth/UCC)**
Toward the end of his reign, King Solomon "did what was evil in the sight of the Lord and did not completely follow the Lord, as his father David had done" (1 Kings 11:6). Solomon's son, Rehoboam, followed his father's evil ways and treated the people harshly. All the tribes of Israel except Judah and Benjamin rebelled and broke away to follow a new king, Jereboam.

(2) *2 Samuel 11:26—12:10, 13–15* **(Epis/Luth)**
Much admired though he was, King David sinned against the Lord by committing adultery with Bathsheba and then arranging for her husband to be killed in battle. In this passage, we hear the rebuke of the prophet Nathan, David's repentance, and Nathan's warning that trouble lies ahead.

Lesson 2
    Galatians 2:15–21 **(Pres/Meth/UCC/Luth)**;
    Galatians 2:11–21 **(Epis)**
Paul's letter to the Galatians, often called the Magna Carta of Christian liberty, deals with the question of whether Gentiles must become Jews before they can become Christians. Here Paul explains the difference between law and gospel.

June 14, 1998
2nd Sunday after Pentecost (Proper 6)
Pres: 11th Sunday in Ordinary Time

Gospel
Luke 7:36—8:3 **(Pres/Meth/UCC/Luth)**;
Luke 7:36-50 **(Epis)**

One of the themes of Luke's Gospel is that Jesus came for *all* people. Even a woman who is known as a sinner is welcomed by Jesus. Remarkably, she shows that she understands the meaning of forgiveness, although Jesus' host, a religious leader, does not.

Theme
Being a Christian means being sustained and molded by Christ.

Thought for the Day
Through God's Spirit who abides in Christians, they willingly fulfill the law. They no longer stand under the demands of the law, but live their lives in accord with God's law through an act of love brought about by the Holy Spirit.

—Hans Schwarz,
True Faith in the True God: An Introduction to Luther's Life and Thought,
Minneapolis: Augsburg Fortress, 1996, p. 107

Prayer of Meditation
Ever-patient God, you have reached out to us in love ever since we, the creatures of your hand, became estranged from you in the Garden of Eden. You sent Moses and Deborah, David and Esther, Paul and Lydia to lead us in faithfulness. You spoke your word to us through the prophets and the gospel writers. Then you sent Christ Jesus to lead, teach, and heal and nothing has been the same since. We thank you that Christ lives in us today. Be our companion as we learn what it means to live by faith in you. In Jesus' name we pray. Amen.

Call to Worship
Leader: We praise you, our God and ruler;
People: We bless your name forever and ever.
Leader: Every day we will bless you,
People: And praise your name forever and ever.
Leader: Great are you, O Lord, and greatly to be praised;
People: Your greatness is unsearchable.

Prayer of Adoration

We are your people, O God, the work of your hand, redeemed with the blood of your son, called by the power of your Spirit. We give you thanks for all you do to sustain us each day. We stand in awe of your persistent love for us. We praise you for welcoming us into your family, to join with the great cloud of witnesses and to be with you forever. We pray in the name of our precious Savior, Jesus Christ. Amen.

Prayer of Confession

Mighty and gentle God, we come before you in sorrow, asking your forgiveness for the ways we have turned from you. You have commanded us to love you above all others and with all our heart and soul and might. Yet, we give greater honor to other people and things than we do to you. You have commanded us to love our neighbors as ourselves. Yet, we walk down the other side of the road when we see someone in need. Forgive us, long-suffering God, for causing you to weep by our disobedience. Create in us new and faithful hearts, that we might follow your commands in all our thoughts, words, and deeds. In the name of the one who died that we might be forgiven. Amen.

Prayer of Dedication of Gifts and Self

Bountiful God, we cannot count all your blessings to us. You made all things, redeemed all creation, and continue to restore the work of your hand. For all that we are and all that we have, we give you our thanks. We come before you, generous God, with a small portion of the many gifts you have showered upon us. Use these meager offerings for the growth of your kingdom—for the spread of your word and the healing of your creation. Receive these gifts, too, as a symbol of ourselves. Use us as instruments of your will—to sow peace, to show your love, and to bring light to those in darkness. In Jesus' name. Amen.

Sermon Summary

Martin Luther sparked a reformation in the Christian church in his search for an answer to the question, "How can I find a gracious God?" Several decades ago, scholars suggested that the modern person's question is, "Is there a God?" But now the latest research shows that people are not asking either of those questions. They are asking instead, "How can I make my life work?" Even though the question has changed, however, the gospel still speaks to us.

June 14, 1998
2nd Sunday after Pentecost (Proper 6)
Pres: 11th Sunday in Ordinary Time

Hymn of the Day

"Alas and Did My Savior Bleed." "If justification comes through the law, then Christ died for nothing," is Paul's clincher in his appeal to the Galatians in today's epistle. This 1707 hymn by Isaac Watts recalls Christ's sacrifice and the mercy and life that lives in us because of it. Watts was a giant among hymn writers of his day, writing some of the most popular verse for worship both in his own time and in ours. This text is sung to many tunes including the "Martyrdom" (sometimes called "Avon"), which is a rolling tune of possible Scottish origin.

Children's Object Talk

Look to Jesus

Object
A Bible, a cross, and a picture of Jesus.

Lesson
Jesus Christ is our Savior.

In the Bible, there's a part called Galatians (turn to this in your Bible). The apostle Paul wrote this letter to some Christians a long time ago.

I found out something very interesting about Paul's letter to the Galatians. There is one name Paul uses lots and lots of times. That name is Jesus Christ. I looked it up and found out that in this short letter to the Galatians, Paul uses Jesus' name over forty times. That is a lot!

Do any of you have ideas about why Paul would use the name of Jesus so often? (wait for responses) Thank you for your good ideas. Your ideas help us to see that Paul thought Jesus was very important.

Jesus Christ is so important, says Paul, that we must not forget him. The Galatians were starting to forget about Jesus. That's why Paul wrote this letter. Paul told the Galatians again that it was Jesus who died on the cross and rose from the dead for them. He reminded them it is because of Jesus that they, and all of us, can trust that God loves us and saves us.

Paul wants all of us to look to Jesus as the one who is our Savior. We can read in the Bible (hold up Bible), we can put a cross in our church and our home to remind us (hold up cross), and we can put up a picture of Jesus too (hold up picture). All of these remind us of the good news that Jesus loves us and saves us.

—*Jeanette Strandjord*

The Sermon

How Can I Make My Life Work?

Hymns
Beginning of Worship: "O Day of Rest and Gladness"
Sermon Hymn: "O Jesus, Joy of Loving Hearts"
End of Worship: "Come, Holy Ghost, Our Souls Inspire"

Scripture
Galatians 2:15–21 (For sermon materials on Luke 7:36—8:3, see the March 1998 and the *1997 May/June Planning Issue* of *The Clergy Journal*.)

Sermon Text
". . . it is no longer I who live, but it is Christ who lives in me . . ." (vs. 20).

When Dave and Marilyn sent their youngest child Kevin away to college, they assumed Kevin would study hard for four years, returning home only for vacations, graduate, and then move on—either to graduate school or a nice job.

Dave and Marilyn were surprised to discover, however, that a degree from an expensive liberal arts college was not Kevin's ticket to a well-paying job. Six months after graduating from college, Kevin moved back into his old room in their home. Dave and Marilyn don't mind giving their son a hand, but it is hard for them. Their empty nest is full again, and the newfound romance they had been enjoying together the last few months seems to be fading quickly. Kevin isn't exactly thrilled with the situation either. Will he ever amount to anything? he wonders. Will he ever be more than Mom and Dad's little boy?

Celeste had gotten married two years after graduating from high school, and she and her husband had bought a nice starter home not far from where they grew up. They had two lovely children, and things seemed to be going just as Celeste had always dreamed. Her husband was doing really well at work, and they decided she didn't need to work as a dental hygienist anymore. Today, Celeste seems to have it all. But . . . But . . . She can't quite put her finger on it. It's just that she's tired —all the time. She feels like she spends most of her time in the car, running her kids to games and

June 14, 1998
2nd Sunday after Pentecost (Proper 6)
Pres: 11th Sunday in Ordinary Time

lessons, taking her elderly mother to appointments and shopping, trying to manage the household to her husband's satisfaction. Celeste often thinks, "If I could just have a day, one day, for myself!" She can't think about it too much, though, or she starts to cry.

When Rodney finished his M.B.A. and was immediately promoted to area manager, he knew he was on his way! Before long, he'd be a vice president. Who knows, maybe he'd even make president by the time he was forty-five. It was a thrill to get up in the morning, a joy to see what the day would bring.

Then that evil empire, the largest rival to his company, appeared on the horizon, and before he knew it, Rodney's company was bought out and he was downsized out of a job. He's been looking for a new job for fifteen months, and it is getting harder for him to believe he'll ever find anything. Maybe he should just go back to school and start over—take up computers. There will always be jobs in computers, he thinks.

Back in the sixteenth century, a man named Martin Luther sparked a reformation in the Christian church in his search for an answer to the question, "How can I find a gracious God?" Several decades ago, scholars suggested that the modern person's question is, "Is there a God?" And now, for many people, the question has changed again.

In 1990, a large midwestern fraternal benefit society sponsored a study to learn about people who do not belong to a church. One of the things the researchers discovered is that people inside and outside the church have very different ideas about the source of the unchurched person's deepest anxiety. People inside the church, people who are already members, think people who are not members are asking themselves the question Nicodemus posed when he came to Jesus alone one night: "What must I do to be saved? But, it turned out in the study, the people who don't belong to churches are actually asking a completely different question. They are asking, "How can I make my life work?" Kevin, Dave and Marilyn, Celeste, and Rodney might be members of churches. But whether they are or not, they are in one way or another asking, "How can I make my life work?"

It's easy to see how the gospel provides the answer to Martin Luther's question. How can I find a gracious God? "We know that a person is justified not by works of the law but through faith in Jesus Christ," we heard in our second lesson today. We are saved by grace through faith in Christ. The perfect, complete answer to a very serious question. But now the question has changed. How can I make my life work? Does the gospel still have something to say?

When the apostle Paul wrote to the young church in Galatia, he was addressing a problem in the church, a problem that on the surface appears to be quite different from the one we are dealing with. Some church leaders insisted that before a Gentile could become a Christian, the person first had to become a Jew. This was not as outrageous a proposal as we might think; keep in mind that as the church began, it was basically a Jewish sect. In fact, in Acts 15 we read about the process the church in Jerusalem went through to decide it would be all right to preach the gospel to Gentiles.

The Galatians needed to know what role the law plays in the life of a Christian. And Paul said,

"I died to the law, so that I might live to God. I have been crucified with Christ; and it is no longer I who live, but it is Christ who lives in me. And the life I now live in the flesh I live by faith in the Son of God, who loved me and gave himself for me" (Gal 2:19-20).

The law no longer has power over us, Paul explained. We now live in union with Christ Jesus, who sustains and molds our life as Christians.

Jesus also speaks to our modern dilemma. How can I make my life work? The trials and tribulations of modern living no longer have power over us. Jesus Christ becomes the whole reason for living. Yes, we all need help with practical matters: how to find enough time in the day, how to put bread on the table and a roof overhead, how to establish and maintain loving relationships with friends and family. But when the focus of living becomes our relationship with God, everything else looks different. Priorities become clear, so it is not as hard to find time for work, play, and prayer. We discover that we have the energy we need to be the loving people God meant us to be. We become wise about who we are and how we are to live.

The question is, "How can I make my life work?" And the answer is, "Through faith in Christ, who lives in us."

—*Beth Ann Gaede*
ELCA pastor, editor, and writer
Minneapolis, Minnesota

June 21, 1998

3rd Sunday after Pentecost (Proper 7)
RC/Pres: 12th Sunday in Ordinary Time

Lessons

Pres/Meth/UCC	1 Kings 19:1–4 (5–7), 8–15a	Gal 3:23–29	Lk 8:26–39
Roman Catholic	Zech 12:10–11; 13:1	Gal 3:26–29	Lk 9:18–24
Episcopal	Zech 12:8–10; 13:1	Gal 3:23–29	Lk 9:18–24
Lutheran	Isa 65:1–9	Gal 3:23–29	Lk 8:26–39

Introduction to the Lessons
Lesson 1
(1) *1 Kings 19:1–4 (5–7), 8–15a* **(Pres/Meth/UCC)**
The prophet Elijah defeated the prophets of Baal by calling down the fires of heaven to consume his offering and then slaughtering the prophets. Elijah's deeds, however, infuriated the wicked Queen Jezebel. In fear and despair, Elijah flees to the wilderness. There God comes to Elijah in a surprising way.

(2) *Zechariah 12:10–11; 13:1* **(RC)**;
  Zechariah 12:8–10; 13:1 **(Epis)**
The prophecies of Zechariah are from the years when the people of Judah were beginning to return from exile in Babylon to their homeland to rebuild their community around Jerusalem. Here the prophet deals with the sorrow and possibilities that have come to Judah through the house of David.

(3) *Isaiah 65:1–9* **(Luth)**
The main issue in the eleven chapters of Isaiah preceding today's lesson is what does it meant to be Israel in a land devastated by foreign powers? The prophet points out in this passage that the people have ignored and even abused the Lord. Nonetheless, God will bring forth a remnant, a portion from the people, who will inherit the land.

Lesson 2
Galatians 3:23–29 **(Pres/Meth/UCC/Epis/Luth)**;
Galatians 3:26–29 **(RC)**

In his letter to the Galatians, Paul addresses through a series of arguments the issue of whether Gentiles must become Jews before becoming Christians. Paul has been explaining that the law was necessary for a time to reveal God's will. But now that Christ has come, we are *all* of us children of God through faith, not the law.

Gospel
(1) *Luke 8:26–39* **(Pres/Meth/UCC/Luth)**

Luke tells just this one story about Jesus ministering outside Jewish territory. The man is healed and then becomes one of Jesus' disciples, declaring in his hometown what God did for him. This story not only demonstrates Jesus' power to heal, but justifies ministry to Gentiles.

(2) *Luke 9:18–24* **(RC/Epis)**

Jesus' ministry in Galilee is drawing to a close. As he prepares to turn toward Jerusalem, Jesus invites the disciples' confession of faith; foretells his coming suffering, death, and resurrection; and cautions all his followers that discipleship will prove costly.

Theme
Because of Jesus, the rules have changed: now *all* people can inherit God's promise.

Thought for the Day
Children and adults all have fun singing this chorus:

> All God's children got a place in the choir.
> Some sing lower, some sing higher,
> Some sing out loud on a telephone wire,
> And some just clap their hands, or paws, or anything they got now.

How do we respond to those who come to worship with us, but whose song is not the same as ours? (Bill Staines, "All God's Critters")

June 21, 1998
3rd Sunday after Pentecost (Proper 7)
RC/Pres: 12th Sunday in Ordinary Time

Prayer of Meditation

Lord of our life, God of our salvation, hope of every nation, grant us peace. Give us peace in our hearts where troublesome thoughts need calming; peace in our church where your children need reconciling; peace in our world where endless war is waging. Give us a taste now of the peace we will know in your heaven when we come to live with you. We pray in the name of the prince of peace, Jesus Christ. Amen.

Call to Worship

Leader: O come, let us sing to the Lord;
People: Let us make a joyful noise to the rock of our salvation!
Leader: Let us come into his presence with thanksgiving;
People: Let us make a joyful noise to him with songs of praise!
Leader: O come, let us worship and bow down,
People: Let us kneel before the Lord, our Maker!
—Psalm 95:1–2, 6

Prayer of Adoration

Marvelous God, all of creation bears witness to your glory. Day and night, sky and sea and earth, flowers and snowflakes remind us of the creative power of your word. We join our songs of praise with those of all your saints and all the heavenly host, but we know that even this mighty choir cannot do justice to the wonders that come from your hand. Receive especially our thanks and praise for the gift of your Son, Jesus Christ, who overcame the powers of sin and death that we might be your children. In his name we pray. Amen.

Prayer of Confession

God of compassion, you desire that we live as your children, but we confess to you that we have not always followed your ways. Today we remember the times when we have not welcomed those whom you are calling into this community. We have been angry and judgmental toward those in need. We have looked past those who are too old or too young for our comfort. We have been suspicious of those whose first language is different from ours. We have ignored those who are "different" from us. Yet we acknowledge that all these, our brothers and sisters, are in need of your healing word. We ask your forgiveness for turning away from your children. Put within each of us the spirit of your compassion, that we may be gracious hosts and willing teachers in this community. In Jesus' name. Amen.

Prayer of Dedication of Gifts and Self

Lord of seedtime and harvest, ruler of factories and offices, protector of highways and seas, shepherd of playrooms and hospitals, you have called each of us to work in your world. You have given each of us the gifts we need to carry out your ministry. Receive these our offerings, fruits of our labors and symbols of our callings. We lay these before you with thanks for all you do to sustain us—for house and home, family and friends, food and clothing. We dedicate these gifts to you and your saving work in the world; we dedicate ourselves to the works of witness and compassion to which you have called us. We pray in the name of Jesus who gave his life for us. Amen.

Sermon Summary

In Paul's culture, sons were special; only sons could inherit family property. Although modern Bible translations tell us "you are all *children* of God through faith" (Gal 3:26), the amazing truth is, because of Christ Jesus, we all now enjoy the role of *sons* of God.

Hymn of the Day

"In Christ There Is No East or West." Again from Paul's letter to the Galatians comes today's hymn expressing the breadth and depth of Christ's transforming love. The verses were written by John Oxenham in 1908, a Congregationalist from England who was a firm believer in the oneness of the human family. His prayer for union is commonly set to two tunes, "St. Peter" and "McKee." "McKee" was written by singer and composer Harry Burleigh who in 1892 was one of very few African Americans to enter the National Conservatory of Music. His tune is spirited and punctuated by a memorable syncopation in the last few measures of each verse.

Children's Object Talk

We Are Children of God

Object

A T-shirt with a team logo, a T-shirt reading "God's Child," signs to hang around the neck of each child reading "God's Child."

Lesson

We are clothed with Christ through our baptism.

June 21, 1998
3rd Sunday after Pentecost (Proper 7)
RC/Pres: 12th Sunday in Ordinary Time

Today I have a T-shirt that has a team name on it. (hold up T-shirt) When a person wears this shirt, we know she's on that team or really likes that team. Maybe someone in your family wears a T-shirt like this.

There are many different teams that people can be on and many different teams that people like. There is one team you, and I, and all people here today are on. The apostle Paul talks about this team in the Bible today. He says we are all children of God. We are all on God's team. When we were baptized, we were *"clothed... with Christ"* (vs. 27).

We are on God's team. That is why I have this T-shirt with me today (hold up second T-shirt reading "God's Child"). It says "God's Child." When you and I were baptized in Jesus' name, God adopted us as his children. God that he loves us, and we are in his family forever. We could all wear a T-shirt like this to remind ourselves of that good news. For today I'll give each of you this special sign that you can put around your neck and wear it over your clothes. (Help children put on signs and recruit an adult helper if it is large group.) There, you look great! You are beautiful children of God!

—*Jeanette Strandjord*

The Sermon

Inheriting the Promise

Hymns
Beginning of Worship: "When Morning Gilds the Skies"
Sermon Hymn: "In Christ There Is No East or West"
End of Worship: "Oh, Happy Day When We Shall Stand"

Scripture
Galatians 3:23–29 (For additional sermon materials on this passage, see the March 1998 and the *1997 May/June Planning Issue* of *The Clergy Journal*.)

Sermon Text
"... in Christ Jesus you are all children of God through faith" (vs. 26).

Although Bible translators certainly need to have a thorough knowledge of the languages they are working with, translating the Bible is not an exact science. Translators need to know more than just the technical meaning of words. They also need to understand the words' cultural connotation, so that the true message is conveyed.

Years ago a team of Bible translators were working in the barren heart of Australia. The work was in many ways heartbreaking because the culture of the people with whom the translators worked was rapidly being destroyed. The lands on which the aboriginal people had lived for centuries was being compressed into hard, sterile dirt, mostly by enormous herds of sheep. The sheep ate every green thing they came upon; their pointy hooves had packed down the fragile earth to the point that few plants could survive; and the rare and precious water holes had been fouled beyond use. Sheep—and the shepherds who cared for them—were much despised by the Australia Aborigines.

So what were the translators to do with the much-loved Twenty-third Psalm, which begins: "The Lord is my shepherd . . ."? For the Aborigines, saying "the Lord is my shepherd" would be about as comforting as if we were to say "God is my druglord." The translators took another look at the culture of the Aborigines and discovered a person who was considered almost a savior to the people. Because the land was mostly desert to start with, and then thanks to the work of the sheep, firewood was hard to come by. People would walk long distances to gather sticks, twigs, and bits of bark and dead leaves to make a little fire. The person who gathered sticks for fires was truly a hero. So in the aboriginal tongue, the Twenty-third Psalm became, "The Lord is my stick-bearer."

An interesting translation problem appears in the passage from Galatians that we heard a little while ago. In the paragraphs before the verses we read, Paul has been explaining the purpose of the laws of Moses. The law functions, he says, to keep us in line, so that we can be counted among the members of God's household. But now that Christ has come, "you are all *children* of God through faith" (vs. 26). We are full members of the household, and we don't need the law to watch over us. The word "children" is not used by modern translators to satisfy those for whom the word "sons" excludes women. "Children" appears even in the King James Version. But there is a good reason to use the word "sons."

One Bible scholar explains:

". . . in the culture in which Paul wrote, a daughter did not have the same status as a son, especially the oldest son . . . While daughters could also inherit property, their property was always at least nominally always under the control of a male relative or patron . . . The best interpretation of [this verse] is most likely

June 21, 1998
3rd Sunday after Pentecost (Proper 7)
RC/Pres: 12th Sunday in Ordinary Time

that all, both male and female, have the equivalent of the legal status of son before God—that is, all stand with Christ as heirs of eternal life. (Carolyn Osiek, "Galatians," in *The Women's Bible Commentary*, Carol A. Newson and Sharon H. Ringe, eds. [Louisville, KY: Westminster/John Knox Press, 1992], p. 334.)

When Paul says, "In Christ, you are all [sons] of God through faith," he means, because of the work Jesus Christ did, because he gave up his life and rose again from the dead to overcome the powers of sin and death, God's people have been granted the highest status available in the household of God: we are like "sons," and therefore we will—all of us—inherit shares in the family estate.

So Paul's analogy describing followers of Jesus Christ as "sons of God" shows what a great gift we have received from God. His analogy also tells us something about how we are to relate to others in God's household. Jesus, Paul tells us elsewhere (Col 1:15, 18), is the firstborn of creation and of all things. By analogy, that means the rest of us are Jesus' younger "brothers." Jesus receives a double portion of the inheritance from God, and we all receive equal shares. None of us is better than another, can claim higher status in God's family, or has the right to exclude another from the family.

At the same time as we rejoice in our good fortune as heirs of God's promises, we need to take a serious look at how we are doing as members of the household. Earlier in our prayer of confession, we admitted: Today we remember the times when we have not welcomed those whom you are calling into this community. We have been angry and judgmental toward those in need. We have looked past those who are too old or too young for our comfort. We have been suspicious of those whose first language is different from ours. We have ignored those who are "different from us."

As God runs the household, however, there is no need for us to try to exclude others or limit the number of heirs who will receive a share of the kingdom. God's kingdom is eternal and infinite, and no matter how many are welcomed into the household, there will always be enough of God's blessings to go around. That is why Paul says, *"There is no longer Jew or Greek, there is no longer slave or free, there is no longer male and female; for all of you are one in Christ Jesus"* (vs. 28). There is no need for distinctions; all are God's children—God's "sons"—and inheritors of the promise of eternal life. Thanks be to God!

—*Beth Ann Gaede*
ELCA pastor, editor, and writer
Minneapolis, Minnesota

June 28, 1998

4th Sunday after Pentecost (Proper 8)
RC/Pres: 13th Sunday in Ordinary Time

Lessons

Pres/Meth/UCC	2 Kings 2:1–2, 6–14	Gal 5:1, 13–25	Lk 9:51–62
Roman Catholic	1 Kings 19:16b, 19–21	Gal 5:1, 13–18	Lk 9:51–62
Episcopal	1 Kings 19:15–16, 19–21	Gal 5:1, 13–25	Lk 9:51–62
Lutheran	1 Kings 19:15–16, 19–21	Gal 5:1, 13–25	Lk 9:51–62

Introduction to the Lessons
Lesson 1
(1) *2 Kings 2:1-2, 6-14* **(Pres/Meth/UCC)**
According to biblical tradition, only two people, Enoch and Elijah, were worthy to be taken by God into heaven without dying. In this story, the power and greatness of Elijah are expressed through the miracle of ascension.

(2) *1 Kings 19:16b, 19–21* **(RC)**;
1 Kings 19:15–16, 19–21 **(Epis/Luth)**
Elijah has fled to the wilderness to escape the wrath of Jezebel, evil queen of Israel, and to seek the Lord's counsel. God finally comes to Elijah in the sound of silence. In this passage, God commands Elijah to anoint three leaders, and we witness the call of Elisha.

Lesson 2
Galatians 5:1, 13–25 **(Pres/Meth/UCC/Epis/Luth)**;
Galatians 5:1, 13–18 **(RC)**
The apostle Paul has been helping gentile Christians in Galatia think through the role of God's law for them. "You are free," Paul says, "but be careful not to abuse your freedom, for you are also called to life in the Spirit."

June 28, 1998
4th Sunday after Pentecost (Proper 8)
RC/Pres: 13th Sunday in Ordinary Time

Gospel
Luke 9:51–62 **(Pres/Meth/UCC/RC/Epis/Luth)**
Jesus, according to Luke, leaves Galilee and begins his journey to Jerusalem where he will be crucified and rise from the dead. We learn in this lesson that the way will not be easy.

Theme
Freedom in Christ gives birth to a new slavery.

Thought for the Day
"The Christian is free because he does not have to acquire salvation by his own works. But because he has already been given salvation as a gift, he is free to work it out in obedience. There is one obligation for Christians, and that is the law of love . . . 'love your neighbor as yourself.'"
—Reginald H. Fuller,
Preaching the New Lectionary: The Word of God for the Church Today,
Collegeville, MN: The Liturgical Press, 1974, pp. 46–47

Prayer of Meditation
God of grace, you heard the cries of your people when they were held in slavery in Egypt, and you chose Moses to lead them to freedom in the promised land. When all creation was groaning in anticipation of your perfect restoration, you sent your Son to set it free. And now we have been freed from the powers of sin and death by the healing blood of Jesus Christ. Show us how to live out our freedom in a spirit of love. Open our hearts to learn and do your will. In Jesus' name. Amen.

Call to Worship
    Leader: Praise the Lord!
    People: Praise the Lord, O my soul!
    Leader: The Lord sets the prisoners free;
    People: The Lord opens the eyes of the blind.
    Leader: The Lord lifts up those who are bowed down;
    People: The Lord loves the righteous.
    Leader: The Lord will reign forever!
    People: Praise the Lord!
—Adapted from Psalm 146

Prayer of Adoration

We praise you, O God, our redeemer and creator. We bless your holy name and sing your praises. You have been our companion in time of need, and with your help we begin this new week, confident that you will be at our side in times of trial and moments of rejoicing. We thank you for the gift of this community, gathered today to hear the story of your love and to learn how to love more boldly and faithfully. We know you will guide us, and for that we offer our songs of thanksgiving. We pray in Jesus' name. Amen.

Prayer of Confession

O perfect Lord, you have freed us from slavery to sin through the gift of your Son who overcame the powers of sin and death by dying on a cross and rising again in triumph. We confess to you that we have not always used your gift of freedom as you intended. We have not put the needs of our brothers and sisters before our own. We have not heeded your warnings against the works of the flesh, and we have failed to bear the fruits of the Spirit. But we belong to you, and we yearn to be guided by your Spirit. Put in us new hearts, that we might be witnesses to the world of your great love and the freedom that all people may enjoy in you. We pray in the name of your Son, Jesus. Amen.

Prayer of Dedication of Gifts and Self

Generous God, we thank you for your many gifts to us: for our physical and mental abilities, for all we need to nourish body and mind, for protection from harm and evil. We thank you for the gifts of creation: for fertile soil, clean water, and fresh air. We thank you for the people who love, guide, protect, and enjoy us. We receive all these things and more with gratitude and offer our humble praise for your overwhelming goodness. Accept now the small portion of your bounty that we have returned to you. Use these gifts to further the work of your reign on earth. Receive them also as symbols of ourselves. Use us to do your will, to love our neighbor and you. In Jesus' name. Amen.

Sermon Summary

God sent Jesus to free us from imprisonment by sin and death. We are also now free from the law. But Christian liberty does not mean we are free from all restrictions and responsibilities. We are still subject to the law of love. Freedom in Christ means the freedom to be of more service to others.

June 28, 1998
4th Sunday after Pentecost (Proper 8)
RC/Pres: 13th Sunday in Ordinary Time

Hymn of the Day

"Spirit of God, Descend upon My Heart." George Croly's words for this hymn speak to both the epistle and the gospel lessons. In Luke, Jesus rebukes those who wish to follow him but have other obligations to tend to. The "holy passion filling all our frame" in verse five is the author's plea to the Spirit to supplant our meaner yearnings described by Paul. Slow and deliberate, this hymn is often used for prayer and meditation.

Children's Object Talk

Love One Another

Object

Six feet of string with a sign saying "Love" attached in the middle.

Lesson

Love holds together brothers and sisters in Christ.

I'm going to hold on to the end of this string, and I'll have (child's name) hold the other end. Can someone read the sign in the middle of the string (wait for response). Yes, it says "love." I put that sign there because that's what the Bible tells us to do. Today it's in the Bible reading from Galatians: *"You shall love your neighbor as yourself"* (Gal 5:14).

Jesus loves (child's name). Jesus loves me. And Jesus asks (child's name) and me to love each other.

Let's see how good you are at listening today. I'm going to say some things to (child's name). If what I say is a loving thing, I want all of you to say "Yeah!" If what I say isn't a loving thing, if it is mean and selfish, I want you to say "Love your neighbor!"

Let's try one just to practice.

"(child's name), you were a great helper this morning." (Wait for the response, "Yeah!") That's right, that was a loving thing. Now here's another one.

"(child's name), I'm not going to share my toys with you." (Wait for the response "Love your neighbor!") That's right, I wasn't being very nice or generous. Let's try one more.

"(child's name), I think you're stupid." (Wait for response.) Right. I don't really think (child's name) is stupid. In fact, he's a talented and wonderful person, and that is what I should have said to him.

You are good at this game. Today and every day, let's practice loving each other by being generous and kind to one another.

—*Jeanette Strandjord*

The Sermon

The Law of Love

Hymns
Beginning of Worship: "Sing Praise to God, the Highest Good"
Sermon Hymn: "Spirit of God, Descend upon My Heart"
End of Worship: "Lord, Dismiss Us with Your Blessing"

Scripture
Galatians 5:1, 13–25 (For sermon materials on Luke 9:51–62, see the March 1998 and the *1997 May/June Planning Issue* of *The Clergy Journal*.)

Sermon Text
"For you were called to freedom, brothers and sisters; only do not use your freedom as an opportunity for self-indulgence, but through love become slaves to one another" (vs. 13).

Taylor and Erin were so-o-o excited. Dad was gong to the hospital to bring Mom and their new baby brother Joshua home. They could hardly wait! For months they had watched the preparations. Dad hauled the crib down from the attic, cleaned it *really* carefully, and went out and bought a new mattress for it. Mom let Taylor and Erin help sort and wash the baby clothes they had once worn; the clothes were so tiny! Taylor and Erin even got to decide which outfit the baby would wear home from the hospital. Finally, they were going to have a new brother. What fun!

Of course, it didn't take long for the enchantment of having a new baby in the house to wear off. Taylor and Erin would rush into the house after playing, yelling as they came in the door. "Is Joshua awake?" But too often, Joshua wasn't awake, and Mom and Dad were saying, "Sh-h-h! The baby is sleeping!" Taylor and Erin learned that having a new brother, as wonderful as it was, meant giving up some things—like playing loud music on the radio when they wanted to dance in the living room. Having a new brother meant sharing some things—like their bedroom. And since they'd gotten a new brother, Mom and Dad seemed to think Taylor and Erin should take on some new responsibilities—like clearing the table and learning to load the dishwasher, picking up their toys more often,

June 28, 1998
4th Sunday after Pentecost (Proper 8)
RC/Pres: 13th Sunday in Ordinary Time

and putting their dirty clothes next to the washing machine after they'd taken their baths each night. Certainly Joshua was a great gift to their family, but having a new brother also meant work!

We'll check back with Taylor and Erin in a few minutes, but now let's turn to our second lesson for today from the apostle Paul's letter to the Galatians. The Galatians were being bothered by people who insisted that before a Gentile could become a Christian, he or she first needed to become a Jew. Gentiles needed to keep the law of Moses, the so-called Judaizers taught, which meant among other things that men needed to be circumcised. As you can imagine, this caused quite a stir in the fledgling Christian communities, and Paul dealt with the issue forthrightly. He wrote to the Galatians, *"For freedom Christ has set us free. Stand firm, therefore, and do not submit again to the yoke of slavery . . . if you let yourselves be circumcised, Christ will be of no benefit to you"* (Gal 5:1–2).

Paul's instructions to the Galatians are quite different from those he gave the church in Corinth, which was struggling with division and disorder, primarily because some people in the community had taken the notion of freedom in Christ to quite an extreme. When Paul wrote to the Corinthians, he gave them explicit directions about a number of matters, including whether Christians should marry non-Christians, whether Christians could eat meat that had been sacrificed to idols, whether women could pray with their heads uncovered, how the community should celebrate the Lord's Supper, and what role gifts of the Spirit should play in public worship.

The guiding principle, Paul taught, is the well-being of the body of Christ. Using the analogy of the human body, Paul explained:

"But God has so arranged the body . . . that there may be no dissension within the body, but the members may have the same care for one another. If one member suffers, all suffer together with it; if one member is honored, all rejoice together with it" (1 Cor 12:25b–26).

Paul did not say anything to the Corinthians about freedom in Christ; he talked instead about doing things "decently and in order" (Gal 14:40).

When Paul wrote to the Galatians, however, he worked with a basic theme: *"For freedom Christ has set us free"* (Gal 5:1). And then he offered the new Christians more general reminders to set the limits of that freedom: *"Do not use your freedom as an opportunity for self-indulgence"* (vs. 13) and *"Live by the Spirit"* (vs. 15). Even Paul's two lists, one describing the works of the flesh and the other the fruit of the Spirit, offer only general guidance when compared to the detailed admonitions Paul laid before the Corinthians.

What are we to make of the differences between these two letters? When Paul wrote to the young churches scattered throughout the Mediterranean region, he clearly tailored his message to the needs of each community. In Corinth, things were more than a bit chaotic. There was trouble in the community, trouble stirred up by insiders who thought "freedom in Christ" meant freedom to do pretty much whatever they pleased. In Galatia, there was trouble, too, but it came from outside the community, and the Galatians were feeling abused and confused by the strange teachings being forced on them.

Both churches, however, really needed to hear the same thing: freedom in Christ is not freedom *from*; it is freedom *to*. Freedom in Christ is not freedom *from* all responsibility or concern for others. Freedom in Christ means having the liberty to enter into a more gracious way of living. Freedom in Christ is about the freedom *to* love, to live by the law of love, or as Paul says, to become slaves to one another out of love for God.

We enter this life of freedom at baptism when the Old Adam is drowned in us, and we rise again to new life. Through baptism, we cease to be slaves to the flesh, to life under the law of Moses. We become slaves to God and through God's Holy Spirit, enter into service to God.

Remember Taylor and Erin? Although they are young, they understand that Joshua, their new brother, is a gift to their family. They are also discovering that enjoying this great gift does not mean doing whatever they want with him. It means loving him—giving up some things, sharing, and being responsible, as they are able, for his well-being. For Christians, enjoying God's great gift of freedom means something similar. We live by God's law of love.

—*Beth Ann Gaede*
ELCA pastor, editor, and writer
Minneapolis, Minnesota

July 5, 1998

5th Sunday after Pentecost (Proper 9)
RC/Pres: 14th Sunday in Ordinary Time

Lessons

Pres/Meth/UCC	2 Kings 5:1–14	Gal 6:(1–6) 7–16	Lk 10:1–11, 16–20
Roman Catholic	Isa 66:10–14c	Gal 6:14–18	Lk 10:1–12, 17–20
Episcopal	Isa 66:10–16	Gal 6:(1–10) 14–18	Lk 10:1–12, 16–20
Lutheran	Isa 66:10–14	Gal 6:(1–6) 7–16	Lk 10:1–11, 16–20

Introduction to the Lessons
Lesson 1
(1) *2 Kings 5:1–14* **(Pres/Meth/UCC)**
Ministries of healing identify God's people, like the prophet Elisha. Realizing God's healing often involves humble acts of obedience in ordinary circumstances, as in the care of Naaman.

(2) *Isaiah 66:10–14c* **(RC)**;
Isaiah 66:10–16 **(Epis)**; *Isaiah 66:10–14* **(Luth)**
Israel learns that the God of love and judgment is best known in the provision of comfort for hurting, grieving people. Where God's people are found, comfort abounds.

Lesson 2
Galatians 6:(1–6) 7–16 **(Pres/Meth/UCC/Luth)**;
Galatians 6:14–18 **(RC)**; *Galatians 6:(1–10) 14–18* **(Epis)**
Followers of Christ extend to others the grace, forgiveness, and comfort that they have received from God through Christ. Christians, like the God they serve, desire good for all people.

Gospel
Luke 10:1–11, 16–20 **(Pres/Meth/UCC/Luth)**;
Luke 10:1–12, 17–20 **(RC)**; *Luke 10:1–12, 16–20* **(RC/Epis)**
The mission of Christians is to bring a message of grace and peace to a world that knows little of either. Calling people to repentance is a means of inviting people into the peaceful presence of God.

Theme
A vision of caring is inspired by Paul's call for sharing.

Thought for the Day
We fulfill God's highest expectations of us when we share one another's burdens.

Prayer of Meditation
God of all comfort, your word abounds with promises of merciful assistance from beyond ourselves, admonitions to engage in ministries of helpfulness to others, assurances of your interest in all our concerns, and stories of healing in a variety of circumstances. During this period of worship, we praise you for your comforting presence, request a personal experience of your compassion, and anticipate the benefits of healing even as we prepare ourselves to live as comforters, healers, and lovers. Amen.

Call to Worship
Let us worship the God of comfort and healing, forgiveness and redemption. As we offer God our praise and gratitude, commit to God our time and talents, and look to God for truth and direction, let us prepare to receive from God the gifts that derive from divine love.

Prayer of Adoration
Sovereign God, we bow in awe before your presence—marveling at your ability to care about all our needs without fatigue compromising your ministry; finding your patience with us amazing, especially as we acknowledge our disobedience, infidelities, and lack of penitence; failing to comprehend the breadth of your compassion or the depth of your mercy. We start to question, probe, voice our wonder. But, speech gives way to silent reverence as we wait for you to speak. Great God, we long to hear your voice and to commit ourselves to do your will. Amen.

July 5, 1998
5th Sunday after Pentecost (Proper 9)
RC/Pres: 14th Sunday in Ordinary Time

Prayer of Confession

God of merciful care, your presence delights us and prompts adoration, but also disturbs us and moves us to confession. We have tried to carry our burdens alone, buying into the myth of self-made persons. We have ignored the benefits of community and even stayed quiet about our needs when speaking with you. Forgive us, God. We need your help. We have worsened our situation at times by attempting to carry burdens we didn't have to bear—burdens resulting from needless doubts, pointless worries, insufficient trust. Forgive us, God. We long for a stronger faith. We have lived such self-absorbed days that we have ignored people around us—sometimes even those closest to us—failing even to recognize their burdens, much less offering them words of encouragement or acts of assistance. Forgive us, God. We want to be ministers of your comfort. Hear our confessions of sin. Affirm our intentions for improvement. With your help, both can be stepping stones to a life more pleasing to you and helpful to others. We speak to you in the name of Christ. Amen.

Prayer of Dedication of Gifts and Self

God, we often feel we have so little to offer as gifts of worship. Our very selves don't seem important enough to set before you in dedication. But you continue to invite our offerings. So, we give you what we have. Here are our words—use them to spread good news and bring encouragement in struggling lives. Here are our thoughts; fill them with insights into opportunities for ministry and the best methods possible for effective service. Here is our work; channel its fruits into support for the church, an extension of missions, and provisions for people who are poor. Here too is our praise; accept it as an indication of the commitment of our lives to you. We pray in the name of Christ. Amen.

Sermon Summary

Paul's admonition for us to bear one another's burdens inspires a vision regarding the basics of Christian belief, the nature of the Christian mission, and the fundamental priority of a Christian congregation.

Hymn of the Day

"Let Us Talents and Tongues Employ." Communion need not only be a solemn remembrance of Jesus' betrayal. It can also be a joyful celebration of the risen Jesus who "calls us in and sends us out" just as he did with his disciples in the story from Luke. Doreen Potter adapted a Jamaican folk tune in 1975, and then asked Fred Kaan, a president of the World Council of Churches, to write a text for it. It was first sung at the 1975 WCC Assembly in Nairobi. The tune, with its infectious melody and calypso beat, will be a favorite with young and old alike. Some hymnals add a repeat to the chorus, which allows everyone a chance to enjoy its escalating praise twice as much. Bells, drums, and handclapping can also help add life to the love of Christ as you sing.

Children's Object Talk

We Boast of the Cross of Christ

Object
A necklace with a cross on it.

Lesson
The cross tells us whom we belong to.

Do you see what I am wearing around my neck today? Yes, it's a necklace and on this necklace is a cross. Do you see any other crosses here today? (Look around your worship space and let the children point them out.)

The cross makes us think of Jesus who died for us. I wear my cross because Jesus means a lot to me. We have crosses up in the church because without Jesus dying and rising from his grave, we wouldn't have a church today. Jesus is very important to us and the church. The apostle Paul talks about that in his letter to the Galatians. He says, *"May I never boast of anything except the cross of our Lord Jesus Christ..."* (Gal 6:14).

Paul wanted you and me to know that it is because of Jesus and his death on the cross that we know God loves us. Sometimes we forget this. We can start to think that we are so good that we don't need Jesus' love and forgiveness. We might start to boast of all the things we've done like coming to church or giving our Sunday school offering. Those are good things, but they don't save us. Only Jesus who died on the cross for us can save us.

Wearing a cross necklace can be one way to remind ourselves that Jesus and his death and rising again are the things we can boast and tell other people about. Looking at the crosses in our church can be a good way to remember, too.

When you were baptized, the sign of the cross was made on your forehead. This was a way of showing how important the cross

July 5, 1998
5th Sunday after Pentecost (Proper 9)
RC/Pres: 14th Sunday in Ordinary Time

of Jesus is. As you leave to be seated today, I'll make the sign of the cross on your forehead once more. This can remind you that it is because of Jesus that we have the promise of God's love and forgiveness.

—*Jeanette Strandjord*

The Sermon

A Guiding Vision

Hymns
Beginning of Worship: "Be Now My Vision"
Sermon Hymn: "Comfort, Comfort O My People"
End of Worship: "Called as Partners in Christ's Service"

Scripture
Galatians 6:(1–6) 7–16 (For sermon materials on Luke 10:1–11, 16–20, see the March 1998 and the *1997 May/June Planning Issue* of *The Clergy Journal*.)

Sermon Text
"Bear one another's burdens, and in this way you will fulfill the law of Christ" (vs. 2).

One day in Nairobi, Kenya, truth sneaked up on me in such a manner that only later did I realize the force and substance with which it hit me. A friend of mine from South Africa closed a meeting with a prayer of benediction. He began by saying, "We thank you God for the privilege of bearing one another's burdens and thus fulfilling the law of Christ." I don't know how the prayer ended. I wasn't listening.

I knew well the inspiration for my friend's words—that verse in Galatians 6 that serves as the text for this sermon. Never before, however, had I really connected bearing other people's burdens with obedience to the law of Christ. For me, law meant prohibitions and additional burdens, not liberation and weight-eradicating love. I certainly had not considered shouldering someone else's difficulties as a privilege for which to be thankful.

The longer the opening sentence of that benediction resounded in my psyche, though, the more I began to feel that it captured the essence of Christian fellowship, the basic work of the church, and the unmistakable sign of people who have sold out to the gospel. Looking at faith from the perspective of Paul's words in Galatians 6:2 enlivens basic components of Christian belief that too often exist only as abstract affirmations. The admonition to share one another's burdens inspires a guiding vision for Christians.

The gospel really is good news. Maybe that statement strikes you as a repetition of the obvious. But a lot of people seem to feel an obligation to make the gospel bad news.

Only when we understand the gospel in a manner that causes us to say, "That's hard to believe; that's too good to be true" have we really begun to understand the gospel at all. No one can run far enough, behave badly enough, or embrace ideas wild enough to separate themselves from God's love. Grace knows no conditions. Placing "conditional" as an adjective modifying the nouns "love" and "acceptance" signals an absence of grace. To be with God is to be at home. To all who are away from home, word comes that the front door has been left open.

The gospel really is good news. The ministry of the gospel is more about laughing or crying while experiencing joy than about biting our lips while doing a duty. What could be more enjoyable than finding a woman who sees herself as unlovable and helping her to discover that she is loved with an incomprehensible love? How could time be better spent than sitting with a fellow who has become bitter about everything and introducing him to the God who can melt away bitterness and replace it with hope? Being on mission for Christ means having a good time—the happiness of seeing a person lost in life discover the way to live; the satisfaction of watching a person clad in rags put on a coat that gives warmth; the festivity of helping an individual who thought life was over discover that life is just beginning.

"Bear one another's burdens, and in this way you will fulfill the law of Christ," the Bible says. Yes. Here is a truth that inspires a true vision of ministry and mission; a vision of church.

When we think of church, Paul's words cause us to see people, all kinds of people. Church is not nearly so much about buildings, programs, budgets, buses, and meetings as about persons, particularly burdened persons.

I often think of the gathered church as a religious counterpart to that Canterbury pub described by Chaucer as a spot where pilgrims came together to swap their stories of pilgrimage. Followers of Christ regularly get together to break bread, drink

July 5, 1998
5th Sunday after Pentecost (Proper 9)
RC/Pres: 14th Sunday in Ordinary Time

wine, retell God's story, and talk to each other about successes and failures, hurts and joys, despair and hope—to cry together and laugh together, to celebrate and grieve, to unload burdens and to pick up burdens.

The church is made up of grace-filled people—individuals who have been touched by grace and who cannot sit still until all people have been touched by grace. A congregation's only hope of being church for others resides in becoming a community of grace. To want to be anything else signals a major problem. The author of the Fourth Gospel called the Christ who brings the church into existence "grace upon grace." How can the church be anything other than a community of grace? Or, how can anything that is not a community of grace be a church?

My South African friend voiced the appropriate benediction for that meeting we attended years ago. The New Testament words on which his prayer was based inspire an appropriate vision for people serious about carrying out the Christian mission and nurturing a Christian congregation. Helped by the apostle Paul, my friend prayed that we would bear each other's burdens, live by grace and with grace, and thus fulfill the law of Christ. And, imagine this, he called the bearing of one another's burdens a "privilege."

So it is. Give us that vision, O God. Grant us the joyful privilege of obeying that law.

—*C. Welton Gaddy*
Northminster Church
Monroe, Louisiana

July 12, 1998

6th Sunday after Pentecost (Proper 10)
RC/Pres: 15th Sunday in Ordinary Time

Lessons

Pres/Meth/UCC	Amos 7:7–17	Col 1:1–14	Lk 10:25–37
Roman Catholic	Deut 30:10–14	Col 1:15–20	Lk 10:25–37
Episcopal	Deut 30:9–14	Col 1:1–14	Lk 10:25–37
Lutheran	Deut 30:9–14	Col 1:1–14	Lk 10:25–37

Introduction to the Lessons
Lesson 1
(1) *Amos 7:7–17* **(Pres/Meth/UCC)**
God measures individuals and nations by the standard of the compassion and justice they extend to others.

(2) *Deuteronomy 30:10–14* **(RC);**
Deuteronomy 30:9–14 **(Epis/Luth)**
God's law is an initiative of grace given for the good of all people. Obedience to this law positively influences every aspect of life.

Lesson 2
Colossians 1:1–14 **(Pres/Meth/UCC/Epis/Luth);**
Colossians 1:15–20 **(RC)**
Meeting Christ, God's gift in whom the fullness of God dwells, results in a discovery of freedom and hope and involvement in reconciling ministry.

Gospel
Luke 10:25–37 **(Pres/Meth/UCC/RC/Epis/Luth)**
The best evidence of a person's love for God and commitment to Christ is service to people in need.

Theme
Christian love has no boundaries.

July 12, 1998
6th Sunday after Pentecost (Proper 10)
RC/Pres: 15th Sunday in Ordinary Time

Thought for the Day
Authentic Christianity involves a life of unlimited love that finds expression in compassionate service among persons in need.

Prayer of Meditation
Holy God, we have gathered eagerly to see who else is here, needing to speak with certain individuals, ready to get on with several items on our social agendas. We even know what we want to think about you, say to you, and offer to you as worship. Stop us, God. Erase our agendas. Create within us an openness to realize what you want from us and an eagerness to give you what you want. Amen.

Call to Worship
As we prepare to worship God, we hear the sound of a screaming siren in the distance and wonder who is hurting; we continue to think of a newspaper headline that nags at our consciences; we find ourselves thinking about a colleague facing big troubles. Let us not engage in worship to escape these realities. Rather, let us lay these concerns before God in worship and seek God's guidance as to how best to respond to them as God's people.

Prayer of Adoration
Great and gracious God, you have not left us alone, though we have run from you and refused to listen to your word. What mercy! You have given us laws that lead us into grace. You have provided us with prophets pointing the way beyond judgment. You have offered us counsel for every aspect of our lives. What compassion! You have insisted on holiness despite our sinfulness, encouraged us toward service amid our selfishness, showed us our potential good when everything was going bad. What inspiration! Great and gracious God, please accept our gratitude and praise. Amen.

Prayer of Confession
As difficult as it is to admit, O God, our record as your servants abounds with causes for repentance. All around us are people in a ditch of one kind or another, for one reason or another. Sometimes we have failed to see them. At other times we saw them too well, having assisted in creating their problematic predicament. Then again, we have decided we don't want to see any more people in a ditch or

have anything to do with them. We just want to take care of ourselves. You must be so disappointed in our careless behavior and compassionless attitude. Like the priest in Jesus' story, we have hurried to times of formal worship instead of pausing to do the work of redemption. Like the Levite in Jesus' story, we have been so eager to enjoy the spiritual music of Zion that we have turned away from sobs and moans emanating from social ditches. Like the Samaritan in Jesus' story . . . God, we have not done much at all like the Samaritan. Please forgive us. And help us do better. We pray in the name of Christ. Amen.

Prayer of Dedication of Gifts and Self
Giving God, we want to give after the manner in which we have received from you. You give us wealth; we give thanks to you and respect to all your creation. You give us care; we dedicate ourselves to care for all for whom you care. You give us law; we commit ourselves to give obedience to your guidance. You give us grace; we devote ourselves to support nothing less than justice in our society, pressing always toward mercy. You give us material goods; we pledge to live as responsible stewards. You give us love and lift us from ditches; we commit ourselves to live in love and assist persons in need wherever we find them. You give us Christ; we give ourselves to him and our efforts to making him known to all people. We speak to you in his name. Amen.

Sermon Summary
Jesus' parable of the good Samaritan presents three different philosophies of stewardship and service. Only one of them, though, characterizes the life of a follower of Christ—a philosophy of generous sharing that finds joy in offering help to needy persons. According to Jesus, such unselfish service defines an individual who has experienced the gift of eternal life.

Hymn of the Day
"O, for a Thousand Tongues to Sing." Jesus' response to the lawyer in the lections for this Sunday inspired the choice of this Charles Wesley classic for today: "You shall love the Lord your God with all your heart, all your soul, with all your strength and all your mind." This hymn gives fine voice to that endeavor. The first line that has since become the popular title was a declaration made by Peter Bohler, a Moravian pastor, that "Had I a thousand tongues, I would praise him

July 12, 1998
6th Sunday after Pentecost (Proper 10)
RC/Pres: 15th Sunday in Ordinary Time

with them all." Bohler's comment was overheard and written into verse by Wesley. This hymn has had the privilege of being the first entry in every edition of the Methodist hymnal ever since. When written in 1739, it ran to eighteen stanzas. John Wesley (and countless other editors) have since distilled the text to its present form.

Children's Object Talk

Mercy

Object
   A piece of tagboard with the word "Mercy" printed on it.
Lesson
   Jesus calls us to show mercy to our neighbors.

In the Bible, Jesus asks us to show mercy to other people. I printed that word "mercy" on this tagboard so you could see it. (hold up board) It is a very important word.

Let's think about this word "mercy." Can you tell me some of the meanings it has (wait for responses). Thank you. In the Bible, Jesus tells us a story that also helps us know what mercy means.

Jesus tells the story of the good Samaritan. The Samaritan was a man from the country of Samaria. One day he was traveling out in the countryside, and he saw another man lying on the ground. This man was very badly hurt. He had been beaten up and robbed. He was cut and bleeding. He wasn't a Samaritan, but a Jew from the country of Judea.

The Samaritan didn't know the man who was hurt. They weren't even from the same country, but the Samaritan went over and helped the hurt man from Judea. He covered his cuts with bandages and took the man to a place where he could rest and get well. The Samaritan didn't even know this man, and he helped to save his life!

Jesus wants you and me to be people of mercy. The story of the good Samaritan tells us that mercy means helping people. We share our food, our medicine, and our money so that people get what they need in order to live. We share with people whom we have only met once, and we may not even know their names. We share with people even if they are from another country or another part of the world.

"Mercy" (hold up tagboard) is a small word, but it gives us lots of sharing and helping to do.

—*Jeanette Strandjord*

The Sermon

Love without Limits

Hymns
Beginning of Worship: "Awake, Awake to Love and Work"
Sermon Hymn: "They Asked, 'Who's My Neighbor?'"
End of Worship: "From the Crush of Wealth and Power"

Scripture
Luke 10:25–37 (For additional sermon materials on this passage, see the *1997 May/June Planning Issue* and on Colossians 1:1–14, see the March 1998 issue of *The Clergy Journal*.)

Sermon Text
"... 'Go and do likewise'" (vs. 37).

Religion seems passionately devoted to minimums. Not Christianity, though. Jesus persistently moved people's focus from minimum requirements to maximum opportunities. The core of Jesus' life and ethic consisted of boundless love, not limited legislation. Nowhere is Jesus' insistence on love transcending law more apparent than in his story about how to treat a man in a ditch when the man is not "one of our kind."

"What must I do to receive eternal life?" That question from a lawyer prompted the unraveling of Jesus' familiar parable. Don't miss the point of the question—insistence on a legal definition; a desire for a law about salvation, a system of religion, a carefully prescribed scheme of service.

Jesus answered the lawyer's question, but his answer elevated the discussion to a completely different level than that on which the question had been asked. The lawyer inquired about a law. Jesus responded with a statement about love—love for God and the love inevitably present when love for God is real; that is, love for neighbor. The legalist was both dissatisfied and insistent, as legalists most always are. He wanted a legal definition of faith, a statement of the minimum requirement for being right with God, and he wasn't about to settle for a commendation of love. "Who is my neighbor?" he demanded to know. "Give me a rule."

Once again, Jesus raised the issue to a higher level of concern. This is when he told the story we know so well.

July 12, 1998
6th Sunday after Pentecost (Proper 10)
RC/Pres: 15th Sunday in Ordinary Time

Jesus spoke about a man whom thieves brutally attacked and left lying in a ditch half-dead. In subsequent hours, at least three different people passed that way. Two of them were only half-alive. The priest and the Levite who saw the victim of the crime knew he had problems. But, so did they. Each hurried along.

We best not be too judgmental here. Our maxims for health and happiness include the counsel, "Don't pick up hitchhikers"; "Watch out for people who look hurt"; and "If it's not in your job description, don't do it." Most of us have passed by someone in a ditch.

The hero in Jesus' story was a Samaritan, a fact that undoubtedly dropped the jaws of Jewish listeners and raised their eyebrows. What did a Samaritan have to do with eternal life or neighborliness? Everybody hated Samaritans. It was as if Jesus had made a hero of an Iranian or a Saddam Hussein soldier in the militia of Iraq.

A traveling Samaritan saw a robbery victim in a ditch and stopped to help. Like his fellow travelers, the priest and the Levite, this man also had problems of his own. But, his compassion for the hurting man took precedence over everything else. So he helped.

The conclusion to Jesus' story frustrated his legal inquisitor even more. Two questions were on the table: How do you get eternal life, and who is my neighbor? Jesus had not touched on either one of them, or at least it seemed that way to the lawyer. Jesus had responded to a request for a law with a story of love. He had answered an inquiry about requirements for eternal life with an illustration of compassion. Jesus described the life of faith not in terms of stern obedience to a prescription, but as a joyful response to personal needs. Jesus addressed the lawyer's interest in narrowing religion by broadening faith.

Through the years, various interpreters of this parable have seen within it three different perspectives on life. None of the three is original with me, but all of them are still very much with us.

The thieves in Jesus' story operated by the philosophy of *what's yours is mine; I'll take it.* Of course, this attitude is not confined to thugs. You can find it in office suites as well as along dangerous roads. Practitioners of this philosophy dress in business clothes as well as soiled rags.

Our society commends the dangerous mentality, *Anything I can get is mine.* Everything is for the taking. Clearly immoral business deals hide behind what is legal. Defenders of such practices tell critics, "That's just the way things are. Welcome to reality."

The priest and the Levite operated by the philosophy of

what's mine is mine; I'll keep it. Give them the benefit of the doubt—each had important things to do. Most people understand that situation. Helping another person takes time and effort. Besides, these two didn't have much to give. When you start to help someone, you never know where it may end up. It's difficult to get out of a situation once you are in it. It's probably best just to take care of your own business and let everyone else fend for themselves.

We're talking about religious people here. Theologically, the priest and the Levite wanted to see the hurting man saved; they just didn't want to help him. They could pray, "God have mercy on this man's soul," but they were not about to touch his bleeding body or comfort his troubled spirit, not even in God's name. *What's mine is mine; I'll keep it.*

Thank God for Samaritans. The Samaritan in Jesus' story lived by the philosophy of *what's mine is God's; I'll share it.* Need called forth uncalculating compassion from this man. Business concerns gave way to bountiful care. The Samaritan did what the hurting man's needs required him to do, not what he was expected to do or obligated to do.

Right here the lawyer's interest in eternal life and Jesus' story about love intersected. Boundaries, minimums, and requirements are not the issue in a relationship with God. The question of discipleship is not "what must I do?" Opportunities define our journeys. "What can I do?" is the question we are always trying to answer. *What's mine is God's; I'll share it.*

Jesus' story does not contain a new definition of neighborliness or a refined law of discipleship. Some would say Jesus never even answered the lawyer's question about eternal life. But he did. Jesus described eternal life as a quality of life dominated by love and characterized by generous sharing. The whole point of Jesus' discussion is love without limits.

Jesus did not challenge us to do as the Samaritan did, but to compassionately meet the needs presented to us. "You," Jesus said to all who heard the parable, "You go, then, and do the same."

—*C. Welton Gaddy*
Northminster Church
Monroe, Louisiana

July 19, 1998

7th Sunday after Pentecost (Proper 11)
RC/Pres: 16th Sunday in Ordinary Time

Lessons

Pres/Meth/UCC	Amos 8:1–12	Col 1:15–28	Lk 10:38–42
Roman Catholic	Gen 18:1–10a	Col 1:24–28	Lk 10:38–42
Episcopal	Gen 18:1–10a (10b–14)	Col 1:21–29	Lk 10:38–42
Lutheran	Gen 18:1–10a	Col 1:15–28	Lk 10:38–42

Introduction to the Lessons
Lesson 1
(1) *Amos 8:1–12* (**Pres/Meth/UCC**)
Not even liturgical acts of corporate worship can prevent desolation among people who fail to practice mercy.

(2) *Genesis 18:1–10a* (**RC/Luth**);
Genesis 18:1–10a (10b–14) (**Epis**)
Hospitality, even to strangers, is a crucial sign of faithful devotion to God.

Lesson 2
Colossians 1:15–28 (**Pres/Meth/UCC/Luth**);
Colossians 1:24–28 (**RC**); *Colossians 1:21–29* (**Epis**)
Jesus reveals the comprehensive love of God that reaches out to embrace all people even through suffering.

Gospel
Luke 10:38–42 (**Pres/Meth/UCC/RC/Epis/Luth**)
Serving God sometimes requires patient listening and learning in one's own life prior to working for good in the lives of others.

Theme
"But the Lord is in his holy temple; let all the earth keep silence before him!" (Hab 2:20).

Thought for the Day
Silently listening to God is as important in the service of God as speaking and acting on behalf of God.

Prayer of Meditation
Our response to almost any situation is "What can I do?" Doing is our middle name. Even now we are having trouble settling down, stilling our bodies and our spirits, quieting our thought and words, agreeing to wait in your presence and become recipients of gifts we can never earn or achieve by ourselves. Prepare us for worship, O God. Help us be still; really still. Help us, God. Amen.

Call to Worship
Most of us have spent the days of the preceding week on the run: keeping engagements, answering phone calls, doing correspondence, juggling family schedules. Stress has been our constant companion, if not our friend. Now it is time to stop racing, internally and externally. I call you to stillness, quietness, and rest. Take a deep breath or let out a long sigh if that will help you. Center on the majesty and mystery of the spiritual life. Prepare to meet God and worship God.

Prayer of Adoration
You know us so well, God. You know our weaknesses and idiosyncrasies as well as our strengths and common traits. You know enough about us to turn away from us with good reason, to give up on a relationship with us with justification, to cease any expectations of our potential for service in the realm of your rule. Yet, you continue to love us, to reach out to us, to call us, to demonstrate a desire to use us for good purposes. You are truly the essence of love and grace, O God. We admire you as we adore you. We like you as well as love you. We want to serve you as well as to enjoy being in your presence. Amen.

Prayer of Confession
God of grace, you instructed your servant Habakkuk to be still and know you as if being still and knowing you are related. We are beginning to understand that relationship. Honestly, we don't know you better because we have not been still, quiet enough to hear your voice, attentive enough to nurture your presence among us, watchful

July 19, 1998
7th Sunday after Pentecost (Proper 11)
RC/Pres: 16th Sunday in Ordinary Time

enough to catch a sign of your will, thoughtful enough to ponder your ways, prayerful enough to attempt communication with you, trustful enough to venture in faith. Staying terribly busy is our choice as well as our necessity. It delivers us from opportunities for caring and saves us from the demands of intimacy. Relationships with our families and friends suffer even as does our relationship with you. Forgive us, God. Save us from an inflated view of self-importance. Deliver us from a messianic identity. Slow us down. Let us learn again, and grow again, and love again that we might live as your people. Amen.

Prayer of Dedication of Gifts and Self

God, whom we worship, when we think of making an offering, we think of money—giving a tithe, making a financial contribution, supporting a church budget, funding a missions enterprise. In a way, this is so easy that it hardly seems a significant act of worship. Besides, we get tax credits for these gifts. When we think of offering you our time, we get in touch with the quality of our dedication. It's difficult to find time to worship even one hour per week. How can we do spiritual reading, engage in Bible study, practice meditation, and offer prayers? There are just so many hours in a day. Though we would like to think we could buy you off with a financial contribution, we know you want from us the kind of personal maturation and spiritual development that take time. O God, with fear and trembling, with hesitancy and a request for help, we dedicate to you our time—not an hour here and there—but all of it. We lay our calendars on the altar. Show us how to live. Teach us how to redeem the time we dedicate to you. Amen.

Hymn of the Day

"Immortal, Invisible, God Only Wise." God's wisdom so often turns human convention on its head, as Mary and Martha find when Jesus invites them to listen to him rather than attend to the household. The Colossians passage evokes the sense of mystery of God's hand as wisdom in the word is revealed for the people. Walter Smith's hymn captures perfectly both the futility of our own wisdom and the overarching grace of God that pierces our darkness. Smith was minister in the Free Church of Scotland in 1867 when he wrote these verses. It was reputed to be a favorite of Queen Elizabeth II, and was the first hymn sung at the service in honor of her sixtieth birthday in 1986.

Children's Object Talk

Never Too Old to Learn

Object

A Bible and a picture of Jesus.

Lesson

We learn from Jesus.

Can any of you guess how old I am? (wait for guesses) Those are all good guesses. I am _____ years old. That is a lot of years and means I've had time to learn many things. I've learned how to read. Some of you have learned that too. I've had time to learn about mathematics and science. Some of you are learning to count and add numbers too.

There are other things to learn as well. I've had to learn about being good to other people and helping them. I've had to learn about telling the truth and being honest. I've had to learn about God and Jesus. That's a lot to learn, and I'm still learning. Now, here's who has been my very best teacher (hold up the picture of Jesus). It's Jesus. When I read about Jesus and what he says in the Bible (hold up picture and the Bible), I learn how much God loves me and wants me to help and care for others.

There's a woman named Mary in a story from the Bible who knows how important it is to learn from Jesus. She takes time to sit by Jesus and listen to him. Jesus is very glad she does. Her sister Martha is too busy to sit by Jesus and listen to him. Jesus tells Martha not to work so hard and to sit down, relax, and listen.

Sometimes, we can get too busy too. We're like Martha, hurrying around trying to do lots of things. We get busy watching TV, playing baseball, and having fun. We get busy drawing and we don't take time to listen to and learn from Jesus. We might even think we are too busy to come to church or Sunday school.

You and I are still learning no matter what age we are. Jesus tells us to take time to listen to him. He will teach us through the Bible, through Sunday school, and church. He's a great teacher.

—*Jeanette Strandjord*

July 19, 1998
7th Sunday after Pentecost (Proper 11)
RC/Pres: 16th Sunday in Ordinary Time

The Sermon

Silent Listening as a Spiritual Discipline

Hymns
Beginning of Worship: "Hear the Voice of God, So Tender"
Sermon Hymn: "How Deep the Silence of the Soul"
End of Worship: "O Savior, Let Me Walk with You"

Scripture
Luke 10:38-42 (For additional sermon materials on this passage, see the *1997 May/June Planning Issue* and on Colossians 1:15-28, see the March 1998 issue of *The Clergy Journal*.)

Sermon Text
"The Lord answered her, 'Martha, Martha, you are anxious and troubled about many things; one thing is needful. Mary has chosen the good portion...'" (vss. 41-42).

During a meeting of a worship committee one evening, a committee member mused aloud, "We need more silence in our services." "How much silence do you want?" I asked. The response surprised me, "At least three minutes." In my mind I hurriedly calculated the implications of that expanse of silence: what will we do about the radio broadcast, how will we handle extraneous noises, will people be uncomfortable? Suddenly I realized that I was reacting negatively to the possibility of more silence in worship when I actually appreciate silence, and at times really long for it. At that point, I let down my defenses and joined in the committees's plans to implement a three-minute period of silence during a Sunday morning worship service.

My reaction to the possibility of silence probably differs little from most people's response to silence in general. We don't have time for it. Or, we run from it. Witness our noisy world.

My experience with that committee member also brings to mind the gospel story of Jesus' visit to the house of Martha and Mary. What an opportunity for spending time with Jesus. However, Martha stayed so busy working, clanging pots and pans, and talking as a part of her commitment to serve Jesus that she could not abide the stillness and silence that would allow her to enjoy Jesus' presence and learn from his wisdom. Martha even became perturbed at her sister Mary for sitting silently at Jesus' feet.

Taken in the house of Mary and Martha, that gospel snapshot with Jesus in the center of it preserves a profoundly important truth. Quiet, still, listening is a spiritual discipline every bit as important as the spiritual responsibilities of speaking and acting. Indeed, if there are not periods of listening, speaking loses substance and acting gives way to fatigue.

To be sure, not all silence qualifies as a spiritual blessing. Welcomed silence may be golden, while the silence of weak evasion is just plain yellow. The silence of a graveyard differs from the silence of a greenhouse. The silence that pervades a room filled with Quakers at worship is nowhere near the same as the silence that hangs over a room filled with tired sleepers.

Silence that qualifies as a spiritual discipline conveys grace, nurtures the soul, and enriches the spirit. It is a silence pregnant with positive spiritual potential. It is the silence that surrounds and pervades being in the presence of God and listening carefully to all God says.

Revelations often go unrecognized because of the loud hurry scurry of innumerable Marthas so bent on doing, they develop spirits unreceptive to listening. Subsequently, they fail to hear, see, or feel the unique amid the constant drumbeats of the familiar. Think of the spiritual implications of that tragic reality.

Listening requires silence. If we can't be silent, we can't listen to ourselves, to each other, or to God. The rumblings of our souls go unnoticed amid our persistence in speaking. Then, out of touch with ourselves, we fragment. Our minds and wills, our convictions and emotions work at cross purposes. In an arena filled with noise, we speak and act in ways that contradict the fundamental beliefs that reside in the depths of our spirits. To be whole, we must find time to be silent.

The issue of silence is bigger than individual concerns, however: more than a matter of personal wholeness and mental health. Silence allows God to sensitize us to society and community. If we are to hear what goes on around us, there must be silence—a hush—within us.

Confucius likened language to a wheel. The spokes, he said, hold the structure together; they are the syntax. But the empty spaces—the silent moments—convey the essence of what is said. How well can we, do we, hear the silence?

Of course, where silence becomes acutely critical is in our relationship with God. Mother

July 19, 1998
7th Sunday after Pentecost (Proper 11)
RC/Pres: 16th Sunday in Ordinary Time

Teresa called God "the friend of silence." Hearing God and speaking for God require long stretches of silence.

Martha was not the only biblical character who had trouble being still enough and quiet enough to hear the divine voice. An Old Testament prophet named Habakkuk longed to hear God speak. But he kept talking, complaining, demanding, questioning. Finally, word came to Habakkuk, "The Lord is in his holy temple; let all the earth keep silence before God." Stated another way, "Habakkuk, if you want to hear God speak, get quiet." Jesus' comment rushes into our consciousness, *"Martha, Martha, you are anxious and troubled about many things; one thing is needful. Mary has chosen the good portion which shall not be taken away from her."* Remember, Mary was sitting quietly listening to Jesus speak.

If we are to hear the counsel of God, we have to emulate the spiritual posture of Mary, stilling the activities and noises that distract our attention and clog our minds. Silence serves as a channel of divine revelation. Silence ministers to our health and wholeness and draws us into the reality of grace.

Like other spiritual disciplines, the practice of silence requires a measure of faith. Faith allows us to give up on sounds: rationalizations of our behavior, explanations of our actions, boasts of our accomplishments, declarations of our intent to follow Jesus, recitals of our achievements, confessions of our sins. Faith allows us to give up on sounds and to give in to the silence in which we, like Mary, learn from Jesus how to encounter God.

The silence of which I speak is not the same as thinking about silence, learning about silence, or talking about silence. It is silence —a cosmic hush, a quiet akin to that which preceded the first moment of creation; silence.

Can we be quiet enough to hear God amid the cacophony of sounds that fill our days? Can we incorporate into our lives a hush that nurtures our faith in Christ and strengthens our spirits? To grow as the people of God, we simply must know and experience in our lives the discipline of quiet listening, patient waiting in silence as practiced by Mary.

Not only does silence convey the will of God, the counsel of God; to us, sometimes silence *is* God's will, God's counsel. Sometimes silence is the whole of God's response to us and ministry for us.

—*C. Welton Gaddy*
Northminster Church
Monroe, Louisiana

July 26, 1998

8th Sunday after Pentecost (Proper 12)
RC/Pres: 17th Sunday in Ordinary Time

Lessons

Pres/Meth/UCC	Hosea 1:2–10	Col 2:6–15 (16–19)	Lk 11:1–13
Roman Catholic	Gen 18:20–32	Col 2:12–14	Lk 11:1–13
Episcopal	Gen 18:20–32	Col 2:6–15	Lk 11:1–13
Lutheran	Gen 18:20–32	Col 2:6–15 (16–19)	Lk 11:1–13

Introduction to the Lessons

Lesson 1

(1) *Hosea 1:2–10* **(Pres/Meth/UCC)**
Not even rank infidelity causes a cessation of God's redemptive love.

(2) *Genesis 18:20–32* **(RC/Epis/Luth)**
God wills and patiently works for good, not evil, for all people.

Lesson 2
Colossians 2:6–15 (16–19) **(Pres/Meth/UCC/Luth)**;
Colossians 2:12–14 **(RC)**; *Colossians 2:6–15* **(Epis)**
The only restriction on Christians is to live out of faith in Christ. But that restriction is a form of freedom.

Gospel
Luke 11:1–13 **(Pres/Meth/UCC/RC/Epis/Luth)**
Individual communication with God about all of life is an important part of the communion that God desires from and seeks with all people.

Theme
Learning the nature and importance of prayer.

Thought for the Day
Communion with God is a vital part of every person's spiritual life.

July 26, 1998
8th Sunday after Pentecost (Proper 12)
RC/Pres: 17th Sunday in Ordinary Time

Prayer of Meditation

Loving God, we identify with the disciples who said to Jesus, "Teach us to pray." Even as we speak to you now, we want to know more about how best to communicate with you that we might sense communion with you pervading our days. In these moments of worship, increase our awareness of ways to deepen our relationship with you. Amen.

Call to Worship

We gather as pursued people. Our creator refuses to give up on us or turn away from us. Even when we have run from God, God has followed us with patient compassion. God's love for us has never ceased. God's grace abounds to this hour. Let us now become aware of the one who takes delight in our well-being, and give to that one worship befitting the wonder and work of holy ministry.

Prayer of Adoration

You are amazing, God, truly amazing. Your majesty overwhelms us and makes us aware of distance between us. Then your desire for intimacy relaxes us and makes us feel at home in your presence. Your expectations for us cause us to think of rules and regulations to be kept. Then your assurance of grace prompts a celebration of freedom and instills a sense of confidence. Your dislike for evil fills us with guilt because we do business with evil on a daily basis. Then your offer of forgiveness lightens the burdens of our wrongdoing, draws us to repentance, and promises us a better future. You are amazing, God, truly amazing. Amen.

Prayer of Confession

O God, you refuse to allow anything to come between us. Not even betrayal and infidelity cause you to give up on us and withhold salvation from us. Why must we be so harshly judgmental, meanly resentful, and sadly hurtful toward other people? Forgive us for not relating to others as you relate to us. O God, you will good for all of us. You want us to enjoy health and happiness, joy in our public and private lives, growth as persons and families. Why do we get such a delight in seeing others fail? Why do we enjoy spreading gossip that inflicts hurt on people so much like ourselves? What gives us pleasure when we see acquaintances struggling with problems from which we are free at the time? Forgive us, God, for not relating to others as you relate to us. We need help and we request it in the name of the one who teaches us to pray. Amen.

Prayer of Dedication of Gifts and Self
From the prayer of Jesus we get insights into the content of the dedication appropriate to you, O God. We give you our words to hallow your name. We devote our behavior to demonstrating the nature of your rule. We dedicate our wills to the implementation of your will. We commit our possessions to assisting other people in your name: sharing daily bread, providing shelter, offering clothes. We devote our vision to seeing the world community in a manner that causes us to speak more of "our" and less of "me" and "mine." We dedicate our consciences to the end that, with your help, we can defeat temptation and avoid doing evil. We commit the content of our days to recognizing and helping others to recognize your sovereignty and love, your glory forever. Amen.

Sermon Summary
The substance of authentic praying consists of faithful loving. Learning to pray to God is not about learning proper words and forms, following specific rules, and repeating prescribed phrases. Learning to pray to God is about falling in love with God and speaking whatever can be spoken out of that love.

Hymn of the Day
"Standing in the Need of Prayer." An African-American spiritual popularized by the great Mahalia Jackson, "Standing in the Need of Prayer" was written by the eminent composer James Weldon Johnson and appeared in the landmark hymnal, *The Book of American Negro Spirituals*. The hymn fits well with Jesus' discourse on how to pray in the Luke passage for today, and can be sung responsively led by a choir or soloist. Like many spirituals, this wonderful hymn adds personal humility to piety while speaking straight to the heart of the human condition.

July 26, 1998
8th Sunday after Pentecost (Proper 12)
RC/Pres: 17th Sunday in Ordinary Time

Children's Object Talk

Big Prayers

Object
None.
Lesson
Jesus teaches us to ask God for whatever we need.

Today I'd like us to think about saying our prayers. What are some times during the day that we pray our prayers? (Wait for responses such as before we eat or at bedtime.)

Yes, those are all important times when we talk to God. Here's a bedtime prayer I learned when I was your age. It starts like this, "Now I lay me down to sleep . . ." Have you heard that prayer before? In this prayer we're asking God to care for us and keep us safe through the night. That's a good thing to ask God, and God does promise to watch over us.

Here's another prayer we pray both at home and at church, "Our Father, who art in heaven . . ." We'll pray that prayer together today during worship. Jesus taught us that prayer. It is called the Lord's Prayer because our Lord Jesus taught it to us.

The Lord's Prayer is a very big prayer. It doesn't just ask God to watch over us at night. It asks for even more. It asks that God's kingdom might come. That means we're asking God to bring us his love and peace and make everything perfect the way God wants it to be. We are praying that our whole world will be perfect. No more sickness, or pain, or fighting, or dying. Wow!

Jesus tells you and me to pray big prayers like this. God is ready to listen to them and wants to give us every good thing.

Let's pray a big prayer right now: Dear God, your kingdom come. Help us to love each other. Let there be peace and no more war. Give us everything we need in life. In Jesus' name. Amen.

—*Jeanette Strandjord*

The Sermon

Enough Said

Hymns
Beginning of Worship: "By Whatever Name We Call You"
Sermon Hymn: "Out of the Depths I Call"
End of Worship: "Great Is Your Faithfulness"

Scripture
Luke 11:1–13 (For additional sermon materials on this passage, see the *1997 May/June Planning Issue* of *The Clergy Journal* and on Colossians 2:6–15 [16–19], see the March 1998 issue of *The Clergy Journal*.)

Sermon Text
"He said to them, 'When you pray, say: Father...'" (vs. 2).

Speaking honestly about prayer usually results in confessing difficulties with praying and identifying problems with knowing how to pray. Even individuals who claim that prayers come easily admit the occasional advent of troubling times when praying seems difficult and receiving answers to prayers virtually impossible. Who of us has not been there?

Moments arrive when we open our mouths to speak a needed confession, to announce an expected profession, or to plead for mercy regarding a problematic situation and nothing happens. Words fail to take shape or sound. A vacuous aridness seems to have replaced all spiritual resourcefulness with us. Both our mouths and our souls are deathly silent.

Anyone who identifies with this predicament can discover a great help in Jesus' words illustrative of the practice of prayer. A later comment from the apostle Paul strengthens our sense of the importance of what we discover in Jesus' words.

Luke probably contains the more ancient text of Jesus' model prayer. The writer of the Third Gospel replaces Matthew's "Our Father in heaven" with the simple assertion, "Father" (see Mt 6:9).

Set alongside the Lucan text this observation from Paul: *"For the Spirit that God has given you does not make you slaves and cause you to be afraid; instead the Spirit makes you God's children, and by the Spirit's power we cry out to God, 'Father!'* [the word is *Abba*] *'my Father!'"* (Rom 8:15).

Both the model prayer from Jesus and Paul's comment about prayer convey a promise about prayer that prods us toward freedom in praying.

Immediately our prayers are freed from a dependency upon words. Jesus was teaching his disciples to pray, not prescribing a specific prayer mandated to be repeated. Jesus pointed his followers toward a type of communication with God rather than demanded an incorporation of special words and specific phrases in every prayer. Jesus offered a model of intimate communication with God, not a spiritual creed or a magical formula for effective prayer. Though we can recite the actual words voiced by Jesus with

July 26, 1998
8th Sunday after Pentecost (Proper 12)
RC/Pres: 17th Sunday in Ordinary Time

great benefit, no real value exists in this repetition.

Authentic prayer cannot be reduced to a formula dependent upon certain kinds of words, particular constructions of words, or a specific number of words. God invites communication from us that contains our own words and conveys our own spirit.

Gerhard Ebeling helped me to see that no other word in Jesus' prayer equals in significance the first word, "Father," a term important because of its communication of intimacy, not because of an emphasis upon masculinity. In a sense, everything that follows in Jesus' prayer is present from its start, inherent in the exclamation, "Father." As a matter of fact, a person who cannot at least begin with "Father" may not be able to get through the remainder of the prayer. Jesus' prayer frees us from a dependency upon words.

Also apparent in Jesus' prayer is a promise that frees us from anxiety about God hearing prayers. If we take our concerns to a loving God, worries about God hearing our prayers are needless. How would a loving father or mother not hear the pleas of one of their children? God's attentiveness to our prayers is assumed, presumed.

Keep in mind Paul's comment about the work of the Spirit in our prayers. If in unconditional honesty our desire to communicate with God gets only as far as the utterance, "Father," whether through the formation of words that audibly leave our mouths or in the silence given expression by the ministry of the Spirit, enough has been said. Should we be unable to say more, saying "Father" is enough. The very presence of God's Spirit who helps us say "Father" gives evidence of God's attentiveness to us.

Apparent now is liberation from any preoccupation with the mechanics of prayer. Look again at Jesus' words in the model prayer. Notice the absence of logistical instructions. We fret far too much over peripheral matters: Is my posture of prayer correct? Should I sit, stand, or kneel when I pray? How did my voice sound? Did I convey a prayerful tone?

Prayer is intimate communion with God. The only rule for such prayer is that there are no rules. We pray to God as sons and daughters of the one to whom we speak, the one whom we love with all our hearts, souls, and minds. Most crucial in an intimate relationship is not an appropriate posture, a prescribed format of speech, or a special voice-inflection, but freedom—the freedom of a child to approach a sensitive, compassionate, trustworthy parent in complete honesty and vulnerability. Liberation from a concern for mechanics appropriate to prayer allows prayer to become all that it can be at any given moment, focusing on God, not on the logistics of our approach to God.

Luke provides an intriguing word-picture of prayer and a prayer, the portrait of a stammering child humbly, honestly, and lovingly reaching out to a caring parent. God's Spirit enables us to speak as our own the confession most characteristic of Jesus' relationship with God—"*Abba*, Father." These are the words of a child. The whole intent of placing the Aramaic "*Abba*" redundantly alongside the Greek word for "father" is to convey the informal, yet intimate repetition of intimacy—"Daddy, Daddy."

Remember, not a hint of sexist chauvinism belongs here, no suggestion of male-oriented elitism in spirituality. The point is intimacy. Prayer is communion between entities in love with each other; communion akin to a conversation between a caring parent and a responsive child.

Sometimes, when we need to speak to God, words fail us. Occasions arise when we simply cannot articulate what we feel. In certain situations, faith weakens. Huge expanses of time elapse when the heavens seem silent, and we are silent.

At such times, all we know for sure about prayer is that we need to pray. However, prescribed forms for prayer strike us as irrelevant and disciplined declarations of prayer as ineffective. What are we to do? Quit praying? No. This is the very point at which recognizing prayer as a loving relationship with God and welcoming the ministry of God's Spirit in nurturing that relationship are so crucial. As best we can, we mutter or think, "Father."

Perhaps we wish we could say more, though we know we do not have to say more. However, the entirety of Jesus' model prayer is enveloped in that one magnificent term of intimacy with which it begins. As long as we address God, God understands us, and our groping for conviction, our struggles with temptation, our pursuit of the heavenly realm, our need for physical provisions. We speak, audibly or silently, with a relationship of intimacy. We are accepted and understood. The very fact that we can say "Father" means that God's Spirit is within us and God's love is around us.

Maybe a time will come when we can say more to God in our prayers—much more. Take heart, though. To be able to address God at all is sufficient. To say "Father" is to say enough.

—*C. Welton Gaddy*
Northminster Church
Monroe, Louisiana

Appendices

Resources for Preparing to Preach

by Dr. David H. Schmidt

The following bibliography offers one person's review of commentaries and overviews that a pastor might consult as she or he prepares the sermon. The first sections cover books that can be used all three years of the Revised Common Lectionary. These are followed by comments about books for the portions of the lectionary covered in this manual. They are grouped by gospels, then epistles, and, finally, Old Testament. An effort is made to include some of the new commentaries coming on the market as well as some standard works that time has shown to be helpful to pastors. In addition, a few of the burgeoning software resources are included as more and more pastors are joining the computer generation.

One-volume Commentaries

Several one-volume commentaries can be used throughout the three-year cycle. *Harper's Bible Commentary*, James L. Mays, gen. ed. (Harper & Row, 1988), published in cooperation with the Society of Biblical Literature, provides good, brief information that reflects the current state of scholarship. There are good overview articles, as well as comments on each book (including the Apocrypha). A second current one-volume work is that of Raymond E. Brown, et al., *The New Jerome Biblical Commentary*, rev. ed. (Paulist Press, 1989). While Roman Catholic in origin, it is a valuable tool for all. Both of these works are now available on a *Logos Bible Software 2.0* CD-ROM, along with *Matthew Henry's Commentary* and the *Bible Knowledge Commentary*.*

Logos Research Systems also makes available the *Harper's Bible Dictionary*. They have recently prepared Doubleday's *Anchor Bible Dictionary* to work with their system. Several software companies provide the *Holman Bible Dictionary* and/or others with some of their packages.

---

*The Logos referred to here is not Logos Productions Inc., publisher of this book, but Logos Research Systems. You may order software by calling them at 1-800-875-6467, or by contacting them through their web page, www.logos.com.

Study of the Psalter
Years A, B, and C

Overviews and Theology

H. J. Kraus' *Theology of the Psalms* (Augsburg, 1986) is a good discussion by a scholar who has also published a major commentary (below). A brief introductory work is Klaus Seybold's *Introducing the Psalms* (T & T Clark, 1990). For a work that invites looking at the Psalms in a new way, see J. David Pleius' *The Psalms: Songs of Tragedy, Hope, and Justice,* The Bible & Liberation (Orbis, 1993). For personal enrichment one might try Donald E. Collins' *Like Trees That Grow Beside a Stream: Praying through the Psalms* (Upper Room, 1991).

Commentaries

H. J. Kraus' *Psalms 1–59* and *Psalms 60–150* (Augsburg, 1987, 1989) is now a standard work full of detail. J. Clinton McCann covers the Psalms in the *New Interpreter's Bible,* vol. 4 (Abingdon, 1996). This volume also includes Job plus 1 and 2 Maccabees in a work designed to give exegetical insight and reflection for today. It is part of a new CD-ROM with vol. 9 of the NIB. James L. Mays' *Psalms,* Interpretation Commentaries (John Knox, 1994), is an expository work that can be used alongside one of the above commentaries.

Study of Acts
Years A, B, and C

Overviews

Mark Allen Powell's *What Are They Saying about Acts?* (Paulist Press, 1991) will provide a good introduction to the state of research on Acts. Richard J. Cassidy has provided a justice-oriented study that follows up on his study of Luke in *Society and Politics in the Acts of the Apostles* (Orbis, 1987) for those who want a fresh perspective.

Commentaries

W. H. Willimon's *Acts,* Interpretation Commentaries (John Knox, 1988), gives a sound expository start for the pastor. E. Haenchen's *The Acts of the Apostles: A Commentary* (Westminster, 1971) is the top scholars' commentary at present. However, Luke Timothy Johnson's *The Acts of the Apostles,* Sacra Pagina 5 (Liturgical Press, 1992), is a recent Catholic study that is a solid alternative that is easier to use. The same might be said for F. F. Bruce's *The Book of the Acts*, New International Commentary on the New Testament, rev. ed. (Eerdmans, 1988). C. K. Barrett's *Acts of the Apostles*, vol. 1, chap. 1-14, International Critical Commentary (T & T Clark, 1993), begins a significant new study on the Greek text. This volume covers most of the texts used this year.

Study of the Gospel Lessons
John (Years B and C)
Overviews
Gerald S. Sloyan's *What Are They Saying about John?* (Paulist, 1991) provides a fine overview of current scholarship. Robert Kysar's *John's Story of Jesus* (Fortress, 1984) will give a good overall review of John. D. Moody Smith's *John,* Proclamation Commentary, 2nd ed. (Fortress, 1986), is an alternative. The journal *Interpretation* (October 1995) offers several fine articles on current Johannine studies.

Commentaries
Raymond E. Brown's *The Gospel According to John*, Anchor Bible 29, 29A (Doubleday, 1966, 1970), has become a standard two-volume work for exegetical study. Couple this with the expository effort of Gerald Sloyan's *John*, Interpretation Commentaries (John Knox, 1988), for a solid set of resources. Gail R. O'Day's "The Gospel of John," *New Interpreter's Bible*, vol. 9 (Abingdon, 1995), is a fresh new study in a volume that includes Luke. This volume is now available for the computer on a CD-ROM that includes the volume on Psalms and Job already mentioned. Charles H. Talbert's *Reading John: A Literary and Theological Commentary on the Fourth Gospel and the Johannine Epistles* (Crossroad, 1992) is a work focusing more on the newer literary criticism. Ben Witherington III's *John's Wisdom, A Commentary on the Fourth Gospel* (Westminster/John Knox, 1995) offers another fresh perspective.

Mark (Year B)
Overviews
Paul Achtemeier's *Mark*, Proclamation Commentaries, 2nd rev. ed. (Fortress, 1986), is a good overview. Frank J. Matera's *What Are They Saying about Mark?* (Paulist Press, 1987) is a fine alternative. A study based on the newer narrative literary critical approach is D. Rhoads and D. Michie's *Mark as Story* (Fortress, 1982).

Commentaries

A recent study by Morna D. Hooker in *The Gospel According to St. Mark*, Black's New Testament Commentary (Hendrickson, 1992), is very helpful. Pheme Perkins' "The Gospel of Mark," *The New Interpreter's Bible*, vol. 8 (Abingdon, 1995), is another new work in a volume that includes a solid commentary on Matthew as well. This volume is now available on a CD-ROM with NIB, vol. 1, that includes Genesis, Exodus, and Leviticus plus introductory articles. Lamar Williamson Jr.'s *Mark*, Interpretation Commentaries (John Knox, 1983), provides an expository study. Eduard Schweizer's *The Good News According to Mark* (John Knox, 1970) continues to provide solid help for the preacher. Ched Myers offers a pair of socioliterary studies that challenge us to take a new look at Mark in *Binding the Strong Man* and *Who Will Roll Away the Stone* (Orbis, 1988 and 1994).

Luke (Year C)

Overviews

Mark Alan Powell's *What Are They Saying about Luke?* (Paulist Press, 1989) offers an excellent overview of what's happening in Lukan studies. F. W. Danker's *Luke*, Proclamation Commentary, 2nd rev. ed. (Fortress, 1987), also provides a good discussion to prepare one for the year. C. Talbert's *Reading Luke* (Crossroad, 1982) offers a literary and theological review with stimulating ideas.

Commentaries

A detailed standard set is Joseph Fitzmyer's *The Gospel According to Luke*, Anchor Bible 28, 28A (Doubleday, 1981, 1985). Add to this the expository work by Fred Craddock in *Luke*, Interpretation Commentaries (John Knox, 1990), for good preaching help. R. Alan Culpepper now covers Luke in the *New Interpreter's Bible*, vol. 9 (Abingdon, 1995). See John commentaries for CD-ROM information. Another helpful new work is Luke Timothy Johnson's *The Gospel of Luke*, Sacra Pagina 3 (Liturgical Press, 1991). Frederick W. Danker's *Jesus and the New Age*, revised and expanded (Fortress, 1988), also is well regarded.

Studies

Walter E. Pilgrim's *Good News to the Poor* (Augsburg, 1981) offers a provocative sermon starter on issues of wealth and poverty. Likewise, J. Massyngbaerde Ford's *My Enemy Is My Guest* (Orbis, 1984) stimulates one on the issues of nonviolence in Luke. Both books invite the preacher to look at the gospel from a new perspective.

Raymond E. Brown's *The Birth of the Messiah* (Doubleday, 1979) offers a detailed study of the infancy narratives. The journal *Interpretation* (October 1994) provides several helpful recent articles on Lukan studies.

Study of the Epistle Lessons
(in order used)

Ephesians

Rudolf Schnackenburg's *Ephesians: A Commentary* (T & T Clark, 1991) translates a fine Roman Catholic study. Markus Barth's *Ephesians*, Anchor Bible 34 & 34A (Doubleday, 1974), provides a detailed study. A new work in a new series will also offer the insights of Pheme Perkins in *Ephesians*, Abingdon New Testament Commentaries (Abingdon, 1996). Ralph P. Martin's *Ephesians, Colossians and Philemon*, Interpretation Commentaries (John Knox, 1991), offers a helpful expository addition.

James

Luke T. Johnson's *Letter of James*, Anchor Bible 37A (Doubleday, 1995), provides a good recent study. S. Laws' *A Commentary on the Epistle of James*, Black's New Testament Commentaries (Hendrickson, 1980), is a recognized alternative. Peter Davids' *Commentary on James*, New International Greek Testament Commentary (Eerdmans, 1982), offers a scholarly look at the Greek text. Two interesting overviews are Pedrito U. Maynard-Reid's *Poverty and Wealth in James* (Orbis, 1987), and Elsa Tamez's *The Scandalous Message of James* (Crossroad, 1990).

Hebrews

F. F. Bruce's *The Epistle to the Hebrews*, rev. ed., New International Commentary on the New Testament (Eerdmans, 1990), is a solid place to begin for Hebrews. Harold W. Attridge's *Hebrews*, Hermeneia (Fortress, 1989), is a fine study on the Greek text, but the book is designed so others can use it without too much trouble. An alternative on the Greek text is Paul Ellingworth's *Commentary on Hebrews*, New International Greek Testament Commentary (Eerdmans, 1993). Ernst Kaesemann's *The Wandering People of God* (Augsburg, 1984) is a well-recognized treatise that might be read along with one of the above commentaries. Barnabas Lindars' *The Theology of the Letter to the Hebrews*, New Testament Theology (Cambridge, 1991), offers a different perspective.

Philippians

Fred B. Craddock's *Philippians,* Interpretation Commentaries (John Knox, 1985), offers a brief expository study. It would need to be supplemented by Gordon Fee's *Paul's Letter to the Philippians,* New International Commentary on the New Testament (Eerdmans, 1995), for a new evangelical work. A study on the Greek text is found in Peter T. O'Brien's *The Epistle to the Philippians,* New International Greek New Testament (Eerdmans, 1991).

1 Corinthians

William A. Beardslee's *First Corinthians: A Commentary for Today* (Chalice Press, 1994) is a new book aimed at the pastor and teacher. Gordon D. Fee's *The First Epistle to the Corinthians,* New International Commentary on the New Testament (Eerdmans, 1987), is a good, detailed, newer evangelical study. C. Talbert's *Reading Corinthians* (Crossroad, 1987) provides a fine literary and theological supplement to any of the above. Graydon F. Snyder's *First Corinthians: A Faith Community Commentary* (Mercer University Press, 1992) offers a good volume from the church perspective of the radical reformation.

Revelation

M. Eugene Boring's *Revelation,* Interpretation Commentaries (John Knox, 1989), provides expository help. Recent exegetical companions include Jurgen Roloff's *Revelation: A Continental Commentary* (Augsburg Fortress, 1993), or Wilfrid J. Harrington's *Revelation,* Sacra Pagina 16 (Liturgical Press, 1993). A recent Latin American study is found in Pablo Richard's *Apocalypse: A People's Commentary on the Book of Revelation* (Orbis, 1995). Another view comes from Allan A. Boesak's *Comfort and Protest: The Apocalypse from a South African Perspective* (Westminster, 1987).

Galatians

Frank J. Matera's *Galatians,* Sacra Pagina 9 (Liturgical Press, 1992), is a recent study that could provide exegetical background for a fine expository work by Charles Cousar in *Galatians,* Interpretation Commentaries (John Knox, 1982). Sam K. Williams' *Galatians,* Abingdon New Testament Commentaries (Abingdon, 1996), is a new study in a new series. Dieter Betz's *Galatians,* Hermeneia (Fortress, 1979), has become a scholarly standard on the Greek text.

Colossians

Ralph P. Martin's *Ephesians, Colossians, and Philemon*, Interpretation Commentaries (John Knox, 1991), provides a good expository start. Markus Barth and Helmut Blanke's *Colossians*, Anchor Bible 34B (Doubleday, 1994), or Petr Pokorny's *Colossians: A Commentary* (Hendrickson, 1991) offer exegetical support. James D. G. Dunn's *The Epistle to the Colossians and to Philemon*, New International Greek Testament Commentary (Eerdmans, 1996), is a fine Greek study.

Study of Old Testament Texts

Isaiah

Expository help for Isaiah now comes from Christopher R. Seitz's *Isaiah 1-39*, Interpretation Commentaries (John Knox, 1993), and Paul D. Hanson's *Isaiah 40-66*, Interpretation Commentaries (John Knox, 1995). R. Clements' *Isaiah 1-39*, New Century Bible Commentary (Eerdmans, 1980), and R. N. Whybray's *Isaiah 40-66*, New Century Bible Commentary (Eerdmans, 1975), provide good, inexpensive commentaries. John N. Oswalt's *Isaiah 1-39* and *Isaiah 40-66*, New International Commentary on the Old Testament (Eerdmans, 1986, 1996), offer an evangelical alternative. Another stimulating study seeking to apply Isaiah to today is Daniel Berrigan's *Isaiah: Spirit of Courage, Gift of Tears* (Augsburg Fortress, 1996).

Jeremiah

Ronald Clements' *Jeremiah*, Interpretation Commentaries (John Knox, 1989), offers a good expository study. R. P. Carroll's *Jeremiah: A Commentary*, Old Testament Library (Westminster, 1986), is one of several solid works to appear in recent years for those wanting more exegetical material. A pair of solid, inexpensive volumes not to be overlooked are Walter Brueggemann's *To Pluck Up, To Tear Down, Jeremiah 1-25* and *To Build, To Plant, Jeremiah 26-52*, International Theological Commentary (Eerdmans, 1988, 1991).

1 and 2 Kings

Richard D. Nelson's *First and Second Kings*, Interpretation Commentaries (John Knox, 1987), provides good expository assistance. Exegetical supplements include G. H. Jones' *1 and 2 Kings*, New Century Bible Commentary, vol. 2 (Eerdmans, 1984), or Donald J. Wiseman's *1 and 2 Kings*, Tyndale Old Testament Commentaries (InterVarsity Press, 1993).

Proverbs

Two new works offer current insights into Proverbs. Michael V. Fox's *Proverbs,* Anchor Bible 18A (Doubleday, 1997), is a replacement volume in that series. Raymond C. Van Leeuwen's "Proverbs," *New Interpreter's Bible*, vol. 5 (Abingdon, 1997), is part of a volume that includes much of the other wisdom literature as well. A fresh overview can be found in Kathleen A. Farmer's *Proverbs & Ecclesiastes,* International Theological Commentary (Eerdmans, 1991).

Job

Expository insights abound in J. Gerald Janzen's *Job*, Interpretation Commentaries (John Knox, 1985). Carol A. Newsom's "Job," *New Interpreter's Bible*, vol. 4 (Abingdon, 1996), is available in the same volume with the Psalms (see there for CD-ROM information). Additional exegetical insight can be found in N. C. Habel's *The Book of Job: A Commentary,* Old Testament Library (Westminster, 1985).

1997–1998 Writers

Sermons and Prayers

Andrea La Sonde Anastos
46 Old Main St.
Deerfield, MA 01342
  Aug. 3, 10, 17, 24, 31, 1997

Thomas W. Currie III
800 Jefferson
Kerrville, TX 78028
  Sept. 7, 14, 21, 28, 1997

Steven L. Davis
8137 E. Quarterhorse Tr.
Scottsdale, AZ 85258
  May 17, 21, 24, 31, 1997

C. Welton Gaddy
2311 Myrtle
Monroe, LA 71201
  July 5, 12, 19, 26, 1998

Beth Ann Gaede
318 Parkway Ct.
Minneapolis, MN 55419
  June 7, 14, 21, 28, 1998

William B. Lawrence
4416 Valley Forge Rd.
Durham, NC 27705
  Nov. 23, 27, 30,
  Dec. 7, 1997

Paul Lundborg
1310 South Hills Dr.
Wenatchee, WA 98801
  Jan. 25, Feb. 1, 8, 1998

Steven D. MacArthur
PO Box 2317
Batesville, AR 72503-2317
  May 17, 21, 24, 31, 1998

Paul Romstad
7501 Newton Ave. S
Richfield, MN 55423
  Dec. 14, 21, 24, 25, 1997

Theresa M. Roos
535 - 20th Ave. N
South St. Paul, MN 55075
  Feb. 15, 22, 25,
  Mar. 1, 1998

Peter Rosenkvist
360 S. Lexington Pkwy.
Apt. 321
St. Paul, MN 55105
  Jan. 18, 1998

John L. Topolewski
141 Carol Ave.
Vestal, NY 13850
  Dec. 28, 1997
  Jan. 4, 6, 11, 1998

Nancy E. Topolewski
141 Carol Ave.
Vestal, NY 13850
   Oct. 5, 12, 19, 26, 1997
   Oct. 26, 1997 (Reformation)

William M. Schwein
6625 N. Sherman Dr.
Indianapolis, IN 46220
   November 2, 9, 16, 1997
   November 2, 1997 (All Saints')

Clyde J. Steckel
2580 Kenzie Terrace #207A
St. Anthony, MN 55418
   Apr. 5, 9, 10, 12, 1998

Gary L. Walling
17300 Van Aken Blvd.
Shaker Heights, OH 44120
   Mar. 8, 15, 22, 29, 1998

Children's Object Talks

Lois Brokering
11641 Palmer Rd.
Bloomington, MN 55437-3437
   Aug. 3–Nov. 30, 1997

Jeanette Strandjord
330 N. Albany Blvd.,
PO Box 127
Spring Green, WI 53588
   Apr. 5–July 26, 1998

Jon Temme
502-10145 - 121st St.
Edmonton, Alberta,
Canada T5N 1K5
   Dec. 7, 1997–Mar. 29, 1998

Preaching Resources

David H. Schmidt
401 Fairmont Dr.
DeKalb, IL 60115

Hymn of the Day Selections

Kent Gilbert
2155 McKee Rd.
Berea, KY 40403

Four-Year Church Year Calendar

	Series B 1996	Series C 1997	Series A 1998	Series B 1999
Advent begins	Dec. 1	Nov. 30	Nov. 29	Nov. 28
Christmas	Dec. 25	Dec. 25	Dec. 25	Dec. 25
	1997	1998	1999	2000
Epiphany	Jan. 6	Jan. 6	Jan. 6	Jan. 6
Ash Wednesday	Feb. 12	Feb. 25	Feb. 17	Mar. 8
Palm Sunday	Mar. 23	Apr. 5	Mar. 28	Apr. 16
Maundy Thursday	Mar. 27	Apr. 9	Apr. 1	Apr. 20
Good Friday	Mar. 28	Apr. 10	Apr. 2	Apr. 21
Easter Day	Mar. 30	Apr. 12	Apr. 4	Apr. 23
Ascension Day	May 8	May 21	May 13	June 1
Pentecost	May 18	May 31	May 23	June 11
Trinity Sunday	May 25	June 7	May 30	June 18
Reformation	Oct. 31	Oct. 31	Oct. 31	Oct. 31
All Saints' Day	Nov. 1	Nov. 1	Nov. 1	Nov. 1

The Minister's Annual Manual

Calendars for 1997 and 1998

1997

JANUARY 1997	APRIL 1997	JULY 1997	OCTOBER 1997
S M T W T F S	S M T W T F S	S M T W T F S	S M T W T F S
1 2 3 4	1 2 3 4 5	1 2 3 4 5	1 2 3 4
5 6 7 8 9 10 11	6 7 8 9 10 11 12	6 7 8 9 10 11 12	5 6 7 8 9 10 11
12 13 14 15 16 17 18	13 14 15 16 17 18 19	13 14 15 16 17 18 19	12 13 14 15 16 17 18
19 20 21 22 23 24 25	20 21 22 23 24 25 26	20 21 22 23 24 25 26	19 20 21 22 23 24 25
26 27 28 29 30 31	27 28 29 30	27 28 29 30 31	26 27 28 29 30 31
FEBRUARY 1997	**MAY 1997**	**AUGUST 1997**	**NOVEMBER 1997**
S M T W T F S	S M T W T F S	S M T W T F S	S M T W T F S
1	1 2 3	1 2	1
2 3 4 5 6 7 8	4 5 6 7 8 9 10	3 4 5 6 7 8 9	2 3 4 5 6 7 8
9 10 11 12 13 14 15	11 12 13 14 15 16 17	10 11 12 13 14 15 16	9 10 11 12 13 14 15
16 17 18 19 20 21 22	18 19 20 21 22 23 24	17 18 19 20 21 22 23	16 17 18 19 20 21 22
23 24 25 26 27 28	25 26 27 28 29 30 31	24/31 25 26 27 28 29 30	23/30 24 25 26 27 28 29
MARCH 1997	**JUNE 1997**	**SEPTEMBER 1997**	**DECEMBER 1997**
S M T W T F S	S M T W T F S	S M T W T F S	S M T W T F S
1	1 2 3 4 5 6 7	1 2 3 4 5 6	1 2 3 4 5 6
2 3 4 5 6 7 8	8 9 10 11 12 13 14	7 8 9 10 11 12 13	7 8 9 10 11 12 13
9 10 11 12 13 14 15	15 16 17 18 19 20 21	14 15 16 17 18 19 20	14 15 16 17 18 19 20
16 17 18 19 20 21 22	22 23 24 25 26 27 28	21 22 23 24 25 26 27	21 22 23 24 25 26 27
23/30 24/31 25 26 27 28 29	29 30	28 29 30	28 29 30 31

1998

JANUARY 1998	APRIL 1998	JULY 1998	OCTOBER 1998
S M T W T F S	S M T W T F S	S M T W T F S	S M T W T F S
1 2 3	1 2 3 4	1 2 3 4	1 2 3
4 5 6 7 8 9 10	5 6 7 8 9 10 11	5 6 7 8 9 10 11	4 5 6 7 8 9 10
11 12 13 14 15 16 17	12 13 14 15 16 17 18	12 13 14 15 16 17 18	11 12 13 14 15 16 17
18 19 20 21 22 23 24	19 20 21 22 23 24 25	19 20 21 22 23 24 25	18 19 20 21 22 23 24
25 26 27 28 29 30 31	26 27 28 29 30	26 27 28 29 30 31	25 26 27 28 29 30 31
FEBRUARY 1998	**MAY 1998**	**AUGUST 1998**	**NOVEMBER 1998**
S M T W T F S	S M T W T F S	S M T W T F S	S M T W T F S
1 2 3 4 5 6 7	1 2	1	1 2 3 4 5 6 7
8 9 10 11 12 13 14	3 4 5 6 7 8 9	2 3 4 5 6 7 8	8 9 10 11 12 13 14
15 16 17 18 19 20 21	10 11 12 13 14 15 16	9 10 11 12 13 14 15	15 16 17 18 19 20 21
22 23 24 25 26 27 28	17 18 19 20 21 22 23	16 17 18 19 20 21 22	22 23 24 25 26 27 28
	24/31 25 26 27 28 29 30	23/30 24/31 25 26 27 28 29	29 30
MARCH 1998	**JUNE 1998**	**SEPTEMBER 1998**	**DECEMBER 1998**
S M T W T F S	S M T W T F S	S M T W T F S	S M T W T F S
1 2 3 4 5 6 7	1 2 3 4 5 6	1 2 3 4 5	1 2 3 4 5
8 9 10 11 12 13 14	7 8 9 10 11 12 13	6 7 8 9 10 11 12	6 7 8 9 10 11 12
15 16 17 18 19 20 21	14 15 16 17 18 19 20	13 14 15 16 17 18 19	13 14 15 16 17 18 19
22 23 24 25 26 27 28	21 22 23 24 25 26 27	20 21 22 23 24 25 26	20 21 22 23 24 25 26
29 30 31	28 29 30	27 28 29 30	27 28 29 30 31

Index of Sermon Texts

Exodus 12:1–14 (5–10), 11–14, Maundy Thursday	329
Isaiah 9:2–7, Christmas Eve	192
Isaiah 43:16–21, Lent 5	314
Isaiah 50:4–9a, Passion/Palm Sunday	321
Isaiah 52:7–10, Christmas Day	200
Isaiah 52:13—53:12, Good Friday	336
Isaiah 62:1–5, Epiphany 2	232
Jeremiah 31:31–34, Reformation	109
Micah 5:2–5a, Advent 4	186
Matthew 6:25–33, Thanksgiving Day	153
Mark 7:1–8, 14–15, 21–23, Pentecost 15, Proper 17	47
Mark 7:24–37, Pentecost 16, Proper 18	54
Mark 8:27–38, Pentecost 17, Proper 19	61
Mark 9:30–37, Pentecost 18, Proper 20	68
Mark 9:38–50, Pentecost 19, Proper 21	75
Mark 10:2–16, Pentecost 20, Proper 22	82
Mark 10:17–31, Pentecost 21, Proper 23	89
Mark 10:35–45, Pentecost 22, Proper 24	96
Mark 10:46–52, Pentecost 23, Proper 25	103
Mark 12:28–34, Pentecost 24, Proper 26	117
Mark 13:1–8, Pentecost 26, Proper 28	138
Luke 3:15–17, 21–22, Epiphany 1, The Baptism of Our Lord	226
Luke 4:14–21, Epiphany 3	240
Luke 4:21–30, Epiphany 4	247
Luke 5:1–11, Epiphany 5	255
Luke 6:17–26, Epiphany 6	263
Luke 9:28–36 (37–43), Transfiguration	271
Luke 10:25–37, Pentecost 6, Proper 10	444
Luke 10:38–42, Pentecost 7, Proper 11	451
Luke 11:1–13, Pentecost 8, Proper 12	458
John 6:24–35, Pentecost 11, Proper 13	19
John 6:35, 41–51, Pentecost 12, Proper 14	26
John 6:51–58, Pentecost 13, Proper 15	33
John 6:56–69, Pentecost 14, Proper 16	40
John 10:22–30, Easter 4	367

John 11:32–44, All Saints' Day	124
John 13:31–35, Easter 5	374
John 14:23–29, Easter 6	381
John 16:12–15, Trinity Sunday	409
John 17:20–26, Easter 7	395
John 20:19–31, Easter 2	351
John 21:1–19, Easter 3	359
Acts 2:1–21, Day of Pentecost	402
Acts 10:34–43, Easter Day	344
Romans 10:5–13, Lent 1	285
1 Corinthians 10:1–13, Lent 3	300
2 Corinthians 5:16–21, Lent 4	307
2 Corinthians 5:20b—6:10, Ash Wednesday	279
Galatians 2:15–21, Pentecost 2, Proper 6	416
Galatians 3:23–29, Pentecost 3, Proper 7	423
Galatians 5:1, 13–25, Pentecost 4, Proper 8	430
Galatians 6:(1–6) 7–16, Pentecost 5, Proper 9	437
Ephesians 1:3–14, Christmas 2	213
Ephesians 1:15–23, Ascension Day	387
Ephesians 3:1–12, Epiphany	220
Philippians 1:3–11, Advent 2	170
Philippians 3:17—4:1, Lent 2	293
Philippians 4:4–7, Advent 3	178
Colossians 3:12–17, Christmas 1	207
1 Thessalonians 3:9–13, Advent 1	161
Hebrews 9:24–28, Pentecost 25, Proper 27	131
Revelation 1:4b–8, Christ the King/Reign of Christ	145

Bro# MIMA8

Advance Order Form

THE MINISTER'S ANNUAL MANUAL FOR PREACHING AND WORSHIP PLANNING 1998–1999

Complete sermon and worship planning helps beginning August 2, 1998, through July 25, 1999

(Available by June 1, 1998)

$23.95

Plus $2.50 shipping and handling
MN Personal Orders, add 6 1/2% sales tax

To Order:

Mail this form to Logos Productions Inc., 6160 Carmen Avenue East, Inver Grove Heights, MN 55076-4422;
Fax your order to: 612-457-4617; or call 1-800-328-0200
(Minneapolis/St. Paul, 451-9945).

MIMA8— Minister's Annual Manual 1998/99	$23.95
shipping and handling (plus MN 6 ½% sales tax if applicable)	
Total	

Payment method (check one):
- ❏ Please bill me   ❏ My check for $_____.___ is enclosed
- ❏ Please charge $_____.___ to my credit card (fill out information below)

Credit card: (check one)   ❏ MasterCard   ❏ American Express
                              ❏ VISA   ❏ Discover/NOVUS

Name (as shown on card)_____
Credit card number_____
Expiration date_____
Signature_____

SHIPPING ADDRESS
ORDERED BY_____
CHURCH_____PHONE(   )_____
STREET_____
CITY_____STATE_____ZIP_____

BILLING ADDRESS
CHURCH_____
STREET_____
CITY_____STATE_____ZIP_____